Charles S. Miley Learning Res. Center
Library
Indian River Community College
Ft. Pierce, Fla.

JANE AUSTEN: THE CRITICAL HERITAGE VOLUME II

THE CRITICAL HERITAGE SERIES

GENERAL EDITOR: B. C. SOUTHAM, M.A., B.LITT. (OXON.)
Formerly Department of English, Westfield College, University of London

For a list of books in the series see the back end paper

JANE AUSTEN

THE CRITICAL HERITAGE 1870–1940
Volume 2

Edited by

B.C. SOUTHAM

LONDON AND NEW YORK: ROUTLEDGE & KEGAN PAUL

First published in 1987 by
Routledge & Kegan Paul Ltd
11 New Fetter Lane, London EC4P 4EE

Published in the USA by
Routledge & Kegan Paul Inc.
in association with Methuen Inc.
29 West 35th Street, New York, NY 10001

Photosetting by Thomson Press (India) Limited, New Delhi
and printed in Great Britain
by T.J. Press (Padstow) Ltd.

Compilation, introduction, notes, bibliography and index
© Brian Southam 1987

Library of Congress Cataloging in Publication Data
(Revised for vol. 2)

Southam, B. C.
Jane Austen: the critical heritage.
(The Critical heritage series)
Vol. II: 1870–1940, has imprint: London;
New York: Routledge & Kegan Paul.
Includes bibliographies and index.
1. Austen, Jane, 1775–1817—Criticism and interpretation.
I. Title. II. Series.
PR4037.S59 1968 823'.7 68–77814

British Library CIP Data also available

ISBN 0–7100–2942–X (v. 1)
ISBN 0–7102–0189–3 (v. 2)

General Editor's Preface

The reception given to a writer by his contemporaries and near-contemporaries is evidence of considerable value to the student of literature. On one side, we learn a great deal about the state of criticism at large and in particular about the development of critical attitudes towards a single writer; at the same time, through private comments in letters, journals or marginalia, we gain an insight upon the tastes and literary thought of individual readers of the period. Evidence of this kind helps us to understand the writer's historical situation, the nature of his immediate reading-public, and his response to these pressures.

The separate volumes in *The Critical Heritage Series* present a record of this early criticism. Clearly, for many of the highly-productive and lengthily-reviewed nineteenth- and twentieth-century writers, there exists an enormous body of material; and in these cases the volume editors have made a selection of the most important views, significant for their intrinsic critical worth or for their representative quality.

For writers of the eighteenth century and earlier, the materials are much scarcer and the historical period has been extended, sometimes far beyond the writer's lifetime, in order to show the inception and growth of critical views which were initially slow to appear.

In each volume the documents are headed by an Introduction, discussing the material assembled and relating the early stages of the author's reception to what we have come to identify as the critical tradition. The volumes will make available much material which would otherwise be difficult of access and it is hoped that the modern reader will be thereby helped towards an informed understanding of the ways in which literature has been read and judged.

B.C.S.

To Doris, for patience and generosity
towards a book that took far too long

Contents

CONTENTS

Preface

This second Jane Austen volume covers the period from 1870 to the early 1940s, from the publication of the *Memoir*, the first biography, to the beginnings of modern criticism in *Scrutiny*. What has made this volume so different from others in the Series is the fact that Jane Austen is alone in English literature in being a popular author as well as a great one, with a considerable cult. The Janeite enthusings are extensive, often amusing, sometimes irritating, yet not to be ignored. Nor can we disregard the acres of journalism and *belle lettriste* appreciation. The sheer volume of all this is daunting and although it may seem an unlikely source, it leads us, nonetheless, to criticism of lasting value. Moreover, this material also shows us how popular taste was shaped; and how, in turn, criticism itself responded to a large audience of common readers.

It was during this period, too, that Jane Austen became recognised as one of the supreme artists of the novel. The serious discussion of her work became an arena for examining central issues in fiction—realism, narrative, the treatment of character, humour, irony and so on; and within these discussions are some remarkable anticipations of modern criticism.

The issues extend well beyond literature. Jane Austen was enrolled in many causes and seen in conflicting roles—sometimes as a heroine of the feminists, sometimes as a champion of domestic values. There were vociferous anti-Janeites including the crusty male brigade. In anglophile America she was treasured as the quintessentially English writer. Yet she was also belaboured in the nationwide debates about a truly native American literature and The Great American Novel.

Lionel Trilling once wrote that the opinions held about her work 'are almost as interesting, and almost as important to think about as the work itself'.[1] Many critics of Jane Austen have found themselves deeply engaged with the novels, attracted or repelled in an intensely personal way—and been prepared to say so. This may

1 '*Emma* and the legend of Jane Austen', 1957

not answer our sense of a necessary critical detachment. But Jane Austen can get the loftiest of Professors to unbend, abandon, for a time, his academic ways and speak from the heart.

The vast range of the Jane Austen literature has meant that the documents selected here can only be a representative selection and there are many sad exclusions, the Garrod-Chapman exchange for one. But in the Introduction I have tried to fill the gaps by way of a descriptive account and to sketch the expanse of humble ground from which the high points emerge.

Acknowledgments

For their help in the preparation of this book, I would like to thank Professor Walton Litz of Princeton; Professor Jane Marcus of the University of Texas; Dr Peter Keating of the University of Edinburgh; Mr Henry G. Burke; Mr George Tucker; Dr Constance Rover; Ms Marsha S. Clark, Charles Patterson Van Pelt Library, University of Pennsylvania; Mr Jeremy Treglown, Editor, *Times Literary Supplement*; Professor Michael Stokes, University of Durham; Mr Fred Lock, University of Queensland; Mr David Gilson; Professor D.W. Harding; the late Sir William Empson; Mr David Doughan, Fawcett Library; Professor Norman Sherry; Miss A. Phillips, Librarian, Newnham College, Cambridge.

All previously unpublished words by Mark Twain quoted in this book on page 75 are © 1987 by Edward J. Willi and Manufacturers Hanover Trust Company as Trustees of the Mark Twain Foundation, which reserves all reproduction or dramatization rights in every medium. They are published here with the permission of the University of California Press and Robert H. Hirst, General Editor of the Mark Twain Project at Berkeley. All citations of such material are identified by the following symbol: † I would also like to thank the following for granting permission for copyright materials to be reproduced in this volume: The Trustees of the Thomas Hardy Memorial Collection in the Dorset County Museum, Dorchester, Dorset, for permission to quote from an unpublished letter from Frederic Harrison to Thomas Hardy; Edward Arnold (Publishers) Ltd for No. 30; Jonathan Cape Ltd and the Estate of Rebecca West for No. 38; Chatto & Windus and the Estate of William Empson for No. 39; Curtis Brown Ltd, London and New York, for No. 40 (Copyright © 1937 by W.H. Auden and Louis MacNeice. Copyright renewed 1965 by W.H. Auden); David Higham Associates Ltd for Nos 33 and 35; The Hogarth Press, Harcourt Brace Jovanovich, Inc., and the Estate of Virginia Woolf for No. 31, from *The Common Reader* by Virginia Woolf (Copyright 1925 by Harcourt Brace Jovanovich Inc.; renewed 1953 by Leonard Woolf); Alexander R. James (Literary Executor) for

ACKNOWLEDGMENTS

No. 8; A.D. Peters & Co. Ltd for No. 36; The Society of Authors as the literary representative of the Estate of John Middleton Murry for No. 29; Times Newspapers Ltd for No. 26.

Introduction

I

Thanks to the review-essays by Scott (*No. 8*)* and Whately (*No. 16*), there was never any serious danger that Jane Austen would be forgotten. She was too well-loved and her admirers too influential for that. But down to 1870, the formal criticism was sparse and thinking remained at a standstill. Scott's account of Jane Austen as an anti-romantic novelist of everyday life and Whately's analytical essay were not superseded. Together, they stand as the source of critical thinking for much of the century. Attention was elsewhere: on Scott, generally regarded as the great novelist of the early period; and from the 1840s onwards, on the Brontës, Thackeray, Trollope, Dickens, Mrs Gaskell and George Eliot as writers dealing with far wider areas of society, deeper levels of experience and social questions more pressing. Beside this literature of more apparent scope and power, Jane Austen was seen at a disadvantage. Slight and provincial, a period novelist of Regency manners, her success seemed limited to the small world of domestic comedy. The subtlety, restraint and concentration of her art were rarely observed, the commanding irony went unperceived; and it was left to a few enthusiasts to keep her name alive. As far as criticism and the public at large were concerned, Jane Austen was a minor writer of a past age. The point is nicely made by the comment Trollope wrote on the end-papers of his copy of *Emma* in 1865: 'It is as a portrait of female life among ladies in an English village 50 years ago that *Emma* is to be known and remembered.'

What changed all this was the *Memoir of Jane Austen* by her nephew, James Edward Austen-Leigh, published in 1870. Until then, the novelist had remained a shadowy figure. The bare facts were in a 'Biographical Notice' that her brother Henry had added to *Persuasion* and *Northanger Abbey* at the end of 1817, a few months after his sister's death. The 'Notice' was enlarged slightly in 1833.

* *Note:* References to documents in the previous *Jane Austen: The Critical Heritage* volume are by number italicised, e.g. *No. 27*. Those to this volume are in roman type.

I

But it was tantalisingly brief and had the materials been available, Macaulay said he would have filled the gap with a short life 'of that wonderful woman'.[1] Tennyson, equally devoted—'He would read and re-read' the novels[2]—fulminated against such revelation. Cherishing her 'as next to Shakespeare', 'he thanked God Almighty that he knew nothing of Jane Austen, and that there were no letters preserved either of Shakespeare's or of Jane Austen's, that they had not been ripped open like pigs.'[3] Such feelings were also reflected within the family. Austen-Leigh was planning a biography in the early 1860s. But some of the nephews and nieces insisted that their Aunt's privacy should be respected and were unwilling to give way in 'the vexed question between the Austens and the Public'.[4] However, this opposition may have eased in 1865 with the death at the age of 91 of Francis, the last surviving of Jane Austen's six brothers. In any event, when the *Memoir* came to be written in 1869, the main facts and circumstances of her life were discreetly revealed.[5]

Welcomed by her admirers, the *Memoir* also had the immediate effect of awakening public interest in an author virtually forgotten. This is not to say that overnight Jane Austen became widely read. But she instantly became an author widely written about, for the biography provided human interest and material for a flood of appreciative essays and reviews, many of them written by devoted readers keen to share their enthusiasm with the world at large.

In itself, the *Memoir* is modest enough, a sketch, the affectionate tribute of an elderly nephew, and offered as no more. Austen-Leigh undertook the work with some misgivings. His daughter Mary records that 'when urged upon the subject', he had replied that 'as there was so little to tell, it appeared to him impossible to write anything that could be called a "life".'[6] Later, he described it as an act of devotion, stemming from his sense of responsibility as one of the oldest members of the family and the only one of his generation present at his aunt's funeral. 'He knew of no one but himself who was inclined to the work' are the opening words of its epigraph. This sounds unpromising. But he was not ungifted as a writer. Working energetically, he completed the book in less than five months.[7] As her favourite nephew, he was well-equipped for the task. His own schoolboy efforts at fiction had won from his aunt a generous appreciation. Those 'strong, manly, spirited Sketches, full of Variety and Glow', she called them; and she had responded half-teasingly, with the classic account of her own very different style: that 'fine' brushwork on 'the little bit (two Inches wide) of Ivory'.[8] To his own recollections he added those of his sisters and cousins and wrote with a natural ease and intimacy; and Virginia Woolf's comment holds true, that the *Memoir* 'reproduced the atmosphere in which' Jane Austen's 'life was lived so instinctively that' it 'can never be superseded' (No. 26).

Although Austen-Leigh had the interest of the family firmly in mind, he addressed himself to readers outside and his presumption of a larger public was confirmed. The *Memoir* was extensively reviewed. The editors of the weeklies and monthlies recognised that there was widespread curiosity about the life of an author so generally forgotten, yet who commanded the admiration, the passionate devotion even, of some of the leading writers and critics of the time—a fact brought home in the *Memoir* itself, where Austen-Leigh collected the tribute of praise, public and private, that had accumulated in the half-century since Scott reviewed *Emma* in 1816.

Nothing could be more charming and unpretentious than the *Memoir* portrait. A labour of duty, it is also a labour of love and draws a touching and human picture of 'dear "Aunt Jane"'[9]—a homely spinster, an amateur, who avoided literary society, whose writing was squeezed in between the household chores and the task of looking after an invalid mother and the joy of being a lovable, available, entertaining, maiden-aunt to a widening circle of young nephews and nieces. Austen-Leigh's testimony on this point is beautifully precise: 'We did not think of her as being clever, still less as being famous; but we valued her as one always kind, sympathizing and amusing.'[10] (Indeed, so much *Aunt* Jane as to prompt the teasing suggestion from Howells that 'We might wish her now to have had a niece or a nephew or two less, if we might so have had a book or two more from her.'[11])

The *Memoir* evokes a comfortable, approachable figure who put down her needlework to pick up her pen—who wrote in the odd moments snatched from the daily round, who scribbled to please herself and entertain the family, who sat quietly in a corner, silently observing the world go by, catching a turn of phrase, the trick of conversation, absorbing the characters and mannerisms of her neighbours and friends, describing their comings and goings, their contretemps, their joys and sadness, their follies and stupidities and failings. But—Austen-Leigh hastens to reassure the reader—there was no

3

intrusion. She never copied, never caricatured. If we are to believe it, 'She herself, when questioned on the subject by a friend, expressed a dread of what she called such an "invasion of social proprieties".'[12]

All we now know about Jane Austen's method of writing, her craftsmanship, her careful revision of the manuscripts and the attention she gave to her proofs, confirms Austen-Leigh's 'dear Aunt Jane' as an endearing fiction. Doubtless, from his angle of vision, from what he had seen and known of her himself as a child (he was born in 1798), and gathered from his sisters, who helped him with the *Memoir*, Austen-Leigh wrote in good faith. Yet he also set out to maintain the illusion of Aunt Jane's ladylike *amateurism*. This was coupled with the idea that the family held first place in her life and that writing was simply a polite accomplishment that she permitted herself at odd moments when time and opportunity offered. In the concluding tribute (at the close of Chapter 11), Austen-Leigh turns away from the writing and locates her achievement elsewhere. 'Her life', we read, 'had been passed in the performance of home duties, and the cultivation of domestic affections, without any self-seeking or craving after applause.'[13]

Austen-Leigh's treatment of this point reflects a peculiarly *Victorian* sensitivity within the family. There was the feeling in some quarters that Aunt Jane, estimable as she was, did not quite come up to the mark. According to her favourite niece Fanny Knight, now the dowager Lady Knatchbull, 'Aunt Jane from various circumstances was not so *refined* as she ought to have been for her *talent*'; 'if she had lived 50 years later she would have been in many respects more suitable to *our* more refined tastes.'[14] This was in August 1869. Shrewdly, Austen-Leigh took note and allows no such objection to be raised. His aunt is rendered to Victorian taste. Her life is mirrored in her art—at least, in its most favourable aspect. The charm 'of her most delightful characters', their 'moral rectitude', 'correct taste' and 'warm affections' were, he declares, 'a true reflection of her own sweet temper and loving heart'.[15] The symptoms and suffering of her long, lingering, last illness pass without mention. 'Finally', as Reginald Farrer observed, in 1917, 'she does not even die for us of anything particular, but fades out, with Victorian gentility, in a hazy unspecified decline' (No. 27).

For the frontispiece, Mr Andrews, the local portraitist at Maidenhead, was encouraged to turn Cassandra's sketch into a vignette of picture-card prettiness. Cassandra drew a face sharp and watchful, with large unmelting eyes and pursed lips. Andrews's Jane Austen is a plump-faced anybody.[16] The novels themselves are discussed in terms equally decorous. In the three later novels, for example, Austen-Leigh pointed to 'a greater refinement of taste, a more nice sense of propriety'.[17] His Jane Austen is unquestionably ladylike, unquestionably the lady amateur, an unconscious and un-labouring genius. Although few of the reviewers swallowed these 'fantasies of propriety' (to quote Farrer again), it was a myth that caught the imagination of the public—and, inevitably, it reap-peared in subsequent accounts, since the *Memoir* remained the main biographical source until the second family biography, *The Life and Letters* of 1913.

Of course, the myth was challenged. The Victorian novelist Margaret Oliphant put her finger on the nub of the matter. It was just as if 'The family were half-ashamed to have it known that she was not just a young lady like the others, doing her embroidery',[18] so different from the open pride that the Oliphant family took in her writing. But the myth was persistent. It was aired again and again in the re-writings of Jane Austen's life served up in popular magazines. It also crops up in such a sober work as *The Civil Service Handbook of English Literature: for the use of candidates for examinations, public schools and students generally* by Austin Dobson. Referring to the *Memoir*, Dobson remarks:

The sketch of her life ... makes more wonderful the genius of the quiet and placid clergyman's daughter, who, living in the retirement of a secluded rural parsonage and a remote rural home, a retirement broken only by the mild dissipation of a four years' residence in Bath,—not brilliant, not bookish,—contrived to write a series of novels which (on her own ground) have not even yet been surpassed.[19]

A standard textbook history, the *Handbook* was first published in 1874, many times reprinted, with a second edition in 1880 and a revised edition in 1897. Throughout, this wording remains unchanged and students by the ten-thousand must have assisted in the transmission of this touching fantasy.

Within the family, it was a long-standing grievance that Jane Austen's gifts had not been sufficiently acknowledged and the promotion of his aunt's reputation is a cause which the biographer duly pursues with determination. In Chapters 8 and 9 the testimo-nials are paraded. There is a roll-call of her admirers, 'the best judges',[20] as he describes them—including Scott, Whately, and Macaulay—their 'golden opinions'[21] marshalled in support. He also compiled a record of favourable quotations from letters, hearsay and other unpublished sources. For during the years of her obscurity, on both sides of the Atlantic,[22] Jane Austen's reputation had been cherished within small literary circles and families rather than in the reviews and histories of literature. Austen-Leigh gave pride of place to the famous 'Big Bow-wow' entry in Scott's Journal for 14 March 1826:

Read again, for the third time at least, Miss Austen's finely written novel of "Pride and Prejudice". That young lady had a talent for describing the involvements and feelings and characters of ordinary life, which is to me the most wonderful I ever met with. The Big Bow-wow strain I can do myself like any now going; but the exquisite touch which renders ordinary commonplace things and characters interesting from the truth of the description and the sentiment is denied to me. What a pity such a gifted creature died so early![23]

First made public in Lockhart's *Life of Scott,* 1837–38, these touching and perceptive remarks at once became the kernel of Jane Austen criticism, the statutory quotation. No article or essay could proceed far without it—not simply because Scott's paragraph carried the stamp of authority but because it pointed to a homely truth which ordinary readers could confirm for themselves. It was a truth with a lasting appeal, as we can see in Ezra Pound's comment that 'People will read Miss Austen because of her knowledge of the human heart, and not solely for her refinement.'[24] Scott's remarks were also prized for the attractive idea that a great writer could be enjoyable, and could be spoken of affectionately as a friend, as well as revered as a genius.

This is the very note of the *Memoir.* The reader is made to feel at ease. A 'prose Shakespeare', the novelist is also a universal aunt, sweet-natured and loving. Her literary domain is familiar ground—the homes, families and the neighbourhoods of the country gentry; and Austen-Leigh takes it for granted that the reader will be able to enjoy the sense of being at one with a select and discriminating audience. In Chapter 8, he recalls that 'To the multitude her works appeared tame and commonplace, poor in colouring, and sadly deficient in incident and interest.'[25] In support of this he quotes a Mr R.H. Cheney, 'one of the ablest men of my acquaintance' who said 'in that kind of jest which has much earnest in it, that he had established it in his own mind, as a new test of ability, whether people *could* or *could not* appreciate Miss Austen's merits.'[26] Whatever Lady Knatchbull might say, whatever lingering doubts there may have been within the family, Austen-Leigh provides a silencing riposte to any questioning of Aunt Jane's social refinement. All else paled in the face of her high literary cultivation and the connoisseurship it commanded. For all his seeming naïvety, Austen-Leigh was a sound judge of what counted. He struck the chord of cultural snobbery with unerring skill. Alongside Scott's 'Big Bow-wow' testimony, the Cheney-test won an immediate and prominent place in the reviewers' stock-in-trade. The notices of the *Memoir* in the *Quarterly Review* for 1870 and the *Athenaeum* for 1871[27] both open with the Cheney-test and it becomes a canon of the Janeite cult,[28] defining its exclusivity and asserting its superiority of taste. Durable and tenacious, it was to reappear in strange places, in versions curiously distorted. 'The appreciation of Miss Austen has come to be one of the marks of literary taste' declared an American study, of 1902, on its final page;[29] and the editor of an American high-school text of *Sense and Sensibility*, published in 1913, concluded the Introduction in terms which must have left its youthful readers baffled:

At the present time her fame is secure, though, like Milton, her popularity seems destined to be confined to the fit and few. Indeed, one eminent man has said, half in jest and half in earnest, that, in order to determine whether a person has or has not ability, one has only to ascertain whether he does or does not like Miss Austen's books.[30]

Equally baffling was the Introduction to another American high-school text, of *Pride and Prejudice*, first published in 1908 (with new editions until 1919), which advised the student that Jane Austen's novels 'are referred to now as models, and are especially acceptable to minds of a high order'.[31]

It was with some success, then, that Austen-Leigh fashioned the sparse and discontinuous critical heritage up to 1870 into a seemingly compact and organised record. The orchestration was immediately effective (although, as we have just seen, with some strange results). Reviews followed and a widespread interest in Jane Austen was awakened. The *Memoir's* first printing of one thousand copies was soon exhausted. In 1871 there came a second, enlarged edition encouraged, according to Austen-Leigh, by 'The notices taken of it in the periodical press'[32] and by letters from the public at large. To the 1870 text were added the most important of the unpublished manuscripts—*Lady Susan*, *The Watsons*, the cancelled chapter of *Persuasion*, extracts from *Sanditon* and further letters. The *Memoir* was reprinted again in 1872 and remained continuously in print thereafter.

An important aspect of Austen-Leigh's success was to draw his aunt in terms so appealing to the family reading-circle. This was a delicate, highly sensitive (and profitable) area of the market, its needs catered for by magazines and journals whose contents were designed for reading aloud *en famille*.[33] Where Hardy later gave offence and George Eliot over-burdened with ideas, Jane Austen seemed to offer the nice balance of principles and entertainment for which Trollope provided a high certification. Addressing an Edinburgh audience in January 1870 (a month after the *Memoir's* publication), he assured his listeners that Jane Austen is 'full of excellent teaching, and free from an idea or word that can pollute. ... Throughout all her works, and they are not many, a sweet lesson of homely household womanly virtue is ever being taught.'[34] Privately, Trollope thought differently, complaining of the 'timidity' and 'cowardice' with which she treated her 'most touching scenes'.[35]

The words of his Edinburgh address carried a particular resonance. Trollope was speaking the language of Ruskin, the Ruskin of *Sesame and Lilies*. This influential tract, published in 1865 and continuously in print for over forty years, intoned the sanctity of the home, the woman's true role and the books by which she should be informed and inspired. While Ruskin had no objection to novels as such, he deplored the effect of their 'overwrought interest': 'The best romance becomes dangerous, if by its excitement, it renders the ordinary course of life uninteresting.'[36] Two years later, he warned of the influence of sensation fiction upon the young. He found the 'connection' between real 'atrocities' and 'the modern love of excitement in the sensational novel' to be 'direct and constant; all furious pursuit of pleasure ending in actual desire of horror and delight in death'.[37] To combat these and other evils of the age he invoked 'the majesty of the influence of good books, and of good women, if we know how to read them, and how to honour'—the 'themes' of *Sesame and Lilies*.[38]

In the *Memoir*, this marvellous collocation of life and literature was to be found. Those aspects of the novels that seemed to put them out of the race—their narrow domesticity, their emptiness of high drama and stirring events, their distance in period, their unrhetorical tone, their undemanding address—now stood out as qualities moral and literary, of high esteem in the Ruskinian ethic. Likewise their author. Austen-Leigh's aunt steps as from a Ruskinian dream: possessed 'of sound sense and judgment, rectitude of principle, and delicacy of feeling, qualifying her equally to advise, assist, or amuse'[39]—an all-purpose recommendation! Ruskin warned of the disease of modern life and the diseased literature that it nurtures, its fictional flower the sensation novel—melodramatic, morbid, city-bound and designed to excite. Austen-Leigh announces the very antidote. His aunt's novels impart what he described as 'the great moral ... namely, the superiority of high over low principles, and of greatness over littleness of mind'.[40] Reviewers were ready to re-render Austen-Leigh in this Ruskinian vein. As one put it, whereas 'In the present age ... when most of the powerful writers employ their power in harrowing our feelings painfully', Jane Austen grants us peace and refreshment, novels of 'quiet humour ... quaint reality ... sober and unexaggerated tone'.[41] The benefits are amusingly recorded in Fitzgerald's note that the eminent orientalist Cowell 'constantly reads Miss Austen at night after his Sanskrit Philology is done: it composes him: like Gruel'; while the painter G.F. Watts turned to Jane Austen at all times: in good health for 'inspiration', for comfort when 'tired or unwell'.[42] The restorative power of the novels was famed. A notable later testimony is found in the memoirs of Margot Asquith:

All sense of fatigue disappears when Jane Austen, with her exquisite sense of humour, unerring ear, and finished style, takes us into her elegant and forgotten world.... (More Memories (1933), p. 255).

In the realm of public debate, the qualities enumerated by Austen-Leigh were seized upon as virtues of rare and high esteem. No other novelist, Victorian or earlier, was prescribed in these salutary terms. Here was an antidote to the unwholesome violence of contemporary fiction, seen at its worst in Wilkie Collins and the Dickens of Bleak House (Ruskin counted up and classified the deaths!). And the unsensationalism in her treatment of love led the reviewers to commend the novelist's 'propriety'. The St Paul's Magazine noted a total absence of the delerious excitement which distinguishes the novel of the present day. The wild pulsation, the strong embrace, the hand-pressure which bruises, the kiss which consumes, all these things, the essentials of the fiction of our period, are absent from Jane Austen's pages; the strongest expression there permitted to a lover is 'dearest', and the most ardent exhibition of passion is a shake of the hands.[49]

This lauding of Jane Austen at the expense of contemporary fiction was, in some quarters, seen as outright provocation and duly answered. The popular novelist James Payn, reviewing the *Memoir* in *Chamber's Journal* (5 March 1870), complained at the activities of the '"goody-goody" people' who condemn 'all that sensational stuff' and 'think it wrong to "waste their time over novels" of any sort, and they only recommend Miss Austen as a sort of alternative medicine, through which eventually the depraved literary stomach might be adapted for really wholesome food'.[44] There was substance to his complaint and Jane Austen was soon to become a pawn in the dispute between the over-delicate Ruskinians and advocates of a more vigorous diet.

It was easy to score off Ruskin and his followers for their wholesale attacks on the 'morbid realism' of the industrial and urban novel, upon the infectious sensationalism of stories of mystery and detection, or the over-wrought pathos of the death-bed scene, beloved of Dickens. Nonetheless, there was a more broadly based sympathy and sanity to Ruskin's positive vision. 'In these days of the book deluge', he stressed the need 'to keep out of the salt swamps of literature, and live on a little rocky island of your own, with a spring and a lake in it, pure and good'.[45] Ruskin advanced 'quietness and repose of manner' as qualities of good literature and urged 'that literature and art are best to you which point out, in common life, and in familiar things, the objects for hopeful labour, and for humble love'.[46] These were the values which the *Memoir's* Jane Austen seemed to celebrate, the refreshment she seemed to offer.

For those anxious about fiction and its effect upon the reader, Jane Austen was to remain in favour, strongly supported by the Ruskinian critique. In 1880, Gissing warned his sister against reading '*too* many novels' and instructed her 'to know all the best; you should get hold of Jane Austen's novels, they are very healthy'.[47] *What Shall I Read?*, 1887, a list compiled for the Girl's Friendly Society, opens with a notable quotation from Lowell—that books 'either beckon upward or drag down'—and the Introduction explores the perennially agitating question—What is 'safe reading'? Ruskin's 'the majesty of the influence of good books, and of good women' is quoted in full and Jane Austen's name follows that of Scott at the head of the safe authors and titles. Three years later, Jane Austen was being recommended by Goldwin Smith at a time when 'A flood of modern fiction pours in, and sensationalism prevails'; when 'the sensation novel gives us murder, and perhaps carnage on a still larger scale, adulteries, bigamies, desperate adventures and hairbreadth escapes.'[48] The six novels continue to be prized by 'clever, illustrious, thinking men', according to *Women Writers*, 1892: 'they find in them a cheerful repose, a freedom from effect, from violent passions, which interests without exciting.'[49]

For the 1870s, Jane Austen met a further need. The serious debate about women's education and the woman's role in marriage and society was already in progress. While *Sesame and Lilies* spoke disparagingly of the 'mission' and 'rights of Woman', it reminded its readers of 'what womanly mind and power are in office', of 'the true dignity of woman' and of woman's 'true queenly power. Not in their house-holds merely, but over all within their sphere.'[50] Jane Austen would not have subscribed to Ruskin's argument. Nonetheless, her heroines display evidence enough of the 'woman-ly mind' and of the woman's 'true dignity'. As a *woman* writer, writing about women and exploring their experiences as indi-viduals in their homes, in society and, in particular, in their relationships with men, Jane Austen was welcomed by Victorian feminists as a fellow-spirit. What they found so sympathetic and refreshing was the absence of any hectoring, any overtly feminist intent, any 'mission'. In the 1840's, she had been hailed as a 'prose Shakespeare'.[51] Now was the moment for this idea to be revived, for *women* to claim her as their literary heroine, their Shakespeare-of-the-novel—always remembering that by some women she was accounted quite un-Shakespearian for the worldliness of her fictional scene and her characters' unspirituality, as we see in a letter from Elizabeth Barrett Browning to Ruskin in 1855 (first published in 1897):

[Miss Mitford] never taught *me* anything but a very limited admiration of Miss Austen, whose people struck me as wanting souls, even more than is necessary for men & women of the world. The novels are perfect as far as they go—that's certain. Only they don't go far, I think. It may be my fault.[52]

But these were private views and scarcely reflected in public debate. Critical discussion in the 1870s is far more responsive to the cause of women and the advocacy of writers such as Josephine Butler—firing her readers with the challenge that 'the dignity of women' was then 'an empty name' and rallying them round 'Our English homes' as 'the strongholds of all virtue'.[53]

II

In Jane Austen's social and moral respectability, as represented in the *Memoir*; in the *un*sensationalism of her stories; in their repute as readable classics of high cultural cachet; in the wholesomeness of their entertainment; and in their focus upon the woman's experience—we can understand why she seemed ripe for rediscovery and recommendation. These are the issues that fill the reviews and essays of the time and they help to explain how it was, more than fifty years after her death, that Jane Austen came to be installed as the literary heroine of the age. In this was a remarkable change. Since Jane Austen's death the critical literature had been thin. There were brief notices of the 1833 Bentley edition and passing references in articles and reviews. Histories of literature and biographical dictionaries provided half-a-dozen entries, some only a paragraph or two long. Prior to 1870, we know of only six essays devoted solely to Jane Austen, the earliest of these dated 1852. The most considerable account had been the two chapters in Julia Kavanagh's *English Women of Letters*, 1862 (*No. 39*). This slender critical tradition was the record alluded to by Austen-Leigh in his citation of 'the best judges', from Scott and Whately onwards to the campaigning of Macaulay and Lewes. Amongst writers and critics the novels were well known, though not invariably admired. There were notable dissenters: Mrs Browning, just quoted; Charlotte Brontë, in her exchange with Lewes and her publisher (*No. 28*); Carlyle, who thought the novels 'dismal trash';[1] Fitzgerald, who found them 'quite unendurable to walk in' (*No. 37*). Yet her admirers were legion—including Mary Russell Mitford, Newman, George Eliot, Trollope, Thackeray, Hallam and Tennyson—and the documentation of this period shows us how very high was Jane Austen's reputation within literary circles.

This was clearly reflected in the reviews of the *Memoir*. In the *Academy*, Edith Simcox noted that 'In the same sense that Keats is the poet's poet, Miss Austen has always been *par excellence* the favourite author of literary men' and she went on to attribute the novelist's 'unassailable place amongst English classics' to her 'delicate execution and subtle analytical power'.[2] But it had been largely a private reputation, recorded in letters and diaries. We see this, for example, in Darwin's letters to his family and friends in the 1830s; in Bulwer Lytton's comment, in 1824, that the novels 'enjoy the highest reputation'; that amongst the Balfours, she was 'a family idol'; in Macaulay's note, 'Read Northanger Abbey; worth all Dickens and Pliny together';[3] in Harriet Martineau's, 'She *was* a glorious novelist';[4] or in the amusing fact that Matthew Arnold, known to his daughters as a 'Mr Woodhouse', read *Mansfield Park* annually to preserve his style.[5] The 'universal note of praise', recorded by Lewes in 1852,[6] was really only 'universal' amongst his own and other such discriminating circles. The interest in Jane Austen was distinctly a minority interest. So the appearance of the *Memoir* was seen as the occasion to pay Jane Austen a public tribute long overdue and an opportunity to make her work generally known. The measure of this can be seen in the thirteen reviews of the 1870 *Memoir* and four of the second edition of 1871, ranging from notices of a thousand words or so to essays upwards of eight thousand. In the *Spectator*, a serious weekly with a large circulation, the editor himself, R.H. Hutton, chose to review both editions and other well-known reviewers, including Anne Thackeray and Margaret Oliphant, saw this as a chance to write at length, Mrs Oliphant to almost sixteen thousand words.

In the circumstances, it was natural that reviews of the *Memoir* were reflective and considered. It was not the case of a new talent to be assessed on the moment, but the opportunity to air judgments long-pondered on a small and distinctive body of writing; judgments which were, moreover, commonly shaped by the established critical tradition stemming from Scott and Whately. So while the general level of criticism is high, amongst the individual pieces we find, nonetheless, a certain uniformity. The accounts tend to be somewhat defined and circumscribed. We see the novels praised for their elegance of form and their surface 'finish'; for the realism of their fictional world, the variety and vitality of their characters; for their pervasive humour; and for their gentle and undogmatic morality and its unsermonising delivery. The novels are prized for their 'perfection'. Yet it is seen to be a narrow perfection, achieved within the bounds of domestic comedy. This consensus account of Jane Austen is fairly represented in Hutton's review (No. 2). The novels are found to be 'exquisitely finished', distinguished for 'their fine, sedate humour and gentle irony'. They are works which 'give us so strong a sense at once of the depth and the limits of the genius'. The 'deeper problems of life' she touches 'so lightly and so gently'. Unlike 'our modern novelists' (naming George Eliot, Thackeray and Mrs Gaskell), she does not '*arraign* either human nature or society for their shortcomings and positive sins'. To the conclusion: 'And thus the limited work she had to do, she achieved with greater perfection and fineness and delicacy of touch than almost any other English writer with whom we are acquainted. Never was a definite literary field so clearly marked out and so perfectly mastered as by Miss Austen.' This style of evaluation—its judgments assured and conclusive—is characteristic of journalist-criticism. Yet it also tells us about the mood of the reviewer, his confidence in placing Jane Austen, his satisfaction at being able to pin-point her achievement with such precision. Not surprisingly, the temptation has proved to be lasting. The lines quoted from Hutton find an uncanny echo, sixty years later, in the Journal of Gide. On 24 January 1929, he was nearing the end of *Pride and Prejudice*

in which Jane Austen achieves perfection, but in which one realizes rather readily (as in Marivaux) that she will never risk herself on heights exposed to too strong winds. An exquisite mastery over what can be mastered. Charming differentiation of the secondary characters. Perfect achievement and easy triumph of decorum. What a charming woman she must have been! Incapable of any intoxication, but almost forcing one to think: it is better thus.[7]

'Wonderful little woman!' Goldwin Smith writes in 1890 (No. 12); and it is this note of *patronising* admiration—a common chord in Gide and Hutton—that lurks uncomfortably in so much of the appreciative criticism.

Nonetheless, amongst many of the 1870 reviewers there was a shared sense of the problem involved in introducing Jane Austen to a wider audience, to whom the novels were unknown. Would a larger public be capable of responding to the 'fineness' and 'delicacy' of her work? And was there anything new to be said?

These questions were posed by T.E. Kebbel in the *Fortnightly Review:*

This is a wonderful triumph of art. Yet it is equally clear that excellence of this kind is no passport to popularity. On the whole, Jane Austen has probably been as much admired as in the nature of things it was possible she should be. Lord Macaulay and Archbishop Whately have done for her reputation all that the most influential criticism can accomplish.

As for the novels themselves, Kebbel comes up with the stock evaluation: 'They are good genteel comedies. They play over the surface of life, and represent its phenomena with the most finished elegance...' He is able to recommend them for 'the quiet fun, the inexhaustible sly humour, the cheerful healthy tone, the exquisite purity, and the genuine goodness which are reflected in every line she wrote.'[8]

There was the occasional unexpected observation. The *Dublin Review* saw 'the levity of Mrs Bennet and her younger daughters' as 'the lively and amusing study, from which the delicate and perfect delineation of Miss Crawford's warped sense of propriety and deficiency of moral tone is afterwards executed'. Alongside Mary Crawford, 'one of the most brilliant of Miss Austen's productions', is placed 'the incomparable Mrs Norris' and Lady Bertram, 'a triumph of art', a 'model of sleek, indolent, contented selfishness'. Although the Catholic reviewer deplored the absence from the novels of true religion and 'spirituality' from the clergyman, she was ready to draw attention, uncensoriously, to Jane Austen's genius in portraying women very far from any Ruskinian or Victorian ideal and quite uncomic in their power.[9] Another insight is Goldwin Smith's reflection on Jane Austen and Shakespeare:

Both are really creative; both purely artistic; both have the marvellous power of endowing the products of their imagination with a life, as it were, apart from their own. Each holds up a perfectly clear and undistorting mirror—Shakespeare to the moral universe, Jane Austen to the little world in which she lived. In the case of neither does the personality of the author ever come between the spectator and the drama.[10]

But such perceptions are rare. Amongst the 1870 reviews there was no real engagement with the idea of Jane Austen as a 'prose Shakespeare'. And there was no glimpse of the writer seen by Tennyson:

Miss Austen understood the smallness of life to perfection. She was a great artist, equal in her small sphere to Shakespeare... There is a saying that if God made the country, and man the town, the devil made the little country town. There is nothing to equal the smallness of a small town.[11]

While the reviewers accepted the *Memoir* portrait of Jane Austen the woman, there was some dissatisfaction with Austen-Leigh's presentation of his aunt as writer. The *Athenaeum,* quoting Jane Austen's remark about working on her little bit of ivory to 'little effect after much labour', comments pointedly 'But of this labour we hear scarcely anything.' 'Something further might surely be attained by referring to her papers.'[12] In the *Academy,* Edith Simcox voiced the same complaint. She lamented the absence of the 'unpublished writings' and pointed to the value of being able to compare the cancelled chapter of *Persuasion* with the published version. This wish was answered in the expanded 1871 *Memoir;* and in her second review she was able to look closely at the manuscript material and observe that 'judgement had a share in her successes, as well as inspiration'.[13] There is a similar attention to the manuscripts in E. Quincey's review of the American edition of the 1871 *Memoir,* published by Scribner's. Under the title 'The Early Writings of Jane Austen', Quincey describes the cancelled chapter as 'the most interesting' of the manuscript remains, *Lady Susan* as 'entirely unworthy of Miss Austen's hand... thoroughly unpleasant in its characters and its details' and *The Watsons* as 'unpromising'. He recognised that the ease and unpretentiousness of the novels was a feat of art: 'for that perfection of artifice which conceals itself and seems nothing but the simplicity of nature and the necessary course of events, there is no story-teller that we know that surpasses Jane Austen.'[14] The wish of the *Athenaeum* reviewer was also answered; and in his notice of the 1871 *Memoir* he declared that 'the real interest of this volume consists in the unpublished fragments'.[15] The 'intrinsic interest' of the manuscripts was also noted in the *Saturday Review.* A solid and well-informed piece, it identifies the literary traditions in which *Northanger Abbey* and *Sense and Sensibility* stand and views Lady Susan as a character appropriate to a 'sensational' novel.[16]

Alongside this attentive and workmanlike reviewing— interesting to us now for historical reasons—there was also critical writing of lasting value, seen on a small scale in Hutton's brief account of the unpublished pieces 'which the public have been so long and so eagerly expecting'. Hutton found *The Watsons* 'full of promise'; the fragment of *Sanditon* indicated that 'the author's humour would probably have taken a broader and more farcical form' than ever before; while in *Lady Susan* he detected a failure of 'form' and 'nerve'. Hutton's explanation of this failure, brief as it is, is a brilliant reconstruction, one of the very best accounts of *Lady Susan* and all the more interesting to us today for having lain untouched by later critics.

The two most important review-articles were those by the Shakespearian critic Richard Simpson and the novelist Margaret Oliphant, both to be found in the previous *Critical Heritage* volume, Simpson (*No. 44*) in full, Mrs Oliphant (*No. 42*) in part. The case of Simpson illustrates the discontinuity of the critical heritage at this time. In any company, he must rank as one of the great critics of Jane Austen. Lionel Trilling has described his essay as

perhaps the very first consideration of the subject undertaken in the spirit of serious criticism—the first, that is, to go beyond mere expressions of delight and regard, or calculations of the distance at which Jane Austen stands from Walter Scott and Shakespeare, to address itself to a description of the novels in their innerness and their largeness of import.[17]

Simpson's account of the writer's mind and intelligence, of the force of her irony and the 'critical spirit' that 'lies at the foundation of her artistic faculty' is unmatched. The essay came anonymously in the *North British Review*, one of the leading periodicals of the day. But it might as well not have appeared. It is listed in several bibliographies of the time—yet no one borrows an idea.[18] It was not until 1957, in Lionel Trilling's Introduction to *Emma*,[19] that Simpson's essay (its author still unidentified) was given its due and his concept of 'intelligent love' introduced to our critical vocabulary, describing so exactly this distinctive aspect of Jane Austen's philosophy of human relationships.

While Simpson was not unsympathetic to the *Memoir* as a *family* tribute and accepted the propriety of 'dear Aunt Jane' as a family portrait, his review presents what is in effect a counter-image, an analytical portrait of the writer's mind, her intelligence, her essentially *critical* genius. In this light, the neglect of Simpson at the time is not so much an index of imperception as of the readiness with which the *Memoir* portrait was received and the ease with which it took possession of the public mind. Quite simply, with 'dear Aunt Jane' about, Simpson's Jane Austen stood no chance. This was the fate, too, of Mrs Oliphant's Jane Austen, a discomforting artist—an un-Ruskinian writer, armed with a 'fine vein of feminine cynicism', 'full of subtle power, keenness, finesse, and self-restraint', blessed with an 'exquisite sense' of the 'ridiculous', 'a fine stinging yet soft-voiced contempt', whose characterisation of Mr Collins is 'amazing in its unity and completeness... cruel in its perfection', whose novels are 'so calm and cold and keen', 'so remorselessly true'.

Mrs Oliphant's understanding of Jane Austen had been anticipated by one earlier writer, the novelist Julia Kavanagh. Her portrait was equally un-Ruskinian and equally un-aunt-like; and not surprisingly, Mrs Kavanagh, although truly one of the 'best judges', was ignored by Austen-Leigh. The *Memoir* contains no hint of what Mrs Kavanagh understood to be Jane Austen's 'really formidable powers', nor of the novelist's satire, its 'touch so fine we often do not perceive its severity'. She was the first critic to challenge the reader with an interpretation of Jane Austen's experience of life: 'she seems to have been struck especially with its small vanities and small falsehoods, equally remote from the ridiculous or the tragic'. Her reading of the novels is wholly different from those of Scott and Whately: 'If we look under the shrewdness and quiet satire of her stories, we shall find a much keener sense of disappointment than of joy fulfilled. Sometimes we find more than disappointment.' One has to ask if any critic, before or since, has pointed more sympathetically to the nature of the experience, for Jane Austen a creative experience, out of which the novels were written. Yet Mrs Kavanagh's account—like the views of Mrs Oliphant and Richard Simpson—was to disappear without trace, submerged by a rising tide of sentimentality and the seas of Janeite idolatory.

For its part in these processes, the *Memoir* was to draw accurate fire from Simpson and Mrs Oliphant. Simpson accepted the Jane Austen of the *Memoir* with resigned good humour, undisturbed by its misdirection. His energies were set upon characterising the writer. For the *Memoir* itself, he had a friendly nod. Not so Mrs Oliphant. Calling upon her own exquisite sense of the ridiculous, her review is itself a little masterpiece of 'fine stinging yet soft-voiced contempt'. Austen-Leigh's Jane Austen, she tells us, is a no one, undifferentiated from 'hosts of sweet women', a compound of myth and cliché. Alongside the nephew's 'dim little lantern', she turns a cold and focussed beam. The Austen family she calls a 'clan', the happy circle something of a prison, 'the sweet young woman' living in the shadow of her numerous brothers. (W. D. Howells looks in this direction, too, in speaking of 'the life of ingrowing family affection which she led among the brothers and sisters, and progressively nephews and nieces').[20]

Like Mrs Oliphant, Hutton (No. 2) objected to the laborious log-rolling of the *Memoir's* Chapters 8 and 9. He was put out by the testimonial style and ran a thirty-two line complaint in his opening paragraph, observing acidly that 'No one with a grain of literary sense doubts her wonderful originality and artistic power' and that 'to tell us that many worthy persons have since enjoyed her writings thoroughly, is like telling us that many have felt the warmth of summer.'

Mrs Oliphant regarded Jane Austen as an unquestionably great writer, of a very special kind—and she doubted that the author of 'books so calm and cold and keen' could ever be really 'popular' with 'the general public, which loves to sympathise with the people it meets in fiction, to cry with them, and rejoice with them'. These are works rather for the 'connoisseur', the 'critical and literary mind'. Nonetheless, Mrs Oliphant accepted that a popularisation of Jane Austen had been achieved, 'by dint of persistency and iteration', awakening (as she puts it so exactly) 'a half-real half-fictitious universality of applause'—and her accusing finger is pointed directly at the *Memoir*: ' "The best judges" have here, for once, done the office of an Academy, and laureated a writer whom the populace would not have been likely to laureate, but whom it has learned to recognise.' Recognition it is, not real knowledge, a point echoed in 1872 by Lady Pollock, accounting the novels 'more esteemed than loved'.[21] Twenty years later, according to Goldwin Smith, many people under fifty had not read Jane Austen. Lip-service was still the order of the day: the novels 'are spoken of respectfully as classics, and as classics allowed to rest upon the shelf'.[22] Even someone as indefatigably stimulating and professional as George Saintsbury groaned at the task of recording these endorsements yet again. The weary and cliché-ridden lines betray his fatigue:

They had no enormous or sudden popularity, but the best judges, from Scott downwards, at once recognised their extraordinary merit; and it is not too much to say that by the best judges, with rare exceptions, their merit has been acknowledged with ever increasing fulness at once of enthusiasm and discrimination to the present day.[23]

III

In locating the source of Jane Austen's high repute, Mrs Oliphant was also looking beyond the *Memoir*. Indeed, there was a considerable record of 'persistency and iteration' in the campaign waged by Macaulay and Lewes since the 1840s, opening with Macaulay's resounding declaration, in the middle of a review of Madame D'Arblay's *Diary and Letters*, that 'Shakespeare has had neither equal or second. But among the writers who, in the point which we have noticed, have approached nearest to the manner of the great master, we have no hesitation in placing Jane Austen, a woman of whom England is justly proud' (*No. 26*). Lewes took up this stunning claim in 1847, in reviewing a batch of English and French novels (*No. 27*) where he slips in a page on Jane Austen, announcing that she and Fielding 'are the greatest novelists in our language' and instructing his reader to mark the 'greatness' and 'marvellous dramatic power' of a writer who is no less than a 'prose Shakespeare'. Mistakenly, or intentionally, he attributes this phrase, of his own devising, to Macaulay, the critical nabob of the day. Lewes's aim was to make his readers sit up and take notice—and how well he succeeded we know from the famous exchange with Charlotte Brontë (*No. 28*). Lewes continued his campaign. In 1851, it was Jane Austen 'incomparable as an artist' (*No. 30*). In 1852, he opened 'The Lady Novelists' with a challenging fanfare: 'First and foremost let Jane Austen be named, the greatest artist that has ever written, using the term to signify the most perfect mastery over means to her end'; and he repeated 'prose Shakespeare', again attributing the words to Macaulay (*No. 32*). Lewes's 1859 essay (*No. 36*) carries a striking commentary on her contemporary reputation. According to Lewes, Jane Austen is familiar only to the 'cultivated reader'; 'beyond the literary circle we find the name almost entirely unknown'. He explains 'that her excellence must be of an unobtrusive kind, shunning the glare of popularity, not appealing to temporary tastes and vulgar sympathies, but demanding culture in its admirers'. Lewes's 'cultivated reader' is not simply familiar with the six novels. He is also knowledgeable about the critics: 'he will perhaps relate how Scott, Whately and Macaulay prize this gifted woman'. To jog the forgetful, Lewes quotes extensively, including the whole of Scott's 'Big Bow-wow' tribute. While he points to the limitations of Jane Austen's art, Lewes sings her praises as loudly as ever. In 'the rare and difficult art of *dramatic presentation*...she has never perhaps been surpassed, not even by Shakespeare himself'. Yet he accepts that 'the appreciating audience of Miss Austen' is restricted 'to the small circle of cultivated minds', 'to critical and refined tastes'. What 'popularity' she has is that of a 'classic'—'but' (he adds pointedly) 'we all know what the *popularity* of a classic means'.

This is the very issue of Mrs Oliphant's complaint. With Lewes and Macaulay and the lesser reviewers who echoed them, she had no quarrel. What she objected to was the move, on one hand, to popularise Jane Austen, on the other, to make a snobbery of her, to elevate her as a cultural shibboleth, to set her up as a mark of exclusive good taste. The *Memoir* was guilty of feeding this. Tongue in cheek, Mrs Oliphant quotes the Cheney-test. She may also have had in mind the kind of article which had recently appeared in the *English-woman's Domestic Magazine* for 1866 (*No. 41*) in which those familiar 'best judges'—Scott, Whately, Macaulay and Lewes—are invoked and deferred to and where Jane Austen is thoroughly 'domesticated': a writer whose principles are 'high and pure', whose comedy is 'genteel', whose morality is 'elegant', whose 'taste' is 'delicate' and 'lady-like', whose humour is of 'a refined and amiable kind'; a writer, we are instructed, not for the public at large but for 'minds of the highest culture'. So it was that Jane Austen began to attract, as Mrs Oliphant puts it, that 'half-real half-fictitious universality of applause'; began to attract a dutiful readership, with an anxious eye upon the opinions of 'the best judges'—a nervousness glimpsed in the journal of Lady Charlotte Schreiber (formerly Guest, notable as the translator of the *Mabinogion*). On 1 July 1876 she records:

I have been studiously reading four of Miss Austen's novels, incited thereto by Macaulay's praise, *Pride and Prejudice, Northanger Abbey, Persuasion, Mansfield Park*. I like the first least of all; I think I like the last best, but I cannot quite make up my mind whether I am alive to their very great merit. For the epoch at which they appeared, some sixty years ago, they are very remarkable.[1]

According to commentators on the literary scene, it was a problem which persisted. In October 1902, the editorial notes of the *Academy* spoke of the difficulty of getting

at the real attitude of this generation towards Jane Austen. She has many genuine and enthusiastic admirers, no doubt; but there is another section of the reading public which accepts her as read. They talk of her with discretion, avoid particular instances, and rejoice in generalities. The fact is that many quite reasonable people find her dull, but they refrain from stating so heterodox an opinion. Perhaps Mr Frewen Lord hits upon the true cause of this when he writes in the *Nineteenth Century*· 'The real superiority of her work lies in her admirable style; the real drawback to enjoying her work is that it is about nothing at all'.[2]

It was James, in 1905, who charted the strange course of Jane Austen's emergence into public view. Its origins he found in 'a beguiled infatuation, a sentimentalised vision, determined largely by the accidents and circumstances originally surrounding the manifestation of the genius'. The over-valuation, as he saw it—that had in recent years carried her 'rather higher, I think, than the high-water mark, the highest, of her intrinsic merit and interest'— he blamed not upon the 'critical spirit' nor the snobbery of the literary public, but on the stiff commercial breeze of the 'publishers, editors, illustrators, producers of the pleasant twaddle of magazines; who found their "dear", our dear, everybody's dear, Jane so infinitely to their material purpose' (No. 22 a).

The innocent seed of this luxurious blossoming was Austen-Leigh's 'dear Aunt Jane'; its immediate outcome, itself the progenitor of yards of 'pleasant twaddle', was the long review-eassay by Anne Thackeray which appeared in the *Cornhill Magazine* in 1871 (No. 3). Warmly addressed to 'All those who love her name and her work', it is heavy with rhapsodical pulsations, syrupy apostrophising and gaspings of delight.

Dear books! bright, sparkling with wit and animation, in which the homely heroines charm, the dull hours fly, and the very bores are enchanting.

Could we but study our own bores as Miss Austen must have studied hers in her country village, what a delightful world this might be...

So transported, Miss Thackeray alights upon the *Memoir:*

For the first time we seem to hear the echo of the voice, and to see the picture of the unknown friend who has charmed us so long—charmed away dull hours, created neighbours and companions for us in lonely places, and made harmless mirth.

Today, we may feel inclined to smile at a manner so patently evocative and to wonder at the cultivated elegiacism of the essay as a whole—with its tearful, threnodic conclusion, its quasi-philosophical moralising from literature to life and death. In this, the essay declares its pretensions as a belated act of justice, an *in memoriam* tribute, a lyrical hagiolatry, touching the strings of Tennyson and Ruskin, deepened with a poignant note of loss and regret personal to the essayist herself. The piece appeared in the August 1871 issue of the *Cornhill Magazine*. Earlier in the year, in March and April, visiting her beloved France, her childhood home, Miss Thackeray found the Germans still in occupation, and witnessed the ruins and devastation. When she returned to England, there came news of revolution and the burning of Paris. Against such a backcloth, the world of Jane Austen must have beckoned as a sanctuary indeed.

Nonetheless, Anne Thackeray's experience of the novels was also founded on a solid bank of common ground. By general consent, the characters possessed a unique vitality. As she put it, they belong 'to a whole world of familiar acquaintances, who are, notwithstanding their old-fashioned dresses and quaint express-ions, more alive to us than a great many of the people among whom we live.' This echoes Austen-Leigh's own tribute in the opening pages of the *Memoir*:

That prolific mind whence sprung the Dashwoods and Bennets, the Bertrams and Woodhouses, the Thorpes and Musgroves, who have been admitted as familiar guests to the firesides of so many families, and are known known there as individually and intimately as if they were living neighbours.[3]

Later in the *Memoir*, Austen-Leigh supported this, his own account, with an American testimony (dating from 1852): 'For many years her talents have brightened our daily path, and her name and those of her characters are familiar to us as "household words".'[4] So while we may find much in Miss Thackeray tasteless and tiresome, it is important to recognise that the essay articulates a widespread experience of the novels, on the one hand of their characters, 'living' and 'familiar', on the other, of their fictional world, depicting an England unsullied by industrial grime and the sprawl of cities. For this unpleasant, contingent reality, one could read Dickens. Anne Thackeray's Jane Austen provides an escape from 'this strange disease of modern life', a haven, seen rosily as the England of yesteryear, more gracious and more genteel, an idyllic retreat for which Miss Thackeray and her readers yearned. These, of course, are the projections of fantasy—Cowells' 'Gruel' or Watt's tranquilliser. But they speak of the power of the novels to catch the readers' imagination and answer their emotional needs. Twenty years later, in analysing Jane Austen's 'charm', R. H. Hutton pointed to the captivation of her 'world' and its capacity to be 'lived in... relieved of the bitterness of the elements' (No. 26). On the wealth of such testimony, Hutton was right to call this 'the true charm of Miss Austen', a 'charm' to which Anne Thackeray and her generation surrendered so readily.[5]

It is also worth putting up with the purple passages to reach Miss Thackeray's comments on Jane Austen's writing. Tricksily phrased they may be—but they signify a real understanding of the novelist's task. When she speaks of Jane Austen's 'gift of telling a story' and her 'gift for organisation', these are cogent points about the writer's narrative method and structural command. Of the novelist's accomplishment, she notes 'this was not chance, but careful workmanship'. She is alert to the vitality of *The Watsons*; and her discussion of the anticipations of *Emma* to be found there is speculation handled with a subtlety and care missing from the elaborate reconstruction set out seventy years later in Mrs Leavis's 'Critical Theory'.[6] Miss Thackeray also has telling points to make about the way in which Jane Austen's presentation of character differs from that of the later Victorian novelists. Of the heroines, she remarks, 'They have a certain gentle self-respect and humour and hardness of heart.' She observes unsentimentally that 'Love', for the heroines, 'does not mean a passion so much as an interest—deep, silent.' Unfortunately, this small yet solid line of commentary awakened no interest, even though the essay was twice reprinted in later collections of her work—*Toilers and Spinners* (1874) and *A Book of Sibyls* (1883). Twaddle not criticism was wanted and the twaddle was expanded. By 1883, as Miss Thackeray notes in the Preface to the second collection, Jane Austen had become a 'dear household name' and the piece was revised accordingly, not with a sharpening of the critical edge but with an apostrophe even more fanciful, affectionate and tearful (appended to No. 3). This was the sure calculation of a literary journalist sensing the public appetite for heavier sentiment and 'finer' writing, and Miss Thackeray's prose swells to the rising commercial breeze.

A Book of Sibyls is dedicated to Mrs Oliphant. Sadly, this was not the caustic Mrs Oliphant of old. Like Anne Thackeray, she too lived by her pen and like Miss Thackeray she had been swept off course—in her case, a truly critical course—by that same commercial breeze. Compared to the Jane Austen of her *Blackwood's* review of 1870, the Jane Austen of her *Literary History of England*, 1882,[7] is temporised, the sharp edges smoothed, the portrait re-drawn to contemporary taste: 'She was pretty, sprightly, well taken care of—a model English girl, simple, and saucy, and fair.' As for the novels, in place of explanation and analysis, Mrs Oliphant is now content to gesture towards the inexplicability of 'genius' and the mysteries of 'witchcraft and magic'. This is not a patch on the chapter she could have written for that *Blackwood's* audience of twelve years before. The falling off, if we call it this, is not in Mrs Oliphant alone, it is also in her readership—less literate, less sophisticated, its appetite whetted for sentimental biography. This seventies-into-eighties view of Jane Austen proved to be potent and persistent. Andrew Lang's 'Letter To Jane Austen', 1884, quotes the best and the worst of Miss Thackeray: alongside her perceptive remarks on the heroines, he gives the 'Dear books' apostrophe, interjecting his own whimsical '"Dear books", we say, with Miss Thackeray...'.[8] This cloying tradition was to live on a further fifty years. In F.W. Cornish's *Jane Austen*, 1913, Miss Thackeray, his cousin, and Mrs Oliphant are named as her most warm and discriminating admirers—not the acerbic Mrs Oliphant, but the perpetrator of 'a model English girl, simple, and saucy, and fair', quoted for our admiration.[9] Cornish then quotes Andrew Lang's own quotation of the 'Dear books' apostrophe.[10] The year before, in his *History of English Literature*, Andrew Lang was still invoking the *Memoir's* 'best judges' and gasping at the wonder of it: 'novels as great in their own style as Scott's, and as imperishable, had been wirtten by a girl of 21'.[11] The shadow of Miss Thackeray stretched even further. In R. Brimley-Johnson's *Jane Austen* of 1930, her 'Dear books' is quoted at the book's opening and close.[12] The enduring life of these words has as much to do with their

25

memorialising force as with the curiosity and quaintness of the idea. In the *Times Literary Supplement* obituary (6 March 1919), Virginia Woolf ended by remarking on Anne Thackeray's 'destiny in the future':

She will be the un-acknowledged source of much that remains in men's minds about the Victorian age. She will be the transparent medium through which we behold the dead. We shall see them lit up by her tender and radiant glow.

So it was that the critical heritage was immobilised, trapped in a mid-Victorian sensibility. Austen-Leigh's portrait, drawn to the taste of the period, was challenged, especially by the reviewers of the 1871 *Memoir* attentive to Jane Austen as writer. But these objections were soon forgotten; 'dear Aunt Jane' won the day. Criticism was not called for. Simpson and Mrs Oliphant were out of step with the public taste for the *in memorialism* of Miss Thackeray, elegant enthusings, fine writing about the 'dear household name'. So while the years 1870–71 did provide a staging-post, a period of consolidation, from which there might have issued a critical heritage refreshed and strengthened, instead, the continuing tradition was *belle lettriste* journalism. Miss Thackeray's touch was sure. She read the public mind and felt its pulse. Her tone—intimate, affectionate, playful, coy and tearful by turns—is perfectly judged. Her essay set the style. A heritage of 'pleasant twaddle', persistent to the turn of the century and beyond, was set in train.

On behalf of the 1870–71 reviewers, it has to be said that the majority were not involved in this kind of popularisation. Most wrote soberly and attentively to the subject, presuming readers familiar with the novels. On the other hand, little in their reviews could be built upon, a limitation which belongs more to the state of criticism than to the incapacity of the reviewers themselves. What was lacking from criticism at this time was the belief—which had existed in some measure for Scott, Whately and Lewes—that the novels of Jane Austen were (to use James's term) *discutable*, 'having a theory, a conviction, a consciousness of itself behind it—of being the expression of an artistic faith, the result of choice and comparison'.[13] While the 1870–71 reviewers speak freely of the 'perfection' of Jane Austen's art, there is no enquiry into the elements of her art. As the American essayist Agnes Repplier was to comment in 1900, quoting Goldwin Smith: '"Metaphor has been exhausted" in depicting the flawlessness of Miss Austen's art and narrowness of its boundaries' (No. 17g). Ideas about her realism and characterisation came straight from Scott and Whately. In crediting her 'fables' with 'compactness of plan and unity of action', Whately provided the ground upon which Lewes was to build his own account, the most developed, of Jane Austen's artistic economy: his claim, for example, in 1852: 'First and foremost let Jane Austen be named, the greatest artist that has ever written, using the term to signify the most perfect mastery over the means to her end' (No. 32); and again, in 1860, when he described *Pride and Prejudice* as 'finely-constructed...what looks so like the ordinary life of everyday, is subordinate to principles of Economy and Selection' (No. 38).

But the *Memoir* and the appreciative literature it inspired put an end to this kind of analysis—indeed, moved against it. The evidence provided by the manuscripts—of the working writer, of her long apprenticeship and development—was ignored in favour of Anne Thackeray's sweet authoress, that 'unknown friend', a genius indifferent to fame or fortune, her scenes and characters 'so natural and life-like that reading to criticize is impossible to some of us—the scene carries us away, and we forget to look for the art by which it is recorded'. Of the Steventon edition of the novels in 1882, the *Saturday Review* remarked that the critic 'feels how comparatively powerless analysis is to lay bare fully the sources of so subtle a thing as literary interest'.[14] A year later, a reviewer of *Portrait of a Lady* and Howells' *A Modern Instance* advised his readers that in treating the 'commonplace' Jane Austen is 'a consummate master' and that 'Her art is too like nature to admit of it being analysed.'[15] In 1897, Adolphus Jack was instructing readers of *Essays on the Novel: as illustrated by Scott and Miss Austen* that 'no critical analysis will reveal anything in her that is not summed up for good in the one word delightful.'[16] At the turn of the century, in his Introduction to *Pride and Prejudice*, E.V Lucas declared, against all the known facts, that 'she wrote her stories with...a pen of considerable celerity'. Upon this fallacy, he proceeded to mount a thesis calculated to hold some attraction for the ordinary reader, on the basis that there is nothing more amusing than to cock a snook at the experts, and none better to do this, in the realm of literature, than Jane Austen herself:

These circumstances baffle the professional critic, who is really at home and in earnest only with the work of conscious literary artificers, and who stands disconcerted and defeated in the presence of the 'divine chit-chat' of this little lady.

Accordingly, the critic is left with 'nothing but superlatives'.[17]

Lucas had no excuse for this profession of ignorance. It was a silly trick. The actual 'circumstances' had been recounted in the *Memoir* and afterwards rehearsed many times. Austen-Leigh had quoted the letters of January and February 1813 in which Jane Austen had confided to Cassandra her frivolous second thoughts on *Pride and Prejudice* and how, in revising it, she had 'lop't and crop't'.[18] Hutton promptly quoted from these letters and told his readers that the *Memoir* 'gives ample proof' 'That Miss Austen did fully appreciate her own power' (No. 2). Simpson underlined the point: 'What she wrote was worked up by incessant labour into its perfect form. ... She was patient as Penelope at her web, unpicking at night much that she had laboriously stitched in the day' (*No. 44*). In reviewing the 1871 *Memoir*, Quincey, following Henry Austen's lead in the 'Biographical Notice', noted that 'her genius was of gradual development' and pointed to the evidence of the manuscripts. Quincey looked to her work 'for that perfection of artifice which conceals itself and seems nothing but the simplicity of nature'.[19] This was a phenomenon observed long before. In 1830, the *Edinburgh Review* (*No. 21*) had remarked on the way in which early readers of Jane Austen had passed her by: 'They did not consider that the highest triumph of art consists in its concealment; and here the art was so little perceptible, that they believed there was none.' It was a point well-made and found its place in *The Book of Authors*, 1869 (No. 1).

After the *Memoir*, there could be no complaint that Jane Austen was uncelebrated. But the celebration carried readers further and further away from the realities of her art towards the figure of Anne Thackeray's song-bird, continued by James: 'Jane Austen, with all her light felicity, leaves us hardly more curious of her process, or of the experience in her that fed it, than the brown thrush who tells his story from the garden bough' (No. 22a). In 1902, James declared Jane Austen 'instinctive and charming' and directed the reader to Flaubert 'For signal examples of what composition, distribution, arrangement can do, of how they intensify the life of a work of art.'[20] Elsewhere, he accounted for the 'little touches of human truth, little glimpses of steady vision, little master-strokes of imagination' as the issue of 'the extraordinary grace of her facility, in fact of her unconsciousness' (No. 22a). The ideas are delightfully drawn. But whether it be in James or Lucas or Anne Thackeray's fellow-twaddlers, the notion was abroad, and happily seized upon, that Jane Austen, a writer of such modesty, artlessness and unconscious perfection, stood beyond the reach of criticism. Faced with Pellew's 'scientific criticism' (No. 7), James was fearful that his delightful Jane, immortal in 'her narrow unconscious perfection of form' (No. 8), might be smothered. Pellew dismantled the myth of the 'unconscious' unlabouring genius. Jane Austen's manipulation of existing fictional styles and types is, for him, evidence of her sophistication as a literary artist. Observantly, he drew upon the *Memoir's* account of where an epistolary 'Elinor and Marianne' stood behind *Sense and Sensibility*. But the chill of 'scientific criticism' could not prevail in a climate so welcoming to James's 'delightful Jane'. W.D. Howells was a champion of Pellew, yet he too forgot the facts of the case for the sake of the fantasy. Thus, by his account (No. 21), *Pride and Prejudice* is a 'masterpiece' 'achieved' 'With the instinct and love of doing it, and not with the sense of doing anything uncommon'. Wonderingly, and fallaciously, Howells describes it as an astoundingly precocious accomplishment, the work of a 'young girl of twenty'; and Jane Austen is drawn, in that same wondering light, as 'that girl who began at twenty with such a masterpiece'.

The figure of a 'young girl' novelist accorded perfectly with the view of Jane Austen as an entertainer, essentially unserious, unfit to be judged alongside writers engaged with the great issues of the hour. For Howells, she was 'a delicate and delightful artist', George Eliot 'of vastly wider and deeper reach'.[21] At the death of George Eliot in 1880, Hutton remarked that her novels 'cover so much larger a breadth and deeper a depth of life than Miss Austen's, that though they are not perhaps so exquisitely finished, they belong to an altogether higher kind of world'.[22] Ten years later, Hutton returned to this theme: 'In Miss Austen's world we are content to live as mere observers, while most of the great novelists of Europe succeed in agitating the heart and stimulating the instincts which lead to passion or action' (No. 14). This was echoed in America, where, in 1891, William Clymer declared that nothing by Jane Austen sets astir '"that vague hum, that indefinable echo, of the whole multitudinous life of man" which should, it has been said, be felt to pervade a great work of fiction'. In this limitation, Clymer says, she can be described as 'provincial'—although Clymer does not himself fall to this trap, for he finds that in this 'limitation lies much of her strength and of her charm' (No. 15). It was seen that George Eliot, Hardy and other later Victorian novelists were not unlike Jane Austen in writing about people ordinary and unknown. But whereas their characters were representative of a class or type, travelling towards 'obscure destinies', signifying historic process, Jane Austen's 'obscure lives' carry no such fateful resonance.

While the image of the 'young girl' novelist accords with James's song-bird, there were other figurings. The *Memoir's* 'dear Aunt Jane' also found an echo in James. His essay 'Matilde Serao' (1901) ended cosily. In retreat from the 'vulgarity' of the romantic novelist, it is to 'dear old Jane Austen' that 'we turn', upon whom 'we have positively laid a clinging hand'[23] (an intimacy that offended Arnold Bennet, for one).[24]

Thus the celebration of Jane Austen evoked diverse and unlikely *personae*, far from the working novelist that the reviewers accurately divined in the *Memoir*. And there came a further distortion when critics used Jane Austen as a sounding-board for their own literary vanities. The 'exquisite'[25] in her art awakened an exquisiteness in her admirers. We find this in the classical connoisseurship put on display by Andrew Lang when he discovered in 'Miss Austen's art . . . that exquisite balance and limit of Greek art in the best period.'[26] Such self-regarding preciousness was later anatomised in Frank Swinnerton's comments on a Janeite of long-standing, A.B. Walkley, for many years the leading theatre critic and essayist for *The Times*. On the theatre, Swinnerton found him competent enough:

But when Mr Walkley comes to the consideration of literature he is so intolerably familiar, as if he winked at Jane Austen and found her a pretty little dear, that he puts himself out of court as a critic. He confounds both Jane Austen and Proust. Reading Proust, he is complacent at his ability to read French and savor the delicious snobbery of Proust. Reading Jane Austen, he fancies himself very much as a refined ironist. Accordingly, Mr Walkley never quite attains to enjoyment of his favourite authors for their own virtues: his attention is too much absorbed by the spectacle of A.B.W. engaged in the act of appreciation.[27]

This was in 1924. Two years later Swinnerton continued these reflections in an article (written soon after Walkley's death) in response to comments in *The Times* about Walkley's 'Gallic love of work that was orderly, shapely and finely finished', of his finding in Proust 'a precision in subtlety', 'which he found no-where else except in the novels of Jane Austen'. Swinnerton replied:

The love of what is shapely and delicate, when it outgrows all other sympathies, is to my mind an indication of an inherent vulgarity; and some months ago I drew attention to what I believed to be this fact regarding Walkley. He was, I said in effect, so refined that he was vulgar. Is the point clear? Certainly, Walkley thought it an essential thing to be refined; and those who were more superficially vulgar than he were regarded with a great deal of distaste.[28]

Swinnerton had in mind passages such as this, from a talk published in *The Nineteenth Century* in April 1922, where Walkley places himself at the heart of the twaddle tradition and basks in the glow of self-congratulation, a sunlight eternal of the Janeite realms:

For us of to-day, then, Jane Austen's novels are more than mere novels, mere yarn-spinning to pass away an idle hour. They belong to the literature of consolation. They are a refuge not only from the madding crowd's ignoble strife, but from the crude and *criard* work which is even more madding than the crowd. This house of rest, built and endowed by Jane Austen, becomes for those who have once felt the peace of it a second home. Some people cannot read her. But all who can, love her. Is there any other novelist, alive or dead, who is so fondly loved? 'Dear books' Jane's novels were to Thackeray's daughter, no mean judge, and that is how all Austenites feel about them.[29]

Walkley did not write in vain. Seven years later, Lady Balfour put much of this passage (down to 'home') at the head of her *Cornhill* essay, 'The Servants in Jane Austen', continuing with an affectionate tribute to him as the rightful possessor of 'a private key' to this 'house of rest'.[30]

IV

The popularisation of Jane Austen after 1870–71 was conducted in reviews and articles increasingly aimed at readers to whom the novels were unknown. Introductory essays, complete with character studies and plot outlines, abound. There was no forum for the kind of serious, sustained analysis that Whately was able to conduct in the *Quarterly Review*, counting upon a classically educated reader, conversant with the Aristotelian distinction between the possible and the probable in art, a reader who was familiar with the novels and who thought about them too. Whately was also able to get quickly into the subject, on the assumption that the reader was a subscriber, had read and digested Scott's review of *Emma* and was ready to continue the discussion from that point. By the 1870s, circumstances so encouraging to the progress of criticism had passed and the critical heritage of these years is thin, a matter of occasional remarks, such as a sentence or two in William Forsyth's *The Novels and Novelists of the Eighteenth Century In Illustration of the Manners and Morals of the Age*, 1871. Although Forsyth is surprised and censorious at 'the constant husband-hunting', he also observes unblinkered that Jane Austen's young men can swear and her clergymen can drink; and he appreciates that she describes love 'with a subtlety of analysis and skill which makes her almost unapproachable amongst novelists'.[1]

From now on, the serious discussion of Jane Austen proceeds by fits and starts, as and when a critic with something new to say gets into print and is attended to. In 1872, for example, Lady Juliet Pollock contributed to *Macmillan's Magazine* a two-part essay on 'Novels and their Times'[2] in which she identified Jane Austen's place in the anti-romantic tradition. Henry Morley also took this approach, writing on 'Recent Literature' in the *Nineteenth Century* (August 1877), commenting that Jane Austen 'replaced the false sentiments and overstrained romance of revolutionary feeling with clear pictures of life and duty, in novels that painted humanity as it lay really about her'. He made the nice historical point that *Sense and Sensibility* and *Pride and Prejudice* 'were in their own way in prose what the *Lyrical Ballads* were in verse, a protest against inflated sentiment and diction'; and he recorded Jane Austen's preoccupation with 'the individual life and individual duty'.[3] Writing in the *Quarterly Review* in January 1873, John Hales noted 'it was a mere fragment of human life that Miss Austen saw with a clearness and an intelligence and a reproductive power that defy panegyric.'[4] But for criticism so dry and reflective there was no welcome. Nor was there any support for the strictures of Leslie Stephen (No. 5). Accepting her 'marvellous literary skill', he found nonetheless the humour of the novels 'excessively mild', 'without a single flash of biting satire', and the novelist herself 'absolutely at peace with her most comfortable world'—a view which perhaps explains his choice of the novels as death-bed reading.

Nonetheless, the *Memoir* had succeeded in entering a claim for Jane Austen's recognition as one of the great English novelists. Successive editions of the *Encyclopaedia Britannica* provide one measure of her advancing status. The 8th edition, of 1854, allowed her to be 'an elegant novelist' and described the six novels as 'pure and spirited delineations of domestic life, with the delicate discrimination of female character which few but of the gentler sex can adequately pourtray'.[5] In the 9th edition, of 1875, she becomes 'one of the most distinguished modern British novelists', the creator of 'the novel of domesticity', whose appreciation, we are advised, calls for 'a somewhat cultivated taste'.[6] A similar note is struck in *A Manual of English Literature* by George Craik. This was a successful textbook history, derived from Craik's much longer work, *A Compendious History of English Literature and of the English Language* first published, in two volumes, in 1861. There, Jane Austen and Maria Edgeworth are linked as 'generally admitted to have been the first female novelists of the last age'.[7] No more is said. But the *Manual*, first published in 1862, announced as a 'text-book for schools and colleges' and for students 'for the Civil Service and other competitive examinations', enlarged on this bare statement. In the 9th edition, 1883, some of the comments are by no means unperceptive: 'there is even an impression of restraint in the limits which she imposes upon herself'; 'her art is shown... above all, in her power of quiet and sarcastic analysis of motives'. Overall, however, the *Manual*, like the *Encyclopaedia Britannica*, describes a writer for the cultivated:

The very nature of her genius forbade her attaining wide popularity; but even if we call her pictures miniatures, there is something in their artistic finish which will always find her an audience fit though few.[8]

Another useful index is Henry Morley's *First Sketch of English Literature*. Morley—who became a Professor of English Literature at the University of London—was a prolific editor and populariser of the English classics and his *First Sketch* remained a standard student textbook for over forty years. In the original edition, 1873, the Jane Austen entry is ten lines long. Only *Sense and Sensibility* and *Pride and Prejudice* are named and most of the space is given to Scott's 'Big Bow-wow' comment. The entry remained unchanged for the 6th edition, 1880. But the 12th edition, 1886, 'New and Enlarged', gave two full pages (about 850 words), mentioning all six novels, some of the minor works, and comparing her work with Wordsworth and Fielding and commenting that 'good sense lies under good art. Every sentence has pith in it, and a quiet humour plays along the lines.'[9]

It was in the 1880s that the first books begin to appear—*Jane Austen and Her Works* by Sarah Tytler (Henrietta Keddie, a prolific romantic novelist) in 1880, the two-volume *Letters of Jane Austen* edited by Lord Brabourne in 1884, a *Jane Austen* volume by Mrs Malden in the 'Eminent Woman' series in 1889, the *Life of Jane Austen* by Goldwin Smith in 1890 and *The Story of Jane Austen's Life* by Oscar Fay Adams, published in Chicago in 1891. In 1882 Bentley brought out the Steventon Edition of the novels—tastefully printed, as it were, in rusty reddish-brown ink and handsomely presented on parchmenty paper with an elaborate binding and, in formal style, every page framed with rules, giving the text a memorial air for an author highly prized.

However, this dignification did nothing for the state of criticism. As Mrs Humphry Ward was to complain in 1885 (No. 9):

Miss Austen's novels are a well-worn subject. We have all read her, or ought to have read her; we all know what Macaulay and what Scott thought of her; and the qualities of her humour, the extent of her range have been pointed out again and again.

Mrs Ward shared Mrs Oliphant's irritation at the parading of 'the best judges' and the elevation of the author as a cultural shibboleth. But Brabourne's presentation of his great-aunt's letters provoked Mrs Ward to a more general lament.

Such editorial performance as this makes one sigh once more for a more peremptory critical standard than any we possess in England. What English *belles-lettres* of the present day want more than anything else is a more widely diffused sense of *obligation* among the cultivators of them—obligation, if one must put it pedantically, to do the best a man can with his material, and to work in the presence of the highest ideals and achievements of his profession.

James, too, had just sounded this note in 'The Art of Fiction', in 1884, where he commented sharply upon the level of what little discussion there was. But both he and Mrs Ward sighed in vain. That 'more peremptory critical standard' was a thing of the past. The present was deplorable, wrote Mrs Ward: 'Taste is laxer, the public easier to please, and book-making more profitable.' Such words found no welcome and it was Mrs Ward's fate, alongside the finest of her predecessors—Mrs Kavanagh, Mrs Oliphant and Richard Simpson—to be forgotten.

Mrs Ward comes with a clear sense both of the novelist's 'great deficiencies' and her true standing as a classsic, indisputably a classic, but a classic 'small' and 'thin'. Like James, she employs the craftsman's terminology—'the workshop which produced the novels', the 'wrestle' of the artist, the 'manufacture' of Catherine Morland. Equally, she applies a writer's commonsense to the composition of *Pride and Prejudice*, puncturing the myth of the prodigy-genius and noting soberly that the novel was probably much revised in the fifteen years between its inception and publication. She detects the earliness of *Northanger Abbey*, its style and spirit 'gay, sparkling and rapid' and discerns 'that buoyant and yet critical enjoyment of life, of which the six novels were the direct outcome'. A woman of her time, Mrs Ward was slightly uneasy as to the lightness of the novels, their 'intellectual and moral framework... of the simplest and most conventional kind'. She pondered the question—how could a writer living 'so narrow a life', 'practically a stranger to... the world of ideas', produce classics of such artistry?

If it had been heeded, Mrs Ward's account of the autobiographical element in the novels—what she calls 'the whole *yield* of Jane Austen's individuality'—could have saved acres of silly speculation. Likewise, the analysis of what Mrs Ward terms 'concentration'—'an exquisite power of choice and discrimination', 'that made Jane Austen what she was'—is a finely pointed account, succinct and original. If there is any precursor, it is T.E. Kebbel's review of the 1870 *Memoir*, where he remarks that

The very narrowness of her range enabled her to concentrate her intellectual vision upon the few types of character which she did meet, with an intensity for which no more extensive experience could have compensated, had it lessened this peculiar power.[10]

However, there was no mainstream of criticism into which Mrs

Ward's ideas could flow; no one to take them up; and her essay disappeared from sight.

Mrs Ward would have been slightly less scathing about the state of criticism had she come across the four or five paragraphs in 'the Editor's Easy Chair' of *Harper's* where William George Curtis remarked on the novelist's 'artistic instinct' and 'the singular beauty of form' which 'preserves' her work.[11] And undoubtedly she would have been less fiery if she had seen the Harvard Prize Dissertation by George Pellew, published in Boston in 1883 under the title *Jane Austen's Novels*. This is the earliest attempt at a systematic historical placing, what Howells was to describe as 'one of the first steps in the direction of the new criticism—the criticism which studies, classifies and registers'.[12] Pellew opposed the current impressionistic school of criticism, which rendered Jane Austen 'as a singular and inexplicable phenomenon, without connection with the past'. He argued that the 'modern critic' cannot be content with this—his job is to be an 'historian'—as he duly is, in a polemical essay of ten thousand words, sketching the literary tradition in which the novels stand.

Pellew sent a copy of his essay to Henry James. In his letter of thanks James raised the politest of eyebrows at the application of what he called 'scientific criticism' to his 'delightful Jane' (No. 8). For all that Pellew is 'scientific' in the method of historical scholarship, there is no lack of critical comment and interpretation in his observation, for example, that Mr Knightley 'represents in a modified form the wise parent, or the omnipresent tutor of the didactic school'. Regarding Elizabeth Bennet he remarks that 'It is the intellectual rather than the emotional side of the feminine character that is brought out...but to have done that well was an important contribution to English literature.' Again, 'It is in her power of creating in artistic form another world, similar to the little world she knew, that Miss Austen's power consists.' Yet Pellew is not everywhere sympathetic. 'Poetry' he does not find. (Compare this with Mrs Ward's comment on the scene in *Persuasion* where Anne Elliot and Wentworth, now reconciled, walk together from Camden Place to Westgate Buildings: 'Jane Austen at once seizes upon the vital points of it, and puts them before us, at first with a sober truth, and then with a little rise into poetry, which is a triumph of style.') Passion, too, is absent from Pellew's Jane Austen, drawing from James a tacit rebuke.

In of course an infinitely less explicit way, Emma Woodhouse and Anne Eliot give us as great an impression of 'passion'—that celebrated quality—as the ladies of G. Sand and Balzac. Their small gentility and front parlour existence doesn't suppress it, but only modifies the outward form of it. (No. 8)

Although some of the reviewers were prepared to mention the novels' elopements, love-children and adulteries, there could be no glimpse of such smouldering fires; 'the maiden lady realism of Miss Austen', as George Moore put it in 1888 (No. 10), was the accepted version of the day; and it was to be another thirty years before Moore chose to make public what he glimpsed of the novels' seething interior life and their author's perception of 'the Venusberg in the modern drawing-room' and the 'truth' that 'We do not go into society for the pleasure of conversation, but for the pleasure of sex, direct or indirect.' 'How', Moore asks, 'should we have discovered it without Miss Austen's help?' (No. 28).

But such speculations were not for the 1880s. After the *Memoir* the first book on Jane Austen, Sarah Tytler's, is designed for the moral instruction of the young. Mrs Tytler makes no claim to originality, the account being 'drawn solely and largely' from the *Memoir*,[13] its declared purpose being to introduce this 'queen of novelists'—Harriet Martineau's phrase[14]—'to an over-wrought, and in some respects over-read generation of young people',[15] by way of resumé, quotation and moralising commentary. Once more, Jane Austen's greatness is certified by the opinions of 'the best judges'. In the *Spectator* (26 March 1881), Hutton rebuked Mrs Tytler. For 'tales in the simplest, purest English', he asked, what need for simplification? What could explanation do for 'the keen and delicate observation, and the good-natured irony and merry hum, of her stories'?[16] Evidently, these strictures did not touch Mrs Tytler's market and in 1884 the book was re-published in *Cassell's Family Library*. Where Hutton and Mrs Tytler were in agreement, and where both were attuned to an important note in contemporary taste, was in seeing Jane Austen as a relaxing and superior alternative to the strains of modern life and its strenuous literature. In the *Spectator* (16 December 1882) Hutton compares the worlds of Jane Austen and Trollope, the one leisurely and domestic, the other all rush and business, with London at the centre of the 'great web'. The change is from 'home rule' to 'social centralisation', a Ruskinian contrast in which Jane Austen comes off best.[17] In the same year the *Modern Review* made a comparison between Jane Austen and Charlotte Brontë, again to Jane Austen's advantage: her novels 'with their quiet humour, their quaint reality... their sober and unexaggerated tone', so welcome 'in the present age, when most of the powerful writers employ their power in harrowing our feelings painfully'. The novels are 'simply and entirely delightful'. As to their author, the *Memoir* is quoted, with the evocation of a Ruskinian heroine: 'We see her always a sweet, serene figure, kindly, cheerful, unimpatient, unambitious.'[18]

There was occasional disagreement. Whilst the *Modern Review* declared that Jane Austen held no appeal for the masses, in the *Argosy* Alice King speaks of the 'many millions, to whom the creations of her genius are as household names' (a numerical puff which must owe more to the *Argosy's* hopes for its own circulation than to any accurate estimate of Jane Austen's following). Miss King gives the Jane Austen myth a full airing. First, the paradox: 'as we glance back at her life, and expect to find something strange and wonderful, we see only a sweet, modest woman walking along a retired commonplace path through the world.' Then the unconscious writer-born: 'she began authorship almost without knowing what the dignity of authorship meant... for writing had been, for her, so much like what singing is for the song-bird.' Finally, a paragon, her fitness for reading *en famille* duly endorsed:

She has left to all time, not only her books, but a picture of what a female author and artist should be: true to home duties, while she is true to her genius; delicate and brilliant in her work, yet without a word having ever dropt from her pen that can offend the blush of modesty, and with the highest moral tone breathing in every line.[19]

This is the *Memoir* portrait re-rendered for the new readership of the 1880s. Despite their repeated assertions of her popularity, the essayists and reviewers were largely catering for readers without knowledge of the novels. Hence the need to reassure the paterfamilias that these were stories 'likely in no way to injure or corrupt the young', as the *Dublin Review* helpfully advised in 1883.[20]

The material of these years shows us that the essayists and reviewers regarded Jane Austen as a good subject to write about, not because they had anything fresh to say but because by now there was a lively public interest in her name. She had the reputation of being a readable and entertaining writer; and, as a writer highly praised, she was a literary figure of some cultural kudos. More particularly, her name was aired in debates about women, including the claim for equal educational opportunity and for the recognition of women's intellectual and creative abilities. At a crude, didactic level, this issue is pressed home in the *Temple Bar*, at the end of a Ruskinian review of the 1882 Steventon Edition:

We should read the best, and ascertain why they are the best. This is a duty for everyone; more especially when we think of the education and reading of women, we might demand, with some show of reason, that among a young lady's accomplishments should be included the power of distinguishing a good novel from a bad one. From this point of view a course on Jane Austen would be salutary.[21]

Not unexpectedly, Jane Austen was also recruited to the feminist cause. Essays contributed by Millicent Fawcett to *The Mother's Companion* in 1887–88 were collected the following year into a single volume, *Some Eminent Women of our Times*, with a Preface to explain that 'The sketches were intended chiefly for working women and young people; it was hoped it would be an encouragement to them to be reminded how much good work had been done in various ways by women.' The account of Jane Austen lays stress upon her sisterhood, her ordinariness as a woman. Great as she was as a writer, 'She was thoroughly womanly in her habits, manners, and occupations.'[22]

A sharp male reaction to this feminist promotion is found in Coventry Patmore's dismissal of Jane Austen as no more than a 'surface' writer, 'as small as she is perfect'. The comparison with Shakespeare he rejected out of hand; and beside the work of his hero Scott ('an original and imaginative artist, which no woman ever was'), he accounted her stories as no more than 'photographed experiences', accurate to perfection yet without a breath of life.[23]

In the mainstream of Jane Austen literature, the important event was Lord Brabourne's two-volume edition of the *Letters* in 1884, dedicated to Queen Victoria herself, in 'the knowledge that your Majesty so highly appreciated the works of Jane Austen'.[24] Brabourne was a great-nephew, the inheritor of letters from Jane Austen to his mother Fanny Knight, together with another batch passed on to her by Cassandra, all of them unknown to Austen-Leigh in preparing the *Memoir*. The collection of ninety-four letters came to Brabourne on his mother's death in December 1882 and he wasted no time in preparing them for publication, with the addition of lengthy sectional headings and five chapters of his own, dealing with the Austen family, its Kentish associations and his views on literature. He shared none of Austen-Leigh's modesty; nor was he sensitive to the view, still held in some branches of the family, that nothing more should be revealed of the writer's life and that enough had been said already in the *Memoir*. Brabourne acknowledged that some of the letters contained 'the confidential outpourings of Jane Austen's soul to her beloved sister, interspersed with many family and personal details which, doubtless, she would have told to no other human being'. Yet he argued that public interest had never been 'deeper or more lively...in all that concerns Jane Austen', and that these letters in particular revealed the circumstances of her own 'ordinary, everyday life'.[25]

Some of the reviewers took him to task, objecting to the editorial cargo burdening the modest epistolary barque. The *St. James's Gazette* complained that 'the editor's work is not well done. It is in the jocose manner; it is at once insufficient and diffuse, and it is very carelessly written.'[26] Brabourne had used the book as an occasion to air his literary opinions and to ride his favourite hobby-horses of genealogy and Kentish history. Not that all his comments are without value and he does add significantly to our store of knowledge about the Austens. His reading of the novels is amusingly opinionated. And he gives Sarah Tytler a rap over the knuckles for treating the reader to so much wearisome paraphrase and commentary when no more is needed, as he puts it, than to hear the novels read aloud. On this score he was writing from a privileged position, since the novels were first known to the family when Jane Austen herself read them aloud, a tradition continued in the next generation.

Naturally enough, Brabourne's view of Jane Austen was wholly uncritical. The *Memoir* gives us 'dear Aunt Jane'; Brabourne 'the inimitable Jane'[27]—an epithet bestowed by one of his old friends, a whiff of incense comfortably familiar, whimsically sentimental and calculated to set the effusions flying. Hence Andrew Lang's 'Letter', a panegyric on those 'immortal' works, fiction 'raised to its highest state of perfection', their author apostrophised in a conclusion that invokes the melodious raptures of Anne Thackeray, to whom the piece is dedicated:

Ah, madam, what a relief it is to come back to your witty volumes, and forget the follies of today in those of Mr Collins and of Mrs Bennet! How fine, nay, how noble is your art in its delicate reserve, never insisting, never forcing the note, never pushing the sketch into the caricature! You worked, without thinking of it, in the Spirit of Greece, on a labour happily limited, and exquisitely organized. 'Dear books...' we say, with Miss Thackeray,—'dear books!'[28]

Not all reviewers went overboard. Some produced comments of value, as we see in the *Academy*, where Thomas Lyster called Jane Austen 'the tiny Molière in prose of genteel society in rural England'.[29] *The Saturday Review* poured scorn upon 'her worshippers' and pointed out that the letters 'contain... the matter of the novels in solution—in a very diluted, and not always a very unmixed solution—but still there.'[30]

In the *Fortnightly Review* for February 1885[31] T.E. Kebbel challenges Brabourne's view of Mr Knightley, Elizabeth Bennet and Darcy. This is one of the very rare occasions in this period when there is any semblance of a debate. Like Brabourne, Kebbel was also interested in localities and social groupings. But there is a world of difference between Brabourne's family-tree history and the illuminating observations that Kebbel had to make on the English-ness of Jane Austen, upon the social gradations of the characters, and upon Jane Austen's special social territory, 'the whole border-land in which the middle and upper classes melt into each other'. In pursuit of local colour, Kebbel trod the paths of Chawton and its neighbourhood, talking to the oldest inhabitants. We can smile at this pedestrian enquiry. Yet his primitive social anthropology alights upon an important truth in the heritage of taste:

while English society remains what it still is, with so much to remind us what it once was, and while the manners of one generation melt so imperceptibly into those of another that the continuity hardly seems broken, so long will the interest in Jane Austen continue to strengthen and expand.

This was a brave prophecy, journalistic too, in common with his large claim that 'All the reading world is now at Miss Austen's feet.' Yet Kebbel was accurate in important matters, such as the dramatic nature of the novels and their particular realism, a quality of vision and representation free from moral direction: 'She takes society as she finds it', an openness of mind that accepts 'Adultery and seduction...among other incidents of human life which cannot be altogether omitted'. In writing this, Kebbel had in mind— remarkably for the time—an audience less censorious than the readership of the *Argosy en famille*.

The official milestone of the 1880s is the entry by Leslie Stephen in the 1885 *Dictionary of National Biography*. In many respects, this is an orthodox account derived from the consensus of 'the best critics'. Yet Stephen registers his distaste at the promotion of Jane Austen, the 'fanaticism' with which she was admired. His Jane Austen is a *writer*, fully conscious of 'the precise limits of her own powers' and subtle in 'the unequalled fineness of her literary tact'.[32] 'Tact', a curious term to meet in literary comment, nicely points the social proximity that Stephen and other critics felt with Jane Austen. Another standard work of reference is *Celebrities of the Century*, 1887, in which the Jane Austen entry is by the popular novelist Hall Caine. In the opening lines he describes her as 'a novelist of the utmost eminence' and mentions a number of the standard commendations (including Scott, Coleridge, Macaulay and Lewes). However, he admits himself baffled by the (by now) routine comparison with Shakespeare:

Variety, and perfect discrimination of the shades of character, Jane Austen shares with the master of human portraiture; but it is difficult to see how this claim can place her even at the feet of Shakespeare...

Perhaps Caine, like Patmore, was irritated by the advertisements for new editions, pressing the Shakespeare comparison. 'Nevertheless', he concluded 'there is a sense in which it is true that within her range of human life she is with Shakespeare.'[33]

In his own land, Pellew had gained no hearing and the *Memoir* portrait continued to be cherished. In *Pen-Portraits of Literary Women*, published in New York in 1887, we are introduced to 'a decorous English gentlewoman, conservative in temper, essentially feminine', 'who wrote merely for her own amusement', whose 'enclosed spot of English ground is indeed little, but never was verdure brighter or more velvety than its trim grass'.[34] The native English version could be just as bad. The heroine of Mrs Malden's *Jane Austen*, 1889 (No. 11), is someone for whom writing was nothing more than 'a pleasant pastime' and writing 'a novel...almost as simple a matter as to write a letter'.[35] Sensitive to the social concerns of her audience, Mrs Malden is careful to point out that

the novelist's parents came of 'good family'[36] and that by virtue of
their 'birth and position' were entitled to mix with the best county
society;[37] whereas the authoress is at fault in making Mrs Jennings
'too vulgar'[38] and Lydia Bennet's elopement is 'a disagreeable
incident, told too much in detail, and made needlessly
prominent'.[39] Much of Mrs Malden's text is plot summary and
extensive quotation. When she cites other critics, it is to reduce
them. Lewes's claim (attributed to George Eliot), 'the greatest artist
that has ever written...the most perfect mastery' (Mrs Malden has
'master') 'over the means to her end' is re-rendered as 'this
completeness, this absoluteness of dainty finish'.[40] Fortunately,
there were reviewers to check this nonsense. In the *Academy*, James
Ashcroft Noble came down heavily on Mrs Malden's method of
summary plus quotation and introduced the proper note: 'Her life
was therefore emphatically the life of a writer.'[41] Regarding the
works themselves, Noble passes beyond matters of surface style
and effect, beyond their so-called photographic realism or accuracy
of miniaturism (the analogies varied from critic to critic) to the
central question of treatment and effect: 'We are charmed always,
but seldom, if ever, deeply moved...' It is by virtue of 'their
combination of various and uncompromising realism with unfailing vivacity and ever-present grace' that the novels are 'unique in
literature'.[42] The reviewer in the *Spectator* (20 July 1889) also
complained—yet another book about Jane Austen, when what was
really needed was criticism capable of providing 'a deeper insight
into the wonderful faculty which produced the novels'.[43]

The appeal was unanswered. What followed, instead, was
another introductory book, modest, yet the best so far—the *Life of
Jane Austen* by Goldwin Smith, 1890, published in London in the
Great Writers series (No. 12). The volumes in this series were
described as 'Critical Biographies'; *Jane Austen* was number
twenty-eight; and the series included books of worth—
Coleridge by Hall Caine, *Milton*, *Carlyle* and *Emerson* by
Richard Garnett, *Keats* by William Rossetti, *Congreve* by Gosse,
and *Crabbe* by T.E. Kebbel. So the inclusion of Smith's volume
signifies the recognition of Jane Austen as a standard classic author,
and the book itself is important in the history of Jane Austen
criticism, in marking what George Saintsbury called the beginning of 'formal criticism' (accepting that Pellew's pioneer work
was unknown). Sober and well-written, it stands, after

Pellew, as the second study of Jane Austen to attempt a sound critical and scholarly approach. Smith consulted the *Memoir* and Brabourne's edition of the *Letters*; he drew upon them sensibly and selectively; his historical account is accurate; his critical views are independent, intelligent and well-argued. Although there is a good deal of summary and quotation, Smith's declared aim was to write something more than a mere 'introduction' à la Malden and Tytler. This was to be a 'guide' to the novels—and here we detect the careful discriminations of Professor Smith, from his long experience of what teaching can and cannot accomplish—'to help as far as we can in the appreciation, or at all events the study of their construction, of the fine touches of art with which they abound, and of the varieties of social character which they portray'.[44]

Smith makes no attempt to sell Jane Austen. The tone—dry and precise—is set in the opening words, 'Miss Austen stands in literary history as one of a group of female novelists of manners.'[45] Although the book is helpfully introductory, Smith assumes a studious reader prepared to face 'literary history'. He rarely falls into the lyrical appreciative mode, although there is surprising floral reference to Fanny Price: 'She has been prettily called by Miss Sarah Tytler a white violet, and the white violet has now attained the fulness of its beauty and fragrance.'[46] This, however, is out of character, for Smith really belonged to the no-nonsense school of criticism and was ready to say so: 'Criticism is becoming an art of saying fine things, and there are really no fine things to be said about Jane Austen.' He saw Jane Austen four square: 'There is no hidden meaning in her; no philosophy beneath the surface for profound scrutiny to bring to light; nothing calling in any way for elaborate interpretation.'[47] In this opposition to the saying of fine things, the book turns in the right direction, even if it sometimes carries him too far in rejecting (a paragraph later) the suggestion that there is a maturity to the late novels which sets them apart from the early three. On the other hand, Smith showed that it was possible to write an account of Jane Austen without feeling obliged to defer to that ubiquitous band of 'the best judges'. Smith was prepared to quote Macaulay's famous eulogy on the marvellous differentiation of the clergymen—and then beg to disagree.

While Smith is notably better than Mrs Malden, there is little of 'that deeper insight' called for by the *Spectator*

44

in 1889. The *Athenaeum* found Smith's book 'disappointing' and declared that 'It is difficult to say anything new about Jane Austen, and it is quite as difficult to say anything which her admirers will deem adequate.'[48] J.M. Robertson (No. 13) commented that 'Strictly speaking' Smith's account does not really amount to a book: 'with a little less exposition of the stories, it might have made a review article in the heroic days of Macaulay and Southey'. Robertson's review carries a number of keen observations: on Jane Austen's 'smiling cynicism'; on her work 'alive with intelligence'; and his vision of her 'disunited families' conveys—unusually for this time—an accurate reading of what is actually in the novels, rather than a conforting impression, so dear to the age, of families happy and united.

Robertson is also valuable as a witness to her readership at this time. Whereas Goldwin Smith wrote indignantly of Jane Austen as a neglected classic, 'spoken of respectfully' but 'allowed to rest upon the shelf', Robertson registered something very different: that 'of late years' she has 'seemed to gain a really wide audience, the reason being that the wide modern development of the novel in the direction of delicacy and subtlety of character-painting' (he mentions Howells and James) 'has greatly multiplied the readers capable of appreciating her art'; and he goes on to remark on 'the modernness of her method'. Smith, to the contrary, observed that 'Jane Austen's tales are known to relate to a by-gone time; they are known to be quiet and devoid of thrilling incident.' 'A flood of modern fiction pours in, and sensationalism prevails.'[49]

V

The publication of Smith's book opens a fresh phase in the critical heritage. Although 'the best judges' continue to be invoked and deferred to, there was now a new authority, Smith himself,[1] and a new undeferential posture. Taking a lead from Smith, reviewers showed themselves ready to enter debate. Hutton (No. 14) takes up Smith's difference with Macaulay. Raleigh, Saintsbury (No. 18) and Cross refer back to him; Saintsbury also glances at Mrs Tytler and Brabourne; and in his Introductions to *Emma* and *Sense and Sensibility* (1896), Austin Dobson cites Brabourne and Smith. *Jane Austen, Her Contemporaries and Herself* (1899) by W.H. Pollock, opens by correcting earlier critics, including Smith, Brabourne and

Macaulay, on matters of fact and opinion. Here we see the beginnings of an enlarged critical forum no longer dominated by the voices mustered in the *Memoir*. A further change is the popularisation of Jane Austen, visibly set in train with a succession of illustrated editions, with introductions addressed to a wider readership. And, on the edges of the scene, there developed a small but vocal literature of dissent amongst those who (like James) felt their personal experience of the novels offended by the babble of the market-place.

These forces are reflected in Hutton's review, 'The Charm of Miss Austen'. In 1870, confident of finding an intelligent and knowledgeable readership (small as it might be), Simpson could refer succinctly to Jane Austen's 'magnetic attractiveness which charms while it compels'. But how universal, how (in that sense) Shakespearean, was her appeal? How widely was she read with understanding? By 1890 the questions raised by Mrs Oliphant twenty years earlier were even more pressing. Just as Smith and Robertson felt the need to measure Jane Austen's readership, Hutton wanted to examine the novelist's appeal, what he calls a 'secret charm for the few...a spell of curious force'. Its substance is hinted at in Virginia Woolf's testimony that a taste for the novels 'was a gift that ran in families and was a mark of rather peculiar culture' (in a paragraph omitted from No. 26). In the promotion that had taken place since 1870, this phenomenon had gained a distinctly social cachet, the idea that the true devotees were not only people of refined literary taste but somehow constituted a select and cultured inner circle. This idea was not new. There is a hint of it as early as 1814–15 in the report by Lady Robert Kerr that *Mansfield Park* was 'Universally admired in Edinburgh, by all the *wise ones' (No. 5(a))*. It is quite unmistakable in Macaulay's account of a dinner at Lansdowne House in 1831:

We chatted about novels. Everybody praised Miss Austen to the skies. Mackintosh said that the test of the true Austenian was Emma. 'Everybody likes Mansfield Park. But only the true believers—the select—appreciate Emma'. Lord and Lady Lansdowne extolled Emma to the skies. I had heard Wilber Pearson call it a vulgar book a few days before.

On a visit to Bath, the following year, Macaulay duly made his pilgrimage to 'all the spots made classical by Miss Austen'.[2] In a letter of September 1833, Maria Edgeworth referred to admiration for Jane Austen as a 'sign of good taste'.[3] But there is a difference between this 'true believers' game in private and its performance in public, which was what Mrs Oliphant objected to in Austen-Leigh's advancement of the Cheney-test.

Thanks to Anne Thackeray and her fellow-twaddlers, by the 1880s the Jane Austen cult was widely advertised. By then, it was a matter of journalistic convenience whether Jane Austen's following was accounted as universal, or small in numbers—either one or the other, as occasion demanded. But on one thing everyone was agreed: the extravagance of the devotion—or, more rarely, the dislike—that Jane Austen aroused. In 1876, Leslie Stephen describes 'Austenolatry' as 'perhaps the most intolerant and dogmatic of literary creeds' (No. 5). In 1884, the *Saturday Review* speaks of 'her worshippers'.[4] A year later, in the *Dictionary of National Biography*, Leslie Stephen defined the source of this appeal as 'The unconscious charm of the domestic atmosphere of the stories, and the delicate subsatirical humour which pervades them.' It was this, he claimed, that had 'won her the admiration, even to fanaticism, of innumerable readers'.[5] There were many, like William George Ward, who read the novels 'again and again, and great portions of which he knew by heart'.[6] In 1886, Sir Francis Doyle described himself as 'one of the regular Austen vassals'.[7] Three years later, Mrs Malden closed her book with a contented reflection on Jane Austen's extremist readership:

Those who do appreciate her novels will think no praise too high for them, while those who do not, will marvel at the infatuation of her admirers; for no one ever cares moderately for Jane Austen's works: her readers either award them unbounded praise or find them insufferably dull.[8]

In this hothouse atmosphere it is useful to have Hutton's sorting out of the reading-public into those 'few' 'who love' the novels; that 'very considerable number of remarkably able men' over whom 'Miss Austen wields no spell at all'; and the 'anti-Austenites' seeking something more expansive, stirring or revelatory than the produce of 'Miss Austen's fine feminine sieve'. Hutton's essay is an attempt to explain the basis of the novelist's minority appeal and to oppose the Janeite snobbery by arguing that our response to her 'charm' is not a test of sensitivity or cultivation but simply a matter of taste. Hutton finds her appeal to reside in the entertainment and relief provided by the 'minute scale and high finish' of a fictional world sufficiently realistic and vital to be 'lived in' free from the pressures and anxieties of real life. In this, Hutton and Smith are at one. Smith's 'lightest of bubbles on the great stream of existence', and Hutton's 'magic mirror', are metaphors that convey a widely held view of Jane Austen's achievement. In both Hutton and Smith, the metaphors are rendered relatively inoffensive by the context of serious and respectful discussion. But they could be used to support a trivialising view of Jane Austen, such as we find in Adolphus Jack's *Essays on the Novel,* 1897, where her art is accounted 'delightful' and the novelist herself 'the mistress of a pretty school...not a master to whom any one would turn to learn about life'.[9] We open the pages of *Pride and Prejudice* to 'bid adieu to a world of sordid cares and troublesome interests';[10] while *Emma* and *Persuasion* are dismissed as 'those prim little moralizings of Miss Austen's later years'.[11] According to Jack, she was a conformist and happy to be so:

This was the society in which she lived perfectly happily, and against which, there is abundant evidence in any one of her books, she never for a moment rebelled. To have, as she phrased it, good principles, to accept the views of other people, to drink tea, and to talk a deal of harmless gossip, this was the sum and end of human perfection.[12]

In these remarks there is more than an echo of Leslie Stephen's Jane Austen—'absolutely at peace with her most comfortable world', a 'delightful world of well-warmed country-houses', drawn so exactly in her 'tea-table' fiction (No. 5).

A rather different figure was being paraded on the biographical front. Oscar Fay Adams, the author of *The Story of Jane Austen's Life* (published in Chicago in 1891), felt that Jane Austen was misunderstood. He set out 'to dispel the unattractive, not to say forbidding, mental picture that so many have framed of her', presenting, in its place 'the winsome, delightful woman that she really was'.[13] Later in the book Adams returns to this theme, declaring that 'In the popular imagination Jane Austen has been enshrined as an exceedingly prim, not to say starched, personage.'[14] And later again: 'Never was the personality of another more amusingly misconceived than Miss Austen's has been by persons to whom her name has been synonymous with what is termed "old maidishness".'[15] (All this suggests how completely Mrs Ward's essay (No. 9) had been forgotten. She had drawn the twenty-year-old writer as 'a pretty, lively girl, very fond of dancing'.)

Adams' biography caught the attention of Arthur Quiller-Couch, a Cambridge don contributing a regular 'Literie Causerie' to the *Speaker*. In April 1893, under the heading 'Our "Incomparable Jane"', Quiller-Couch ranked himself alongside Howells as 'one of her devotees'.[16] Referring to the detailed bibliography in Adams, he named 1870 as 'the year decisive of Jane Austen's fame',[17] with its outburst of reviews, among which he picked out Simpson's in *North British* (without giving Simpson's name). Mrs Malden's tone he found 'still half militant, half apologetic',[18] whereas Adams' biography he welcomed:

Other biographers leave us with the impression that she was slightly prim, old-maidish, addicted to papa, potatoes, poultry, prunes and *prism*; whereas in fact she was light-hearted, gay-humoured, at times almost 'giddy', and always fond of dancing and dress.[19]

It was, Quiller-Couch declared, 'the sprightliest portrait extant ... also the truthfullest';[20] a Jane Austen for the 1890s, we might add.

VI

A distinctive note to the American criticism of Jane Austen was slow to emerge. This was not because of unfamiliarity. The novels were readily available in America, with American editions from 1832–33 onwards. These were mildly bowdlerised, with the removal of 'Good Lord!', 'Good God!', 'Good Heavens!', 'By Jove!' and other such genteel profanities. According to the standard literary guide, Allibone's *Critical Dictionary of English Literature and British and American Authors*, first published in Philadelphia in 1859, the 'novels are held in high estimation'. Scott's 'Big Bow-wow' passage is quoted together with a few lines from the final paragraph of Whately's 1821 review, to the effect that her 'works may safely be recommended' as being 'unexceptionable' and for 'combining instruction with amusement'.[1] A similar reassurance was being conveyed thirty-five years later in one of the earliest textbook histories, *An Introduction to the Study of English Fiction*, 1894, by William Simons, a Professor at Knox College. Simons concludes his account with the claim that 'Next to Scott', no works of that period 'are so generally familiar or read with so much real appreciation to-day as quiet, homely, wholesome Jane Austen'.[2] If this sounds familiar, it is because much of the literary journalism current in America was reprinted from British sources and what there was of American authorship tended to be British in orientation. Occasionally, American reviewers would comment on the Englishness of Jane Austen and refer to the cultured American readership to whom she most appealed. But these are usually remarks in passing and play no real part in critical discussion. In *Harper's New Monthly Magazine* for July 1870 the reviewer of the *Memoir* is thoroughly English in his observation that the 'novels are again coming into vogue with readers of quiet and refined tastes.'[3] A similarly English emphasis is found in the *Portrait Gallery of Eminent Men and Women* by Evert A. Duyckinck, published in New York in 1873. The seven-page entry gives Scott's 'Big Bow-wow' paragraph, draws heavily upon the *Memoir*, speaks of her readers as persons of 'taste and refinement'[4] and recommends Anne Thackeray's *Cornhill* piece. There is no reference to an American homeland readership; and the entry might well have been penned on the other side of the Atlantic: 'it is because we see the persons of our acquaintance reflected in their various moods upon her page, that we enjoy and admire her books.'[5] Longfellow was one such admirer. In 1877, he reported that a letter from his wife read 'just like a chapter in one of Miss Austen's novels' and that an account of his own affairs was 'Another chapter from another of Miss Austen's novels'.[6] For these readers, at least, the distance in time and place consituted no divide. To judge by Goldwin Smith, the situation was little changed in 1890. He understood himself to be addressing a readership on both sides of the Atlantic and assumed a community of taste and interest, if not of knowledge:

It may be safely said that not only the guide but the introduction is needed by a great mass even of pretty-well-read people on both sides, and especially on the American side, of the Atlantic.[7]

William Clymer however, was less kind to his fellow-countrymen, observing that as a paramount 'artist' of the novel, Jane Austen makes no 'deep impression' upon 'the present inartistic generation of Americans' (No. 15).

Many of those readers described in *Harper's* as of 'quiet and refined tastes' and in Duyckinck as of 'taste and refinement' belonged to the colonial remnant whose affections and loyalties inclined towards the 'classical' literature of the mother country rather than to the recent literature of America itself. The implicit tensions come through clearly in Emily Dickinson's diary, where she quotes from the *Springfield Republican's* announcement that Thomas Higginson's novel *Malbone* was to be serialised in the *Atlantic Monthly* and that an early critic had reported that

'its whole tone and style are admirable, and that it differs from most American fictions in having its scenes laid wholly among cultivated people'. In this respect it will resemble the often praised but little read novels of Jane Austen.[8]

Higginson himself found no problem in reconciling his admiration for Jane Austen with an enthusiastic dedication to the future of an 'uncultivated' 'democratic' American people.[9] 'Literature as an Art', an essay published in 1867, ended: 'We, a younger and a cruder race, need still to go abroad for our standard of execution, but our ideal and our faith must be our own.'[10] This 'standard of execution' he discerned in Jane Austen—her writing 'simple, direct and graphic',[11] the novels seeming 'as if they were written yesterday', with Trollope, Howells and James amongst her 'lineal successors'.[12] Yet he saw a national difference:

in English books and magazines everything seems written for some limited circle. ... But every American writer must address himself to a vast audience, possessing the greatest quickness and common-sense, with but little culture.[13]

In 1879, Howells wrote to James Lowell rejoicing that his country was on the way to having a 'school of really native American literature'.[14] The idea of The Great American Novel was already in the air and the distance between the two national literatures became a topic of debate.[15] As Higginson put it, 'The living realities of American life ought to come in among the tiresome lay-figures of average English fiction.'[16] Higginson excepted Jane Austen. But for some Americans, Jane Austen's 'limited circle' could be foreign and oppressive, as Emerson confided to his Journals, in 1861:

I am at a loss to understand why people hold Miss Austen's novels at so high a rate, which seem to me vulgar in tone, sterile in artistic invention, imprisoned in the wretched conventions of English society, without genius, wit or knowledge of the world. Never was life so pinched and narrow.[17]

Something of this complaint is reflected in Pellew's comment that the world of the heroines, with its 'meagre possibilities', was 'too limited for their full development'. Having in mind the humdrum domestic setting of the novels, American critics would sometimes reach for the word 'provincial'. More rarely, in this very provinciality they glimpsed their essence. When William Clymer (No. 15)—matching James in the breadth of his reference to European literature—describes Jane Austen as 'provincial' for her remoteness from the 'world of ideas' he regards this as a purely aesthetic issue: 'That is her limitation. In the recognition of that limitation lies much of her strength and of her charm.' Gertrude Stein rejoiced at the very compactness and insularity of English life, whose 'description', in Jane Austen, 'of the complete the entirely complete daily island life had been England's glory'.[18] Most critics, however, were uneasy about the absence of open space—literal and metaphorical.

For American literary nationalists Jane Austen's cultivated scene was too pallid, too constrained, too refined, too downright unheroic. Riddled with the intricacies of class and snared with manners, it was a baffling realm of social artifice, in Edith Wharton's words, 'a kind of hieroglyphic world',[19] remote from the 'clearer social atmosphere' (Higginson's phrase)[20] and native idealism of the New World. Where in England's island culture was an equivalent Frontier of the West, a realm of romance, danger and raw reality? What remained to fight for and explore? The pioneering spirit could find no satisfaction here. Jane Austen's boundary was drawn too soon. Her vistas, far from democratic, terminated in pleasure grounds or a landscaped scene. It was, remarked James, a 'confined circle in which her muse revolved',[21] a complaint raised—for him—with unusual bluntness: 'Why shouldn't it be argued against her that where her testimony complacently ends, the pressure of appetite within us presumes exactly to begin?'[22] In the seasons of literature he found her held in a perpetually 'arrested spring'.[23] The 'touches of human truth', the 'glimpses of steady vision', the 'master strokes of imagination' were incontestably there—but, for him, all were incontestably 'little'.[24] Similarly the heroines, with their 'small and second-rate minds... Their small gentility and front parlour existence' (p. 180). This was the writer who stood modestly in his personal pantheon as the founder of the novel of 'domestic tranquillity'.[25]

Other Americans were untroubled by such limitations and differences. Indeed, some found their spiritual home, an America lost, in Jane Austen's England. Sarah Orme Jewett —whose New England is finely rendered in her many regional essays and stories—recounts how she turned again to *Persuasion* in 1902 and was carried back to the world of her childhood:

Yesterday afternoon I amused myself with Miss Austen's *Persuasion*. Dear me, how like her people are to the people we knew years ago! It is just as much New England before the war—that is, in provincial terms—as it ever was Old England. I am going to read another. *Persuasion* tasted so good! I haven't read them for some time.[26]

In public, alongside Higginson, Jane Austen had a redoubtable pair of champions: William Dean Howells, whose vigorous tones sounded a mainly bass to the silvery Philadelphia Austenianism of Agnes Repplier (comically associated in H.L. Mencken's description of Howells as 'an Agnes Repplier in pantaloons').[27] Both were literary journalists, skilled essayists and reviewers as well as novelists. Although Miss Repplier, a shrewd and critical admirer of Jane Austen, is now totally forgotten and Howells—perhaps her most eloquent and wholehearted champion (more so even than Lewes)—almost wholly forgotten, both of them once enjoyed a large popular following and played a leading part in educating the public taste for Jane Austen, in Britain as well as in America. Each in their different ways showed how it was possible to talk about a novelist intelligently and engage in debate, not as an academic exercise, but as an activity that any educated reader might be expected to follow and enjoy.

In Jane Austen, Howells, like Scott, found the healthy truthful realism of everyday, commonplace experience. For his fellow-countrymen, he was able to celebrate this as a manifestation of the democratic principle. Moreover, twenty years in developing his own variety of the American novel of realism had sharpened his understanding of the precise nature of Jane Austen's achievement. His regular column in *Harper's Monthly* provided the opportunity to air these views. In November 1889, discussing the 'form' or rather the 'formlessness', of English fiction, he asked, 'How, for instance, could people who had once known the simple variety, the refined perfection of Miss Austen, enjoy anything less refined and less

perfect?'[28] He pointed to the decline of the novel, away from Jane
Austen, down through 'the mania of romanticism' from Scott to
George Eliot. The *Harper's* essays were assembled and reshaped as
Criticism and Fiction, published in 1891 (No. 16). In this, Jane
Austen stands supreme and Realism is defined not as a mere literary
effect but as a literary principle:

Realism is nothing more and nothing less than the truthful treatment of
material, and Jane Austen was the first and last of the English novelists to
treat material with entire truthfulness. Because she did this she remains the
most artistic of the English novelists...

Such emphatic and particularising rhetoric was required, since Jane
Austen's 'realism' was a cliché, bandied about, its meaning taken as
read, simply and crudely attached to the effect of lifelikeness or
verisimilitude. Occasionally, there was some thoughtful extension
of the idea, as in James Noble's comment, carrying Howellsian
discriminations and weight, in the *Academy* for August 1889: 'It is
in virtue of their combination of uncompromising realism with
unfailing vivacity and ever-present grace that the novels of Jane
Austen are unique in literature.'[29] Or there is Leslie Stephen on the
superiority of Jane Austen's 'finer kind of realism', superior to that
of Defoe because it 'combines exquisite powers of minute perception with a skill which can light up the most delicate miniatures
with an unfailing play of humour'.[30] At this time, James was one of
the few critics to suggest that this was an equivocal area:

I am perfectly aware that to say the object of the novel is to represent life
does not bring the question to a point so fine as to be uncomfortable for
any one. For, after all, may not people differ infinitely as to what
constitutes life—what constitutes representation? Some people, for instance, hold that Miss Austen deals with life, Miss Austen represents. Others
attribute these achievements to the accomplished Ouida.[31]

In the same year, 1888, Higginson reported the Parisian discovery
that Jane Austen was

the founder of that realistic school which is construed to include authors so
remote from each other as the French Zola and the American Howells. The
most decorous of maiden ladies is thus made to originate the extreme of
indecorum.[32]

William Clymer (No. 15) saw an affinity with Maupassant, yet also
made a more sober connection, seeing her work bridging the
Romantic period, joining 'the realistic study of manners taught her by

Richardson and Fielding' with 'the strain of realism that marks Thackeray and Trollope' as their 'descendants'.

Long ago, Scott had used the word 'truth' in speaking of Jane Austen's possession of that 'exquisite touch which renders ordinary commonplace things and characters interesting from the truth of the description and the sentiment'. Tennyson put a similar emphasis upon the word in declaring his admiration for 'George Eliot's genius and insight into human character, but maintained that she was not quite so truthful as Shakespeare or Miss Austen'.[33] Yet neither Scott nor anyone else had insisted upon a simple and direct relationship between the aesthetics and the morality of fiction. Hence there was some justice to Howells's attack on the state of criticism in England as 'provincial and special and personal', criticism which expresses 'a love and hate which had to do with the quality of the artist rather than the character of his work'.[34] Howells does not address these comments specifically to the writing about Jane Austen, but he might fairly have done so. In old age, Howells was himself to fall to this same provincialism, speaking warmly of a novelist 'good as she was great' and of 'the loveliness of her own soul' as manifested in her creations.[35] Nonetheless, his own 'love' left his critical faculty unblunted, as we see in the studies of the heroines which came out in *Harper's Bazar* in 1900–01 (No. 21), essays that display the fine understanding that Howells possessed as a writer-critic.

While Howells presented himself in *Criticism and Fiction* as a full-blown literary theorist, ready to do battle in the cause of realism, Miss Repplier—a familiar essayist in the tradition of Lamb, Hazlitt and Leigh Hunt—remains on the side-lines, diffident, yet quick to engage herself on behalf of Jane Austen. A derisive commentator upon the extravagance of Janeite sentimentalism, she deployed a bland irony even upon the enthusiasm of Howells himself. She never wrote about Jane Austen at length; some of her remarks are mere snippets; yet they voice the cultivated colonial view, still audible in old Philadelphia at the turn of the century. They establish her right to stand alongside the early Mrs Oliphant, Mrs Ward and Alice Meynell in that small band of dissident admirers, none of whom were prepared to let Janeite nonsense pass unchallenged. Tongue in cheek, Miss Repplier questions the exclusiveness of Howells's regard for the novelist's 'truthfulness', fearful that this will lead to a new shibboleth as silly and offensive as the

Cheney-test (No. 17b). She questions the wisdom of recommending (as so many writers did) 'the fine, thin perfection' of the novels
as suitable reading for the young (No. 17b). In 'Three Famous Old
Maids', she opposes the then-prevalent autobiographical interpretation of Fanny Price and Anne Elliot.[36] She recalls Anne Thackeray's
much-quoted, greatly-admired exclamation: 'Could we but study
our bores as Miss Austen must have studied hers in her country
village, what a delightful world this might be!' Responding literally
and truthfully, she answers, no, not delightful at all; they would
leave us 'vastly weary of their company' (No. 17d). She observes
the way in which the novelist 'reveals to us with merciless
distinctness the secret springs that move a human heart' through
merely 'the casual conversation, the little leisurely, veracious
gossip'. Parodying the terms of Janeite appreciation, she ascribes all
this to the 'Miraculous', before which we can only 'bow our heads,
and pay unqualified homage at its shrine...' (No. 17c). At times,
the wit is mordant. In a gently charming piece on 'Guests', she
turns to the world of Jane Austen, 'who, with relentless candor, has
shown us how usefully guests may be employed as an antidote for
the ennui of intellectual vacuity.'[37]

In 1897, Miss Repplier described Jane Austen's art, 'now the
theme of every critic's pen', as 'incomparable'.[38] However, her
admiration was not unqualified. Three years later, in *The Critic*
(No. 17g), she referred to the novels as being 'destitute of passion'
and questioned their pre-eminence in English fiction. She also
commented on the current state of Jane Austen criticism, voicing
her objection to the 'bellicose enthusiasm' of 'a little school of
critics' who 'endeavored to exalt these half-dozen admirable novels
by denying them competitors, by reducing all English fiction to
one common denominator—*Emma*.' No names are given. But one
of the culprits is surely Howells; and possibly Goldwin Smith (here
mentioned), whose opening sentence to Chapter 5 advertises the
claim: 'Some will think that of all Miss Austen's works *Emma* is the
best.' Miss Repplier more than once makes it clear that her vote
goes to *Mansfield Park*. It is this novel, not *Emma*, that she takes
down 'for the fiftieth time', to enter once more into the theatricals
(No. 17e) or to delight in its 'gifts' (No. 17f). In this, Miss Repplier
was in a proud minority, for the critics' choice was overwhelming-
ly for *Emma*.

Agnes Repplier was a literary aristocrat but no snob. She spoke for a cultured minority, a group she described (in relation to the early readership of *Pride and Prejudice*) as 'that "saving remnant" to whom is confided the intellectual welfare of their land'.[39] The complacent superiority of the professional Janeites, such as the Austen editor Augustine Birrell, she scorned:

He dwells rapturously over certain well-loved pages of 'Pride and Prejudice' and 'Mansfield Park', and then deliberately adds, 'When an admirer of Jane Austen reads these familiar passages, the smile of satisfaction, betraying the deep inward peace they never fail to beget, widens, like "a circle in the water", as he remembers (and he is always careful to remember) how his dearest friend, who has been so successful in life, can no more read Jane Austen than he can read the Moabitish Stone.'[40]

Much later, in 1931, she provided her own explanation for the Janeite phenomenon:

Jane is not for all markets, and this circumstance lends a secret and unworthy zest to her faithful followers. They do not want to share their pleasure with their neighbours. It is too intimate and too individual. (No. 17i)

By that time the evidence had amassed. But she may well have been thinking back to the rallying Janeitism of those early editors, to Augustine Birrell, whom she quoted with contempt forty years before. In the decade up to 1900, these 'faithful followers' were growing in numbers. That very year, Howells observed it to be

a constantly, almost rapidly increasing cult, as it must be called, for the readers of Jane Austen are hardly ever less than her adorers: she is passion and a creed, if not quite a religion (No. 21).

That was America. In England, Jane Austen could be a religion. An aristocratic admirer, the Earl of Iddesleigh, proposed 'a magazine...devoted entirely to Miss Austen...We are never tired of talking about her; should we ever grow weary of reading or writing about her?'[41] Though the magazine never came, Lord Iddesleigh's enthusiasm blossomed into hagiography. Two years later, in 'The Legend of St Jane', he celebrated 'a loving worship of the most fascinating of saints' and the 'sacred spots' 'where our divinity visited Earth'.[42] His own home, 'Pynes', near Exeter, he believed to be the original for Barton Park in *Sense and Sensibility*.

On a plane similarly elevated, W. L. Phelps, introducing an American edition of the novels in 1906, averred that 'One of the sincere joys of existence is to discuss with kindred souls the characters and fortunes of the men and women born into life eternal on the pages of Jane Austen!'[43] Unfortunately, not all Janeite dedication was so pure. Hints of the Cheney-test, of an exclusive snobbery, intrude. Her admirers began to regard the world of the novels as a version of Home Counties existence, of gracious living, of 'courtesy and breeding', to quote Lady Mary Sackville's Introduction to a book of *Selections* in 1913. In this province of appreciation, disagreement amongst her 'Genuine admirers' is not an issue of criticism but of etiquette, 'a breach of good manners impossible in her presence'.[44] In the person of Mr Collins, Jane Austen entered the slang of the Edwardian house-party, a 'Collins' being the customary letter of thanks from the departed guest (as *Chamber's Journal* explained to its readership in 1904).[45] Miss Repplier ridiculed these attitudes. Howells mocked them persistently. But they remained proof against laughter and scorn on both sides of the Atlantic and carry the history of criticism and taste into the annals of caste and culture—an amusing twist to Lionel Trilling's observation that the reader of Jane Austen can find 'that he is required to make no mere literary judgment but a decision about his own character and personality, and about his relation to society and all of life.'[46]

VII

The critical heritage was also swayed by forces in the book trade. The marketing of Jane Austen, in the 1880s and 1890s particularly, was both an intrusion and a stimulus. Purists might lament the taint of commerce; yet commerce paid for critical introductions and edited texts. The novels had been available at low prices since 1849, and were included in the Tauchnitz paperback series. However, the first really popular edition was not until 1883, when George Routledge brought out all six novels in paper-board bindings, with pictorial front covers garishly coloured, the individual novels priced at 2s. boards or 2s.6d. cloth. According to Andrew Lang's 'Letter' of 1884, 'You are not a very popular author; your volumes are not found in gaudy covers on every bookstall.'[1] Nonetheless, the venture must have been encouraging enough for Routledge to put the titles into his Sixpenny Novels series. There was an illustrated *Mansfield Park* in twenty-six weekly parts in 1885, followed by

Sense and Sensibility in 1886 and *Pride and Prejudice* in 1887. Soon there was a distinct shift up-market to stylish, even luxurious presentation. Sets were designed for the bibliophile taste in ornamentation and fine detail—with decorated bindings and end-papers, elaborate title-pages and gilt edges—even for ordinary trade editions. The pages themselves were frequently embellished with a full repertoire of headpieces, tailpieces, ornamental initials and typographical devices quaint and curious—quite out of character with the novels themselves and at odds with the severity of the original editions.

With the Jane Austen boom came trade warfare. For an edition of *Pride and Prejudice* in 1894, George Allen secured the leading illustrator of the day, Hugh Thomson, an artist of the Macmillan stable. Macmillan countered by commissioning Thomson to illustrate the other five novels and Charles Brock (an artist in the Thomson style) for *Pride and Prejudice*, so that a complete Macmillan illustrated edition should be on the market as rapidly as possible.

On the character and effect of these illustrations it is worth remarking that while Dickens was lucky enough to have Cruikshank and Hablot K. Brown to capture the Dickensian grotesque and macabre, Jane Austen was landed with illustrators capable of little better than period costumery and prettification and quite unable to catch the spare precision and economy of her vision. The illustrations were inescapable. To George Allen's *Pride and Prejudice*, Hugh Thomson contributed no less than 160, reproduced year after year in different editions—in Macmillan's Illustrated Standard Novels, in the Macmillan 'Peacock' series, in the same publisher's Illustrated Pocket Classics, reprinted into the late 1930s. The 1894 *Pride and Prejudice* sold over 11,500 copies in the first year, with an additional 3500 copies going to America. In the *Academy*, Arnold Bennett remarked on the 'delightful little pen pictures' to Thomson's *Mansfield Park*. But he went on to ask why they were there at all:

... we do not think that those who are sealed of the tribe of Jane Austen want her stories illustrated. Who that knows Anne Elliot can accept any presentment of her, however well conceived? Jane Austen's art cannot be aided.[2]

Bennett said much the same thing again on the publication of

Thomson's *Northanger Abbey* and *Persuasion* in 1898: 'Jane Austen's stories are too true and vivid on the literary plane to need, or to be in a position to gain by illustration.'[3] On the Brock brothers' illustrations to *Sense and Sensibility*, also 1898, the *Academy* pronounced: 'We have long been convinced that Jane Austen's characters refuse to fit any artist's mould.'[4]

In the same year, the Thomson's *Pride and Prejudice* came under further scrutiny in the 'Reputations Reconsidered' series running in the *Academy*. This was a light-hearted critical forum. Three friends—lounging at their ease in a Norfolk inn, after a good day's walking—discuss this 'pretty edition' and its illustrations, welcoming some, objecting to others. Saintsbury's Preface (No. 18) also comes under fire. Robinson ('an ardent young student') complains at his invention of 'so horrible a word as "Janeites" and "Austenians" is nearly as bad... what expressions for a Professor of Literature to apply to a writer of so pure and simple a style as hers'. Smith ('from the City'), however, applauds Saintsbury's relaxed style as a refreshing change in critical writing.[5]

There were also sumptuous limited editions, in bindings especially handsome, printed on larger pages of handmade paper, and extra-illustrated with the illustrations in a high proof state. For such collectors' pieces there was a keen market. When a student at Cambridge in 1899, E.M. Forster determined to spend his College prize money on one of these fine editions. On his way to the University Library to look over their Jane Austens, he bumped into Oscar Browning (a Fellow of King's College) who whisked him off to his rooms, claiming to have copies 'far nicer'. But Forster disagreed and next day made his own choice of a set 'in 10 volumes. It is such a lovely edition, in green cloth with beautiful print and paper.'[6] However, such enthusiasms were not universal. In 1897, Agnes Repplier reflected on 'the beautiful and costly editions'[7] then available and James identified in 1905 'the stiff breeze of the commercial', 'the special bookselling spirit'. Wryly he contemplated the scene: 'the body of publishers, editors, illustrators' 'who have found their "dear", our dear, everybody's dear, Jane so infinitely to their material purpose, so amenable to pretty reproduction in every variety of what is called tasteful, and in what seemingly proves to be saleable, form.' He was less concerned about the exploitation of Jane Austen than about the confusions of value that follow: the 'tide' of 'appreciation' which has risen, as he puts it, 'rather higher, I think, than the high-water mark, the highest, of her intrinsic merit and interest'.[8] Recalling his gentle scepticism at Pellew's 'scientific' criticism, we can suppose that James found one aspect of this over-appreciation to be the seriousness with which her editors now addressed their task, prefacing the novels with considerable introductions, sometimes with a quantity of historical detail. In this respect, at least, away from the *Academy* style of journalism, the discussion of Jane Austen takes on some 'scientific' ballast, and for the first time the student of the novels is offered the rudiments of scholarship.

Scholarly trappings are much in evidence in the earliest of these 1890s editions, the ten-volume set published by Dent in 1892 under the editorship of Reginald Brimley Johnson, an enthusiastic scholar-amateur who came to be regarded as the leading Austen expert until the arrival of R.W. Chapman in the early 1920s. Attractive and successful, this edition was reprinted again in 1892 and four times more by the spring of 1897. Headed by the charming (and unauthentic) 'Zoffany' portrait, illustrated by William Cooke, and with ornaments by F.C. Tilney, it was an item for the fastidious book-lover and offered such decorative features as a two-colour title-page, top edges gilt, and Ex Libris panels. The bindings carry elaborate gold die-stamping. The title of the novel is presented within a regal cartouche, topped with the Austen family crest (a stag rampant). If this is the touch aristocratic, the touch personal is added by the signature 'J. Austen' in facsimile, bottom right, also in gold. The illustrations, printed in a rich dark sepia, on parchmenty paper, are individually leaved with protective tissue. The hint of preciousness in all this decorative elaboration is heightened by the diminutive size of the volumes. The pages are only 4¼ by 6¾ inches, giving the whole an effect, as it might be described, of tasteful daintiness. To this is added a confusing dash of the quaintly antique in gothic black-letter chapter-heads, the numerals so mannered as to remain indecipherable. If all this offends the purist bibliophile, it is a confection which displays a vigorous (if broadsided) marketing instinct. And to attract the collectors, there was a limited edition, on larger, handmade paper, with illustrations to superior impression, 100 copies for the home market, 50 for America.

With this attention to appearance there also comes a concern for bibliographical exactitude. The novels are listed with their dates of composition and first publication. There is a note that 'In this edition the novels will be printed in the order of publication, and from the text of the last editions revised by the author',[9] for access to which thanks is given to the Rev. A. Austen-Leigh. Volume 1 of *Sense and Sensibility,* the opening volume of the set, carries a note on the copy-text used and the editor's policy in textual emendation. (Unfortunately, these good intentions were frustrated, since the printers buried the resurrected authentic texts beneath misprints of their own!) This bibliographical concern inspired the first steps in serious textual criticism, two articles in the *Cambridge Review* for 1893 by the great classical scholar A.W. Verrall, hailed by Geoffrey Keynes as 'the dawn of true Jane Austen scholarship'.[10] They reveal that close reading is by no means an innovation of modern critical method, as we also see in William Clymer's 'scrutinizing' examination of the passage announcing the death of Mrs Churchill and in his further comment on Louisa Musgrove's fall: 'Read hastily, it is tame; read attentively, it is as rapid and close in construction, and as fully provides for every character at every moment as if it were Scribe's' (No. 15). For book-collectors, the abundance of bibliographical information held a special fascination. But its presence within handsome reading editions carries a whiff of pedantry, an air of indulgent bibliographicalism; and in the later Jane Austen editions there is a distinct shift away from the amassing of such detail. Indeed, some editors roundly declared their aversion to any kind of fact-grubbing. In his Introduction to *Sense and Sensibility,* 1896, Austen Dobson mentioned Scott and Whately but was happy to tell the reader that he knew of no other contemporary reviews and that as for the origin of the book's title, well, that was 'one of those minor problems which delight the cummin-splitters of criticism'.[11]

In 1896 came the Methuen edition, whose editor E.V. Lucas carried the anti-scholarly argument even further, declaring that the professional critic was baffled, could only stand 'disconcerted and defeated in the presence of the "divine chit-chat" of this little lady'.[12] The reader is left either to 'idolise Miss Austen or pass her by: there is no middle way'.[13] For her idolaters, there is the delight of a special and exclusive bond: 'Among English novelists she is the very darling. Everyone believes fondly that by no one else is she quite so thoroughly appreciated.'[14] To the World's Classics edition of *Emma* in 1907, Lucas wrote an Introduction similarly affected. Having agreed with 'the best critics' that of all the novels this is her best, 'her ripest and her richest', he continues airily,

But with the merits of Miss Austen's great novel I am not here concerned. They will be patent to the reader, before whom a very delicious banquet is spread; and, indeed, to praise it now would be an offence.[15]

While we can dismiss this as the ineptitude of a journalist-editor, paid to do a job, nonetheless Lucas's introductions were there to guide his readers and inevitably played a part in shaping the public view of Jane Austen. His advice, when offered, proposed a curiously one-sided approach: Emma Woodhouse is commended as 'her most complete character-study', of all the heroines, the one 'which probably contains most points of resemblance to the girl reader'.[16] Elsewhere in the Introduction to *Emma* Lucas practises, with excruciating skill, the manner of the critic whimsical. Writers who have praised Jane Austen enter as 'the great intellects whose darling she has ever been'; and her enthusiasts are 'those very numerous persons who take Miss Austen's words as seriously almost as life itself'.[17] In 1906, R. Brimley Johnson opened his Introduction to *Sense and Sensibility* on the same lines, quoting from the *Memoir* that 'there was scarcely a charm in Jane Austen's most delightful characters that was not a true reflection of her own sweet temper and loving heart',[18] and elaborating this with a claim that the virtues and attractions of the heroines were manifestations of the author herself. Brimley Johnson was also responsible for another kind of distraction, a topographical Hampshire Edition, remarked on dryly in the editorial column of the *Academy*, in October 1902:

Within the front cover there is to be a map (in the old style, showing trees buildings, and hills) of the country or town in which the scenes of the story occur, prepared from views and guide-books of the period; and within the back cover the particular neighbourhood inhabited by the principal characters, which may, or may not, have ever actually existed, is illustrated in a similar style, giving the relative sizes, distances, and positions of houses and walks according to the author's descriptions. The scheme is likely to lead to rather interesting results, and maps always have their own particular charm.[19]

In the same vein was the Publisher's own Note that 'The colour' of the binding cloth 'is navy blue, in recollection of her keen interest in the profession of her two sailor brothers'.[20]

Fortunately, there were other editors around able to resist such silliness. With Joseph Jacobs we are in another world. His Introduction to an illustrated edition of *Emma*, first published in 1896 (and reprinted five times by 1904) is a serious essay, opening with a well-documented account of the novel's composition and publication and continuing with a discussion of the reviews by Scott and Whately, observing, with accuracy, that 'Whately struck the note of subsequent criticism.' He quotes Goldwin Smith, to disagree with him, advancing his own opinion that even a 'genuine admirer' might accept that some of Miss Bates's speeches 'would not be the worse for curtailment'.[21] He draws attention to the evidence of development in the three later novels, noting in *Emma* that 'the style is everywhere carefully subordinated to the needs of the narrative, while the slender thread of the intrigue is followed with the closest tenacity.'[22] He reports Emma's view of Highbury's village street, commenting that this is topography 'not only clearly seen, but touched in with the true economy of line'.[23] He notes that Emma is a character

so subtly and gradually developed, that by the time she has come to see the errors of match-making, and has reached the luminous moment when 'it darted through her with the speed of an arrow, that Mr Knightley must marry no one but herself', we are almost prepared to forgive her for being rude to Miss Bates.[24]

Jacobs was prepared to face readers of his popular edition with ideas and analysis; and he maintained this critical stance, adding a late 'Postscript' to the post-1898 reprints, showing his readers how unsympathetic Charlotte Brontë was to *Emma* and its author, quoting her letter of April 1850 (*No. 28(c)*), which appeared in print towards the end of 1896. This was the famous judgment delivered to her editor after reading *Emma* and finding there nothing more than a delineation of 'the surface of the lives of genteel English people... a Chinese fidelity...', and the novelist herself 'a complete and most sensible lady, but a very incomplete, and rather insensible (*not senseless*) woman'. Jacobs advised his readers, half-a-century later, that these opinions were 'unjust'.[25]

Another thoughtful and un-Janeite editor was William Leask, whose 'Biographical Introduction' to *Pride and Prejudice* in 1900 opens on a sternly anti-biographical course: 'All that is really known of her is but a few dates and some facts of little importance.

They shed no light on her art, her method of composition, or her attitude to the history and development of the Novel.' His opening paragraph continues, on another unexpected tack, with the pronouncement that while 'she is recognised as the first of female novelists' nonetheless 'Her public is small, and doubtless will remain so.'[26] At a time when the commercialisation of Jane Austen was at its height, Leask was determinedly against the tide of fashion.

George Saintsbury was the one critic-editor who succeeded in pleasing all parties. At first, his Preface to *Pride and Prejudice* seems to echo all that is worst in Lucas. There is a fanfare in full Janeite style (according to the OED, the word is first found here), announcing this the work of a Janeite for his fellow-devotees and delivered with a presumption of their shared sympathies and indulgence. The writer and his readers are members of the same club. The critic is no gentleman unless he declares his passion for the writer and her heroines—a convention observed by someone as grand as Bradley (No. 24). Artful and mannered, Saintsbury enters a fantasy of life and marriage with Elizabeth Bennet. Twenty years later, he was to dedicate himself even more quaintly: 'proud as I am to be an Austen Friar, a knight (or at least a squire) of the order of St Jane',[27] a fancy aired (of all places) between the sober covers of his textbook history of *The English Novel*, 1913.

These postures may be tiresome; yet they were not, in the event, inimical to sound criticism. As an introductory discussion, Saintsbury's Preface is lively and demanding. It assumes a reader able to follow, for example, his claim that 'Mr Collins is really *great*'—not, we should note, great *in vacuo*, but great alongside the creations of Addison, Fielding and Swift. With conscious daring— for this readership, at this time—Saintsbury places Jane Austen 'as near to Swift in some ways' as to Addison in others and he demonstrates the Swiftian effects in Jane Austen's prose.[28] While Saintsbury was an arch-Janeite, a master at the game, it was an indulgence kept within bounds. His placing of Jane Austen, in the open territory of literature, English and European, is as strict and purely critical as anyone could wish. His Janeite devotion is disciplined to the point of analysing how Elizabeth Bennet is drawn to engage the reader and allows no place for the snobbery of the Cheney-test. This comes out clearly in the short section—severely historical and analytical—he gives to Jane Austen in *A History of*

Nineteenth Century Literature, 1896.[29] Fielding and Richardson are identified as the progenitors of her method; and Jane Austen, the mother of the nineteenth-century novel, is neatly distinguished from Scott, the father of the nineteenth-century romance.

If Jane Austen found favour with such an influential popularising critic as Saintsbury, her reputation was also assisted by a swing in taste away from sensation fiction, at one end, and from social-problem fiction, at the other.[30] A contributor to the *Edinburgh Review* in 1892[31] cited Mrs Ward's 'obnoxious theories', her 'New views of life' and 'militant propagandism' in *David Grieve*, contrasting them unfavourably with Jane Austen's reliance 'for her success on her feminine gifts of keen and faithful observation'. Here was an escape from heavy 'didactic purpose' and the 'great questions of the hour'. Jane Austen offered relief that was both entertaining and substantial; and, in their elegance the novels were seen as a decided improvement upon the 'loose baggy monsters' of Victorian fiction. There was, as H. G. Wells commented in 1897, an evident 'beauty of form' to Jane Austen and this he explained as a technical accomplishment standing historically between the primitive structures of eighteenth-century fiction and the 'curse' of 'plot' that dogged Victorian serial publication:

The earlier novelists seem to have shaped their stories almost invariably upon an illustrative moral intention, and to have made a typical individual, whose name was commonly the title of the novel, the structural skeleton, the sustaining interest of the book. He or she was presented in no personal spirit; Tom Jones came forward in the interests of domestic tolerance, and the admirable Pamela let the light of restraint shine before her sex. Beauty of form does not seem to have been sought by the earlier novelists—suffice it if the fabric cohered. About the central character a system of reacting personages and foils was arranged, and the whole was woven together by an ingenious and frequently complicated 'plot'. The grouping is at its simplest and best in the gracefully constructed novels of Jane Austen.[32]

In the 1890s, the novels were also being recommended for the lessons in behaviour they held for young ladies of the new generation. Charlotte Yonge contributed an essay on Anne Elliot to *Great Characters of Fiction,* 1893,[33] a volume dedicated to cultivating the reader's 'critical faculty', so enabling 'her' (rather than him) to reject the 'silly trash' of cheap fiction. The essay itself argues the superiority of the traditional womanly values over the new belligerent feminism. Anne is applauded as a 'gentle, submissive girl of the earlier years of the century'; and, as a class, the heroines are praised as 'maidens... without aspirations after a career, leading quiet lives in their homes, dutiful and refined'. By the end of the decade, there was talk of a Jane Austen 'renascence'. A contributor to the *Westminster Review* found refreshment in

the contemplation of a peaceful, homely, healthy existence like that of Jane Austen! It is, indeed, this peaceful, homely element in her writings that gives them the place they are rightfully reclaiming in English literature.[34]

Wells gives an acid reflection on these attitudes at the close of Chapter 11 of *Ann Veronica*, 1909, where the heroine, in prison for her suffragette activities, thinks to herself:

The wrappered life—discipline! One comes to that at last. I begin to understand that Jane Austen and Chintz covers and decency and refinement and all the rest of it. One puts gloves on one's greedy fingers. One learns to sit up...

In Nebraska, Willa Cather was telling readers of the *Courier* in 1895 why Jane Austen 'was in some respects the greatest' of the women novelists (No. 20). The gender difference weighed heavily with some critics and was elevated into a mode of discrimination. Jane Austen's supremely 'feminine gift', according to Saintsbury lay in her 'habit of minute and semi-satiric observation natural to womankind'.[35] Craik announced that she held 'the most secure place in the roll of our female novelists';[36] and in 1913 Chesterton (No. 25) introduced a chronological bias, speaking of the eighteenth-century novel as 'male' and the nineteenth-century 'female'.

Howells, in *Munsey's Magazine* in 1897, continued his 'realist' advocacy to the American public:

When you come to Jane Austen, there is nothing more faithful than her work. She is one of the very greatest of English novelists, for that reason, and decidedly my favorite. She wrote very few books, but every one of them was very good. All were of the quietest, and you might say the narrowest life, the life of the small country gentry, but every fact was perfectly ascertained, every phase truthfully reflected.[37]

Howells's embracing concept of realism, moral and aesthetic, emerges as the leading idea in subsequent American text book and literary-historical approaches. In part, this followed naturally both from his eminence as a realist writer and the force of his advocacy.

It was a tradition which lasted into the present century, certainly down to 1938, when Thornton Wilder wrote 'A preface for *Our Town*', touching upon the 'secret' of her art within the realist tradition:

Most works in realism tell a succession of such abject truths; they are deeply in earnest, every detail is true, and yet the whole finally tumbles to the ground—true but without significance.

How did Jane Austen save her novels from that danger? They appear to be compact of abject truth. Their events are excruciatingly unimportant; and yet, with *R. Crusoe*, they will probably outlast all Fielding, Scott, George Eliot, Thackeray, and Dickens. The art is so consummate that the secret is hidden; peer at them as hard as one may; shake them; take them apart; one cannot see how it is done.[38]

But the tide was not one-way. It was during this boom period of the 1890s that there appeared one of the shrewdest depreciations, 'The Classic Novelist' by Alice Meynell (No. 19), in which Jane Austen is found to be a classic of doubtful status, her art being 'of an admirable secondary quality', the little masterpieces 'now and then marred', concerned with the 'trivial', marked by feelings of 'coldness' and 'dislike', the novelist herself 'a mistress of derision rather than of wit and humour'. A year later, in 1895, Alice Meynell struck again in reviewing a volume of Austen family charades. To borrow her own terminology, Miss Meynell displays herself as a feline 'mistress of derision', assailing the family pieties by way of their feeble word-games and mocking Mr Andrews's beloved *Memoir* portrait: 'The only real and credible thing is the dress. Jane Austen had the hesitating *coquetterie* of her time... the low Empire bodice (which also betrays the most untaught dressmaking) is filled up by an indefinite "tucker".' In the same derisive tone she turns to a clumsy and unconvincing sketch of Steventon Rectory, remarking acutely that, by contrast,

Miss Austen always lays out the pleasure-grounds of her novels with a kind of cool professional pleasure. She plants and shuts out—no doubt with evergreens—everything in the shape of farmstead and hayrick, and leads 'a road of smooth gravel, winding round a plantation to the front'. She has a respect for the drawing-room windows, and is sensitive as to their 'view'. 'The pleasure-grounds were tolerably extensive', she says more than once with temperate appreciation. There is always a shrubbery.[39]

Orthodox views were under scrutiny in the other boom taking place at this time, the boom in the study of English Literature itself. This phase of the critical heritage, as viewed from North America, was accurately charted by the Yale Professor, William Lyon Phelps, in the Introduction to an edition of the novels published in New York in 1906, where he provided an account of her fortunes over previous decades:

After the publication of the *Memoir* by her nephew in 1870, which came at the psychological moment, the books and articles on Jane Austen began to bloom in every direction. About 1890, what was called a 'revival' took place; it was really nothing but the cumulative growth of her fame. Many new editions appeared; and an instance of how she was regarded as a master of style may be seen in the fact that for some years every Harvard Freshman was required to read one of her books for rhetorical purposes. She had sufficient vitality to survive even such treatment.[40]

In Britain, too, Jane Austen was on the syllabus. Students at University College, London, were fortunate in having W.P. Ker as their Professor, as we can judge by this extract from his Jane Austen lecture (c. 1899), discussing the connection between the novelist's 'intelligence' and 'perfection':

There is no name for the dominant quality in Miss Austen's work, except perhaps intelligence. It is not *wit* in the ordinary limited sense of the word; *wits* in the wider sense is nearer it. It is the philosophic faculty, not as that is commonly imagined, but as it is described by Plato—the faculty of taking both a comprehensive and a discriminating view of every subject. It is this that makes her stories so vivid, because it is this that keeps her from sacrificing the general life of the story to any one character. It is closely related to the dramatic faculty, but it has a wider range. It is that which does justice to all the characters and to each part of the story; which recognizes all the different ways in which the same things appear to different people. It is something more than the ordinary faculty of neat construction, of handiness in shaping a piece of work. The perfection of Miss Austen's novels is not mere harmony or proportion or correctness— not the old pseudo-classic perfection of adherence to the rules. On the contrary, it is such a vivid understanding of the fabric of life that the representation of this fabric is itself kept moving and changing like life itself. 'The same set of events appearing differently to different people' is a formula that might be used to describe her stories.[41]

What this 'fabric of life' meant to its readers is encapsulated in the lines of 'Clerihew' Bentley published in 1905:

69

The novels of Jane Austen
Are the ones to get lost in.[42]

Two years later, in 1907, James warmed remarkably, finding a niche for Jane Austen alongside Shakespeare, Cervantes and Fielding and the other 'fine painters of life'.[43] If anything could be called an authoritative recognition, this was it. In the eyes of the public, amongst academics and in the esteem of her peers, it seemed that Jane Austen's place was secure.

VIII

The growth in the formal study of literature at the turn of the century created a new channel for criticism. Textbook histories proliferated. Some were hack-works. Yet eminent Professors and men-of-letters were ready to pronounce judgment and the most important of their works remained in print, unchanged, for many years. Prominent among these were Raleigh's *The English Novel*, 1894; *English Prose Selections*, 1896, edited by Henry Craik; *Modern English Literature*, 1897, by Edmund Gosse; and the leading American work, *The Development of the English Novel*, 1899, by Wilbur C. Cross. Like Saintsbury, Raleigh and Gosse address readers who know the novels and are capable of following an informed level of discussion. Raleigh places the novelist alongside Shakespeare: 'the sameness of artistic impersonality, of serene abstraction from life, that characterises both writers equally'; and he opposes the familiar idea of the perfect but limited artist with the claim that 'The world of pathos and passion is present in her work by implication.'[1] Raleigh also comments on the method of her narrative and irony and the 'medium' of her style, the 'craft' of the transitions between 'life' and 'conventions'. On these matters, he writes with the economy and precision of a critic knowledgeable and long practised.

In this respect, his conclusion reads oddly, that 'her work shows scant traces of development; her first novel is as completely modelled and as perfectly life-like as her last.'[2] Beside Raleigh, Gosse is a touch journalistic; and Raleigh's pages may have been in his mind when he too invokes a Shakespearian Jane Austen. But his brisk conclusion, placing the form of her novel in a European perspective, is one of the refreshing currents that ensured that views on Jane Austen at this time did not stultify and showed that the *Memoir* mould could be broken.[3] This is also true of Craik.[4] Sceptical of 'gentle Jane', the favourite aunt, he pushes this image aside to grasp the human nature of the writer herself, in the manner of Julia Kavanagh and Mrs Oliphant, asking the reader to consider the pressure of experience which stands behind her characters (the 'years of provocation under the torture of some domestic Mrs Norris') and inviting the reader to register the 'sarcasm' and 'cynicism' deployed upon the characters at the end of *Sense and Sensibility*. As befits a historian of prose, Craik attends particularly to matters of style and there is a fine concluding paragraph on Jane Austen's debt to Johnson.

Reprinted no less than twenty-six times between 1899 and 1923 and in print for many years later, Cross was the standard history of the novel for generations of American students. His approach to Jane Austen, indicated in the sectional title 'The Critic of Romance and Manners', points to a world of 'pure comedy' distinguished by 'a delicate psychological humour akin to the higher comedy of Shakespeare' where the spectator watches 'the mistaken and mistaking actors'. In this vein, Cross reveals his familiarity with the best of the earlier criticism, from Scott onwards; and he reviews this material historically, remarking that 'The assertion of Macaulay in 1843, that she ranks with Shakespeare in the dramatic delineation of character, put the seal on the Jane Austen cult.' Cross was also attentive to the most recent views, quoting, for example, a few lines from Charlotte Brontë's recently-published *Emma* letter. He follows Howells in treating Jane Austen as a 'realist'—that is, the drier, analytical Howells of *Criticism and Fiction*. The distinction has to be made because in *Harper's Bazar* for May 1900 Howells opened one of the most fulsome accounts of Jane Austen that we have (No. 21).

Nothing could be further from textbook history, although the enterprise—to sketch the development of the English and American novel through its heroines—sounds academic enough. It stemmed from Howells's seemingly idiosyncratic belief that 'a novel is great or not, as its women are important or unimportant'; and in successive issues of *Harper's* he took his readers through the women of late-eighteenth- and nineteenth-century fiction, from Fanny Burney's Evelina to the heroines of Mrs Humphry Ward. In this roll-call, as in *Criticism and Fiction*, Jane Austen stands alone. She sets the mark for 'the serene veracity which is the sole law of beauty and lord of all moods and times'. She provides 'the norm and prophecy of most that is excellent in Anglo-Saxon fiction since her time'. Surveying the work of over a hundred years, Howells identifies 'what is still almost an ideal perfection in the art of Jane Austen'. To catch some sense of the authority and persuasiveness with which these ringing claims were delivered, one has to turn the page after page of *Harper's* or the five-hundred pages of the two-volume *Heroines of Fiction* into which the series was gathered in 1901, with a multitude of illustrations. Altogether, at a popular level, these three essays still constitute the most ambitious and resounding claim on behalf of Jane Austen's supremacy in the realm of fiction.

Addressing a wide magazine readership, Howells quotes the key scenes in full and provides a good deal of resumé-commentary, a level of literary journalism he accomplishes without strain, writing about the heroines with evident enthusiasm and affection. Yet sometimes his comments are those of a writer-critic addressing his peers, as, for example, in the relaxed analytical comment on *Emma*:

Among her quiet books it is almost the quietest, and so far as the novel can suggest that repose which is the ideal of art *Emma* suggests it, in an action of unsurpassed unity, consequence, and simplicity.

Or on *Persuasion*, 'imagined with as great novelty and daring as *Pride and Prejudice*'. Or that Emma Woodhouse is possibly 'the most boldly imagined' of the heroines, 'for it took supreme courage to portray a girl, meant to win and keep the reader's fancy, with the characteristics frankly ascribed' to her—a point which has fascinated later critics. Again, there is a modern note to his observation that Emma 'is charming in the very degree of her feminine complexity'. *Sense and Sensibility* he finds 'the most conventional, the most mechanical of the novels', yet with 'moments of being the greatest'. In Fanny Price, we are shown that 'goodness is charming', 'another proof', according to Howells, 'of Jane Austen's constant courage, which was also her constant wisdom, in being true to life'.

The form of the *Harper's* essays is popular introduction and celebration.[5] In 1895, Howells had confessed that Jane Austen's books, 'late in life, have been a youthful rapture with me'.[6] So it is that the 'youthful rapture' finds eloquent and enthusiastic expression. Yet it is the eloquence and enthusiasm of a mature writer; and the force of these essays is to stake a critical claim as assertive and demanding as that advanced ten years before in *Criticism and Fiction* (quoted here on page 54). Now the claim is spelt out anew.

Jane Austen was indeed so fine an artist, that we are still only beginning to realize how fine she was; to perceive, after a hundred years, that in the form of the imagined fact, in the expression of personality, in the conduct of the narrative, and the subordination of incident to character, she is still unapproached in the English branch of Anglo-Saxon fiction.

An opportunity for revaluation, or at least for reviewing critical opinions of the last ninety years, was afforded in 1902 by Moulton's *Library of Literary Criticism*. The Jane Austen section runs to fourteen pages, gathering the classic early statements and more recent items, including Howells, up to 1900. Although some of the extracts present Jane Austen the writer, the dominant figure is still the gentle domestic Jane of the *Memoir*; and the note of sentimental biographicalising is established from the beginning. The opening words from *Pen-Portraits of Literary Women* (see page 42) set the tone: 'No other Englishwoman of letters ever lived a life so entirely uneventful...'. Moulton finds no room for criticism that can surprise or disconcert; and it is instructive to see what happens, in this context, to Agnes Repplier's Jane Austen: 'the central figure of a little loving family group, the dearest of daughters and sisters, the gayest and brightest of aunts, the most charming and incomparable of old maids'. Yet in 'Three Famous Old Maids',[7] the essay to which these are the concluding words, the flavour is tart and ironic. Far from being affirmed, the image is held in question. But this was an angle of vision so rare and uncongenial, and the domestic Jane Austen of the *Memoir* so firmly enshrined, that it comes as no surprise to find Miss Repplier recruited, in Moulton's hands, to the very cause she subverts.

Moulton's anthology contributed nothing to the state of Jane Austen criticism, which continued on its familiar wayward course, moving by fits and starts, seemingly indifferent to the platforms and points of vantage provided by Simpson, Howells and the others. Howells provoked disagreement. But it was only the semblance of debate, as we see in contributions to *Nineteenth Century* in 1902–3. Walter Frewen Lord objected to Howells' 'divine' Jane Austen and to the wholesale eviction, in *Criticism and Fiction*, of Dickens, Charlotte Brontë, Thackeray and George Eliot. Contemptuously, he labelled Jane Austen a 'feminine' writer[8]—to which a Miss Gladstone retorted vigorously, possibly inspired by

Heroines of Fiction, calling for Jane Austen's account of the woman's point of view to be taken seriously.[9] Clearly, the editor of *Nineteenth Century* considered Jane Austen a lively issue of general interest, to be treated at length—even if neither opponent had anything new to say.

IX

At the turn of the century, the debate in America is reflected in the joshing that went on between Howells and Mark Twain. Howells' 'honored prime favorite' was Twain's 'prime abhorrence' (No. 23e) arousing in him an 'animal repugnance'.[1] Twain set out out to represent himself as Jane Austen's most ferocious and dedicated enemy, an offensive aimed more widely against the Anglophile tradition in American culture—enshrined in the view held by Howells and others that the literature of his own country was a condition of English literature. In this contest, Twain's antipathy can be read as a rejection of the Englishness of Jane Austen and her following (he held an equally derisive view of *Middlemarch*).[2] Towards the end of his life, Twain took Jane Austen as one of his stock jibes and the items collected here (No. 23), dating from 1896 to 1909, show how much he enjoyed needling his Austenite friends, Howells in particular. Occasionally Howells retaliated. We catch a glimpse of this literary horseplay in a letter of May 1903, where he threatens to visit Twain on his sick-bed and 'have it out' with him about Jane Austen. 'If you say much more I'll come out and read Pride and Prejudice to you.'[3] It was a campaign that Twain also conducted in public. After a New York dinner in 1906—'a pleasant party and good talk'—he reported his disagreement with a Mrs Riggs: 'She respects Jane Austin, whilst it is the one desire of my heart to dig her up.'[4]

Twain claimed to be at the mercy of his feelings, to be so maddened by her books, so incapable of concealing his 'frenzy from the reader' that he was defeated in his wish 'to criticize Jane Austen', having 'to stop every time I begin' (No. 23 b). This mock-confession, made in 1898, was first quoted by his friend Brander Matthews, in 1920.[5] On the evidence before him, Matthews constructed an explanation for Twain's phobia. It was a case of Jane Austen's Home Counties miniaturism jarring with the largeness of his Southern vision: 'the clever spinster of Winchester' at odds with 'the robust humorist of Hannibal, Missouri'; his 'ingrained democracy...outraged' by her 'placid and complacent acceptance of a semi-feudal social organization, stratified like a chocolate layer-cake...'.[6] According to Lionel Trilling, 'The *animality*' of Twain's 'repugnance is probably to be taken as the male's revulsion from a society in which women seem to be at the centre of interest and power....'[7]

These speculations are credible enough. Yet Matthews was mistaken in one particular, in supposing that 'Twain never did write a criticism of Jane Austen'. In fact, around 1909 Twain did start a 'Jane Austen' essay (as yet unpublished)[8] in which he made a serious attempt to identify the gulf between them, picturing himself 'a barkeeper entering the Kingdom of Heaven'.[†] He accepts that others find a 'secret charm'[†] and is ready to apply himself once again. The fragment runs to just over seven hundred words, giving us little to go on. Unlike his other occasional remarks, however, the piece is not a derisive joke. In the short stretch given to the character of *Sense and Sensibility* ('manufactures',[†] unable to 'warm up and feel passion'[†])—Edward Ferrars 'an unpleasant shadow',[†] Elinor Dashwood 'a wax figure',[†] Willoughby 'criminal and filthy,[†] and so on—Twain raises issues which are unquestionably critical. Other readers, too, have expressed their doubts about the feelings that exist amongst these characters, have questioned the success with which they are drawn, have speculated about the judgment that the novel delivers. It is our loss that Twain never chose to expand upon the collision between his Bowery barkeeper and the 'Presbyterian'[†] world of Jane Austen. Howells passed a kindly last word: 'Yes, Clemens was a good judge of books except when it came to Jane Austen; there he fell down.'[9] But this only leaves us to wonder if Howells had ever seen this fragment.

Twain was not the only American impatient with the characters of *Sense and Sensibility*. In his Introduction to the 1906 New York edition Phelps writes, no less scathingly, that 'Edward Ferrars is spineless, Willoughby is a stage villain, and Colonel Brandon is depressing.'[10] Yet, on Jane Austen's achievement as a whole, Phelps was with Howells, regarding her as 'fully as conscientious an artist and fully as courageous and firm in her realism as was Flaubert...'[11] In these, and other comments, Phelps opposes

[†]See p. xiii above.

James's notion of Jane Austin as a genius artless and unaware. Of *Northanger Abbey* he commented:

Such a work, written in the very bloom of youth, is conclusive evidence of the self-conscious purpose of its author; it proves that she knew exactly what she wanted; that her purpose in art was fixed, definite and unalterable.[12]

The voice of Howells is also heard later, in a successful textbook by Phelps, *The Advance of the English Novel* (published in New York in 1916, reaching a fifth edition by 1917; and published in London in 1919), where Jane Austen is presented as 'an absolute realist' and the novels as 'a profound and accurate criticism of life'.[13]

Another American textbook drawing a Howellsian Jane Austen is Richard Burton's *Masters of the English Novel*, published in New York in 1909. Chapter 5 is entitled 'Realism: Jane Austen' and the novelist herself is described as 'a princess among truth-tellers',[14] 'the literary godmother of Trollope and Howells'.[15] Burton supports the 'assertion' (credited to Howells) 'that she leads all English novelists in that same truthful handling'.[16] His own significant observation is that in each of the novels, 'the lesson has been conveyed by the indirection of fine art'.[17] In England, the best of the textbook tradition begun by Saintsbury and Raleigh is continued in *The Age of Wordsworth*, 1905, by C.H. Herford,[18] and, at a more popular level by Thomas Seccombe and W. Robertson Nicoll in *The Bookman Illustrated History of English Lterature*, 1906.[19] Herford relates Jane Austen to the Romantic Movement and declares that 'she criticises her society from the inside'. He writes of the place of 'breeding' and 'character' in 'the moral chiaroscuro of her work', remarking that 'The wonderful Bennet household, for instance, is imagined with more comic force than psychological consistency.' Sophisticated commentary at this level is also to be found, somewhat surprisingly, in the *Bookman*. The section is headed by a quotation from Raleigh (beginning 'Satire is the element in which she lives') and Raleigh is judiciously quoted again on the presence in her work of 'The world of pathos and passion'.[20] While Seccombe and Nicoll provide their readers with the basic biographical information, their commentary is unusually critical of 'the social and mental atmosphere in which Jane Austen lived, moved, wrote, and had her being—the thoroughly unspiritual atmosphere of a comfortable country rectory...' In this world imprudent marriage [was] the one unpardonable sin, 'elegance' a cardinal virtue, vulgarity sternly ostracised (witness Mrs Elton and the Thorpes), dissent and every kind of stupidity are squalor successfully ignored.

In this radical critique, they observe that Jane Austen's fictional 'department' of life was not completely

actual, because the normal activity of human beings is virtually excluded, and all the characters are parasitical beings subsisting upon the labour of others in a kind of cloistered and subdued lotus-land free from the gusts of hunger and passion.

Nonetheless, this scathing judgment does not hamper their historical sense and the reader is invited

to appraise her vivacity and her exquisite literary malice by comparing her work with that of the writers to whom her line of relationship is clear: Richardson, Burney, Edgeworth, the Trollopes, and the Oliphants and their successors.

Altogether, this is an account which must have given the *Bookman* readership something to chew upon; whereas, sad to say, it was E.V. Lucas who was invited to provide the Jane Austen entry for the 11th edition of the *Encyclopaedia Britannica*, 1910,[21] where the *Memoir* tradition is staunchly upheld:

During her placid life Miss Austen never allowed her literary work to interfere with her domestic duties: sewing much and admirably, keeping house, writing many letters and reading aloud.

As for criticism, Lucas is content to call the roll of the *Memoir*'s 'best judges' and invoke Scott's 'Big Bow-wow' passage. His own comments are banal: 'an admirably lucid and flowing prose style which makes her stories the easiest reading'. By this account, the last forty years of criticism were as nothing.

Disappointingly, the reawakening interest in women novelists could lead to conclusions similarly backward-looking—as we find in *Woman's Work in English Fiction: from the Restoration to the Mid-Victorian Period* by Clara H. Whitmore, published in London and New York in 1910. A student of Ker and Wilbur Cross, she claimed in the Preface that 'nearly all the books on literature have been written from a man's stand-point'[22] and expressed her determination to redress the balance. But it was a false prospectus. Her Jane Austen is far from new. There is no evidence of the distinctive 'women's view-point' claimed in the Preface and her final words resurrect the 'family-reading' Jane Austen of the 1870s: 'So the public, tired of the brilliant scenes and conflicting passions of other novels, has in the last few years turned back to the simple, wholesome stories of Jane Austen.'[23]

X

Another backward-looking curiosity is Arthur Ransome's view that 'the whole of her work is so intimate and particular in expression that it would almost seem to be written in a letter to the reader.' This oddity is worth quoting because it comes in Ransome's *History of Story-Telling: Studies in the Development of Narrative*, 1909.[1] Despite the promise of the title, little is said about 'narrative'; whereas a real advance is made in *Materials and Methods of Fiction*, a pioneering work of technical analysis by Clayton Hamilton. Published in New York in 1909, it carries a considerable introduction by Brander Matthews, announcing that 'We are beginning to take our fiction seriously and to inquire into its principles,'[2] an intent reflected in the chapter titles—Narrative, Plot, Characters, Setting, The Point of View in Narrative. In Chapter 5, Characters, Hamilton quotes from *Emma* to illustrate Jane Austen's method of portraying a character through the conversation of others (ch. 33, where Mrs Elton chatters to Emma Woodhouse about Jane Fairfax) and the self-revelation that can occur in the same situation (ch. 21, when Emma and Mr Knightley discuss Jane Fairfax). Chapter 7, The Point of View in Narrative, concludes 'although written by Jane Austen in the third person, the story is really seen by Emma Woodhouse and thought in the first.'[3]

Hamilton discerns a similar effect in *Pride and Prejudice* where Elizabeth Bennet alone is analysed at any length and the other characters portrayed as Elizabeth sees them. Hamilton's approach was welcomed. In 1918 came an edition revised and enlarged for student use, now entitled *A Manual of the Art of Fiction*. To meet the widening 'study of prose fiction' at American universities this edition was provided with Review Questions and Suggested Reading, and sub-headings to the main text. Clearly, higher education in North America had engaged gear with the practice of criticism, with consequences not to be sneered at. Finally, in 1939, now called *The Art of Fiction*, *Materials and Methods* made a third appearance, with further editorial apparatus.

In England, the important advance was A.C. Bradley's lecture first given in 1911 to the ladies of Newnham College, Cambridge, and repeated in the same year to members of the English Association in London. The printed version came with extensive notes and it is this text (No. 24) which, for the next thirty years, stood, in place of Scott and Whately, as the prime document for the serious study of Jane Austen. Yet such was the Janeite grip that even Bradley felt obliged to open the lecture on a suitably disarming note. To establish a popular level of *rapport*, he claimed to speak as one of the 'faithful' and entered into the spirit of the hour, chivalrously declaring of Elizabeth Bennet, 'I was meant to fall in love with her, and I do.' The substance of the lecture, scholarly and systematic, is untroubled by such playful fancies. Bradley reminds his listeners that the novels stand in two distinct groups and discusses their development with this chronology in view, referring also to the manuscript materials, including the cancelled chapter of *Persuasion* and the letters, and to other literary and historical evidence. Such scrupulous attention takes us back forty years, to the best *Memoir* reviews of 1870 and 1871. Where Bradley is totally original is in his discussion of Jane Austen's morality and religion, in crediting the novels with 'wisdom', and in finding a strong attachment to Johnson and Cowper. Although he joins the majority of critics in naming *Emma* as the best of the novels, his admiration for *Mansfield Park* is unusual and his brief account of Mrs Norris—'this intolerable woman had strong affections'—is quite startling. Yet Bradley finds no reason to disagree with the accepted view that the 'novels make exceptionally peaceful reading'. His conclusion on this point is curiously precise, quite personal in its final emphasis: 'She troubles us neither with problems nor with painful emotions, and if there is a wound in our minds she is not likely to probe it.' What was it in Bradley, and in Jane Austen, that should prompt an idea so bizarre?[4]

Bradley's place in the critical literature was soon on record. A 1912 edition of *Pride and Prejudice*, edited by Katharine Metcalfe and published by the Clarendon Press, included a group of four 'Criticisms'. In this select gathering, Bradley is quoted on the source of Jane Austen's 'ironical amusement', alongside Scott's 'Big Bow-wow' passage, Macaulay's comparison with Shakespeare (from *No. 28*) and a few lines of Southey quoted in Chapter 9 of the

Memoir. If Miss Metcalfe was alert on the critical front, she was perceptive too on editorial matters, for here was the first edition of any of the novels to return accurately and with editorial judgment to the three editions of *Pride and Prejudice* published in Jane Austen's lifetime. There was historical authenticity, too, to the appearance of the book—with facsimile title-pages of the original three volumes; the original chapter numbering, volume by volume; a Regency typeface and layout, including catch-words at the foot of each page. This elaborate period reconstruction is matched by a modern scholarly apparatus of equal elaboration, including a considerable appendix, entitled 'Jane Austen and Her Time' with sections headed: Travelling and Post, Deportment, Accomplishment, and Manners, Social Customs, Games, Dancing, Dress, and General Language.

In all its singularity, this volume stands out in curious isolation. Why was there no continuation, with a similar scholarly treatment for the other novels, to form what might have been the Clarendon Jane Austen? The puzzle is solved in the circumstances of the book's genesis. It was planned with R.W. Chapman (employed at the Clarendon Press since 1906) and in 1913, Katharine Metcalfe, a tutor at Somerville College, became his wife.[5] Ten years later came *The Novels of Jane Austen. The text based on Collation of the Early Editions* by R.W. Chapman, published at the Clarendon Press. The text of *Pride and Prejudice* was printed directly and unchanged from the setting of Katharine Metcalfe's 1912 edition; and we can see that this volume served as the prototype in virtually every detail for Dr Chapman's magisterial edition of 1923.

Miss Metcalfe also provided a very elaborate, if old-fashioned, Introduction, with some quaintly Jamesian and *Memoir*-like suggestions: that 'the simple creativeness of her mind forbade self-consciousness' and that 'to her writing was an altogether secondary matter.'[6] Following Bradley, however, in sketching Jane Austen's character and life, she made good use of the letters ('the best preface to knowledge of the books');[7] and there is an excellent and seemingly original section in which she compares the 'delicacy' of Jane Austen's comedy of manners with that of Chaucer: their 'minds...curiously like each other', revealing the same 'delicate irony...sly humour...irresistible wickedness...subtlety...worldliness..detachment' (but not 'aloofness').[8]

The liveliest and most original textbook account appeared in Oliver Elton's *Survey of English Literature*, 1912.[9] As a university teacher, Elton understood what students required by way of biographical and bibliographical fodder (for example, he brings out the point of 'First Impressions' as an allusive *literary* title). Yet there was no muffling of his personal views—in detecting 'a governessy tone' and a note of 'sourness' to *Sense and Sensibility*; in tracing the progress, in *Persuasion*, from satire, through high comedy, to idyll; in finding fault with *Emma*. Elton establishes fresh and important understandings: that in *Mansfield Park* 'the "instruction" is swathed in irony'; that the novelist 'resolves' the 'didactic' 'into the art of the comedian'. His view of Jane Austen as a woman writer was not new ('feminine to a profound degree', he calls her). But hitherto no male critic had qualified his admiration with a chauvinism so severe and open. Not a Shakespeare but a 'feminine Congreve', touched with coldness, a distinct unlikeableness; a literary embodiment, he concludes, of 'the woman our enemy'.

Across the Channel, Halevy devoted a section to 'Women Novelists' in *A History of the English People in 1815*. The first French edition was 1912, the English translation 1924. The paragraph he gives to Jane Austen—quoting contemporary reviews— is well-informed. Halevy's single descriptive-critical comment is strongly reminiscent of Tennyson's view of 'the country town', which, like Halevy, he saw as her chosen territory.

The petty jealousies and hatreds, the littleness and the meanness which characterized social relations in the country and the provincial town, were portrayed by Jane Austen with a merciless, if unembittered pencil.[10]

Remarkably, Halevy identifies Jane Austen as a novelist of 'the new England', observing the passing of 'old' Georgian England and the coming of the 'new' Regency world. Notwithstanding the nineteenth-century setting of the three later novels, Jane Austen was persistently treated as an eighteenth-century writer.[11] That the later novels are concerned with change in contemporary society was a point only Howells had made before (see page 225); indeed, it was often specifically denied, as in the *Nation* in 1913:

For Jane Austen must remain as a brilliant episode in English literature, or more exactly perhaps, an interlude. She picked up the art of fiction where it had been dropped, and carried it on, unconscious of the change of culture about her.[12]

In 1913 came the definitive biography, *Jane Austen: Her Life and Letters: A Family Record* by William and Richard Arthur Austen-Leigh (son and grandson of the author of the *Memoir*). It took in material from Brabourne's edition of the *Letters*, *Jane Austen: Her Homes and Her Friends* (1902) by Constance Hill and *Jane Austen's Sailor Brothers* (1906) by J.H. and E.C. Hubback. The Austen-Leighs announced that the *Life* was 'intended as a narrative, and not as a piece of literary criticism';[13] and the special family sentiment, strong in the *Memoir*, comes across in their hope to have conveyed 'even a small part of the feeling which we ourselves entertain of the charm of her personality—a charm almost as remarkable in its way as the brightness of her genius'.[14] But the authors took care to avoid the sentimental strain of the *Memoir* and they set out to dispel its myths. The 1870s had been left with the picture of a reclusive amateur, happily innocent of her own genius, held in bonds of close affection within the bosom of the family—an image which had delighted the essayists and their public. The Austen-Leighs set their faces against this; and their Preface announced a polite but unmistakable programme of correction. They would treat 'the emotional and romantic side of her nature—a very real one'; 'Then, again, her nephews and nieces hardly knew how much she had gone into society, or how much, with a certain characteristic aloofness, she had enjoyed it'; 'A third point is the uneventful nature of the author's life, which, as we think, has been a good deal exaggerated.'[15] These revisionist claims—towards a livelier, more sociable Jane Austen, seeing her in girlhood instead of the long twilight of early old-maidishness—were also advanced by their use of the so-called 'Zoffany' portrait,[16] a delightful and relaxed picture of a young girl of 14 or 15. This attractive picture is wholly different from the Andrews portrait in the *Memoir*, which represented a woman in her thirties, set in spinsterhood, and which had given rise to some strange and sentimental rationalising:

there is something singularly refreshing in the story of that unassuming life... there is something singularly restful in the picture of that serene and cheerful lady, who never grew old, with her bright eyes and her full round cheeks, playfully adopting a spinster's cap as a symbol of old-maidhood at an age when many women draw lovers round them still, sitting in her quiet family circle. . . .[17]

Nothing here fits the 'Zoffany' portrait, which although not now

accepted as a picture of Jane Austen, could very well stand for the
vivacious young woman we read about in her letters of the
1790s—Mrs Ward's 'pretty, lively girl, very fond of dancing' in the
flesh (No. 9).

The *Life* also gave her writing due prominence, not just the fact
of being a writer, but the business of getting published, its failures
and successes, of dealing with proofs, the excitement of publication
itself and of hearing how the books were received. It was a
corrective successfully delivered. As the *Yale Review* noted: 'It will
serve to explode for good and all three still current errors: that Miss
Austen was a woman without passion, a novelist without experience of life, and a writer careless of the fate of her work.'[18] For
scholars and literary historians, the *Life* provided more of the
essential bare bones of fact and circumstance; for the critics, it
delivered materials towards the portrait of a writer, a figure to
whom Chesterton's daring aphorism, written the same year, can
credibly attach. In comparison with George Eliot and the Brontës,
he claimed, 'Jane Austen knew much more about men than either
of them. Jane Austen may have been protected from truth: but it
was precious little of truth that was protected from her' (No. 25).
The remark is based upon Chesterton's reading of the novels, not
the *Life*. But at last the biography had been brought within distance
of the writer's domain. The importance of this reclamation was
confirmed in the *Athenaeum*:

It was high time for this act of piety, for the casual writer is abroad,
inventing, perverting, and improving, and some interesting matter
concerning the family has already reached the stage when myth and
tradition are apt to merge.[19]

Yet the demythologising process of the *Life* could do little to
curtail the existing varieties of interpretation and response. There
was, for example, already in motion the youthful feminist rejection
by Rebecca West:

For want of emotional experience Jane Austen's imagination never
developed virility. And, though of course her comic characters had human
failings, her heroes (that is, the men she regarded from a sexual point of
view) were 'strong gods'.[20]

These 'strong gods' Rebecca West had elsewhere defined as the
'men' in books written 'by spinsters...for spinsters'.[21] Ezra Pound

also connected the limitations of the novels to the limitations in their author's experience:

Professors to the contrary notwithstanding, no one expects Jane Austen to be as interesting as Stendhal. A book about a dull, stupid, hemmed-in sort of life, by a person who has lived it, will never be as interesting as the work of some author who has comprehended many men's manners and seen many grades and conditions of existence.[22]

And Walter de la Mare discovered a tame and complacent Jane Austen: a 'serene, observant mind', a 'quiet, unimpassioned heart', a writer capable of living 'contentedly on in the society of the mediocrities whom she portrays to the life'.[23]

A very different kind of demythologising was conducted by Howells.[24] The publication of the *Life* led him to reflect acidly on the growing bulk of memoirs and studies and new editions. Like James before him, he viewed this accumulating literature with an amused and sceptical eye. The body of his essay, recounting the misadventures of a band of American devotees come to honour Jane Austen's tomb at Winchester, is a classic item of Austenian pastiche, recounting these real-life events in the style of a fictional episode. Within the pastiche lies a further joke, a parody of the 'pilgrimage' essay. The pilgrim traveller's-report from Europe was a popular feature in American cultural reviews and magazines from the 1860s onwards, some of the finest coming from Henry James.[25] On the 'Jane Austen' version of the European Literary Grand Tour, the shrines are Steventon, Chawton, Bath, Southampton, Portsmouth, Lyme Regis and other spots immortalised by the novelist's life and writings. Winchester is the holy city, its holy-of-holies the modest memorial slab set in the Cathedral's north aisle.[26] Many were the fond 'pilgrimage' chronicles recounting such transatlantic journeys, the discovery of this unregarded spot, and homage paid.

Aside from this amusing excursion in literary styles, Howells has a serious case to make about the character of Jane Austen criticism, in which he detects 'a certain chill, creeping paralysis of respectability', the critics 'sobered, not to say awed, in the presence of her fame'. His list of critics 'who seem to be always her eulogists', 'such eminently qualified persons', recalls Mrs Oliphant's sharp comment about 'the best judges' having 'done the office of an Academy'. However, while Mrs Oliphant was annoyed at seeing a great writer foisted upon an unappreciative public, forty years later Howells believed that the critics were now a stumbling block and it was no thanks to them that Jane Austen enjoyed 'the ever-widening honor and affection of mature men and women'. What he sought was a criticism enlivened 'with bursts of naturalness and even light-heartedness'; what he found in the *Life* was a work 'very tasteful, very gentlemanly, very nice' but doing nothing 'to remove the sense of polite distance at which the reader has been held by her biographers'. Here, he plays the amused Yankee contemplating a foreign salon of 'upper-class worshippers' (accepting that the two resident Americans on his list—Oscar Fay Adams and the Canadian-American Goldwin Smith—had qualified as honorary Britishers through their strong cultural sympathies). His criteria for good criticism are vague. But the effective demonstration is in his own writing and in the remarkable essay by Farrer (No. 27) which shows the possibilities of maintaining an acute critical edge to eulogy charged with the very 'bursts' that Howells was asking for.

Many subscribers to the *Times Literary Supplement* must have been taken aback by the considerable review (No. 26) that led the front page on 8th May 1913. It began on an intimate and familiar note ('the *Life* gives depth and perspective to the figure we see in our mind's eye'). *Memoir*-like, the author's personal qualities are enumerated. However, the anonymous reviewer, Virginia Woolf, was soon providing something quite unexpected—not an account of the *Life* but an estimate of the 'damage' done by the novelist's 'conservative spirit', the 'chief damage' being to the men. For many *TLS* readers, this was the first occasion upon which anyone would have ventured to address them on Jane Austen's 'defects'— characters 'which bore us frankly', pages which 'have to be skipped'. While there was some comfort in the reviewer's emphasis upon the novelist's 'greatness as an artist', many readers must have been puzzled by a passing reference to the 'curious atmosphere of symbolism' thrown over the scene in *Mansfield Park* 'where Maria and Henry Crawford refuse to wait for Rushworth, who is bringing the key to the gate'. (It was to be another thirty or forty years before Jane Austen's 'symbolism' became a commonplace of criticism.) Another intriguing reference came at the end, to Jane Austen as a writer who remains 'A little aloof, a little inscrutable and mysterious'. If this review was not to break the spell of Jane

Austen's famed 'perfection', at least a challenge had been delivered to the image of the perfect and limited miniaturist.

Whereas Virginia Woolf deplored the 'conservative spirit' in Jane Austen, an American reviewer of the *Life*, Paul Elmer More[27] saw this as the centre of her imaginative gravity and found the high point of her achievement in the idyllic realms of *Emma* and *Mansfield Park*, where

we are transported into a world that seems to have been the same from everlasting to everlasting, into a kind of ideal centre of calm which was conceived, and for a time and in certain places actually realised, by the eighteenth century.

More's account of the Austen family and of the novelist's life and works is evidently the vision of an Anglophile American in love with the past. It is nonetheless an important step towards identifying the cultural and intellectual traditions in which the novels stand.

As to the soundness or otherwise of More's sense of history, no one spoke. But if we are to test it alongside any other statement, it would be a short essay by Chesterton, 'The Evolution of Emma', 1917,[28] treating the continuities of social culture which run forward from Jane Austen and the 'evolution' of 'That unique and formidable institution, the English Lady' perpetrating Emma's mistakes on a large and public scale. There is a typical Chestertonian joke in this, accompanied by a fine Chestertonian insight: that Jane Austen 'understood the intricacy of the upper middle class and the minor gentry, which were to make so much of the mental life of the nineteenth and twentieth centuries.'

A more precisely literary-historical placing of the *Life* came from Robertson Nicoll in the *British Weekly*. Whilst expressing his admiration for the book, he was quick to point out that 'we still need an estimate of Jane Austen from a master hand' and regretted that Macaulay had never written his short biography. He referred back, also, to Simpson's essay, calling it 'A very ambitious article'. 'But one looks in vain for a complete estimate which shall set Jane Austen's novels in relation with the age she lived in and the conditions of her work.'[29]

That was the reviewer's pipe-dream. Close to hand was depressing reality in the pages of the latest standard account, the *Jane Austen* volume, by F. W. Cornish, in the *English Men of Letters* series, also published in 1913. On the biographical side, it is up-to-date, drawing upon the *Life*. But its style of critical appreciation belongs to the 1880s, to the whimsicalities of Andrew Lang and the twaddle of Anne Thackeray and the later Mrs Oliphant, all three quoted for our admiration. Jane Austen is prized for her 'finish'. Her writing is a 'miracle'. 'She never drops a stitch.'[30] Her 'faults are obvious. Her style is remarkable rather for exquisite choice of words than for skill in composition or distinction of language. Her plots, though worked out with microscopic delicacy, are not in high degree original or ingenious.'[31] 'Her novels make no display of idealism, romance, tenderness, poetry, or religion.' He concludes: 'She has no need to construct her characters, for there they are before her, like Mozart's music, only waiting to be written down.'[32] No better and no worse, one must admit, than much being written at this time. The point is neatly illustrated in Cornish's reflections on Jane Austen's 'philosophy of life', concluded with a quotation from Walter de la Mare's notice of the *Life* in the *Edinburgh Review* for July 1913:

As for philosophy of life, she would have laughed at the idea of her having any. She was an observer and a learner, not a thinker; too busy taking note of the actual to spend much attention in moralising on the ideal.

If I may quote her most recent critic: 'It was, as she said of Elizabeth Bennet, her business to be satisfied, her temper to be happy. She practised an instinctive self-control as a duty. She was her own clear-sighted, unprejudiced, unafflictive mistress. She knew that social existence consisted for the most part of trivialities, of the follies of the well-intentioned, the infelicities of the discontented, of "a monstrous deal of stupid quizzing and commonplace nonsense", but she viewed and appraised it all against the still background of her own life... She could be happy anywhere... The present authors repudiate the notion that Jane Austen was a stranger to the emotional and romantic side of life, that her experience was shallow and stagnant. The most trying storms in life are those in a teacup. Not all life's heroes rest in Westminster Abbey'.[33]

Cornish was read in 1913 by the positivist Frederic Harrison, who found it (as he wrote to Thomas Hardy) 'A wretchedly poor book'. His letter continued:

She was a heartless little cynic was Jane, penning satires about her neighbours whilst the Dynasts were tearing the world to pieces, &

consigning millions to their graves. A relation of hers even was guillotined in 1793, her brother was in the fleet that fought at Trafalgar—& not a breath from the whirlwind around her ever touched her Chippendale *chiffonier* or *escritoire*.[34]

Although at this time there was no developed feminist critique, the *Englishwoman* provided a forum for women contributors. In literary matters, at least, the tone was by no means sympathetic. In October 1910, readers were advised of the 'Weakness of the Woman novelist' and warned that 'A woman is apt to fall in love with her own characters, feel for them, and speak through them.'[35] A month later, Moyra Humphries delivered a stern admonition:

Girls who complain that life is dull should read Miss Austen's novels. They will find there a society which existed without games or sports, with very occasional visits to London, with country-house visiting, but without what we know as country-house gaieties.[36]

In the issue for June 1913 the *Life* was reviewed under an unpromising title, 'The Incomparable Jane'. But this hint of idolatory does not trouble the review itself. Engenia Newmark remarks bluntly that the book is 'quite devoid of charm' and that for all its biographical detail, 'we know little more of the novelist'. Four months later came 'The Emancipation of the Heroine', a misleading title, for W. Lyon Blease maintained that Jane Austen's 'young women, lively and attractive as they are, are still the quiet suppressed young females of the eighteenth century'.[37] 'There is the same passivity, the same waiting for the gentlemen to ask them.'[38] This was refuted in January 1914 by Madeleine Hope Dodds, who read the confrontation between Elizabeth Bennet and Lady Catherine de Bourgh very differently:

a plea for independence of thought. . . . It is one of the curious anomalies of criticism that Miss Austen's heroines are censured nowadays for being prim and colourless, while in her own time they were regarded as dangerously wilful and headstrong, setting a bad example to other young women. Of the two, earlier opinion is the more correct. Under their demure air, they all hide strong characters and independent minds.[39]

In the same issue T.O 'Meara spoke up for women authors, pointing to the unexpected strengths of Jane Austen:

Jane Austen was the secluded daughter of an eighteenth-century parson-age, and Dickens was a man of the world: yet consider his method of handling such an incident as Little Em'ly's elopement; and then consider the gleeful relish with which Miss Austen, an early Shavian satirist, squeezes the last drops of ironically humorous effect out of the affair of Lydia Bennet! Contrast the attitude of the Peggotty family in the face of their disaster with the attitude of the Bennet family... Thackeray, too, was a man of the world, specialising in snobs; but it was Miss Austen who conjured up Mrs Elton and Mr Collins, before whom all other snobs grow dim...[40]

Four years later, in 1918, Helen Wodehouse examined the 'defined and framed world' of the novels and the relationship of this world both to the author and reader and to qualitites in the writing—'a certain security and quietness of movement and coolness of temper'. Unusually, this analysis is advanced by comparisons with a contemporary novelist, Arnold Bennett; and with some interplay between the Napoleonic war-time of Jane Austen's England and the war-time of 1918. But the ghost of 'dear Aunt Jane' intervenes; and in the last few lines there sounds a Janeite rhapsody evoking the high yesteryear of Anne Thackeray and her 'Dear books'.

The major account of English literature at this time was the massive *Cambridge History*. This carries a 'Jane Austen' chapter[41] by the literary journalist Harold Child.[42] There are one or two surprises: that, for example, 'the great blot' on *Pride and Prejudice* 'is the author's neglect to lift Darcy sufficiently above the level of aristocratic brutality'.[43] Child thought highly of *Mansfield Park*: 'the finest example of her power of sustaining the interest through a long and quiet narrative'.[44] He speaks of the development of Fanny Price as 'one of Jane Austen's finest achievements in the exposition of character' and remarks on the 'artistic truth' of 'the effect of Crawford's advances upon Fanny'.[45] Beyond this, however, the chapter is lame and colourless. The familiar commendations are to hand: the novelist's 'artistic perfection'[46] (twice), works of 'balance and proportion'[47] (three times), the 'touchstone of good sense',[48] to his concluding sentence—'Through all alike, there runs the endearing charm of a shrewd mind and a sweet nature.'[49] Sadly, this chapter was reprinted, unchanged from 1915 until as recently as 1953. For generations of students and ordinary readers this tepid and unpenetrating view was the authoritative 'Cambridge' account of Jane Austen's writing and character.

Readers of *The Voyage Out*, also first published in 1915, came across something far more breezy in Chapter 4, with Mr Dalloway's vigorous championing of Jane Austen as 'incomparably the greatest female writer we possess', because 'she does not attempt to write like a man. Every other woman does; on that account I don't read 'em'. Mrs Dalloway's retort, that it is 'no good your pretending to know Jane by heart, considering that she always sends you to sleep', sounds like a Stephen family joke. But there was an unequivocal tribute in Virginia Woolf's technical recourse to Jane Austen. The tribute of tutelage, imitation or, at best, assimilation, is also seen in the novels of Forster and, mixed with Jamesian elements, in those of Edith Wharton. In the next decade all three were to write about Jane Austen with the special insight of attentive pupils. There was the growing perception, too, of a less comfortable novelist. In 1914, Lytton Strachey observed her 'caressing mischief'[50] (on another occasion Strachey said it was 'Passion' he found in Jane Austen[51]). In the same year, Saintsbury defined her

peculiar quiet irony, a little like Addison's, but more evasive and of a finer quality—in fact, a counterpart of Swift's in power, with all the savagery, and the gloom, and the coarseness taken out.[52]

This was in *A First Book of English Literature*, a school book, much reprinted. In 1915, Arthur Waugh found a style of 'clear and *nervous* restraint'.[53] Saintsbury, in 1916, noted that the writer's 'cruelty' is a 'cruelty' which 'only gives poignancy to the wit'.[54] But these insights were quite out of step with the Janeite image of a mild and sunny-tempered humorist at ease with her world. As yet there was no debate on these matters. The seeds of this were to come in 1917, the centenary of Jane Austen's death.

XI

This event was anticipated in January 1916 by a letter to the *Times Literary Supplement* from 'The Valley of Rocks and Wolves, Tibet'. The letter was signed by Reginald Farrer, that strange genius of the Alpine flower. It appealed to 'all members of that large and elect band which owes its chief and unfailing literary happiness to Jane Austen'. Describing himself as 'not the least ardent worshipper of the Divine Jane', he proffered his idea 'as to the aptest tribute we can pay to the unquestionable supreme artist in English fiction'. His suggestion, outlined in some detail, was to establish a fund for the assistance of retired governesses. Alongside this, he called for a new edition of Jane Austen—'a great memorial edition...sumptuous, stately, final, and as perfect as care of editors, printers, binders, and publishers can make it'. The edition was to include the minor works and each volume was to have 'its prefactory paean, not couched in the timid and half-apologetic vein of some editors, but inspired with the discreet and solemn rapture of the hierophant'; and he went on to name Henry James, H.G. Wells, E.M. Forster and Edith Wharton among the desired contributors.[1]

The joke went down well. In those dark years of the war it was a welcome fantasy and excited a lively correspondence. For behind the Janeite front was a real critic, a voice as distinctive as Simpson's. We catch it, momentarily, in his letter, when he comments on the Jane Austen of *Lady Susan*, 'arid and odious in the prematurity of youth', revealing 'fully that pitilessness which is the bedrock of her genius'; on *The Watsons*, 'that dropped fragment of the Portsmouth-Bath mid-period of Jane Austen's life, in which one guesses her to have been inwardly *désoeuvrée* and unhappy, and infertile accordingly'; on *Emma*, 'so close is the web of this incomparable book that the beginner may well find it difficult and only on the third or fourth reading does it begin to reveal its real mine of wealth, unexhausted and inexhaustible, to the ninety-ninth'; and in his suggestion that to explain 'one of the most vital episodes', 'Lovers Vows' should follow the text of *Mansfield Park*—as duly it did in Chapman's magnificent Clarendon Press edition—which so precisely fulfils Farrer's desiderata for the 'great memorial edition' that his grandiose vision, launched half-in-jest, seems, on the face of it, to have provided the inspiration for Chapman's editorial scheme. In fact, as we know, it really derived from Katherine Metcalfe's *Pride and Prejudice* of 1912.

The principal event of the centenary, in official terms, was a meeting of the Royal Society of Literature at which the formal 'Appreciation' was delivered by Montague Summers. Summers knew the minor fiction of the period very well and was able to speak with authority: 'alone in her greatness of reserve and consummate power, but not alone historically, one of a long procession of female novelists'.[2] However, Summers had nothing to say about the nature of this 'reserve' or 'power'. Instead, he launched into a thorough-going Janeite eulogy, distinctive only for its theological reference and a theatricality reminiscent of Sir Edward Denham: 'To-day the world is divided into the elect and the profane—those who admire Jane Austen, and those (one shudders to speak the phrase)—who do not.'[3] He claimed that 'it is only in recent years that she has begun to come into her own'[4] and complained, Denham-like again, that the novelist had been insufficiently praised:

her appointed panegyrists themselves, prove timid, they venture and do not dare, they eulogise and are lukewarm, speak of her faults and she had none…genius impeccable…writing so faultless…touch so unwavering …achievement so complete…work of so exquisite a rarity that if sheer perfection be the standard we must place her first of all English novelists.[5]

Later in 1917 came the great essay by Farrer (No. 27). Following the precedent of Scott and Whately, it appeared in the *Quarterly Review*. It began in the guise of a Janeite *jeu d'esprit*, its title arch and dilettante, its opening heavy with playful clubmanship. The irony of the occasion is caught in the epigraph from *Mansfield Park*. Of all times, this was no moment for lounging and chitchat. Yet, as Farrer explains in his opening paragraph, it was nonetheless Jane Austen's finest hour, when the novels could provide relief from the horrors of war. Farrer saw the need to entertain his readership and we have to understand his concern to ease the pressures of the time. The artful manner—a blend of the archaic and the bluff and breezy—enabled him to talk about literature seriously whilst seeming to shrug it off. These tactics of style limit him not at all and the body of the essay presents a subtle and highly concentrated appraisal of Jane Austen's art, identifying and analysing its strengths and weaknesses within a perspective of European literature.

Farrer's piece has been described as the best short introduction to Jane Austen[6] and it holds an important place in the historiography of criticism. Avowedly, Farrer was addressing the Janeites. So there is no boring them with academic debate. Yet the essay is, in effect, a detailed rejoinder to the existing critical literature. The unspoken agenda is to dispose systematically of the traditional myths and fallacies and to reclaim the writer and her works for sensible discussion. Occasionally, the critics enter the essay, once as 'the cruder critics'; and Macaulay, Goldwin Smith and Charlotte Brontë are mentioned by name. It is clear, however, that Farrer knew the criticism thoroughly and saw the need to halt the sentimental and mistaken nonsense which had been accumulating since the *Memoir*. Farrer's own Jane Austen is announced in the adjective 'inexorably' (in the footnote to the opening page) and in his swift disposal there of her reading-public. The terminology is all of a piece—'radiant and remorseless Jane', 'dispassionate but pitiless'. No trace here of 'gentle Jane', of what Farrer describes as the 'lay-figure, comfortable and comely, but conveying no faintest suggestion of the genuine Jane Austen'. The biographical fallacy is disposed of. The Shakespeare association is examined and redefined. The domestic myth is dismantled: there are no happy families in Jane Austen. 'These fantasies of propriety' are dissolved. Likewise the 'theory', as Farrer describes it, of the 'limited' writer. Likewise the criticism of her men: 'it would be quite a mistake to call her men pallid or shadowy'.

The received Jane Austen is now replaced by a great and 'conscious' novelist: the 'greatest artist in English fiction', a writer of 'intense concentration' (as Mrs Ward had observed (No. 9)), displaying an 'intense preoccupation with character', whose heroines are in possession of 'minds'. In describing the novels, Farrer is attentive to their development: with 'the looser mesh' of the early novels, the increasing density and subtlety of meaning, *Emma* as the great novel but 'not an easy book to read', with its 'manifold complexity', its 'complicated wonderfulness'. The writer's art is defined in terms of 'technical problems', 'technical mastery', 'technical triumphs'. His formulation of the 'problem' of *Emma* reminds us of the modern rhetoric of fiction;[7] his account of the 'radical dishonesty' and the 'sheer bad art' of *Mansfield Park* reminds us of Mrs Leavis and Marvin Mudrick; and again in his discussion of *Lady Susan*.[8] His account of the 'woven pattern of Austenian irony' and of the author's mastery over her material takes us back to Simpson; and to Simpson again in the observation that Jane Austen's prime concern is 'with character unfolded through love'. Elsewhere we are reminded of Mrs Kavanagh, the early Mrs Oliphant and Lewes. Howells, too, we hear ('The real thing is her only object always... She is consumed with a passion for the real'); and it is upon the Howellsian 'real' that the essay ends. It is this intelligent and unsentimental tradition that Farrer now recovers and continues.

Alongside Farrer it is instructive to place another war-time document—a letter dated 23rd October 1917, from Professor Raleigh to Chapman, an Oxford friend, then on active service in

Salonica. Raleigh had just been reading *Pride and Prejudice*.

She knows a lot; and I believe she knows what she doesn't know. At least, I shouldn't like to believe that she thought she knew anything about married people or young men. Her married people are merely a bore or a comfort to the young—nothing to each other. Her young men, my Gawd! I will only take Darcy and Bingley. Of course they have no profession—they have money. But there is no scrap of evidence, no indication, that they can *do* anything, shoot a partridge, or add up figures, or swim or brush their hair. They never talk of anything except young women, a subject taboo among decent young men. (I find that women mostly don't know that men never talk intimately about them. Jane didn't know this). Well, Darcy and Bingley have only one interest in life—getting married, and marrying their friends one to another. It is incredible, immense, yet it deludes you while you read. As for the young women, they are marvellous and incomparable, so that Jane is a swell all the same. But, her young men would be black-balled in any Club...[9]

Away from the lecture-hall, Raleigh delivers himself unguardedly not on the novelist as writer but the novelist as woman, as he viewed the species; and the men are judged as inhabitants of Raleigh's own clubland world. The extraordinarily 'social' character to his commentary is peculiarly English, peculiarly male, peculiarly of its period; and a backhanded testimony to the power of the characters to insinuate themselves into Raleigh's vision of the world.

The other centenary pieces were unremarkable, rehearsing the familiar testimonies to Jane Austen's greatness and popularity, a point well-made by George Moore (No. 28) who confessed his puzzlement that the essayists 'could have written so much and said so little', and wondered why 'this very trite appreciation should be expanded into many columns when so much remained unwritten about this delightful writer'. Remarking that 'it is the criticism of the fellow-craftsman that counts', Moore promptly came up with a writer's comment of enduring worth: 'that Miss Austen was the inventor of a new medium of literary expression...the formula whereby domestic life may be described.' This fruitfulness of definition is seen again in his comment that *Pride and Prejudice* 'tends towards the vase rather than the wash-tub'. Moore's critique of *Sense and Sensibility* is unmistakably that of a fellow-novelist. Alert to its local weaknesses and failures, he greets it (the only critic to do so) as an account of 'a disappointment in love': 'never was one better written, more poignant, more dramatic'. His attention to Jane Austen's treatment of 'the agony of passion' may well have been fired by Farrer's discussion. His comment—'it is here that we find the burning human heart in English prose narrative for the first, and, alas, for the last time'—possesses the same historical perspective that we find in Farrer; and a similar breadth of reference to the European novel. On the other hand, the final words—the witty and daring association of 'Miss Austen's spinsterhood' with her revelation of 'the Venusberg in the modern drawing-room'— are surely his alone.

Frank Swinnerton also gives a *writer's* view of Jane Austen.[10] Like Farrer, he successfully combined the ease of good journalism with analytical and reflective criticism; and Swinnerton's Jane Austen, a writer of both simplicity and complexity, seems to owe something to both Moore and Farrer: 'She stands apart, portraying intensively very simple forms of domestic life, which yet, in the later books especially, permit of a highly complicated series of emotional relationships...' While Farrer's voice also sounds in Swinnerton's account of the 'intricate relationships' of *Emma*—'the work of a comic genius, at its height of lucidity and penetration'— his comments on the Crawfords ('the most interesting young people in the book') and the conclusion of *Mansfield Park,* an ending not to our liking, yet (contradicting Farrer) 'artistically right and true', are distinctly his own.

Howell's final word was the Introduction he contributed in 1918, at the age of 81, to the Harper edition of *Pride and Prejudice*. There he gave full play to Janeite sentiment, now elevated to a critical principle—that the qualities of the heroines are those of the author herself, that they share 'the loveliness of her own soul'; that 'good as she was great' as a writer, so was she as a woman.[11] If this is a version of biographical fallacy, Howells was surely aware of it, boldly indifferent to it, confident that his readers would be delighted and strengthened in their Janeite convictions when they read, for example, that in the heart of Elizabeth Bennet is revealed 'the heart of Jane Austen, who is almost one with her, and was always writing herself into her, in her irony, her playfulness, her final dignity of heart and mind'.[12] Whether or not we object to this sustained identification, no one can be blind to the modesty with which Howells handles this method; nor to his unerring grasp of

Jane Austen's artistry—in his appreciation of her as 'so entirely the most ironical'[13] of English novelists; in his differentiation amongst her 'fools'; in his account of her style and method (in *Pride and Prejudice*, 'the open simplicity of the design');[14] in his clear appraisal of the failures and weaknesses in her handling of character and plot; his recognition of a 'playfulness' within her irony, an element which contrives to impel our sympathy for its victims:

Playfulness was the note of her most delightful nature, and in her perpetual irony it gives that prime quality of her talent a charm which satire never has. We have only to call it satire in order to feel its difference from all other irony, and to find in it a sort of protesting pity, a sort of latent willingness that the reader shall come to the rescue against it.[15]

The ideas of Howells seem to pervade the appreciative literature of the 1920s. But the echoes are not always second-hand and soft-centred. There is the ring of truth, an unsentimental conviction, to Frank Swinnerton's testimony that he could not read *Pride and Prejudice, Emma* or *Persuasion* 'without responding with personal emotion to the entirely personal beauty of the chief characters'.[16]

Elsewhere, however, Janeitism persisted at a curiously primitive level, the literary and biographical strands still confusingly intertwined, their unravelling laborious. In 1922, these issues were raised with some authority in Mary Augusta Austen-Leigh's *Personal Aspects of Jane Austen*. Miss Austen-Leigh was a daughter of the author of the *Memoir* and inherited his concern that Aunt Jane's reputation should be protected. In 1919, she contributed an article to the *Quarterly Review*, which became Chapter 5 of the book. This piece, redolent of Anne Thackeray, was feelingly addressed to 'Jane Austen's earnest adherents', those for whom it is not enough

to know her books—in some cases almost by heart. They desire to know herself also, they seek after a more intimate acquaintance with their unseen lifelong friend, Jane Austen, who, more than one hundred years ago, was laid to rest, early on a summer morning, within the walls of Winchester Cathedral.[17]

The article sought to identify the theme of Repentance in the novels and to challenge the account of Jane Austen's religion given in a recent French study (*Jane Austen: sa vie et son oeuvre* by Léonie Villard, 1915). Miss Austen-Leigh then saw the need for a fuller refutation and decided to write a book—dedicated 'To all true lovers of Jane Austen and her works'—providing additional biographical information to correct 'critics of the present day' who continue to write of Jane Austen's 'Narrow experience', her reclusiveness, her life lacking in incident and 'the consolations of culture': and who continue to claim, in the face of the *Memoir* and the *Life and Letters*, that 'concerning her personal character and private interests we know remarkably little'.[18] The pointlessness of this debate and the clumsiness of Miss Austen-Leigh's own performance were seized upon in scathing reviews by Virginia Woolf and Katherine Mansfield. Writing in the *TLS*, Virginia Woolf pointed out that while 'her chief admirers', novelists themselves, from Scott to George Moore, have praised Jane Austen 'with unusual discrimination', amongst the ordinary reviewers, instead, there is 'incorrigible stupidity'. 'Ever since Jane Austen became famous they have been hissing inanities in chorus' about her dislike of dogs and children, her indifference to England and to public affairs, etc. etc.[19] Katherine Mansfield's message was the same: Ignore these meaningless controversies and attend to the writer herself. Katherine Mansfield ended by touching upon her own experience of reading Jane Austen, an experience which she generalises into a working axiom, Cheney-like in its own way: 'the truth is that every true admirer of the novels cherishes the happy thought that he alone—reading between the lines—has become the secret friend of their author.'[20]

Twenty years later, this was a 'truth' which Mary Lascelles was to endorse, prominently, in the closing lines of *Jane Austen and Her Art*.[21] Another truth for Katherine Mansfield was Virginia Woolf's falling short of Jane Austen. Reviewing *Night and Day* in 1919, she remarked on the temptation 'to cry Miss Austen up-to-date'. But there was an essential difference:

With Miss Austen, it is first her feeling for life, and then her feeling for writing; but with Mrs Woolf these feelings are continually giving way the one to the other so that the urgency of either is impaired.[22]

In the *Nation*, H. W. Massingham made a similar comparison;[23] and her Diary tells us how much these remarks stung Virginia Woolf.[24]

Miss Austen-Leigh's protest and the amusing commentary that it provoked are part of a growing chorus of complaint at the continuing confusions and stupidities. It was a matter of sufficient interest to call for an article in *The Times*. On 21st April 1920, A.B. Walkely pointed out that 'The amusing parlour-game' of guessing the identity of the fictional places in the novels is 'a part of the larger misconception of imaginative work' in the 'perpetual search for the "originals"'[25] of the characters. He reminded his readers of a recent correspondence in the *TLS* seeking the location of Highbury; and, more recently, enquiring for the original of Mansfield Park.[26] Yet Walkely was himself not above addressing readers of *The Times* on matters equally ridiculous. Eighteen months later, he contributed a piece entitled 'Jane's Chiffons: Flowers and Fruit. The Universal Passion', to this conclusion: 'Finally, the incomparable novelist shared the universal passion of her sex for the best silk stockings.'[27] For the effusions of Miss Thackeray and her ilk, James found the word 'twaddle'. What would have been his word for this!

XII

This same year, 1921, in *The Craft of Fiction* Percy Lubbock called for a new enquiry into Jane Austen the writer. It was time to halt the repetition of time-worn truths: 'That Jane Austen was an acute observer... we know, we have repeated, we have told each other a thousand times; it is no wonder if attention flags when we hear it all again.'[1] Instead, Lubbock urges the reader 'to study the craft, to follow the process, to read constructively'.[2] His final words set the aim: 'The author of the book was a craftsman, the critic of the book must overtake him at his work and see how the book was made.'[3] In the event, Lubbock did not examine Jane Austen in this way. A follower of James, he was familiar with the passage in which his master had declared Jane Austen 'instinctive and charming' and sent the reader elsewhere to analyse the novelist's art. However, James's pronouncement was soon to be tested in the editorial scholarship of Chapman, first advanced in a front-page article, 'The Textual Criticism of English Classics', which Chapman contributed, anonymously, to the *Times Literary Supplement* for 20th March 1919.[4] Here, Jane Austen's name stands alongside other much-edited classic authors—Shakespeare, Jonson, Donne, Boswell and Dr Johnson—and Chapman mentions having seen 'the late Dr Verrall's copy of "Jane Austen" (a modern reprint)'. Having compared Verrall's marginal suggestions with the texts of the first editions, Chapman reported that 'Some of them seemed to be unnecessary or unhappy; of those which seemed probable, almost all were found to be readings of the first edition.' This was Chapman's sighting-shot. The barrage then followed—a leading article, entitled 'Jane Austen's Methods', occupying the front and second pages of the *TLS* for 9th February 1922.[5] It gave notice that hitherto the study of Jane Austen had been haphazard and amateur. Now was the time for critical and systematic scholarship. Chapman proceeded to detail the principal misunderstandings that had dogged the discussion of her work so far. It was a shrewd tactical document. Seemingly a dispassionate and disinterested analysis, this was really a statement of intent, preparing the way for the immensely detailed and bibliographically precise editions which Chapman was soon to issue from the Clarendon Press.[6] These were to include the minor works and manuscript fragments as well as the six novels, thereby providing the means to satisfy what was described in the *TLS* as the curiosity of critics about the writer's workshop, a field 'yet open to research'.

Chapman pointed to the fallacies and illusions: that she was a 'purely natural genius, living in an illiterate circle, and owing little to books'; 'that she knew little of the world'. 'On the point of sexual irregularity she is, indeed, remarkably free from "spinsterly" prudishness.' He drew attention to the inclusions and exclusions in her portrait of society. He pointed to her knowledge of English and foreign literature. As to the corpus of her work, he emphasised the importance of establishing the chronology of composition, which he set out as fully as could be determined, with the warning that it is 'unusually obscure'. These concerns are reflected in the elaborate apparatus to the Clarendon edition. Here is 'the great memorial edition' Farrer had called for.[7] It is a remarkable enterprise, properly described as monumental (the large-paper, limited edition being especially splendid); historically important as the first such edition of any of the major English novelists. With Miss Metcalfe's *Pride and Prejudice* as the model, Chapman set out to provide the present-day reader with the experience of reading enjoyed by Jane Austen's contemporary audience (although it must be said that the large-paper *de luxe* edition looks rather over-blown alongside the modest volumes that Jane Austen would have known). Each novel carries a facsimile title-page of the first edition and the text is divided according to the three-volume structure of their original publication, with two volumes each for *Persuasion* and *Northanger Abbey*. The binding, typeface and lay-out of the pages, including catch-words at the foot, have a Regency air. This styling was regarded as a major selling point and featured strongly in the advertising. What we value, of course, is Chapman's promise of textual accuracy 'based on full collations, made, it is believed, for the first time, of all the editions published in the author's lifetime'.[8] Through the notes and appendixes Chapman also set out to provide something towards the ideal of 'complete enlightenment'.[9]

Although we may wonder at the sheer extent and elaboration of the Clarendon edition—with its procession of notes, appendixes, indexes and general indexes—Chapman made good the promise of his *TLS* piece. Here indeed is the necessary foundation for scholarship. For the first time, the student was able to work with trustworthy texts and follow the variants. As Chapman demonstrates, the collation of texts is not exclusively a task of bibliographical scholarship. Textual emendation and reconstruction call for literary intelligence. The changes made to 'the mention of a natural daughter' in the first and second editions of *Sense and Sensibility* enable us to follow the editorial reasoning behind Chapman's comment on Jane Austen's freedom from '"spinsterly" prudishness'. Never again could the novels be regarded as texts innocent of scholarly interest; and Wilbur Cross, in the *Yale Review*, made the point that 'no one has ever before brought out a critical edition of the major works of a great English novelist...Mr Chapman has clearly set the pace for all who would deal critically with our novelists.'[10]

The *TLS* welcomed the Regency pastiche in the style of the text and described the six volumes as 'the most scientific edition of Jane Austen, and it is the most beautiful'. The reviewer also reflected upon the kind of criticism appropriate to an author so established and well-loved:

She is a classic of very sound security, and her books are not only contemplated but loved. Is there anything to be done but to enjoy them? There may yet be something to be done—not overdone—in the way of a really critical study of her art, but to one's frank enjoyment there seemed nothing to be added.[11]

However, these, and the other welcoming reviews, incensed George Sampson. In the *Bookman* for January 1924 he protested that Jane Austen had become a sedulously overpraised writer. She has become a piece of literary cant, so that professed admiration for Jane Austen is as much a sign of respectability as the Conservative bills in the windows of really nice suburbs in election time.[12]

He questioned the familiar dicta from Scott, Macaulay, Goldwin Smith and A.C. Bradley, in particular, the comparison with Shakespeare:

How thin appear the little projections of Jane Austen when tried by this true standard! Where is her first-rate imagination, or her first-rate experience, or her experiencing nature?... Jane Austen is the feminine Peter Pan of letters. She never grew up. In her world there is neither marrying nor giving in marriage but just the make-believe mating of dolls.

In her characters, Sampson could see 'no sex at all'; in the novelist herself, no trace of 'a developing experience'. 'Her last story is as unreal as her first.'[13]

Chapman's editions of the manuscripts—*Lady Susan* and *Sanditon* in 1925, *Plan of a Novel* and *Two Chapters of Persuasion* in 1926 and *The Watsons* in 1927, complete with manuscript facsimiles and a detailed notation of the additions and corrections—take us as close to the heart of the creative process as we are likely to reach. They banish James's fantasy of the writer's 'light felicity', the author 'shelved and safe, for all time'. Chapman proved the frailty of such judgments. Unshelving the novelist, he exposed her to an examination less bemused. Nowhere is this change more amusingly registered than in E.M. Forster's review (No. 30). Behind the Janeite self-mockery—the archness and the cosy tone—is a real reversal of attitude, an openness to reading an *edited* Jane Austen, with all that implies in attention to the task.

The contribution of scholarship to the insights of criticism is not easily defined; and, indeed, it can be argued that critical insight has no necessary dependence—an issue neatly raised in G.K. Chesterton's Preface to *Love and Freindship*.[14] Published in June 1922, it was not informed by Chapman's *TLS* article; and Chesterton makes several excusable errors of fact—one being his supposition that the volume contains 'the earliest work of Jane Austen' (when, in fact, much of the then-unpublished *Volume the First* is earlier). Despite, then, his ignorance of the juvenilia as a whole, his disclaimer to scholarship, and the fact that this Preface is avowedly popular and addressed to readers at large, Chesterton nonetheless seizes upon the value of this material. He recognises that the discovery of the manuscript is 'more than the discovery of a document; it is the discovery of an inspiration', revealing 'the psychology of the artistic vocation', the young writer possessing 'an instinct for the intelligent criticism of life'. Chesterton sees this as 'the first of the reasons that justify a study of her juvenile works'—a call that might have come from Chapman himself! As to 'Love and Freindship' itself, Chesterton greeted it as a piece 'to laugh over again and again as one laughs over the great burlesques of Peacock or Max Beerbohm'.

Virginia Woolf, too, was an attentive reader of the minor works and reviewed *Love and Freindship* in 1922,[15] *the Watsons* in 1923;[16] and Chapman's edition of the novels, in the same year, was the occasion for the essay 'Jane Austen at Sixty'.[17] All three pieces were then conflated into her best-known 'Jane Austen' essay, which appeared in *The Common Reader* in 1925 (No. 31). The novelist is drawn as a formidable artist, exercising 'an almost stern morality' upon 'deviations from kindness, truth, and sincerity'. Like Chesterton, Virginia Woolf encouraged the reader to read reflectively and analytically. Of *The Watsons,* she comments, 'The second-rate works of a great writer are worth reading because they offer the best criticism of his masterpieces'; and from this point we move into a detailed account of Jane Austen's 'difficulties' and 'the method she took to overcome them'. This is the commentary of a writer-critic, of someone who can speak with personal experience of 'complexities in the writer' and 'the complexity of her scenes', of the new elements in *Persuasion*—'a peculiar beauty and a peculiar dullness', the 'dullness... which so often marks the transition stage between two different periods'. Putting herself in the novelist's place, Virginia Woolf is confident in connecting 'aesthetic fact' with 'biographical fact', of venturing into speculation about the future, had Jane Austen lived on, to be 'the forerunner of Henry James and of Proust'.

There is the same assurance to Forster's review of *Sanditon*[18] which pursues this very question of the novelist's further development. Although he detected 'a new cadence' in the prose and 'topography... screwed much deeper than usual into the story', he concluded that the fragment 'is reminiscent from first to last', a throw-back to the juvenilia. This was to stand as the controlling judgment for the next forty years. It is a pity, in this respect, that

Frank Swinnerton's review[19] of 'this latest Austen treasure' was not more widely known. Swinnerton thought highly of the fragment. He saw Jane Austen's development continued yet further and found 'matter... of great and mature excellence': 'an additional pungency to the satire' together with 'a delicacy and sureness unsurpassed in any other of her works'. Against Forster, Swinnerton declared himself a 'Sanditonian'. He was not alone in this. In the *Yale Review*, Wilbur Cross observed 'Everywhere throughout the fragment there is promise of consummate art.'[20]

XIII

With these editions of the novels and the minor works and the mass of attendant reviews, Jane Austen's name was as much in the air as that of a popular living author, and, as ever, spoken of with familiarity and affection. Wilbur Cross continued to minister to the flame in the pages of the *Yale Review*. In 1922, he was delighted to find the novelist 'none the less "divine"' in *Love and Freindship*.[1] Three years later, reviewing *Sanditon*, he was again able to celebrate 'the cult of "the divine Jane"'.[2] Meanwhile, Kipling's short story 'The Janeites', 1924, added a patriotic dimension to the cult. Artillerymen at the front escape from the Inferno of war in recalling the novels, 'Jane' being the *non pareil* for 'a tight place'. Kipling's mild joke is to allot the single critical observation to a drunken mess-waiter, who remarks that Jane Austen did not die 'barren': 'she *did* leave lawful issue in the shape of a son; and his name was 'Enery James.' When it was taken into the next Kipling collection, *Debits and Credits*, 1926, the story was followed by 'Jane's Marriage', a poem telling of her reunion in Paradise with Captain Wentworth and ending with a rousing poetic toast 'unto England's Jane!'. Agnes Repplier called the poem 'vivacious' (No.17i). But from Mary Webb, there came a wicked riposte, 'Our Immortal Jane'. Deceptively Janeite, the piece soon discloses a cutting edge:

It must be, to most of us, a keen regret that we can never meet Jane Austen, except in a problematical heaven. And what would the angels think of that trenchant wit, that ladylike Falstaffianism? For she had a kind of elfin ribaldry. Would she sit at the Celestial Banquet as she did at the Hampshire tea-parties, with a perfectly solemn face and an infinitely amused mind? There... would she inaugurate with some officiating angel the kind of cat-and-mouse game which she played with Mr Collins, following his foibles with unescapable keenness and gentle ridicule through the aeons of eternity?

While this celestial evocation is a delicately malicious send-up of Kipling, Mary Webb was sensitive to the life of the characters—'the subtle completeness of Jane Austen's people... Mr Collins is with us like a familiar friend... she really possessed her chosen souls, who flowered for her, petal by petal, in their shrewdness or inanity'; Mr Bennet, 'at once quiet and deadly'. In the novels she found 'solidarity', in the novelist 'stamina'. 'Independent, robust, she expresses feminine intuitions with masculine brevity. Her girls are real for all their primness.'[3]

How fresh is Mary Webb's reading alongside a standard 'woman's' account: *Women Writers of the Nineteenth Century*, 1923, by Marjory Bald. The Preface announces the focus of the study to be upon 'the complete humanity of each woman', yet the text itself displays the vocabulary and vision of the twaddle school: 'this dainty flawless art... It possesses an inexhaustible magic.'[4] The novelist is rendered in terms equally unreal: 'Without obtrusive effort or exertion of visible influence she gave to her world what it most required—an example of reserved and ordered serenity.'[5] The gallic version of this pacific Jane Austen is discovered in Legouis and Cazamian's textbook *History of English Literature* (the English translation published in 1927):

All Jane Austen's work is transfused with the spirit of classicism in its highest form, in its most essential quality: a safe, orderly harmony among the powers of the mind, a harmony where of necessity the intellect is paramount. So classical, so delicately shaded is that method, that we are strongly reminded of the art of the great French analysts.[6]

But this was not the 'spirit' observed by Herbert Read, who found it 'hard to concede the full meaning of classicism to Jane Austen's universe of undertones' (No. 33).

Hardly surprising, then, that Arnold Bennett, writing in his *Evening Standard* column in July 1927, should regard Jane Austen as 'dangerous ground' (No. 34) and that three years earlier Virginia Woolf should have warned her *Athenaeum* readers of those 'twenty five elderly gentlemen living in the neighbourhood of London who resent any slight upon her genius as if it were an insult offered to the chastity of their Aunts'.[7] However, it was not the season for slights and there was little need for these elderly gentlemen to rouse themselves. The establishment line, as we follow it in the Transactions of the Royal Society of Literature, continued to be avidly Janeite. At a meeting of the RSL on 23rd February 1927, the Shakespearian scholar Dr Caroline Spurgeon read a fulsome eulogy, endorsing the association of Jane Austen's name with that of Shakespeare and emphasising why 'she is so characteristically English'. Dr Spurgeon also placed Jane Austen in a new category: 'more than a classic; she is also one of a little company—few, but very fit—whose work is of the nature of a miracle.'[8] When, later that year, the address was published in the annual volume of Transactions, the volume editor, Margaret Woods—who admitted in her Preface to being of 'the Tribe of Jane'—expressed her confidence that 'All good Janeites will welcome Dr Caroline Spurgeon's appreciation' and she went on to rejoice at 'the multitude and ardour of her adorers!'[9]

But the membership of the RSL was not Janeite to a man. One exception was H. W. Garrod, Professor of Poetry at Oxford, who answered Dr Spurgeon with a 'Depreciation' read to the Society in May 1928.[10] Opening on a note of mild buffoonery, Garrod presents himself as the Professor unprepared, who comes 'in lightness of heart', not having read the novels for years and relying, for this occasion, upon 'a faulty memory'. There is no pretence at a sustained argument. He is the professor unbuttoned, sans cap and gown, confessing to unreasoning dislike, expressing his 'shameful irritations'. And the lecture parades his 'why I do not like her' in a manner disarmingly frank and facetious—as it may have been, on the night—with its succession of slangs and sallies. Garrod is a spokesman for the view that Jane Austen's concern is with 'Manners' and not 'the human heart', that finds in the novels a 'parochialism' 'worse than worldliness', a detachment complacent and founded on ignorance. Yet the antipathy rings true. Garrod was affronted that 'a slip of a girl' (as he calls Jane Austen at the end of his lecture) should be so venerated—a reaction that compares so badly with Elton's,[11] who admitted his dislike, was unsettled by her women's vision, yet admired her for being 'feminine in a profound degree'.

Clearly, Garrod was in the grip of powerful feelings. Lionel Trilling has suggested a 'sexual protest';[12] John Bayley that 'in re-reading her' Garrod 'discovered something about his own outlook on life that made it urgently necessary to depreciate hers'.[13]

Undoubtedly, the tone that comes through is a grudging, indignant anger at Jane Austen's fame and popularity. Another personal motive can be seen in Garrod's jealous stewardship of English Literature. As an Oxford Professor, he saw himself as an appointed guardian; and doubtless he felt under a special obligation to perform this duty within the portals of Literature's own Royal Society, whose pass had been so lately sold. This, too, was the hour. For in the world outside, Garrod observed 'a somewhat notable boom in Miss Austen', which his 'Depreciation' was calculated to deflate.

Appropriately, the 'Reply' came from the moving force behind this recent 'boom', none other than Chapman himself.[14] Appropriately, too, it was delivered at a meeting of the RSL, in November 1929. However, it fell far short of being the grand rebuttal. Chapman, following Garrod's lead, played the same game, purporting to have bestirred himself as little as his opponent. His 'Reply', he says, was 'almost entirely written on a railway journey and from memory'. So it reads. Like Garrod, Chapman offers no sustained argument, merely countering his opponent, point-by-point, his manner airy and disdainful. The only developed passage is his confession to being one of the 'lovers of Jane Austen'. He explains that his feeling for Mr Woodhouse and Miss Bates, like his feeling for Emma Woodhouse, 'is one of personal affection at least as much as it is one of critical appreciation of supremely skilful miniature-painting.' In this vein, he opposes Garrod: 'He has made Jane Austen odious; it is sufficient confutation to reply that she is loved as not many authors have been loved.'

Chapman described Garrod's attack as a 'lampoon'. The academician's lampoon stung Chapman to an academician's riposte. Whatever feelings had been stirred, their exchange of views is donnish, a literary bout between Oxford opponents. As to critical insight, we could be back in the 1880s and certainly far from the level of thought which Middleton Murry (No. 29) brings to the method of Jane Austen's comedy of manners or Herbert Read to the analysis of her prose (No. 35). Although Read finds her narrative style that of an essayist rather than a novelist, and hence inadequate to handle dramatic action, the seriousness of his attention is not in doubt. When Herbert Read wanted to characterise the novelist's limitations (No. 33), in countering what he described in 1926 as 'the present sophisticated rage for Jane

Austen', he quoted from the correspondence of Charlotte Brontë; and it is in her letters to G.H. Lewes and her publisher's reader, W.S. Williams, in 1848 and 1850 (*No. 28*), that we find a 'Depreciation' that shows up the slightness of Garrod's attack. Or there are the few lines in which D.H. Lawrence delivers a sharp historical definition of 'the mean Jane Austen', a novelist of 'personality' rather than 'character':

This, again, is the tragedy of social life today. In the old England, the curious blood-connection held the classes together. The squires might be arrogant, violent, bullying and unjust, yet in some ways they were *at one* with the people, part of the same blood-stream. We feel it in Defoe or Fielding. And then, in the mean Jane Austen, it is gone. Already this old maid typifies 'personality' instead of character, the sharp knowing in apartness instead of knowing in togetherness, and she is, to my feeling, thoroughly unpleasant, English in the bad, mean, snobbish sense of the word, just as Fielding is English in the good generous sense.[15]

Whatever one's view of these remarks, there is no question about Lawrence's engagement with the issue; and the challenge of these few lines has meant more to later criticism than the whole of Garrod's lecture. And distaste did not blind Lawrence to Jane Austen's power as a novelist. In the Introduction to *The Mother*, 1928, by Grazia Deledda, he wrote: 'We can hardly bear to recall the emotions of twenty or fifteen years ago, hardly at all, whereas we respond again quite vividly to the emotions of Jane Austen or Dickens, nearer a hundred years ago.'[16]

XIV

The substance of Garrod's 'somewhat notable boom' and Read's 'present sophisticated rage' was apparent. Alongside the scholarly editions of the novels and the minor works, academic studies began to appear: in 1924, in a single volume, a translation of part of *Jane Austen: sa vie et son oeuvre* by Leonie Villard, accompanied by *A New Study of Jane Austen (interpreted through 'Love and Freindship')* by R. Brimley Johnson; in 1927, *Jane Austen* by R. Brimley Johnson; in 1930, *Jane Austen: Her Life, Her Works, Her Family, and Her Critics* by R. Brimley Johnson. In 1929 came the first substantial *Bibliography*, by Geoffrey Keynes; and in the same year Mary Lascelles' introduction to a World's Classics edition of *Mansfield Park* set new standards of criticism and scholarship. The days of the slipshod amateur essay were numbered.

In the learned journals, there was an increasing flow of articles and notes. Scholarly interest had never been so high. Chapman's editorial work had prompted many lines of enquiry, such as Michael Sadleir's investigation of the Gothic novels mentioned in *Northanger Abbey*. The Professor of Philosophy at Manchester, S. Alexander, used his lecture on 'The Art of Jane Austen'[1] as an opportunity 'to record a lifelong devotion'. Yet mingled with this note of affection was a close adherence to Bradley's historical division of the novels into the early and the late. Lubbock, too, was another guide, and Clara Linklater Thomson's *Jane Austen: A Survey*, 1929, was a brave early attempt to answer his call for an examination of 'the craft of fiction'. Miss Thomson's book was later overshadowed by Miss Lascelles' *Jane Austen and Her Art* which appeared in 1939. Earlier, in *Some Great English Novels: Studies in the art of fiction*, 1926, Orlo Williams had argued that the kind of 'analysis' which Lubbock conducted on other authors 'may very profitably be applied to Miss Austen's novels, and none more so than to *Emma*';[2] and he went on to consider 'the whole architecture of the story'. Adjusting the metaphor, he writes of its 'seven well-balanced movements',[3] its 'alterations of key and measure, of poignant solos and triumphant tutti'.[4] The comparisons are with Purcell and Mozart; in *Emma* he finds 'such bright and graceful music, so pure in form, so delicate in texture'.[5]

At this time, however, the critical debate was not around the 'art' of the novel but upon character, a debate set in motion in March 1923 by Arnold Bennett's declaration that 'The foundation of good fiction is character creating and nothing else.'[6] With this challenge he attacked *Jacob's Room* (1922). Clever, 'packed and bursting with originality', 'exquisitely written'. All this he allowed. Nonetheless, he commented, 'the characters do not vitally survive in the mind'. Virginia Woolf replied with 'Mr. Bennett and Mr. Brown'. The debate widened, involving writers on both sides of the Atlantic, and moved on from 'character' in the novel to the issue of 'life' itself, a matter on which Virginia Woolf and Forster crossed swords.

Accordingly, the issue now becomes Jane Austen's mastery of the novel of character, with renewed attempts to fasten upon the Shakespearian quality of the characters and their capacity to enjoy a continuing existence in the reader's imagination, free of the page. The grand exercise in this vein is J.B. Priestley's account of Mr

Collins in *The English Comic Characters*, 1925 (and, on a smaller scale, in *English Humour*, 1929), extending a tradition that goes back to Macaulay (No. 26). The heart of Priestley's case resides in a single paragraph.

Although we feel that we know what he will do and say next, yet he always goes beyond our expectations just as absurd people in real life do; we know the kind of thing he will say, yet could not say it for him (as we could with a lesser comic character), for his absurdity is always a little in advance of what we can possibly imagine. Thus he is, as Mr Saintsbury once remarked somewhere, a creature 'of the highest and most Shakespearian comedy'. And being a person of such great lineage, he does not exist simply for the sake of the story (though he plays his part in it), does not fall into his place in the group, but exists in his own right and compels his creator to indulge him all over the place, just as Falstaff blackmailed Shakespeare for scene after scene.

The reference to Saintsbury is no more than just, for his Preface to *Pride and Prejudice* (No. 18) seems to provide the meat of Priestley's essay.

The life of the characters was also to occupy Forster. In the spring of 1926, he was invited to give the Clark Lectures at Trinity College, Cambridge. This he did, early in 1927, and the lectures were published the same year as *Aspects of the Novel*. An insight upon his preparation for these lectures is found in Forster's Commonplace Book. Setting down his ideas for the lecture on 'Round versus Flat characters', Forster noted:

Jane Austen—infelicitously described as a miniaturist on ivory. Carves cherry stones if you like. But even Miss Bates has a mind, even Elizabeth Eliot a heart. Discovery that Lady Bertram has a moral outlook shocked me at first. I had not realized the solidity of an art which kept such an aspect in reserve, and placed her always on the sofa with pug.[7]

In the lectures as published, Forster took Jane Austen as the prime example in his distinction between 'flat' and 'round' characters: all hers, he says, 'are ready for an extended life, for a life which the scheme of her books seldom requires them to lead'. He stresses the consciousness of her art: that the characters are 'highly organized' and related to one another and to their setting in a 'closely woven fabric'. A similar observation had been made some years earlier by Frank Swinnerton in discussing the 'close mesh of human sensitiveness' that composes the 'intricate relationships' of *Emma*.[8]

In *The Structure of the Novel*, 1928, Edwin Muir opposes Forster on several fronts.[9] Yet he too sees Jane Austen as a supreme artist, in this case not of the novel of character but of 'the dramatic novel', in which 'character is action, and action character' (telescoping James's definition in 'The Art of Fiction': 'What is character but the determination of incident? What is incident but the illustration of character?').

The most illuminating analysis was provided by Edith Wharton. In *The Writing of Fiction*, 1925 (No. 32), it was to *Emma* she turned for 'the most perfect example in English fiction in which character shapes events quietly but irresistibly'; and she noted the way in which the characters 'evolve... softly, noiselessly' ('evolve' was the word used by Scott, referring to the play of Jane Austen's dialogue 'in which the characters of the speakers evolve themselves with dramatic effect' (*No. 8*). Scott's observation may have prompted Walter Pater's attention to 'that kind of quiet evolution of character through circumstance, introduced into English literature by Miss Austen'[10]).

Edith Wharton returned to Jane Austen again in two important essays in the *Yale Review*. The first of these, 'The Great American Novel' (July 1927), makes a caustic attack upon Sinclair Lewis's *Main Street* and the 'main street' school of criticism, a narrow, nationalistic body of opinion, a hundred years old, which insisted that the Great American Novel 'must always be about Main Street, geographically, socially and intellectually'. Her reply to this updated version of the old nationalist argument involved the question of Jane Austen's provincialism:

If it be argued that the greatest novelists, both French and English, have drawn some of their richest effects from the study of narrow lives and parochial problems, the answer is that Balzac's provincial France, Jane Austen's provincial England, if limited in their external contacts compared to a Main Street linked to the universe by telephone, motor, and wireless, nevertheless made up for what they lacked in surface by the depth of the soil in which they grew.[11]

Edith Wharton may have come across Virginia Woolf's treatment of this question in the *Yale Review* for October 1926, in the essay 'How Should One Read a Book', comparing the world of *Robinson Crusoe* with the polite society of Jane Austen:

But if the open air and adventure mean everything to Defoe they mean nothing to Jane Austen. Here is the drawing-room, and people talking, and by the many mirrors of their talk revealing their characters.[12]

Not all American critics who acknowledged 'the depth of the soil' were so wholehearted in their praise. Conrad Aiken, although devotedly anglophile in his cultural affinities, fastened upon the 'old-fashionedness' of Virginia Woolf and Jane Austen in tones distinctly equivocal. Beneath the surface of admiration, suave and diplomatic, sounds an undernote of reservation, within which lurks a fleck of irony reminding us of very different attitudes, from Emerson onwards, towards the gentility—as it was perceived—of Jane Austen's fictional world:

The aroma of 'old-fashionedness' that rises from these highly original and modern novels—from the pages of *Jacob's Room, Mrs Dalloway*, and now again from those of *To the Lighthouse*—is a quality of attitude; a quality, to use a word which is itself nowadays old-fashioned, but none the less fragrant, of spirit. For in this regard, Mrs Woolf is no more modern than Jane Austen: she breathes the same air of gentility, of sequestration, of tradition; of life and people and things all brought, by the slow polish of centuries of tradition and use, to a pervasive refinement in which discrimination, on every conceivable plane, has become as instinctive and easy as the beat of the wing. Her people are 'gentle' people; her houses are the houses of gentlefolk; and the consciousness that informs both is a consciousness of well-being and culture, of the richness and lustre and dignity of tradition; a disciplined consciousness, in which emotions and feelings find their appropriate attitudes as easily and naturally—as *habitually*, one is tempted to say—as a skilled writer finds words.[13]

Virginia Woolf's own account of English society touched on aspects less reverential and antique. She found complexity and richness, not constraint, as she wrote in 1928:

The novelist, and the English novelist in particular, knows and delights, it seems, to know that Society is a nest of glass boxes one separate from another, each housing a group with special habits and qualities of its own...[Jane Austen] restricts herself to her own special class and finds infinite shades within it.[14]

Edith Wharton spoke for the idea of a special English or European culture. 'Jane Austen's provincial England' along with the 'provincial France' of Balzac were worlds apart from her own country:

the dense old European order, all compounded of differences and *nuances*, all interwoven with intensities and reticences, with passions and privacies, inconceivable to the millions [E. W.'s fellow-countrymen] brought up in a safe, shallow and shadowless world.[15]

Edith Wharton's second *Yale Review* essay, 'Visibility in Fiction', appeared in March 1929. The 'visibility' in question is 'the aliveness of the characters', 'the novel's one assurance of prolonged survival'.[16] The great novelists are Balzac, Jane Austen, Thackeray and Tolstoy, the creators of characters who 'have broken away from the printed page and its symbols, they mix with us freely, naturally; and so do a host of minor figures who have mostly escaped out of the same tales'.[17] This 'gift of giving visibility' she calls 'the rarest in the novelist's endowment',[18] and examines as a matter of artistry, testing the idea 'that visibility is achieved simply by the author's own intense power of seeing his characters in their habit as they lived'—only to reject it:

Who ever actually *saw* a Dostoevsky or a Turgenev character with the eyes of the flesh? And as for Jane Austen's, one almost wonders if she ever saw them bodily herself, so little do their physical peculiarities seem to concern her.

Yet 'We certainly do not think of Jane Austen's characters as disembodied intelligences, though she has favored us with such scant glimpses of their physical appearance.' Even 'the least' of her 'creations' is 'tangible, substantial, solidly planted on the earth that we ourselves tread'.[19] Theirs is a sustained visibility, not just evoked 'for a moment'.[20] In the concluding paragraphs, Edith Wharton makes no attempt to force a solution, to resolve the 'trick'. Instead, the reader is led back to her favoured conjecture (reminiscent of Mrs Ward (No. 9)) of artistic intensity and concentration; and she places Jane Austen, without strain, in an European perspective:

Balzac, Jane Austen, Thackeray, Tolstoy: almost invariably, when these touched the dead bones they arose and walked. Not only stood, struck lifelike attitudes, did the Madame Tussaud business with an uncanny air of reality, but actually progressed or retrograded, marked time or spurted forward, in our erratic human way; and came out at the end of their tales disfigured, altered, yet still the same, as we do when life has thoroughly dealt with us. These four novelists alone—with Proust perhaps as an only fifth—could give this intense and unfailing visibility to their central characters as well as to the episodical figures of the periphery; and it is plain that, though their results are identical, and Mr Woodhouse is as warm to the touch as Henry Esmond, the procedure in each case was profoundly different. To say this is perhaps to acknowledge that the problem is insoluble, the 'trick' not to be detected; yet we may still conjecture that a common denominator is, after all, to be found in the patient intensity of attention which these great novelists concentrated on each of their imagined characters, in their intimate sense of the reality of what they described, and in some secret intuition that the barrier between themselves and their creatures was somehow thinner than the page of a book.[21]

Just as Edith Wharton was annoyed by 'main street' criticism, so Virginia Woolf was resistant to the 'woman's world' thesis: the proposition that as women have led restricted lives, so their experience and art is similarly restricted. This was an argument aired in the nineteenth century whenever the discussion touched upon the woman novelist's *métier* and the areas she was qualified to treat. The debate was alive again in the 1920s and a dogmatic voice was that of Elizabeth Drew in *The Modern Novel*, 1926. She had no time for the equality argument. For her, the gender difference was as absolute artistically as it was genetically:

but when all is said, and in spite of the feminists with the queen bee in their bonnets, the fact remains that the creative genius of woman remains narrower than that of man, even in the novel. Just as, though Jane Austen is supreme in her own line, she is not as great as Fielding...In spite of equal education and equal opportunity, the *scope* of women remains still smaller than the scope of men...the eternal platitude seems the eternal truism that, just as it is still in her close personal relationships that woman most naturally uses her human genius and her artistry in life, so it is still in the portrayal of those relationships that she perfects her most characteristic genius in writing.[22]

This is the background of debate to Virginia Woolf's account of what it means to be a woman writer, in *A Room of One's Own*, 1929,[23] and 'Phases of Fiction' of the same year. It is in 'Phases of Fiction' that the Shakespeare: Jane Austen likeness is suggestively aired, both writing 'without hate, without bitterness, without protest, without preaching'; both unknowable in their writing yet pervading every word they wrote.[24] There is an instructive contrast between Virginia Woolf's tone and the fanciful sentence with which J.B. Priestley closes his section on Jane Austen in *English Humour* (1929): 'Her real triumph is the happy perfection of her art, upon which humour plays like the sunlight upon some flawless antique marble.'[25] Virginia Woolf had no time for such exquisiteness. For her, the novels were proof of the triumph of art over circumstance and spoke movingly of what it cost to be a woman writer. Yet this special, personal meaning is not derived at the cost of sentiment or partiality. The greatness of Jane Austen, as she describes it, analytically, in 'Phases of Fiction', 1929, is a matter of the novelist's technique—of 'form', or 'architectural quality', of 'the use of dialogue', of arrangement and relationship. And as far as Virginia Woolf brings Jane Austen herself into the discussion, as a personal presence within the novels, it is to speak of her 'absence', her 'aloofness', of writing 'unstained by personality'. Thus Jane Austen is clear of the hazard that faces all writers and for women writers is an especial trap, a habitual proclivity, as she defined the problem in 'Women and Fiction', an essay published in 1929:

The desire to plead some personal cause or to make a character the mouthpiece of some personal discontent or grievance. The genius of Jane Austen and Emily Brontë is never more convincing than in their power to ignore such claims and solicitations...[26]

The Jane Austen of 'Phases of Fiction' is the cool, uncosy novelist, the master of a classic style, working on the knife-edge of language, a feat finely described in a lesser-known passage (1925)[27] where Virginia Woolf relates the structuring of *Emma*—its turning-point a single sentence of 'modest, everyday prose'—to the *Electra* of Sophocles:[28]

His Electra stands before us like a figure so tightly bound that she can only move an inch this way, an inch that. But each movement must tell to the utmost, or, bound as she is, denied the relief of all hints, repetitions, suggestions, she will be nothing but a dummy, tightly bound. Her words in crisis are, as a matter of fact, bare; mere cries of despair, joy, hate

> Alas! unhappy me! I have died this day.
> Strike, if you can, a double blow.*

But these cries give angle and outline to the play. It is thus, with a thousand differences of degree, that in English literature Jane Austen shapes a novel. There comes a moment—'I will dance with you,' says Emma—which rises higher than the rest, which, though not eloquent in itself, or violent or made striking by beauty of language, has the whole weight of the book behind it. In Jane Austen, too, we have the same sense, though the ligatures are much less tight, that her figures are bound, and restricted to a few definite movements. She, too, in her modest everyday prose, chose the dangerous art where one slip means death.

(*Virginia Woolf quotes the original Greek, here translated, of lines 674, 1415).

After this sensitive, highly personal commentary, we are brought down to earth with Arnold Bennett's treatment of Jane Austen in 'The Progress of the Novel', an essay which opens the first issue of *The Realist* in 1929. Summarily, Bennett lumps her in with those novelists—an undistinguished majority—who choose to ignore the world beyond their 'imaginary wall'.

The pretence upon which she worked involved a more or less complete blindness to all sorts of phenomena within the tiny expanse itself...she only saw what it suited her to see; and her job was thereby drastically simplified.[29]

This, anyway, was Bennett's public dismissal. In private, he was less damning and more interesting. On re-reading *Mansfield Park* a year earlier, he wrote in his Journal: 'a fine novel. One or two pages of Zola's or rather Huysman's realism in it.'[30]

The championing of Jane Austen—specifically as a woman writer—was also being conducted by Rebecca West (No. 36). Ridiculing the 'comic patronage' of Jane Austen as a limited, decorous and unpassionate novelist, she finds heroines 'haggard with desire or triumphant with love' and points to the analytical mind of a writer who shared the intellectual world of Hume and Gibbon. How far from Lawrence's 'unpleasant' 'old maid' of 1930, who, in turn, is remote from the novelist evoked by T.F. Powys. In *Unclay*, 1931, Jane Austen stands as a wellspring of feeling. When Mr Hayhoe reads *The Watsons*, he thinks of death and of those who went 'too early. There was his favourite—Jane. 'Twas enough to make any man sigh to think of her. Oh! why had she not been permitted to write a few more books! What good titles she could have found, what charming characters!'[31] And by reading *Pride and Prejudice* to her, Hayhoe plans to reform Daisy Huddy.

In this same year, 1931, another kind of simplicity was on show in *Introductions to Jane Austen* by John Bailey, collecting his volume introductions to the Georgian Edition of 1927, now revised and extended. Bailey—an Oxford don, here published by his own University Press—maintained a determinedly old-fashioned Janeite pose, scorning the labours of scholarship. In the Preface, he declared:

my object has not been to make discoveries—I doubt if there are any to make—still less to use Jane as an excuse for the display of things so unlike her as learning and research about sources and parallels; but simply to share with others my enjoyment of the most enjoyable of authors.[32]

His Jane is a natural genius. She wrote 'well because she could write well and liked it, and all the better because she did not know how well she wrote'.[33] The woman and the artist are one: 'in her tiny field it is the truth and not an exaggeration to say that she and her art are perfect.'[34] Given the vagaries of the Jane Austen literature, it is no surprise to hear a voice so defiantly anti-critical. Despite his disclaimer, Bailey did exaggerate. The point was made politely by Percy Lubbock in his review of Bailey's *Introductions*.[35] He concluded that the time had come to end the repetition of the old and obvious truths, to move beyond controversy (did he have the Garrod-Chapman exchange in mind?): 'there is nobody who demands a calmer and clearer atmosphere for the display of the subtle movements of her art.'

Lubbock was asking for the kind of aesthetic criticism which was to appear a few years later in *Jane Austen and her Art*. Immediately, however, the most important initiative took a different direction. In the Preface to an edition of *Northanger Abbey* in 1932 (No. 38), Rebecca West presented Jane Austen as a writer of 'quite conscious' 'feminism'. *Northanger Abbey* itself is viewed as a critique of 'the institutions of society regarding women', 'the fruit of strong feeling and audacious thought'. The novelist and the novel are seen in a light entirely new: the novelist as a critic of society, the novel as 'disconcerting'. But all this went unnoticed. Anyone seeking an authoritative statement on *Northanger Abbey* would be referred to Michael Sadleir's Introduction to the Oxford University Press's World Classics edition of 1930—largely an account of the Gothic romances mentioned in the novel—derived from his paper to the English Association in February 1927, published as a pamphet later that year. The accepted emphasis, then, was *literary* historical and there was no context in which Rebecca West's *historical* account (in the Preface to the humble Traveller's Library edition) could find a place.

A similar fate awaited Ida O'Malley's study of women and society, *Women in Subjection: a study of the lives of Englishwomen before 1832*, 1933. Chapter 8, entitled 'Jane Austen and the Middle-Class women of her day', stresses her significance to 'the women's movement' and brings out Jane Austen's importance as an historian of the woman's predicament, of those 'quite ordinary ladies who accepted their pleasant airy cages as a natural home'. It also examines her importance in overturning the 'legend that women are not intellectually creative'. But like Rebecca West, Miss O'Malley went unheard and this line of historical interpretation found no takers. At a popular level, Janeitism still held sway. Even such a serious study as C.L. Thomson's *Jane Austen* could awaken the drivel of journalism: 'Jane Austen's true lovers can never talk nor read too much about her. She has that quality of inexhaustibleness which belongs only to the very great.'[36] So ran the comment of the *Spectator* in February 1930, showing that the 'quality of inexhaustibleness' was not confined to the novelist alone but was shared, down the years, by all too many of her admiring reviewers.

XV

The publication in 1932 of the complete *Letters*, edited by Chapman, was an event with critical as well as biographical implications. Most of the letters were known from the *Life and Letters*, which quoted them extensively. Although Garrod had dismissed the letters as a 'desert of trivialities punctuated by occasional clever malice',[1] many readers looked to them for a glimpse of the writer's private self and they were not disappointed. However, the self-revelation could be upsetting: the letter-writer displayed herself as a far from 'gentle Jane'. In the *TLS*,[2] Forster announced that the letters were marked by 'Triviality, varied by touches of ill-breeding and sententiousness', by a 'lack of feeling', the eyes of their writer 'observant and hard'. Nonetheless, he found a way to preserve Jane Austen's image undented, separating 'Miss Austen' the writer of the letters from 'Jane Austen' the author of the novels. Accordingly, the precious bonds of Miss Austen's family (those 'accidents of birth and relationship') provide the 'groundwork' of Jane Austen's six novels. Harold Nicolson likewise found the letters 'trivial and dull', a 'desert of family gossip'. But unlike Forster he saw the letter-writer and the novelist as one, the letters suggesting a woman with

a mind like a very small, sharp pair of scissors, attached by a pink ribbon to a very neat and maidenly work-basket. Such an impression can only have a damaging effect upon our appreciation of the novels. The letters are so like the worst in Jane Austen...She emerges diminished from this correspondence.[3]

Source-hunters lighted upon the letters in pursuit of originals for the characters and places, a pastime authoritatively endorsed. The *Virginia Quarterly Review* remarked that the letters 'contain the raw materials that went to the creation of Miss Bates, Henry Crawford, Anne Elliot, and all the rest.'[4] In private, Virginia Woolf read the letters diagnostically, suspecting that the suppression of her sexual self played a part in limiting Jane Austen's achievement:

What I shall proceed to find out, from her letters, when I've time, is why she failed to be much better than she was. Something to do with sex, I expect; the letters are full of hints already that she suppressed half of her in her novels—Now why? But I've only read 30 pages.[5]

A few days later she reported 'The letters are to me fascinating— for what they don't say largely.'[6] Unluckily, Virginia Woolf never expanded on these ideas, although she told Chapman in 1936 that she had 'often thought of writing an article on the coarseness of J.A. The people who talk of her as if she were a niminy priminy spinster always annoy me.'[7]

Yet the letters did nothing to diminish Jane Austen in the eyes of her devotees. A contributor to the *Saturday Review of Literature* reported himself still 'terribly in love with Jane Austen'[8] and the *Virginia Quarterly Review* advised that 'the Janeite is grateful'.[9] Unlike Forster, they found nothing wrong with the rectory 'drainage'. The whiff in the air was incense—'the incense which patient contact alone can communicate', according to David Rhydderch, who provided, in 1932, a Janeite account of the Jane Austen industry. In 1932 there also appeared a 'depreciation'—the chapter entitled 'Jane Austen's Unheavenly World' (quoting the final sentence of Alice Meynell's fierce attack, No. 19)—in *The Facts of Fiction* by Norman Collins. The chapter opens:

It would seem impossible to overpraise the singular genius of Jane Austen. But with alarming accumulation of hyperbole it has been done. Though well intentioned, it probably began unintentionally.

Collins locates the source of this overvaluation in the 'silliness' of Macaulay's association of Jane Austen with Shakespeare. Against Macaulay he quotes at length Charlotte Brontë's letter to Williams

(*No. 28(c)*) ('Anything like warmth... (*not senseless*) woman'); and continues with his own analysis of the novelist's faults and limitations. That her domain is 'the miniature'. That she displays not 'perfection' but 'competence'. That her prose (quoting Alice Meynell again) is 'a mouthful of thick words'. Collins admits some qualities. As remarkable as 'the limitations' of her 'vision' is its 'brightness of definition'. 'She is perfectly feminine in her range of experience; and in her competence of reporting feminine experience, perfectly masculine' (an idea from Edith Wharton). However, the phrase-making loses its sparkle in a smart and silly conclusion: 'Knowing the sad, quiet life of Jane Austen, we can almost forgive the excessive praise that she has received; it is a post-dated cheque that has been duly honoured.' The joke, for what is, is mild enough—and as trivial as Alexander Woolcott's twaddly welcome for *Volume the First* in 1933:

England's Jane, the frail, diffident little spinster who saw little in this world beyond the hedgerows of her own countryside and died when she was forty-two, but left behind her pages profound in their penetration, agleam with a delightful mockery, fashioned with an incomparable art.[10]

Sharper notes are sounded in the Bloomsburyite battles, with Virginia Woolf pitched against Jane Austen and found wanting. Wyndham-Lewis remarked in 1934 that 'Miss Woolf is charming, scholarly, intelligent, everything that you will: but here we *have* not a Jane Austen.'[11] The following year this line of attack was continued by Frank Swinnerton in *The Georgian Literary Scene*:

Virginia Woolf is essentially an impressionist, a catcher at memory of her own mental vagaries, and not a creator... she is too sensitive, highly intelligent, and playful in mind, to have the emotional depth of an imaginative person... Jane Austen was wiser and less anxiously exploratory; but Jane Austen had more creative imagination than cultivated brains. How odd that Virginia Woolf cannot see this.[12]

The most celebrated critical event of the 1930s was the Leslie Stephen Lecture[13] delivered at Cambridge in 1936 by Lord David Cecil. It is an event which invites two comparisons: one, going back fifty years, to Stephen's Jane Austen entry in the *DNB*, 1885; the other returning twenty-five years, to Bradley's lecture to the English Association. What all three have in common is a sense of occasion—that the moment had arrived for a summation of Jane Austen's achievement. Necessarily, Stephen's *DNB* entry is highly compressed. The points are laid out in judicial style, sentence-by-sentence:

No writer ever understood better the precise limits of her powers...All critics agree to the unequalled fineness of her literary tact...The unconscious charm of the domestic atmosphere of the stories, and the delicate subsatirical humour which pervades them, have won her the admiration, even the fanaticism, of innumerable readers.[14]

In the Leslie Stephen Lecture, Cecil effects a placing of the novelist similarly judicial. Although his appeal is to the common-sense and common experience of his listeners, the manner is no less categorical, and the Cheney-test is rephrased for the 1930s:

...yearly the applause of posterity has grown louder. There are those who do not like her; as there are those who do not like sunshine or unselfishness. But the very nervous defiance with which they shout their dissatisfaction shows that they know they are a despised minority. All discriminating critics admire her books, most educated readers enjoy them; her fame, of all English novelists, is the most secure.

Bradley brought scholarship to Jane Austen, reminded his listeners of the chronology of composition, of the manuscript materials and the evidence of the letters. His lecture—for all its Janeite touches, its personal flavour and confessed devotion—is notably systematic. Cecil was equally conscious of the need for a corrective to Janeite enthusings. Perhaps, too, he had in mind Virginia Woolf's complaint (made in reviewing Forster's *Aspects of the Novel*) that 'fiction has had no rules drawn up on her behalf, very little thinking done on her behalf.'[15] His admiration is declared analytically and the analytical process underlined ('we turn to analyse our admiration'). 'Laws' are invoked ('the laws that govern the art' of 'the novel') and in pointing to a unique technical accomplishment he stands in the neo-Jamesian Lubbock tradition. Scrupulous in defining her limits, his further aim was to establish Jane Austen's claim to be 'one of the supreme novelists of the world'—for the 'universal significance' conveyed in the characters and in the author's view of life, in which a universal standard of values is to be found. Around this scheme, Cecil constructs an account which touches upon the author's mind, the life of the novels and the life of their age. His purpose in this somewhat four-square approach was to rescue Jane Austen criticism from mere impressionism and the worst excesses of subjective interpretation. For some readers this worked. Reviewing the lecture, Elizabeth Bowen praised its 'detachment' and avoidance of 'a possessive whimsicality' which so often 'tinged' appreciations of Jane Austen. She also observed that Jane Austen 'is a difficult subject for criticism, likely to make its methods pompous and unwieldy.'[16] Virginia Woolf also liked the lecture. In thanking Cecil for a copy of the text, she wrote that she was 'reading it with great pleasure... you pack so much into such a shapely nutshell ... you get one asking questions (my test of criticism) about what one doesn't know at all...'[17]

The most weighty endorsement came from Chapman.[18] In *Time and Tide*, he called the lecture 'the best general account... perhaps the first that can be called adequate to the subject'. He congratulated Cecil for 'saying the right things, and leaving nothing essential unsaid. He will not think this grudging praise; it is as much as Jane Austen could have given him.' But Chapman also pointed out that 'Lord David's description of her time as mostly spent "in the drawing-room, sewing and gossiping" does less than justice to the variety of her experience'. In fact, it could be said that Cecil's account of Jane Austen's life perpetuates the very myths that the authors of the *Life and Letters* set out to dispel. His opening sentence—'Jane Austen, it would appear, did not take her work over-seriously'—is totally at odds with the evidence produced by Chapman in the 1920s and would surely have been contested, fifty years earlier by reviewers of the *Memoir*. Chapman also questions Cecil's short way with 'those who do not like her; as there are those who do not like sunshine or unselfishness'. This is the Cheney-test revived with a vengeance; and one has only to think of that notorious anti-Janeite, Mark Twain, to observe its hollowness. Cecil's conclusion—that if in doubt about 'the wisdom of one of my actions', it would not be Flaubert, Dostoievsky, Balzac, Dickens, Stendhal or Tolstoy he would consult but Jane Austen; and that if he incurred her 'disapproval', he would be 'seriously upset', would 'worry for weeks and weeks'—presumes a bond with his audience. This light-hearted signing-off—informal and intimate—treads on the verges of whimsy. Yet the essence of the matter is not unseriously intended. While Cecil underlines his *critical* purpose with 'rules', 'laws', method and analysis well to the fore, he concludes as he began, as a devotee addressing his fellow-devotees on a common cultural ground.

The essay by Elizabeth Bowen commissioned for *The Saturday Review of Literature* in 1936[19] is a quick round-tour of impressions and ideas. There is no attempt at systematic exposition or development. If we call it a piece of literary journalism, nonetheless it formulates some of the central paradoxes of Jane Austen's genius and achievement:

No woman had ever less the provinciality of her sex, no lady less the provinciality of her sphere.
To underrate a deliberately quiet life is, absurdly, to confuse experience with knowledge.
Accident—the accident of her birth—dictated the scene and scope of her novels but did not restrict their power.

Clearly, at this time, and for this audience, Miss Bowen felt it necessary to clear the ground of some ancient fallacies. Yet there is no dilution to the level of discussion. The third sentence continues: 'She was a very rare example—perhaps Proust was another—of intelligence articulating with the social personality'—an observation which assumes some acumen on the part of her readers; and again in her analysis of Darcy, 'Compound of passion and snobbery, he is a Proustian figure'; and of Henry Crawford, who 'counters the moral rhythm of *Mansfield Park*—which is at once the most intellectual and most nearly insincere novel she wrote'.

The earliest steps in semantic analysis were taken in an essay on 'Sensibility' by Caroline Thompson in *Psyche* (vol. xv, 1935) and in the sharp response by William Empson in the next issue, 1936, from which I quote the few lines and footnote that relate directly to Jane Austen (No. 39). Semantics aside, the most interesting point is Empson's agreement with George Moore and Farrer on the power with which Marianne Dashwood's suffering is drawn. (Virginia Woolf also noticed this: 'And the love so intense, so poignant'; entry for 31 March 1940 (*The Diary of Virginia Woolf* (1984), v. 277).) The revelation of the novelist as a strong and uncosy writer is continued in Auden's *Letters from Iceland*, 1937 (No. 40), where Jane Austen is seen mock-modishly, as a Marxian analyst, concerned with 'The economic basis' of her society, and as a post-Modernist, beside whom 'Joyce seems innocent as grass'.

The understanding of Jane Austen as a major European novelist is further developed in *The March of Literature*, 1938, by Ford Madox Ford.[20] Ford addresses the book to young students, writing as an 'artist-practitioner', calling it 'the book of an old man mad about writing—in the sense that Hokusai called himself an old man mad about painting'. Ford sets himself against 'hounds of the professorio-academic pack', observing that while the 'public has always loved her as they love a delicious aunt', 'The academic critic despises Jane Austen because her subjects are merely domestic.' This is the 'old man's' knockabout. But when he turns to questions of writing and its effect, Ford applies himself seriously. We see this in the final three or four paragraphs where he looks at 'the effect of ordinariness set against ordinariness in a slightly different plane' and the way in which the world of the novels is engaged with our own experience. It is clear that 'gossip' held a particular value for Ford. The notion that in reading the novels we are overhearing 'gossip' may seem odd and trivial. Yet when we connect this to his view of Jane Austen's 'consummate' and 'delicate' art, beside which even Henry James appears 'heavy-handed', and to the 'vividness' of the novels, the idea of gossip takes on a suggestive and revealing point, as it does with Agnes Repplier (No. 17c).

In 1938 there also appeared a new biography, *Jane Austen* by Elizabeth Jenkins. Although the book makes no claim to a place in the critical literature, it is distinctly a *literary* biography in its focus upon the growth and education of a writer, concerned with 'Her powers of mind, the strength of her creative imagination'.[21] Thus the central event of Jane Austen's life is shown to be the composition of the novels and her literary antecedents are given more prominence than her family forebears. Miss Jenkins sets her face against 'the folly and the uselessness of attempting to establish definite connections between the world she lived in and the world of her imagination'.[22] At the same time, she deploys the knowledge of a social historian to good effect in pointing out that it is not only the 'failings' of *Sense and Sensibility* 'but, more important, its background and its atmosphere', which 'relate it to the earliest period of her novel-writing'.[23] We have to refer back to Halevy (see above, p. 81) to match this informed level of literary-historical observation. While Halevy had identified a nineteenth-century Jane Austen, in *Literature and Society* (1938) David Daiches interprets 'The picture that emerges from her novels' as 'essentially an eighteenth-century one'; and claims that 'the new forces are not yet visible and the old standards still prevail.'[24] Given this head-on contradiction between literary historians of a historical bent, it is not surprising that the historical placing of the novels remained so uncertain.

XVI

In 1939, the formal study and criticism of the novelist was set on a new footing. The publication of *Jane Austen and Her Art*, by Mary Lascelles was hailed by the *Times Literary Supplement*, where it was treated, remarkably, to a first leader as well as a lengthy review (both by Harold Child).[1] This was fitting recognition since this was the first book to provide a full-scale account of Jane Austen based upon thorough historical and biographical scholarship; and on the critical front Miss Lascelles broke fresh ground in applying James's ideas on the 'art' of the novel. The Preface points to a further critical-historical dimension, explaining the origin of the book in the fact that 'the professed critics'—Bradley, Saintsbury, Raleigh, John Bailey and Chapman are named—work on a scale 'so small that the reader does not see how they have reached their conclusions until he has patiently found his own way to them'. A 'generation of critics' whose opinions carry conviction, they 'leave us at the beginning of the exciting "how?" and "why?" of analysis'.[2]

The lecture by Bradley is identified as providing the main inspiration: 'while quotations' from it 'might well head most parts of this book I should not have realised all that they meant if I had not written it.'[3] Bradley's influence may be present, too, on a larger scale, in her decision to open the book with a chapter on 'Biography'—not a summary of the novelist's life but a detailed account of her composition, work-by-work, from the earliest of the juvenilia, through to *Sanditon*, within a biographical framework. Bradley had stressed the need to recognise the gap between the earlier and the later group of novels and Miss Lascelles provides just such a scheme. Harold Child, the anonymous reviewer in the *TLS* (17th June 1939), remarked that the nature of Jane Austen's writing does not invite our attention to its 'art'; yet, when we do turn to it, here is a book in which to 'study these acts of creation from the roots upward'.[4] This point attaches equally to Chapter 2, 'Reading and Response', which calls to mind the comments of Simpson, seventy years earlier: 'She began by being an ironical critic...imitating and exaggerating the faults of her models... This critical spirit lies at the foundation of her artistic faculty... she was a critic who developed herself into an artist.' Although Simpson's essay was apparently unknown to Miss Lascelles, her chapter might well have been written in exemplification of his terse insights.

These two chapters are the necessary preliminaries—necessary not only in terms of the book's argument but because satisfactory accounts of these areas did not exist elsewhere—to Part Two, the treatment of 'Jane Austen's Art'. Here (as Miss Lascelles says in her Preface), she takes issue with Professor Stoll's statement that 'all narrative art seems... to aspire towards the condition of drama' and with Lubbock in *The Craft of Fiction*:

[When] the most illuminating writer on the art of the novel tries to drive a wedge between the 'art of narrative' and the 'art of fiction'—then it is surely time to look into the story-teller's peculiar problems.[5]

At this point, Miss Lascelles anticipates the objection that it is not worthwhile 'to study narrative art in so simple a form as that which it assumes in Jane Austen's novels' and connects this with the comment of Herbert Read (see above, page 289) that (as she puts it) 'admirers of this sort of simplicity' are 'disagreeably eccentric'. Miss Lascelles also glances at 'the more common charge—that my subject was herself disagreeable'.[6] No names are mentioned. But presumably she was thinking of what Harold Nicolson and Forster had to say on the publication of the *Letters* in 1932.

Jane Austen and Her Art is too well-known to need documentation here. No one can be unaware of its acutely *critical* nature—generally, in its mode of agrument and analysis; more particularly, in the dialogue it maintains with the existing literature. In this, it comes close to providing an allusive historiography. The James-Lubbock approach to the art of the novel is linked with other traditions and styles of criticism.

In the book's concluding paragraph, a mixed and miscellaneous critical heritage is drawn together and extended. The citations connect Raleigh in *The English Novel*, James writing to Mrs Humphry Ward in 1899 with Katherine Mansfield in 1920.

What distinguishes Jane Austen's manner of inviting us to share in the act of creation but a greater delicacy of intimation? Her invitation is not conveyed directly at any given moment—when it might be summarily refused. It is implicit in all her dealings with us, in what Raleigh called 'a certain subtle literary politeness that is charm itself', above all in her mood of hospitality. 'The truth is,' Katherine Mansfield writes, 'that every true admirer of the novels cherishes the happy thought that he alone—reading between the lines—has become the secret friend of their author'. How has it come about that we feel so towards this most reserved of writers? That very reticence may suggest a partial explanation: '...the personality of the author,' Henry James says, '...however enchanting, is a thing for the reader only, and not for the author himself...to count in at all'.[7]

If, in 1939, there remained any lingering doubt as to the value of scholarship and rigorous critical analysis in the understanding of Jane Austen, the question was called to a head in these pages. While Miss Lascelles scorned John Bailey's nonsensical tribute ('She wrote well because she wrote well...'), there was no suggestion that she shared Lord David Cecil's confidence that the nature of Jane Austen's achievement was so generally understood and agreed upon, nor did she share his trust in the operation of 'laws' and 'rules'. Child recognised the book for what it was: 'not only a masterly study of one of the finest artists in English literature but also an outstanding contribution to the criticism of the craft of fiction'.[8] What Child failed to mention, however, was its response to the tenacious myths documented so fully in this volume, myths not all of them silly and sentimental, some spun by the master of the 'art' of fiction himself. James's Jane Austen, 'instinctive and charming', 'with all her light felicity', we can leave to his pages and enjoy. But about her 'process' and 'the experience in her that fed it', a succession of critics, from 1870 onwards, has (unlike James) been far from incurious. Miss Lascelles' success was to portray Jane Austen as a *writer*; to anatomise the writer's art, without removing from its modesty; to examine her 'charm' without removing from its effect; and to preserve the cherished Jane Austen, leaving intact what James called 'the extraordinary grace of her facility'.

All this falls within the experience of the common reader. Yet the book as a whole calls for a reader conversant with literary and critical history, a reader who, like Miss Lascelles, is not satisfied with the dogmatic pronouncements of the old-style men-of-letters, who shares with her an appetite for following the sometimes intricate paths of analysis. This, the reviewers warned their audience, is not every reader. While Winifred Husbands in the *Modern Language Review* saw it as a book for 'all lovers of Jane

Austen', it was a book to be 'studied' nonetheless.[9] One of a type of 'highly technical studies in literary art' said Edward Sackville-West in the *Spectator*.[10] There was a hint of protest too. 'Perhaps we may think here and there that our critic's analysis is too much like dissection, a pinning-down of brilliant butter-fly wings', wrote Emma Salter in the *Contemporary Review*.[11]

The reviewers signalled their discomfort at seeing the discussion carried away from the home-ground of the common reader to become a communication between academics, increasingly demanding and increasingly specialised. While the Jane Austen on view was still the novelist of old, the possibility of a continuing tradition of popular criticism now seemed to be at an end. In the Leslie Stephen lecture, David Cecil had done his best to keep this tradition alive for the 1930s, setting the familiar, beloved figure within a framework of critical rules and laws. But the attempt there to mix the 'theory' of the critic with the affection of the devotee was only a partial success, and in the light of Miss Lascelles' book it was clear that any continuing discussion of the novelist's art called for a refinement of analysis that the broad brush could never attain.

XVII

A further blow to the popular tradition was struck in D.W. Harding's essay 'Regulated Hatred: an aspect of the work of Jane Austen'. Originally given as a talk to the Literature Society of Manchester University in March 1939 and printed in *Scrutiny*,[1] little changed, a year later, this is a key document in the shaping of modern approaches to Jane Austen. Like Mary Lascelles, Harding was attentive to the detail of the novelist's art. But, unlike Miss Lascelles, he revealed a writer of deep and powerful emotion (Harding was trained as a psychologist), whose 'hatred' was regulated through language and devices of style. While the coda of Miss Lascelles' book celebrates the bonds of intimacy and affection between writer and reader, Harding warns us of something very different—of a 'complex intention' involving an amusing yet cruel deception. The Janeites, rejoicing in the comfort and security of her fictional world, fall unwarily for the traps of style; pass by, in their bemusement, the 'unexpected astringencies' within the text. That they are the novelist's prime target, Harding drives home in a calm and sardonic equation:

her books are, as she meant them to be, read and enjoyed by precisely the sort of people whom she disliked; she is a literary classic of the society which attitudes like hers, held widely enough, would undermine.

These traps of style Harding illustrates in a number of passages; and with an extract from *Northanger Abbey*, he argues the need for an historical understanding of the text. Although this historical approach was not taken up, Harding's attention to tone and the regulation of language was to become the dominant approach to Jane Austen. Moreover, his view of the writer as subversive, attacking her society from within, an Audenesque secret agent, was an image of some fascination and novelty. In 1938, David Daiches had attributed to Jane Austen 'the intelligence and the clarity of vision to realise' the 'pettiness' of her world, 'perhaps only half consciously'.[2] There is no such qualification to Harding's claim and, not unexpectedly, it raised an outcry. One distinguished critic complained to *Scrutiny* of the author's 'communist' views;[3] while Chapman saw it as an essay 'in iconoclasm' with which he declared himself 'out of sympathy'.[4] It polarised the critics. On one side was the Harding camp, embracing the new, caustic Jane Austen; on the other, those who remained faithful to the 'gentle-Janeism' (as it was described)[5] of Mary Lascelles.

Harding was well aware of his heresy, of the pieties offended. His contest was with views long-embedded and fiercely cherished. The opening of the essay is a dismembering of the 'popular impression' of Jane Austen—the novelist as 'delicate satirist' blessed with an 'inimitable lightness of touch', the novels as a place of urbane and secure refuge from everyday life. The Janeites are flayed as 'precisely the sort of people whom she disliked'. Harding's performance is amusing and tactically clever. Yet it is a point at which the critic begins to construct his own version of history. What does Harding make of the arch-Janeite Saintsbury, who discovered a Swiftian Jane Austen and speaks of her 'cruelty'? Or the arch-Janeite Farrer, who saw a 'pitilessness which is invariably salted with dislike or contempt' and found the novelist 'the most merciless, though calmest of iconoclasts; only her calm has obscured from her critics the steely quality, the inexorable rigour of her judgement' (No. 27)? Or the arch-Janeite Forster, who (Harding-like) announced that 'The Jane Austenite possesses little of the brightness he ascribes so freely to his idol. Like all regular churchgoers, he scarcely notices what is being said'; and then promptly moved to an analysis of the text (No. 30)? Quite simply, those were Janeites unbemused and attentive, Janeites whose devotion allowed them to detect a hardness of heart and a sharpness of tongue. Of these Janeites, inconvenient to Harding's case, we hear nothing.

Equally, Harding has nothing to say about those earlier writers who, in addressing the public at large, represent a Jane Austen wholly at odds with his caricature of the 'popular impression' and remarkably close to his own *un*gentle Jane. Witness Julia Kavanagh in 1862: 'With the keenest insight into the meanness of human motives, Miss Austen preserved the greatest command over her formidable powers. She seldom or never draws a character we can hate: she is too calm, too dispassionate, too self-possessed to be bitter or eloquent. Delicate irony is her keenest weapon', her satire deployed 'with a touch so fine we often do not perceive its severity' (*No. 39*). Eight years later, there is Margaret Oliphant's Jane Austen, a writer 'full of subtle power, keenness, finesse, and self-restraint', her books 'so calm and cold and keen', her 'contempt' 'fine stinging yet soft-voiced', her fictional world 'so remorselessly true' (*No. 42*). In the same year, Richard Simpson names 'irony' as the condition of Jane Austen's art, with 'the critical spirit... at the foundation of her artistic faculty', a writer 'full of subtle power' (*No. 44*). Knowing nothing of Mrs Kavanagh, Mrs Oliphant, Mrs Humphry Ward, Richard Simpson, Farrer and the others, Harding supposed that *un*gentle Jane was *his* discovery and that the earlier critical literature could be safely ignored.

In effect, 'Regulated Hatred' closed the door; and soon after, in the 'Critical Theory of Jane Austen's Writing', by Mrs Leavis, which appeared in *Scrutiny* between 1941 and 1944, the bolts were shot. Mrs Leavis sought to establish the case for Jane Austen as a novelist fully conscious of her artistic aims and hard-working in their pursuit; and to this end, the 'Critical Theory' opens with an attack upon the 'miracle' view of the novels, as the pernicious error of the hour.[6] The assault is vigorous and entertaining. But it takes no account of the solid line of 'anti-miracle' criticism that extends from the earliest reviews of the *Memoir* down to *Jane Austen and Her Art*, published as recently as 1939. Unfortunately, no one corrected Mrs Leavis; the 'Critical Theory' passed as fact; and the discovery of an unmiraculous Jane Austen was logged as a discovery of the present day—see Arnold Kettle's comment in *An Introduction to the English Novel*, 1951:

There is no longer, especially after Mrs Leavis's articles, any excuse for thinking of Jane Austen as an untutored genius or even as a kind of aunt with a flair for telling stories that have somehow or other continued to charm. She was a serious and conscious writer, absorbed in her art, wrestling with its problems... There is nothing soft about her.[7]

Yet were these matters ever in doubt? Did enlightenment have to wait upon Mrs Leavis? Readers of this volume will know otherwise—that in the very first review of the *Memoir* (No. 2), these same points were spelt out by Hutton with a particularity and force that would have embarrassed Mrs Leavis and Professor Kettle and amused their students:

...how well she estimated her own real powers... No one with a grain of literary sense doubts her wonderful originality and artistic power. To dispute it now is simply to prove that the disputant does not know what he is talking about... That Miss Austen did fully appreciate her own power,—appreciate, we mean, in the sense of truly estimating it, both what it could do and what it could not,—and did also appreciate the stupidity of those who did not understand her at all, and yet pretended to give her advice, this book gives ample proof...

Like Harding, Mrs Leavis seeks to pit the force and originality of her case against the stupidity of the embedded views. Harding renders the 'popular impression', Mrs Leavis the 'classical account'—in which the writer stands as

a certain kind of novelist, one who wrote her best at the age of twenty (Professor Oliver Elton), whose work 'show no development' (Professor Garrod), whose novels 'make exceptionally peaceful reading' (A.C. Bradley); one scholar writes of her primness, another of her 'sunny temper', with equal infelicity, and all apologise for her inability to dwell on guilt and misery, the French Revolution and the Napoleonic Wars.[8]

To this, Mrs Leavis adds a second construct, the 'conventional account', according to which the novelist is 'prim, demure, sedate, prudish and so on, the typical Victorian maiden lady'.[9]

The 'popular impression' and the 'classical' and 'conventional' accounts are useful devices, providing the critic with energetic points of departure, Aunt Sallies to be assailed and derided as a prelude to his own account. But they are devices which can backfire. In the case of 'Regulated Hatred', the reader is left to suppose a critical vacuum, that until Harding declared himself there was a total silence on the matter of *un*gentle Jane. Mrs Leavis's 'accounts' are equally unhistorical, equally misleading. Looking further at the critics referred to in the 'classical account' we can produce a variety of Jane Austens, some of them not at all laughable, some of them casting shadows across Mrs Leavis's argument and showing that earlier critics had thought hard on the very questions treated in the 'Critical Theory'. As to the 'conventional account', one is left to wonder where, in 1941, it would have been possible to find a reader of Jane Austen who could suppose the novelist to be 'the typical Victorian maiden lady'? Could such an image have survived the publication of the *Letters* in 1932? Or of the juvenilia in the 1920s? Or, indeed, a single reading of the novels themselves, in which seduction, elopement, adultery and illegitimacy stand as facts of life—'facts on which the maiden novelist in her rectory parlour had looked unperturbed', as Edith Wharton put the matter?[10] Seduction can be comic, as reviewers of the 1871 *Memoir* spotted in *Sanditon*. These were Victorians who would have laughed Mrs Leavis's 'Victorian maiden lady' out of sight. So would Farrer, who spent several pages on the glaring fact that Jane Austen was not Victorian. But the readers of *Scrutiny* knew nothing of these views, were told nothing of them, were left to suppose the earlier critics of Jane Austen had said nothing worth saying and that criticism of Jane Austen really began on the pages of *Scrutiny* in the early 1940s.

The documents collected in this volume show up the *Scrutiny* version of literary history as critical fiction. The revelations of the 1940s turn out to be the commonplaces of the 1870s. Had Mrs Leavis read the *Memoir* reviews of that time, she would have seen that her series of articles was not an act of revelation but of reclamation; and that a debt of acknowledgment was due to the reviewers and essayists of long ago. The elaboration of method and the construction of the 'Theory' are new. The insights are old.

This Critical Heritage volume closes on a cheerless note. Although *Jane Austen and Her Art* went some way towards providing a link with the past and transmitting the earlier traditions of criticism, Miss Lascelles only quoted to her purpose and mentioned none of the outstanding critics of the *Memoir* period and after. Nor did she mention Farrer. Like Harding, he too remarked upon the novelist's 'art of conveying emotion without expression', found to the highest degree, he said, in *Persuasion*—not in the regulation of 'hatred' but of love. But Farrer was forgotten. The *Scrutiny* critics wove their own tapestry. So it was that much of the finest criticism remained unknown. That Jane Austen's 'playfulness' (as Howells termed it) and her gifts as an entertainer were at one with the 'formidable powers' described by Julia Kavanagh, this understanding was lost sight of, and, as we quit the scene, criticism was set, one-sidedly, on promoting an *ungentle* Jane.

Notes

I

1 G.O. Trevelyan, *The Life and Letters of Lord Macaulay* (1876), ii. 466, quotes Macaulay's Journal, 1858: 'If I could get materials I really would write a short life of that wonderful woman.' In Winchester Cathedral, finding himself 'by the plain marble slab, which covered the remains of Jane Austen', Macaulay decided 'Here's a woman who ought to have had a National monument' (*Mrs Brookfield and Her Circle* (1905), C. & F. Brookfield, ii. 337).

2 *Alfred Lord Tennyson: A Memoir by His Son* (1898), ii. 371. His friend Allingham reported in 1867 that Tennyson was 'a great novel reader, very fond of Scott, but perhaps Miss Austen is his prime favourite' (*William Allingham's Diary* (1907), edd. H. Allingham & D. Redford, p. 156). His knowledge of the novels may have dated from as far back as the early 1830s. Hallam was an Austen enthusiast and corresponding with Emily Tennyson in January 1833 about *Emma*, which he was then re-reading 'with the greatest enjoyment' (*Letters of Arthur Henry Hallam* (1981), ed. Jack Kolb, p. 717).

3 *Autobiography of Henry Taylor* (1885), ii. 193, reporting what Tennyson told Julia Margaret Cameron in 1860. These words were soon quoted, prominently, in the final paragraph of *Jane Austen* (1889) by Mrs Malden (see below, p. 189); and, prominently again, in the Tennyson memorial issue of the *Illustrated London News* for 15 October 1892, p. 492.

4 Caroline Austen (sister of James Edward Austen-Leigh) used these words (quoted by R.W. Chapman, *Jane Austen: Facts and Problems* (1948), p. 140).

5 Some omissions or concealments may be the result of ignorance rather than design. Austen-Leigh had access to only some of the surviving letters and Cassandra had destroyed or censored all the letters she considered as touching too closely upon her sister's private life. But Austen-Leigh certainly exercised his own judgment in avoiding family scandals or shames, such as the existence of George, her mentally defective brother, Henry Austen's bankruptcy and his aunt's acceptance and overnight rejection of the proposal by Harris Bigg-Wither. There is some bowdlerisation, too, in his quotations from the letters. These matters are dealt with in R.W. Chapman, *Jane Austen: Facts and Problems* (1948), ch. 10; and in the Introduction and Notes to the *Memoir* included with the Penguin English Library text of *Persuasion* (1965), edited by D.W. Harding.

It was also Austen-Leigh's intention to skirt the romantic episodes, in particular the flirtation (in 1795–96) with Tom Lefroy, who was still alive when the *Memoir* was in planning. His death early in 1869, aged 92, removed the problem of offending him personally. But within the family it was still dangerous ground, and Austen-Leigh chose to steer clear of the anecdotes and rumours circulating amongst the Lefroys and so avoid any controversy on this still delicate matter (an issue explored by Deirdre Le Faye, 'Tom Lefroy and Jane Austen', The Jane Austen Society *Report* 1985, pp. 8–10).

6 Quoted in *Jane Austen's Family Through Five Generations* (1984), Maggie Lane, p. 244.

7 Between 30 March and early September 1869 (Lane, p. 245).

8 Letter to him 16 December 1816, *Letters*, pp. 468–9.

9 *Memoir of Jane Austen* (1926), ed. R.W. Chapman, p. 150.

10 *Memoir*, p. 3.

11 'Editor's Easy Chair', *Harper's Magazine*, November 1913.

12 *Memoir*, p. 157.

13 *Memoir*, p. 175. Austen-Leigh's account of this point was frequently copied, sometimes almost verbatim, as in *The Book of Noble English-women*, 1875, by Charles Bruce: 'Her life was passed in the performance of home duties and the cultivation of domestic affections', p. 325.

14 Undated letter (written 23 August 1869), 'Aunt Jane', *Cornhill Magazine*, clxiii (1947–49), pp. 72–3. This delicacy persisted to the next generation. In editing the letters for publication in 1884, the novelist's grand-nephew Lord Brabourne silently changed 'Bowel' to 'Stomach' and omitted lists of physical complaints.

15 P. 2.

16 However reading pictures is a subjective business. Hutton (No. 2) found the Andrews portrait 'very remarkable', 'very attractive and expressive' and gives eleven lines to its interpretation. To him, it spoke 'of the *ease* of power, and of power well appreciated by its owner'. He would not have seen Cassandra's drawing. Whereas Agnes Repplier wished that 'Cassandra's pudding-faced likeness (which could never have been a likeness)...had been consigned to eternal oblivion' (No. 17i).

In 1870, an elderly lady who remembered Jane Austen from her own childhood, was not impressed by the Andrews version: 'Jane's likeness is hardly what I remember there *is* a look, & that is all—I remember her as a tall thin *spare* person, with very high cheek bones great colour—sparkling Eyes not large but joyous & intelligent. The face by *no means so broad* & plump as represented...' (reported by D.G. Le Faye, *TLS*, 3 May 1985, p. 495).

17 *Memoir*, p. 155.

18 *Autobiography and Letters* (1899), ed. H. Coghill (1974), p. 24.

19 P. 184.

20 *Memoir*, p. 136.

21 *Memoir*, p. 137.

22 At the end of Chapter 9, Austen-Leigh gives in full a letter from a Miss Quincy of Boston dated January 1852 to Admiral Sir Francis Austen, communicating to the Austen family that 'the influence' of his sister's 'genius is extensively recognised in the American Republic' (pp. 151–2). The correspondent was Eliza Susan Quincy. According to her sister, Mrs Robert Waterston, who visited Admiral Austen in 1856, in America the novels were regarded 'as household words'. (See Section X, note 25.)

23 *Memoir*, p. 149. I have followed the *Memoir* wording, which differs in small details from the more accurate version given in *No. 17*, of which Cassandra Austen made a copy. Scott actually wrote 'Big Bow-wow', the form I have given in later references. A good period discussion of the difference between Scott's romantic, historical fiction and Jane Austen's 'domestic novel' is in R.H. Hutton's *Sir Walter Scott* (1887), pp. 103–4; and, to Scott's advantage, in a signed article by Coventry Patmore, 'Comparing small things with great', *St James's Gazette*, 22 January 1886, reprinted in *Courage in Politics* (1921).

24 'The Rev. G. Crabbe, L.L.B', *The Future*, 1917; reprinted in *Literary Essays of Ezra Pound* (1954), ed. T.S. Eliot, p. 279.

25 *Memoir*, p. 136.

26 *Memoir*, p. 136. It was long-lived, certainly into the 1920s, going by Middleton Murry's record.

I remember an intellectual dinner party at which it was announced, without any manifest ill-effects upon the company, that the real test for literary taste was an admiration not for Jane Austen (as some one had suggested) but for Dickens. (*Pencillings* (1923), p. 32.)

27 cxxviii. 196; 15 July 1871.

28 The best analysis of the 'cult' is in the opening pages to '*Emma* and the Legend of Jane Austen' by Lionel Trilling (first published 1957, Introduction to the Riverside Edition of *Emma*; reprinted *Emma: Casebook Series*, 1968, ed. David Lodge, pp. 148–50).

29 *Charlotte Bronte, George Eliot, Jane Austen: Studies in Their Works* (1902), Henry H. Bonnell, p. 474.

30 New York, edited by Edwin L. Miller (Assistant Principal, Central High School, Detroit), p. 12.

31 New York, edited by Josephine Woodbury Heermans (Principal, Whitter School, Kansas City), p. xvii.

32 *Memoir*, unnumbered first page of Preface.

33 Some hint of these dangerous waters is given by Wilkie Collins. Commenting on the anti-fiction brigade, he wrote of them 'canting "national morality" and their blustering "purity of hearths and homes"' (*My Miscellanies* (1863), i. 77).

34 'On English Prose Fiction as a National Amusement', *Four Lectures* (1938), pp. 104, 105. The illusion of an inoffensive Jane Austen was rooted and persistent. See, for example, Margot Asquith's Jane Austen: 'comedy without foot-lights, conduct without crime, and love without sex...' (*More Memories* (1933), p. 255).

35 'I cannot but notice Miss Austen's timidity in dealing with the most touching scenes which come in her way, and in avoiding the narration of those details which a bolder artist would most eagerly have seized. In the final scene between Emma and her lover,—when the conversation has become almost pathetic,—she breaks away from the spoken dialogue, and simply tells us of her hero's success. This is a cowardice which robs the reader of much of the charm which he has promised himself—' (From comments Trollope wrote on the end papers of his copy of *Emma* in 1865 (reprinted in *Emma, Casebook Series* (1968), ed. David Lodge, p. 51).)

36 Second Edition (1865), p. 163.

37 'Effect of Modern Entertainments on the Mind of Youth' (c. 1867), *Works* xvii. 468.

38 *Sesame and Lilies*, p. vi.

39 P. 99.

40 *Memoir*, p. 153.

41 Reference mislaid.

42 *The Letters of Edward Fitzgerald* (1980), edd. A.M. & A.B. Terhume, iii 260. Letter to W.F. Pollock, 24 December 1870; M.S. Watts, *G.F. Watts: The Annals of an Artist's Life* (1912), p. 15.

43 *St Paul's Magazine* (1870), v. 632–3.

44 P. 158.

45 *The Elements of Drawing* (1857), in *Works*, xv. 226.
46 Ibid., p. 228.
47 *Letters of George Gissing* (1927), edd. A. & G. Gissing, letter dated 25 June 1880.
48 *Life of Jane Austen* (1890), pp. 65, 187.
49 By Catherine J. Hamilton; p. 193.
50 Second Edition (1865), pp. 124, 126, 122.
51 G.H. Lewes, *No. 27*.
52 *The Letters of Elizabeth Barrett Browning* (1897), ed. F.G. Kenyon, ii. 217.
53 Josephine Butler, *Women's Work and Women's Culture* (1869), Intoduction, pp. xxxvi, xxxix.

II

1 Journal entry for 7 March 1845, quoted by G.E. Fasnacht, 'Acton on books and reading', *TLS*, 6 May 1955, p. 244.
2 Vol. 1 (1870), p. 118.
3 Journal entry for 12 August 1854 (G.O. Trevelyan, *Life and Letters of Lord Macaulay* (1876), ii. 379). Earl of Lytton, *The Life of Edward Bulwer Lytton*, (1913), i. 457; Arthur James Balfour, *Chapters of Autobiography* (1930), p. 39. The copies in the family library, in Bentley's 'Standard Novels' series, were 'worn' and 'dirty' with 'fair wear and tear'.
4 Diary entry for 23 October 1837 (*Harriet Martineau's Autobiography* (1877), iii. 199). Another comment was to dub Jane Austen 'the Queen of Novelists, the immortal creator of Anne Elliot, Mr Knightley, and a score or two more of unrivalled intimate friends of the whole public...' When this diary entry was published (i. 100), it was immediately picked up and quoted by Sir Jerom Murch (President of the Bath Literary and Philosophical Association) in *Mrs Barbauld and her Contemporaries* (1877), pp. 20–21.

    Significantly, what was not picked up was Harriet Martineau's reference to the novels, any one of which, she wrote, 'may be taken as a specimen of her powers, a manifestation of her mind' (*Westminster Review* (October 1837), xxviii. 43–4).
5 Park Honan, *Matthew Arnold: A Life* (1981), pp. 377, 60. Cardinal Newman is also reported to have said that 'he read through *Mansfield Park* every year, in order to perfect and preserve his style' (C.F. Harrold, *John Henry Newman* (1945) p. 421). According to his wife, the elderly Thomas Hardy, when reading the novels, was 'much amused at finding he has *many* characteristics in common with Mr Woodhouse', Michael Millgate, *Thomas Hardy: A Biography* (1982), p. 531.
6 *No. 33.*

7 *Journals of André Gide 1889–1949* (1967), ed. Justin O'Brien.

8 Vol. 13 (1870), pp. 187–93.

9 Frances Hoey, *Dublin Review* (1870), lxvii. 447.

10 *The Nation*, New York (1870), x. 124. The *Memoir* was published in New York by Scribner's.

11 *Tennyson: Memoir* (1897), ii. 96. Tennyson is reported as having made the remark on 25 January 1870 when Anne Thackeray was present. Could this have been prompted by the just-published *Memoir*? Commissioned to review the book, she might have taken the opportunity to sound Tennyson's views, as a known enthusiast. Anyway, Tennyson later felt it necessary to explain the Shakespeare comparison: 'I am reported to have said that Jane Austen was equal to Shakespeare. What I really said was that, in the narrow sphere of life which she delineated, she pictured her characters as truthfully as Shakespeare. But Austen is to Shakespeare as asteroid to sun. Miss Austen's novels are perfect works on a small scale—beautiful bits of stippling.' Wilfrid Ward, *Problems and Persons* (1903), quoted by N. Page, *Tennyson: Interviews and Recollections* (1983), p. 10.

The only earlier critic to focus on the smallness of everyday life in the novels was Julia Kavanagh: 'every-day men and women, with their selfishness; their good nature; their small vices and very small minds. One stroke of the pen sets them before us' (*No. 39*).

An historical gloss is found in Mountstuart E. Grant Duff's observation: 'If the 1833 movement did nothing else, it rescued the country districts of England from the sort of society which is described by Miss Austen, in reading whose works we are often seduced by the marvellous skill of the artist to forget the ghastly dreariness of the world in which she lived' ('Manning and the Catholic Reaction of our Times', *Edinburgh Review*, 1896; reprinted *Out of the Past* (1903), i. 146–7).

12 8 January 1870, No. 2202, pp. 53–4.

13 1 August 1871, pp. 367–8.

14 *The Nation*, New York (1871), xiii. 164–5.

15 15 July 1871, pp. 70–71.

16 22 July 1871, pp. 118–19.

17 *Sincerity and Authenticity* (1972), p. 81.

18 The *North British Review* essay is listed, unattributed, in the bibliography to *Jane Austen*, 1890, by Goldwin Smith; also in the bibliography to *The Story of Jane Austen's Life* by Oscar Fay Adams (Chicago), 1891. It is recommended by Henry H. Bonnell, in *Charlotte Bronte, George Eliot, Jane Austen* (USA), 1902. W. Robertson Nicoll referred enigmatically to the essay: 'I know of one article on Miss Austen which is really luminous, and which I believe to be by Lord Acton, but I mean to keep

the secret of its hiding-place—for reasons' (reprinted in *People and Books* (1926), p. 95). Nicoll's piece must have been written pre-1913, for in his review of that year of the *Life and Letters*, 1913, he refers again to the essay: 'a very ambitious article appeared in the *North British Review* which I wrongly attributed to Lord Acton' (*A Bookman's letters*, 1919, p. 166, reprinting an unidentified review).

19 Riverside Editions, Houghton Mifflin Co., Boston.
20 *Pride and Prejudice* (1918), Introduction, p. ix.
21 'Novels and Their Times' II, *Macmillan's Magazine*, September 1872, p. 3.
22 *Life of Jane Austen*, 1890, p. 65.
23 *History of Nineteenth Century Literature*, 1896, p. 128.

III

1 *Lady Charlotte Schreiber: Extracts from her Journal 1853–1891*, ed. The Earl of Bessborough (1952), p. 134.
2 11 October 1902, p. 384.
  The final quotation is taken from 'Jane Austen's Novels', *Nineteenth Century*, October 1902, p. 669.
3 P. 2.
4 P. 151. This letter is discussed in Section 1, note 22.
5 The testimony is voluminous, e.g. Jane to Thomas Carlyle, 5 August 1852, recounting a drive to Sherborne House in a gig: 'Nothing could be more pleasant than so *pirring* through quiet roads in the dusk—with the moon coming out. I felt as I were *reading about myself in a Miss Austen novel!*' (*I too am here: Selections from the letters of Jane Welsh Carlyle*, edd. A. & M. McQueen Simpson (1977), p. 182). Mrs Russell Barrington, one of whose two sisters married Walter Bagehot, to whom she writes, in about 1858: 'It had been the habit of our sisterhood to read Jane Austen's books periodically aloud to each other, especially *Pride and Prejudice* and *Sense and Sensibility*, and the characters in them had become our intimate acquaintances...On arriving at Herds Hill [W.B.'s home] it was as if one had stepped back into the world of a hundred years ago, a world of Jane Austen's novels. A delightful world it was...' (*Life of Walter Bagehot* (1916), Mrs Russell Barrington, p. 265).
6 'A Critical Theory of Jane Austen's Writing', *Scrutiny* (1941–42), x. 75–84.
7 Vol. III, ch. 6.
8 Reprinted from *St James's Gazette*, 1884 in *Letters to Dead Authors*, London 1886, pp. 75–85; New York 1889; new London edn. 1892. The book was dedicated to Anne Thackeray.

 9 P. 235.
10 P. 235.
11 P. 536.
12 Pp. 10, 253.
13 'The Art of Fiction', 1884.
14 lvi. 827–8.
15 *National Review,* i. 265.
16 P. 280.
17 Published by Methuen, 1900: pp. xxi, xxi–xii, xxiv.
18 P. 105.
19 *Nation* xii (1871), pp. 164–5.
20 'Gustave Flaubert', 1902; reprinted, *The House of Fiction,* ed. L. Edel, p. 207.
21 *Heroines of Fiction* (1901), ii. 44.
22 Reprinted from *Spectator, Brief Literary Criticisms* (1906), p. 182.
23 *North American Review* (March 1901), clxxii. Reprinted in *Notes on Novelists* (1914), p. 248.
24 *Academy,* 6 April 1901, p. 308: 'He concludes on a note of unashamed insularity...'.
25 A rewarding Empsonian exercise lies in tracing the shifts in tone and meaning following Scott's original use of the word. In 1885, Mrs Humphry Ward wrote that 'condensation in literary matters means an exquisite power of choice and discrimination' (No. 9). That usage, like Scott's, seems properly to focus upon Jane Austen's consummate gifts as a writer with a specific mastery in the use of language. Whereas the devotees use 'exquisite' to suggest Jane Austen's genius as a miniaturist, a creator of works-of-art flawless and finished to a point of rare perfection. The appeal of this 'exquisite' art is regarded as so refined and delicate that its discovery and appreciation call for more than a touch of the 'exquisite' on the part of the critic himself.
26 *History of English Literature* (1912), p. 539.
27 'Mrs Woolf Again', *Bookman* (New York, 1924), reprinted in *A London Bookman* (1928), p. 148.
28 'A.B. Walkley', *Bookman* (1926), p. 264.
29 P. 636.
30 Lxvii (1929), p. 696.

IV

 1 Pp. 337, 334.
 2 See Section II, note 21.
 3 Vol. ii. 139–41.

4 'Chaucer and Shakespeare'; reprinted in *Notes and Essays on Shakespeare* (1884), p. 72.

5 Vol. iv. 251.

6 Vol. iii. 101–2.

7 Vol. ii. 534.

8 P. 515.

9 P. 912. The 1870s and 1880s were Morley's heyday. Thereafter, sales slackened. The 1901 edition of the *First Sketch* was announced as the 'Thirty-fourth thousand'; the 1912 edition had only advanced to the 'Thirty-sixth thousand'.

James and Mrs Ward were not alone in this. Ten years before, in the *Atlantic Monthly* (1873), xxxii. 371, the anonymous review of Anne Thackeray's *Old Kensington* had voiced the same complaint:

The English and American public of novel readers have, it would seem, a vague, unwarrantable impression that the novel is but a careless, easy-going kind of composition, in which certain principles of dramatic writing may often with advantage be set aside, and seldom need to be regarded.

On 25 April 1884, Walter Besant delivered a lecture on 'The Art of Fiction' at the Royal Institution in London. Besant set out 'to consider Fiction as one of the Fine arts...governed and directed by general laws'. As 'the great Masters of the Art' he named 'Fielding, Scott, Dickens, Thackeray, Victor Hugo' (not Jane Austen). As a book, the lecture was published and appeared as late as 1902 (Brentano's, New York; Chatto & Windus, London), the text unchanged but with an Appendix added advising young writers how to get published.

10 *Fortnightly Review* (1870), xiii.

11 January 1881, pp. 308–9.

12 Preface to Pellew's *Poems*, Boston (1892), p. vii. Pellew died that year and Howells's Preface is by way of being an obituary tribute. Notwithstanding this weighty commendation, Pellew's essay seems to have disappeared from view. Thomas Sergeant Perry, editor of the *North American Review*, sent a copy to John Addington Symonds, who returned a letter of thanks on 15 July 1883, remarking 'there is considerable literary promise in its fresh and unaffected style' (*Selections from the Letters of Thomas Sergeant Perry*, ed. E.A. Robinson, New York (1929), p. 251).

There was a single contemporary reference, a notice of only a few lines, in *Englische Studien*, viii (1885). The only other mention was in the bibliography to Adams, *The Story of Jane Austen's Life*, Chicago (1891).

13 P. viii.

14 Quoted p. 49.

15 P. vii.

16 Pp. 414–15.

17 Pp. 1609–11.

18 Vol. iii (1882), pp. 394, 387.

19 Vol. xxxiv (1882), pp. 187, 189–90, 192.

20 3rd Series, x. 123.

21 Vol. lxii (1882), p. 365.

22 Pp. v, 139.

23 'Comparing Great Things with Small', *St James's Gazette*, 22 January 1886.

 The comparison with Shakespeare astonished other readers. After hearing Tennyson enthuse about Jane Austen 'as next to Shakespeare', Julia Margaret Cameron wrote to Henry Taylor (*c.* 1860), 'I can never imagine what they mean when they say such things' (Henry Taylor, *Autobiography* (1885), ii. 193).

24 Thirty years earlier, on 7th March 1858, the Queen recorded in her diary: 'Began reading *Jane Eyre* to my dear Albert, having finished *Northanger Abbey,* one of Miss Austen's admirable novels' ('Queen Victoria and "Jane Eyre"', *Brontë Society Transactions* (1956–60), xiii. 296). 'Admirable' as Queen Victoria may have regarded Jane Austen, during her reign the author's presentation copy of *Emma*, dedicated and inscribed to the Prince Regent, languished in the Servants' Library at Windsor Castle!

25 Pp. xii–xiii.

26 20 November 1884, p. 7.

27 Pp. xii–xiii.

28 See Section III, note 8.

29 Vol. xxvi (1884), p. 334.

30 15 November 1884, p. 637.

31 'Jane Austen at Home', pp. 262–70; reprinted *Littell's Living Age* 1885, clxiv. 680–5.

32 Vol. ii. 260. That Leslie Stephen wrote the entry presumes no especial choice on his part, since, as *DNB* editor, he contributed several hundred.

33 Ed. Lloyd C. Sanders, pp. 74–5.

34 Helen Gray Cone & Jennette Leonard Gilder, i. 193–220.

35 P. 3.

36 Pp. 6, 8.

37 P. 14.

38 P. 73.

39 P. 99.

40 P. 209.

41 Vol. xxxvi (1889), p. 96.

42 P. 97.
43 Vol. lxiii (1889), pp. 80–81.
44 P. 65.
45 P. 11.
46 P. 152.
47 P. 185.
48 12 April 1890, p. 467.
49 *Life of Jane Austen*, p. 65.

V

1 His opinions were repeated over many years. His comment on *The Watsons*—'a mere exercise'—was quoted in the *TLS*, as late as 1 February 1923, p. 67.
2 18 July 1831. *The Letters of Thomas Babington Macaulay*, ed. Thomas Pinney (1974), ii. 72; 13 June 1832, ii. 130–31.
3 Letter of 10 September 1833, quoted in *Maria Edgeworth: A Literary Biography* (1972), Marilyn Butler, p. 446.
4 15 November 1884, p. 637.
5 1885, ii. 260.
6 W. Ward, *William George Ward and the Oxford Movement* (1889), p. 36.
7 *Reminiscences and Opinions of Sir Francis Hastings Doyle* (1889), p. 353.
8 *Jane Austen* (1889), p. 210.
9 P. 280.
10 Pp. 254–5.
11 P. 271.
12 P. 250.
13 P. iii.
14 P. 45.
15 P. 62.
16 8 April 1893, p. 402.
17 P. 400.
18 P. 401.
19 P. 401.
20 P. 402.

VI

1 Vol. i. 82–3.
2 Boston, p. 62. There were geographical-historical issues in the precedence of Scott, who was favoured, for example by the heavy Scottish settlement in the South.

3 P. 226.

4 P. 409.

5 P. 414.

6 23 July 1877, *The Letters of Henry Wadsworth Longfellow* (1982), ed. Andrew Hilen, vi. 286.

7 *Life of Jane Austen* (1890), p. 65.

8 Diary entry 9 December 1869, *The Years and Hours of Emily Dickinson* (1960), ed. Jay Leyda, ii. 134.

9 *Atlantic Essays*, Boston (1871), p. 19.

10 'Literature as an art' (1867), *Atlantic Essays*, p. 47.

11 *Women and Men*, New York (1888), p. 113.

12 P. 157.

13 'A Plea for Culture' (1887), *Atlantic Essay*, p. 19.

14 *Selected Letters of W.D. Howells* (1979), edd. G. Arms & C.K. Lohmann, ii. 231, 22 June 1879.

15 A fiery contribution came from the Columbia Professor Brander Matthews in *Americanism and Briticisms*, 1892. This was reviewed by Augustine Birrell in the *Speaker* (reprinted in *Essays about Men, Women and Books*, 1894, pp. 199–204), where he ridiculed Matthews's cultural chauvinism, quoting him: 'it cannot be said too often or too emphatically that the British are foreigners, and their ideals in life, in literature, in politics, in taste, in art are not our ideals.' Birrell chided Matthews for 'scolding' his fellow-countrywoman Agnes Repplier for quoting British authors (including Jane Austen) but mentioning no Americans.

16 'Literature as an Art', *Atlantic Essays*, p. 66.

17 *Journals of Ralph Waldo Emerson: 1856–63* (1913), edd. E.W. Emerson & W.E. Forbes, ix. 336–7.

18 *Lectures in America* (1935 (edn. 1957)), p. 18.

19 Quoted in *Edith Wharton and the Novel of Manners* (1975), G.H. Linberg, p. 1.

20 'Americanism in Literature', *Atlantic Quarterly* (January 1870), xxv. 63.

21 No. 22b.

22 No. 22b.

23 See Section III, note 23.

24 No. 22a.

25 *Nation*, New York, 9 November 1865.

26 Sarah Orme Jewett was born in 1849 and was about 53 when this (undated) letter was written in 1901–2. *Letters,* ed. Annie Fields, Boston, 1911, p. 185.

In her own writing, these cultural and literary affinities were unmistakable. As Higginson commented, 'types of the old New English gentry' inhabit her books and her New England hamlets hold an element of higher breeding and more refined living' ('Local Fiction' (1896) in *Book and Heart* (1897), pp. 61, 65).

27 H.L. Mencken, *Prejudices: First Series*, 1919 (edn. 1932), p. 56.

28 No. 16.

29 17 August 1889, p. 97.

30 'Charlotte Brontë', *Cornhill Magazine* (1877), xxxvi; reprinted in *Hours in a Library* (1907), p. 282.

31 *Partial Portraits* (New York, 1888), p. 228 (London, 1894).

32 *Women and Men* (1888), p. 156.

33 Reported by Wilfred Ward, *Problems and Persons* (1903), 'Tennyson: a Reminiscence', pp. 196–217. But Leslie Stephen has it that Tennyson said this directly to George Eliot herself: 'He greatly admired her insight into character, "but did not think her so true to nature as Shakespeare and Miss Austen"' *(George Eliot* (1902), p. 192).

34 Not surprisingly, a storm of criticism met the book on its publication in Britain, with Andrew Lang and William Archer leading the opposition (documented in *Criticism and Fiction and Other Essays* (1959), edd. C. M. & R. Kirk, pp. 93–4).

35 Introduction, *Pride and Prejudice* (1918), p.v.

36 *Lippincott's Monthly Magazine*, 1891, xlvii; reprinted *Essay in Miniature* (1892).

37 'Guests', *In the Dozy Hours* (1894).

38 'The Royal Road of Fiction', *Varia* (1897).

39 See n. 35 above.

40 'A Plea for Humor', in *Points of View* (1891), pp. 18–19.

41 Vol. xlvii. 811.

42 *Monthly Review*, vii. 159–60.

43 New York, p. xxx.

44 Pp. ix, xv.

45 27 August 1904, pp. 611–12. Students of linguistic anthropology will want to follow the use of this word in *The Letters of Sir Walter Raleigh* (1926). Raleigh was a tuft-hunter with a facetious turn of mind and his disquisitions upon the 'Collins' are instructive and amusing, see especially his discussion of the variants, the 'anti-Collins' and the 'Super Collins' (ii. 466).

46 '*Emma* and the legend of Jane Austen' (1957), reprinted in *The Emma Casebook* (1968), ed. David Lodge, p. 149.

VII

1 See Section III, n. 8.

2 6 November 1897, p. 374.

3 *Academy*, 5 February 1898, p. 148.

4 *Academy* (1898), lv. 70.

5 5 March 1898, pp. 262–4.

6 *Selected Letters of E.M. Forster: 1879–1920* (1983), edd. Mary Lago & P.N. Furbank, i. 23–4. In 1924, reviewing the Clarendon edition, Forster welcomed the authentic, historical illustrations: 'they purge his mind of the lamentable Hugh Thompson [sic]. Never again will he tolerate illustrations which illustrate nothing but the obscurity of the artist' (from passage not given in No. 30).

7 'The Royal Road of Fiction', *Varia* (1898), p. 215.

8 No. 22a.

9 P. lx.

10 *Jane Austen: A Bibliography* (1929), p. xxii.

11 *Pride and Prejudice*, pp. xxi–xxii.

12 P. xxiv.

13 P. xxv.

14 P. v.

15 P. xiv.

16 P. v.

17 P. xv.

18 P. 2. The *Memoir* text is 'her' not 'Jane Austen's'.

19 11 October 1902, p. 384.

20 P. vii.

21 P. x.

22 P. xi.

23 P. xv.

24 P. xi.

25 P. xvi. It is useful to recall that Mrs Browning's similarly caustic remarks to Ruskin (quoted in Section I n. 51) written in 1855, were first published in 1897.

26 P. iii.

27 P. 304.

28 P. xvi.

29 The *History* was a very popular work. In 1905, there was a new and revised edition which included 72 plates. This edition reached a tenth impression by 1923 and the last edition, 1924, carried the text unchanged from 1898.

30 Oscar Wilde lent his support to these views in his popular *Woman's World* column. In January 1889, he declared that 'Women seem to me to possess just what our Literature wants—a light touch, a delicate hand, a graceful mode of treatment, and an unstudied felicity of phrase.' George Eliot's style he found 'far too cumbrous' and Charlotte Brontë's 'too exaggerated'. ('Some Literary Ladies', *Woman's World*, January 1889; reprinted in *A Critic in Pall Mall* (1910), p. 129.)

Elsewhere, he voiced his preference for novels which give pleasure to 'the artistic instincts', rather than fiction of the 'reformers', 'pamphleteers' and 'earnest sociologists', drawing our attention 'to social anomalies, and social forms of injustice'. (*A Critic in Pall Mall*, p. 211 (an undated comment, culled from one of his reviews)).

31 Unsigned review of *The History of David Grieve*, April 1892.
32 'The Novels of Mr George Gissing', *Contemporary Review*, August 1897.
33 Ed. M.E. Townsend. The solecism 'Elliott' appears throughout; and there is a delightful printer's creation, 'Bellynch Hall'.
34 Janet Harper, 'The Renascence of Jane Austen', *Westminster Review* (1900), cliii. 442.
35 *History of Nineteenth Century Literature* (1896).
36 Prefatory eassy, *English Prose Selection*, Vol. v, 1896.
37 April 1897.
38 Thronton Wilder, *American Characteristics and other Essays,* ed. Donald Gallup (1979), p. 101.

In 'Noting the Nature of France', Wilder wrote 'Jane Austen was pure storyteller and her works are outlasting those of apparently more formidable rivals i.e. Meredith and George Eliot, who used fiction as the vehicle for their reflections' (*New York Times*, 8 January 1939) Gallup, p. 118.
39 *Pall Mall Gazette*, 25 July 1895, reviewing *Charades &c. written a hundred years ago by Jane Austen and her family* (1895), ed. M.A. Austen-Leigh.
40 P. xxxiii. Unfortunately, more commonplace views abounded. William J. Long thanked Phelps for his advice in the preparation of *English Literature: its history and its significance for the life of the English-speaking world* (Boston, 1909), a textbook for schools. Jane Austen (pp. 437–9) is announced as a writer of 'charm and genius...so lately rediscovered...' Scott's 'Big Bow-wow strain' is quoted. The single American angle is in the comment that 'Her works have an exquisite perfection that is lacking in most of our writers of fiction.' The entry is unchanged in the 1919 edition.

Long was also the author of *Outlines of English and American Literature* (Boston, 1917), where he writes of Jane Austen (pp. 245–8) 'as a forest flower... the little woman... is ranked by critics among the five or six greatest writers of English fiction', whose appeal is to 'mature readers (especially those who are interested in human nature)'. There is no mention of 'art' and no specifically American perspective to the entry.
41 'Jane Austen', *On Modern Literature: Lectures and Addresses by W.P. Ker* (1955), edd. T. Spencer & J. Sutherland, p. 115.

42 Edmund Clerihew Bentley, *Biography for Beginners* (1905), unnumbered pages.
43 Preface, *The Princess Casamassina* (New York Edition, 1907); *The Art of the Novel: Critical Prefaces by Henry James* (1934), ed. R.P. Blackmur, p. 67.

VIII

1 P. 263. This was an idea that attracted attention and we find it taken up by later writers. It heads the *Bookman* account, 1906, see page 76; and Amy Cruise quotes the passage in *English Literature Through The Ages* (1914 and reprinted), pp. 446–7 (1922 edn).
2 P. 266.
3 This account gained wide circulation; there was a new, revised edition in 1905 and a tenth impression of the book was issued in 1923.
4 *English Prose Selections* (1896), vol. v, Prefatory essay, Jane Austen Section.
5 The enterprise began life as a series of lectures, 'Heroes and Heroines of Fiction', which Howells gave in the Fall and early Winter of 1899.
6 *My Literary Passions* (New York, 1895), p. 247.
7 See Section VI, note 35.
8 'Jane Austen's Novels', Walter Frewen Lord, October 1902, pp. 665–75.
9 'Another View of Jane Austen's Novels', Annie Gladstone, January 1903, pp. 113–21.

IX

1 Quoted by Lionel Trilling, 'Mansfield Park', in *The Opposing Self* (1955), p. 209.
2 Twain to Howells, 21 July 1885: 'I bored through Middlemarch during the past week, with its labored & tedious analyses of feelings & motives, its paltry & tiresome people, its unexciting & uninteresting story, & its frequent blinding flashes of single-sentence poetry, philosophy, wit, & what-not, & nearly died from the over-work. I wouldn't read another of those books for a farm.' *Mark Twain—Howells Letters* (1960), edd. H.N. Smith & W.M. Gibson, ii. 533–4.
3 *Mark Twain—Howells Letters* (1960), edd. H.N. Smith & W.M. Gibson, ii. 769. Letter of 1 May 1903.
4 Quoted by Alan Gribben, *Mark Twain's Library: A Reconstruction* (1980), i. 33.

5 'Mark Twain and the Art of Writing', *Harpers Magazine* (October 1920), pp. 635–43; reprinted in *Essays on English*, 1921.

6 *Essays on English*, p. 265.

7 As Note 1 above.

8 MS DV 201 (De Voto numbering), in the Mark Twain Papers, The Bancroft Library, University of California, Berkeley.

9 *Selected Letters of W.D. Howells* (1983), edd. G. Arms & C.K. Lohmann, vi. 116, 29 June 1917.

10 P. xxxvii.

11 P. xliii.

12 P. x.

13 P. 91.

14 P. 102.

15 P. 122.

16 P. 175.

17 P. 108.

18 Pp. 106–8.

19 Vol. ii. 416–23: Chapter Six, 'Jane Austen, some lady Novelists, her contemporaries, and others'.

20 *The English Novel* (1894), pp. 263, 65.

21 Vol. II. ii, p. 936.

22 P. iii.

23 P. 178.

X

1 P. 150.

2 P. xxi.

3 P. 128.

4 The tranquillising effect of the novels, their refreshing and restorative power, is a constant theme of the appreciative criticism. In 1913, writing from Canada, Rupert Brooke told Cathleen Nesbitt how he turned to Jane Austen in 'A bad fit of home-sickness' (*Letters* (1968), ed. G. Keynes, pp. 479–80).

5 According to *The Times* Obituary (22 April 1960) by Dr L.F. Powell, Dr Chapman planned the complete Clarendon edition in 1912 with his wife's assistance. The obituary by Mary Lascelles for *Proceedings of the British Academy* (1961), xlvii. 362, records that Katherine Metcalfe's proposal to edit *Pride and Prejudice* from the original editions was recommended to the Delegates of the Oxford University Press by Walter Raleigh, an adviser to the Press, influential as the first holder of the Chair of English Literature at Oxford (since 1904) and regarded as an authority on the novel for his 'short sketch of its history', much reprinted since its first appearance in 1894.

6 P. iii.

7 P. vii.

8 P. xxii. Did Miss Metcalfe's comments provide the stimulus for 'Two masters of Comedy', an unsigned leading article in the *Times Literary Supplement*, 25 August 1927, pp. 565–6? The argument follows hers very closely, also some of the phrasing. The contributor was M. Gray (unidentified).

9 Vol. i. 191–201.

10 1924, pp. 449–50.

11 We see this in Arnold Bennett's popular guide, *Literary Taste: How to form it* (1909), p. 100, through to the edition revised by Frank Swinnerton, published as a Pelican Special in 1938 (p. 138).

12 17 May 1913, in a review of the *Life and Letters*.

13 P. viii.

14 P. 400.

15 P. vii.

16 According to the evidence marshalled in the *Life and Letters* (pp. 62–3), the picture was painted in 1790/91, when Jane Austen was 15. Sir Oliver Miller, the present Surveyor of the Queen's Pictures, has expressed his doubts about its attribution to Zoffany and the belief that it was painted before 1800. His conclusion is that 'On all counts, therefore, the portrait should be dismissed from the iconography of Jane Austen' (*The Jane Society Report*, 1983, pp. 15, 17). R. W. Chapman also dismissed the picture: 'It is a portrait of a young girl which can be dated by the costume to about 1805 (when J.A. was thirty) or later' (*Jane Austen: Facts and Problems* (1948), p. 213.) But the case has recently been re-opened. The *Sunday Times* for 12 May 1985, p. 13, quotes the arguments of the present owner of the Zoffany portrait, Mr Henry Rice (a direct descendant of Edward Austen) and art historian Madeliene Marsh, that the picture is indeed of Jane Austen; that, for a child's dress, the style is of the period 1775–95; and that the artist 'is clearly not Zoffany, but almost certainly' Ozias Humphry, 'perhaps commissioned by Francis Austen'.

17 *Speaker*, 26 February 1898, p. 262.

18 Henry Seidel Canby, April 1915, p. 612.

19 10 May 1913, p. 513.

20 *The Freewoman*, 1 August 1912. There was a running discussion at this time on the relationship between sexuality and creativity.

21 *The Freewoman*, 11 July 1912, 'Spinsters and Art': 'how many books are written by spinsters, how many more for spinsters. In all these men are drawn as strong gods'; and she ended the piece with a harsh axiom: 'a spinster is usually a sentimentalist, and therefore incapable of art'.

22 In a review of Robert Frost's *North of Boston* (1914), *Poetry*, December 1914.

23 In a review of *Life and Letters*, *Edinburgh Review* (July 1913), ccxviii. 186, 187.

24 'Editor's Easy Chair', *Harper's*, November 1913.

25 Such 'pilgrimage' essays are to be found in *Atlantic Monthly*, *Scribner's North American Review*, *The Nation*, *Harper's*, *Lippincott's* and other magazines. Their hey-day was from 1860 to 1910 and their high point, in literary terms, is seen in the work of Mark Twain, Howells and James. James was the grand tourist, his essays reprinted from the magazines and, in turn selected in different combinations, for successive volumes (see *Transatlantic Sketches* (1875), *Foreign Parts* (1883), *Portraits of Places* (1883) and *English Hours* (1905)). Alongside these real pilgrims were the fictional varieties, again, strongly represented in the European novels of James, and epitomised in the title of *The Passionate Pilgrim* (1875).

Thus the 'pilgrimage' essay is a voluminous genre, with an honourable pedigree; and the sub-group relating to Jane Austen is an important biographical/appreciative offshoot. The most notable example, signed A.M. Waterston, appeared in *Atlantic Monthly* for February 1863. Opening with a visit to 'the Old Cathedral of Winchester' and the grave within, it takes the reader on a privileged and informed tour of the Austen territory, concluding with a visit to the home of Admiral Austen, none other than Francis Austen, the novelist's brother.

A.M. Waterston was in fact Mrs Robert Waterston (née Anna Quincy), sister of the Miss Quincy quoted in the *Memoir* (see Section I, note 21). From documentation in *Austen Papers 1704–1856* (1942) by Richard Arthur Austen-Leigh, ch. 10 'Austens and Quincys', we know that Mrs Waterston visited Frances Austen in June 1856. She advised him of her travels: 'To day we leave London, and go to Winchester a pilgrimage to *her* resting place which has given more interest to me in the old Cathedral, than all its buried Kings.'

Another notable 'pilgrimage' essay, eight thousand words long, appeared in *Harper's New Monthly Magazine* for July 1870, complete with a portrait of Jane Austen and three illustrations. Like the *Atlantic* essay, this too opens with the pilgrim's arrival at Winchester in search of the obscure memorial slab. It is this literary tradition that Howells affectionately plays with.

26 The seeking-out of the slab—noting its simplicity, obscurity and the general indifference with which it was regarded—is one of the distinguishing features of the 'pilgrimage' essay. Indeed, much was made of this typically English modesty as something to be treasured. The view of the English press was slightly less respectful, though self-congratulatory nonetheless: 'With truly English reticence, the flat stone under which she lies bears no record of her life's work. For all the

information which the passing stranger can gather from the inscription which marks her grave, Jane Austen might have been the most commonplace spinster that ever tended dogs and canary birds under the shadow of an English cathedral' (*Spectator*, 2 July 1898, p. 23, a notice of *Sense and Sensibility*, The Winchester Edition). The comment is fair. On the slab, Jane Austen is styled 'youngest daughter of the late Revd. George Austen'; and the only hint of her achievement as a writer is in the guarded reference to 'the extraordinary endowments of her mind'. The brass plate set in the wall nearby, which does record her authorship, was put there by Austen-Leigh in 1872, out of the proceeds of the *Memoir*. The memorial window above was erected in 1900.

27 *Nation*, 2 October 1913.

28 *New Witness* (1917), vol. x; *Living Age* (1917), ccxciv; reprinted *The Uses of Diversity* (1920).

29 Reprinted in *A Bookman's Letters* (1913), pp. 165, 166.

30 Pp. 232–3.

31 Pp. 235–6.

32 P. 236.

33 P. 49.

34 Unpublished letter dated 10 November 1913.

35 P. 319.

36 P. 78.

37 P. 207.

38 P. 201.

39 'Cecilia's Godchild', pp. 56–67.

40 'Books Masculine and Feminine', p. 52.

41 In Volume xii, 1915.

42 Harold Hannyngton Child (1869–1945), literary journalist, voluminous contributor to *TLS*, reviewer of *The Art of Jane Austen* by Mary Lascelles (see below, p. 124). In the Cambridge History, Child is styled 'Sometime Scholar of Brasenose College, Oxford'.

43 P. 237.

44 P. 238.

45 P. 238.

46 P. 242.

47 P. 242.

48 P. 242.

49 P. 244.

50 Review, 'The Novels of Dostoevsky', *Spectator*, 11 April 1914.

51 *Dialogues of Alfred North Whitehead* (1934), ed. Lucien Price, p. 30. The Bloomsburyite intimacy is conveyed in a remark by Strachey in a letter of 3 May 1925: recounting a scene and snatch of dialogue he witnessed at the Zoo, he comments 'the whole

scene was decidedly Jane Austen' (*Bloomsbury/Freud: The Letters to James and Alix Strachey 1924–1925* (1986)), edd. Perry Mewel and Walter Kendrick, p. 255).

52 P. 193.

53 In 'Fiction in the Nineteenth Century', originally an article, unidentified, in the *Academy* or *Daily Chronicle* (date unknown); reprinted in *Reticence in Literature* (1915), p. 94.

54 *Peace of the Augustans* (1916); World Classics Edition (1946), p. 13.

XI

1 January 1916, p. 9.

2 'Jane Austen: An Appreciation', given 24 October 1917, *Transactions of the Royal Society of Literature*, n.s. 36, 1918, pp. 4–5.

3 P. 8.

4 P. 14.

5 Pp. 15–16, 32.

6 Walton Litz, *Jane Austen: A Study of her Artistic Development* (1965), p. 39.

7 In *The Rhetoric of Fiction* (1961), Wayne C. Booth notes that 'probably the best discussion of this double-edged problem is buried in Reginald Farrer's essay' (note to p. 245).

8 Marvin Mudrick, *Jane Austen: Irony as Defense and Discovery* (1952).

9 *Letters of Sir Walter Raleigh*, ed. Lady Raleigh (1926), ii. 232. Swinnerton discussed Raleigh and his letters in his monthly London letter to the New York *Bookman* (reprinted in *A London Bookman*, 1928). He admired Raleigh's 'good judgement' and 'good analyses' but found them 'destructive... cold, factitious... and hard' (p. 248).

10 'Jane Austen', *Athenaeum*, 5 and 19 September 1919; reprinted *Bookman* (New York), vol. i, 1919–20; and adapted as Introduction to *Pride and Prejudice*, 1923. Frank Swinnerton (1884–1983), journalist, critic and novelist, was one of the earliest critics to relate the criticism of Henry James to Jane Austen. But Swinnerton held his own view of her as a 'conscious' and 'profound' artist.

11 P. v.

12 P. xix.

13 P. ix.

14 P. xi.

15 P. vii. Austen-Leigh remarks upon her 'playfulness of spirit' in the *Memoir*, p. 175.

16 Review of *The Watsons* concluded by L. Oulton (1923), reprinted in *A London Bookman* (1928), p. 45.

17 'Jane Austen: a personal aspect', *Quarterly Review*, ccxxxii. 301–17.
18 P. 8.
19 28 October 1920, p. 699.
20 *Athenaeum*, 3 December 1920, pp. 758–9.
21 P. 219.
22 *Athenaeum*, 21 November 1919. Virginia Woolf was conscious of a deficiency in her writing and admitted to it in 'A Sketch of the Past' (an unpublished autobiographical fragment, dating from the end of her life), in which she named Jane Austen with Trollope and 'perhaps Thackeray and Dickens and Tolstoy' as 'real' novelists who had succeeded in conveying both conscious life and non-being (when 'One walks, eats, sees things, deals with what has to be done'). She concluded, 'I have never been able to do both' (in *Moments of Being* (1970), ed. Jeane Schulking, p. 70).
23 *Nation*, 29 November 1919.
24 See *The Diary of Virginia Woolf: Vol. I: 1915–19* (1977), ed. A.O. Bell: entries for 28 November and 5 December 1919.
25 P. 14.
26 In issues for March 18, 25; April 1, 8, 15.
27 30 December 1921, p. 8.

XII

1 Pp. 272–3.
2 Ibid.
3 P. 273.
4 Pp. 141–2; reprinted in *The Portrait of a scholar and other Essays written in Macedonia 1916–1918*, pp. 65–79. There, we learn that Chapman wrote the article while serving at the front, for it carries the note 'Y4 (Smol Hill) July 1918'.
5 Pp. 81–2.
6 In January 1920, Chapman was appointed Secretary to the Delegates of the Oxford University Press; in effect, he had the powers of a publisher.
7 It would be amusing to suppose that Farrer's letter was the inspiration of Chapman's edition. However, according to Chapman himself, he planned the Oxford Jane Austen with his wife Katharine Metcalfe but was then delayed by the war and his young family.
8 P. ii.
9 P. i.
10 Vol. xvii (1928), p. 381.

11 1 November 1923, p. 723.
12 Vol. lxv. 191.
13 P. 193.
14 Pp. ix-xv.
15 *New Statesman* (1922), xix. 419–20.
16 *New Statesman* (1922–23), xx. 662, 664.
17 *Nation* (1923), xxxiv. 433–4.
18 *Nation*, 21 March 1925; reprinted *Abinger Harvest* (1936).
19 *Bookman* (New York) 1925; reprinted *A London Bookman* (1928).
20 Vol. xv (1925–26), 389.

XIII

1 Vol. xii. 413.
2 Vol. xv (1925–26), p. 387.
3 *The Bookman*, February 1927, pp. 256–8.
4 Pp. v, 13.
5 Quoted Chapman, *Critical Bibliography*, p. 45.
6 Edn. 1957, p. 965. The first sentence of this extract was treated to a wide circulation in *A Short History of English Literature* by Ifor Evans, p. 235. First published in 1940; in the 1983 edition Penguin claimed sales of 750,000 copies.
7 A glimpse of these 'elderly gentlemen' is given in a letter (2.8.1923) from the American Mr Justice Holmes to an English judge, Sir Frederick Pollock: 'The other day Laski wrote glorifying your Saint Miss Austin [sic]. I must get *Pride and Prejudice*: but have I dared confess to you that the last time I tackled her I found her—let me whisper it very softly—a bore?' (*Holmes-Pollock Letters*, ed. Mark De Wolfe Howe (2nd ed., 1961) (2 vols. in one), ii. 120).
8 *Essays by Divers Hands* (Transactions of the Royal Society of Literature), 1927, vii. 82.
9 Pp. xi-xii.
10 *Essays by Divers Hands* (1928), viii. 21–40.
11 See p. 81.
12 See Bibliography, Trilling on *Emma*.
13 'The "Irresponsibility" of Jane Austen', in *Critical Essays on Jane Austen* (1968), ed. B.C. Southam, p. 1. One clue to Garrod's 'outlook on life' may lie in the biographical facts. Garrod (1878–1960) was a distinguished classical scholar who moved to English studies in the 1920s. He spent much of his life at Oxford, unmarried, where he had rooms in Merton College for over fifty years.
14 *Essays by Divers Hands* (1931), xi. 17–34.
15 *Apropos of Lady Chatterley's Lover* (1930), p. 58.
16 P. 7.

XIV

1 Originally given as a lecture at the John Rylands Library (14.3.1928); printed in the *Bulletin of the John Rylands Library* (vol. xii, no. 2, July 1928) and reprinted as a separate pamphlet in 1928.

2 Pp. 166–7.

3 P. 167.

4 P. 177.

5 P. 178. These musical analogies were not taken up at the time. Recently, Brigid Brophy has, to great effect, compared the work of Jane Austen with the music of Mozart.

6 'Is the Novel Decaying?', *Cassells' Weekly*, 28 March 1923. This article, together with 'Mr Bennett and Mr Brown' and the continuing debate, is documented in *Virginia Woolf: The Critical Heritage* (1975), edd. Robin Majumdar & Allen McLaurin, pp. 112–37.

7 *E.M. Forster: Commonplace Book* (1985), ed. Philip Gardner, pp. 15–16. The section on Jane Austen is pp. 45–53 of *Aspects*.

8 See p. 95.

9 Pp. 42–7, 56–9. E.F. Benson also reviewed *Aspects* critically. 'We resent Lady Bertram being classed as a "round" character merely because she saw the elopement of Julia and the infidelity of Maria "in all its enormity". That does not make her round: it is indeed a noble manifestation of her adorable flatness which rivals that of Mr Woodhouse.' ('A literary mystification', *Spectator*, 29 October 1927.)

10 *Guardian*, 28 March 1888.

11 P. 650. She was not alone in this attack. Edmund Wilson commented on American critics who 'forget critical standards in their devotion to the great common causes: the cause of an American national literature in independence of English literature, and the cause of contemporary American ideas as against the ideas of the last generation' ('The All-Star Literary Vaudeville', 30 June 1926 (source not given), reprinted in *A Literary Chronicle* (1956), p. 77).

12 Vol. xvi, No. 1. Reprinted in *The Second Common Reader*, 'How should one read a book?'.

13 'The Novel as Work of Art', *Dial* (Chicago), July 1927, p. 41.

14 *Life and Letters*, October 1928; reprinted in *The Second Common Reader*, 'The Niece of an Earl'.

15 *Yale Review*, July 1927, p. 650.

16 P. 180.

17 P. 484.

18 P. 484.

19 P. 485.

20 P. 487.

21 P. 488. The question of the sparcity of detail that is provided in the novels and the need for the reader to respond to that detail is argued by Nabokov in *Lectures on Literature* (1980) (the lectures were actually delivered in the 1950s). In a prefatory section, 'Good Readers and Good Writers', Nabokov wrote, 'We must see things and hear things, we must visualize the rooms, the clothes, the manners of an author's people. The color of Fanny Price's eyes in *Mansfield Park* and the furnishing of her cold little room are important' (p. 4). His lecture notes for *Mansfield Park* include a map he prepared of Sotherton Court, a sketch of the layout of Mansfield Park, an account of Fanny's horse rides and a map of England tracing the action of the novel in the movement of characters and the changes of scene.

    These ideas are also pursued in 'Jane Austen's Sleight-of-hand' by Margaret Lane, *Jane Austen Society Report 1962*: reprinted *Purely for Pleasure* (1966), pp. 95–107.

22 P. 116. Gender as an artistic determinant is a subject which inspires some of the most asinine and hilarious comments on Jane Austen. In the 1890s, A.B. Walkley tried to explain his preference for the portrayal of her older men: 'This is accounted for, no doubt, by the fact that spinsters who write novels have the best chance of observing the foibles of the other sex in their papas and uncles' (*Frames of Mind* (1899), pp. 110–11). The answer to this kind of nonsense is to be found in ch. 31, 'Men's Novels and Women's Novels', in *Women and Men* (New York, 1888), by T.W. Higginson.

23 'On Jane Austen', pp. 99–102.

24 *Bookman* (New York), vol. lxix; reprinted *Granite and Rainbow* (1958), pp. 114–19.

25 P. 137.

26 *The Forum*, March 1929.

27 'On not knowing Greek', *The Common Reader* (1925). I cannot discover that this essay was published separately or when it was written.

28 Farrer made a similarly striking classical comparison between Jane Austen and Euripides (p. 271).

29 P. 4.

30 Entry 18 July 1928, *The Journals of Arnold Bennett, 1921–28*, ed. Newman Flower (1933), iii. 267.

31 P. 121.

32 P. v.

33 P. 25.

34 P. 22.

35 *Times Literary Supplement*, 12 November 1931.

36 14 February 1930, p. 236.

XV

1 See Section XIII, note 10.
2 10 November 1932.
3 *New Statesman*, 26 November 1932, p. 659.
4 1933, ix. 291–3.
5 Letter to Ethel Smyth, 20 November 1932, *The Letters of Virginia Woolf, 1932–35* (1979), ed. Nigel Nicolson, v. 127.
6 Letter to Ethel Smyth, 29 November 1932, v. 131.
7 20 November 1936, vi. 87.
8 14 January 1933.
9 As note 4.
10 'A Treat for Janeites', *McCall's Magazine*, December 1933; reprinted in *Long, Long Ago* (1963), p. 204.
11 *Spectator*, 2 November 1934.
12 P. 393.
13 *Jane Austen* (1935); reprinted *Poets and Storytellers* (1949).
14 *Dictionary of National Biography* (1885), ii. 260.
15 *New York Herald Tribune*, 16 October 1927; shorter version, quoted here, *Nation*, 12 November 1927, pp. 247–8.
16 *Spectator*, 12 July 1935.
17 23 May 1936, vi. 22.
18 *Time and Tide*, 27 July 1935; reprinted in *Johnsonian and other Essays and Reviews* (1953), pp. 197–201.
19 'Jane Austen: artist on ivory', 15 August 1936; reprinted in *The English Novel* (1936), ed. Derek Verschoyle and *Novelists on Novels* (1962) ed. Louis Kronenberger.
20 See pp. 715–17, 736–7 (1947 reprint).
21 P. 37.
22 P. 80.
23 P. 60.
24 P. 207.

XVI

1 Pp. 356, 357.
2 P. v.
3 P. v.
4 P. 357.
5 P. v.
6 P. vi.
7 Pp. 219–20.
8 P. 356.

9 Vol. xxxv (1940), pp. 399–401.
10 27 October 1939.
11 Vol. clvi (1939), p. 509.

XVII

1 *Scrutiny*, vii (March 1940), pp. 346–62.
2 *Literature and Society* (1938), p. 207.
3 Private communication from the author.
4 *Critical Bibliography*, p. 52.
5 Marvin Mudrick, *Jane Austen: Irony as Defense and Discovery* (1952), footnote to p. vii, where 'Regulated Hatred' and Farrer's essay are cited as 'The valuable—if brief—general introductions to Jane Austen'; and *Jane Austen and Her Art* is said to contain 'much perceptive comment persistently marred by an infusion of outline-softening gentle-Janeism...'

   Professor Mudrick announces his critical bearings in a twin epigraph: 'It seems vain to expect that discourse upon novelists will contain anything new for us until we have really and clearly and accurately seen their books' (Percy Lubbock, *The Craft of Fiction*) and the lines from 'Regulated Hatred' quoted here on page 128.
6 *Scrutiny*, X (1941–42), pp. 61–2.
7 P. 90.
8 P. 61.
9 P. 62.
10 *The Writing of Fiction* (1925), pp. 62–3.

1. Critical Views

1869

Jane Austen section, *The Book of Authors*, 1869, ed. W.C.
Russell, 402–3.

A standard collection of critical opinions, several times
reprinted. These quotations, together with those assembled in
the *Memoir* formed the inheritance of earlier views readily
available after 1870. Sources have been added within square
brackets. I have been unable to locate the source of the
sentence attributed to Lewes. In the *Westminster Review*, July
1852, he said something very similar: 'the greatest artist that
has ever written, using the term to signify the most perfect
mastery over the means to her end'.

Shakspeare has neither equal nor second. But among the writers
who... have approached nearest to the manner of the great master
we have no hesitation in placing Jane Austen, a woman of whom
England may justly be proud. She has given us a multitude of
characters, all in a certain sense commonplace, all such as we meet
every day. Yet they are all as perfectly discriminated from each
other as if they were the most eccentric of human beings.
—*Macaulay*. [*Edinburgh Review*, January 1843]

Miss Austen is only shrewd and observant—*C. Brontë*. [letter to
G.H. Lewes 12.1.1848]

One of the greatest writers, one of the greatest painters of human
character, and one of the writers with the nicest sense of means to
an end that ever lived.—*G.H. Lewes*.

By the way, did you know Jane Austen, authoress of some
novels which have a great deal of nature in them? nature in ordinary
and middle life, to be sure, but valuable from its strong
resemblance and correct drawing? I wonder which way she carried
her pail?—*Scott to Joanna Baillie*. [letter 10.2.1822]

Miss Austen has never been so popular as she deserved to be.
Intent on fidelity of delineation, and averse to the commonplace

tricks of her art, she has not in this age of literary quackery received her reward. Ordinary readers have been apt to judge of her as Partridge, in Fielding's novel, judged of Garrick... She was too natural for them. It seemed to them as if there could be very little merit in making people act and talk so exactly like the people they saw around them every day. They did not consider that the highest triumph of art consists in its concealment; and here the art was so little perceptible that they believed there was none.—*Edinburgh Review*, July 1830. (T.H. Lister)

2. R.H. Hutton on the *Memoir*

1869

From an unsigned review, 'The Memoir of Miss Austen', *Spectator*, 25 December 1869, 1533–5.

Richard Holt Hutton (1826–97) was a prolific literary journalist and man-of-letters; from 1861 onwards, joint-editor of the *Spectator*. For his contemporary readership, this judgment of Jane Austen would have been seen as an authoritative placing of the novelist.

This little volume will be eagerly read by the now, we hope, very numerous admirers of Miss Austen's exquisitely finished novels, and not without real pleasure, though also with considerable regret to find how very little biographical material for any complete picture of her, remains in her family. Mr Austen-Leigh has done all in his power; he has prefixed a very attractive and expressive portrait of his aunt; a great deal of pleasant gossip about the manners and times in which she was brought up; a very sensible and amusing letter by her great-great-grandmother, written from Constantinople (where her husband was ambassador) in 1666 to her daughter (Miss Austen's great-grandmother), proving that the excellent sense and sobriety of the novelist had been handed down to her through four generations at least; a few amusing anecdotes about Miss Austen's great-uncle, the Master of Balliol, Dr Theophilus Leigh, showing that real wit as well as sound sense was indigenous in the elder branches of the family; a few lively family letters of Miss Austen's own, showing how dear to her her own creations were, and how well she estimated her own real powers; a few delightful reminiscences of her by nephews and nieces; and one piece of very good literary banter, a sketch by Miss Austen of the novel she should be compelled to write if she followed the suggestions of her many counsellors; and, finally, one or two treasured family traditions of Miss Austen's private explanations of matters referred to in the novels, but not there completely elucidated. The only thing that we could have well spared in Mr Austen-Leigh's little book is his chapter of "testimonies" to Miss Austen's originality and power as a novelist, which is, to our minds, out of place and out of taste. No one with a grain of literary sense doubts her wonderful originality and artistic power. To dispute it now is simply to prove that the disputant does not know what he is talking about. Hence the chapter in question is a little too like a publisher's list of testimonies from the press to the worth of some bran-new writer's book. Who would not smile to see a biographer of Sir Walter Scott place at the end of his memoir testimonies by critics however respectable,—unless, indeed, they were artists as great as Goethe, for example,—to Sir Walter's eminence as a writer of romance? We do not, of course, object to hear the testimony of so great a master of the craft as Sir Walter Scott to Miss Austen's skill, especially when he speaks of his infinite inferiority to her in all the subtleties of discrimination between the finer shades of human character. But when a biographer of Miss Austen cites the approbation even of Archbishop Whately, or Robert Southey, or Dr Whewell, for his heroine's works, and still more when he quotes the praise of persons of so very slight a literary weight as the late Marquis of Lansdowne or the late Lord Carlisle, we feel jarred by a certain deficiency in his perception of the true dignity of his subject. It *is* of some interest to know how stupid was the audience to whose ears Miss Austen made her first appeal,—how little they could understand the delicate truth and humour of her pictures. But to tell us that many worthy persons have since enjoyed her writings thoroughly, is like telling us that many have felt the warmth of summer. Specific testimony of that kind implies that the fact attested needs attestation,—that it is not matter of common notoriety and universal recognition, which, as regards Miss Austen's merits, we are happy to say that it is. But with this only exception, it seems to us that Mr Austen-Leigh has made out of his very slender materials a very welcome and pleasant little volume, which all admirers of Miss Austen will eagerly read.

We learn from it that Miss Austen lived, like most of the upper-middle class of that age, in a world which was not one of by any means high pressure, in spite of the great political events brewing and bursting on the Continent of Europe. It could not certainly be said of *her*, in spite of the date of her birth (1775), and that she was just old enough to understand how vast and fearful was the French Revolution when it burst upon the world,—

> 'But we, brought forth and reared in hours
> Of change, alarm, surprise,—
> What shelter to grow ripe is ours?
> What leisure to grow wise?'

For Miss Austen's novels and her life,—so far as we learn its tenor from this volume,—was one of perfect calm, and it was to this calm that we owe that fine, sedate humour and gentle irony which imply a settled standard of life, and an estimate of human follies quite unmixed with bitterness of motive or scepticism of inference. There was no mockery in Miss Austen's irony. However heartily we laugh at her pictures of human imbecility, we are never tempted to think that contempt or disgust for human nature suggested the satire...

A real enjoyment (which had no malice in it) of the futilities and false hits of what is called human intelligence, and an apt power of just so far generalizing, and putting sufficient emphasis upon, its mistakes, as to sharpen the outline and bring it out clear against sober reason, was in her not only not extinguished by her love for those whom she laughed at, but probably somewhat sharpened by it...

It is a great comfort to us to have so complete a verification of the theory we have always cherished,—that Miss Austen's personal character was a sort of medium between the heroine of *Pride and Prejudice*, Elizabeth Bennet, and the heroine of *Persuasion*, Anne Elliot,—that she had all the vivacity of the one and all the gentleness and sweetness of the other. Her own great favourite, it appears, among her heroines, was the former; but was she quite aware that there is in Elizabeth Bennet just the very slightest touch of that want of refinement which we may fairly attribute to the influence of such a mother,—and indeed, in some sense of such a father as hers, for Mr Bennet, dry and keen as is his humour, is too indifferent to the feelings of the persons he meets to have the manners of a perfect gentleman,—and to the general effect of the society of Meryton? Anne Elliot, though without the bright and mischievous playfulness of Elizabeth Bennet, is a far more perfect lady, has far more of the grace and refinement which we find from this short biography were the most distinguishing characteristics of the writer. The portrait prefixed to the volume,—a very remarkable one,—entirely bears out this double likeness to Anne Elliot and Elizabeth Bennet. It is a small head, with very sweet lively eyes, and a fullness about the face which seems to speak of health and spirit, but the air of high breeding and gentleness of nature is deeply impressed upon it. It is refinement, playfulness, and alertness, rather than depth of intellect, which the face seems to express. The little head is carried with great spirit, with a certain consciousness of seeing rapidly beneath the surface of life, and with an air of enjoying its own rapidity of vision, that speaks of the *ease* of power, and of power well appreciated by its owner. That Miss Austen did fully appreciate her own power,—appreciate, we mean, in the sense of truly estimating it, both what it could do and what it could not,—and did also appreciate the stupidity of those who did not understand her at all, and yet pretended to give her advice, this book gives ample proof...

Slight as the memoir is, then, we are heartily grateful for it. It is always a pleasure to know that any popular writer *was* what he or she 'must have been,'—so much easier is it to construct for ourselves a 'must have been,' than to draw a really sound inference as to the 'was.' But the inference is easier and more likely to be true when an author's works give us so strong a sense at once of the depth and the *limits* of the genius which created them, as Miss Austen's. It is impossible to suppose that the deeper problems of life weighed very oppressively on a mind which touches them so lightly and so gently as Miss Austen's. It is clear she did not at any time *arraign* either human nature or human society for their shortcomings and positive sins, as our modern novelists, George Eliot, or Thackeray, or even Mrs Gaskell, either do, or try to do.

She was content to take human society and human folly as they were, and to like while she laughed, instead of arraigning because she loved. And thus the limited work she had to do, she achieved with greater perfection and fineness and delicacy of touch than almost any other English writer with whom we are acquainted. Never was a definite literary field so clearly marked out and so perfectly mastered as by Miss Austen.

3. Anne Thackeray on Jane Austen

1871

From an essay, 'Jane Austen', *Cornhill Magazine*, 1871, xxxiv. 158–74. Reprinted in *Littell's Modern Age*, 1871, ccx. 643–53; *Toilers and Spinsters*, 1874, 35–71; *A Book of Sibyls*, 1883, 197–229.

Anne Isabella Thackeray (1837–1919), eldest daughter of the novelist, was a novelist, essayist and biographer. According to Virginia Woolf, she was 'the un-acknowledged source of much that remains in men's minds about the Victorian age' (see page 26).

A review of the 1817 *Memoir*, this is, in effect, a *belle-lettriste* essay (running to 9000 words), by far the most influential of all the popularising accounts of Jane Austen. It opens with an extract from the conversation in Chapter 9 of *Pride and Prejudice*, where Bingley and Elizabeth are discussing the 'study' of 'character'.

Appended is a passage illustrating the heightened sentimentalism of the revised version printed twelve years later in *A Book of Sibyls*.

These people belong to a whole world of familiar acquaintances, who are, notwithstanding their old-fashioned dresses and quaint expressions, more alive to us than a great many of the people among whom we live. We know so much more about them to begin with. Notwithstanding a certain reticence and self-control which seems to belong to their age, and with all their quaint dresses, and ceremonies, and manners, the ladies and gentlemen in *Pride and Prejudice* and its companion novels seem like living people out of our own acquaintance transported bodily into a bygone age, represented in the half-dozen books that contain Jane Austen's works. Dear books! bright, sparkling with wit and animation, in which the homely heroines charm, the dull hours fly, and the very bores are enchanting.

Could we but study our own bores as Miss Austen must have studied hers in her country village, what a delightful world this might be!—a world of Norris's economical great walkers, with dining-room tables to dispose of; of Lady Bertrams on sofas, with their placid 'Do not act anything improper, my dear; Sir Thomas would not like it;' of Bennets, Goddards, Bates's; of Mr Collins's; of Rushbrooks, with two-and-forty speeches apiece—a world of Mrs Eltons... Inimitable woman! she must be alive at this very moment, if we but knew where to find her, her basket on her arm, her nods and all-importance, with Maple Grove and the Sucklings in the background. She would be much excited were she aware how highly she is said to be esteemed by the present Chancellor of the Exchequer, who is well acquainted with Maple Grove and Selina too. It might console her for Mr Knightly's shabby marriage.

All these people nearly start out of the pages, so natural and unaffected are they, and yet they never lived except in the imagination of one lady with bright eyes, who sat down some seventy years ago to an old mahogany desk in a quiet country parlour, and evoked them for us. Of her ways and belongings we read for the first time in this little memoir written half a century after her death. For the first time we seem to hear the echo of the voice, and to see the picture of the unknown friend who has charmed us so long—charmed away dull hours, created neighbours and companions for us in lonely places, and made harmless mirth...

So we gladly welcome one more glimpse of an old friend come back with a last greeting. All those who love her name and her work, will prize this addition, small as it is, to their acquaintance with her. *Lady Susan* is a short story complete in itself. It is very unlike her later works in many respects, and scarcely equal to them, but the *Watsons* is a delightful fragment, which might belong to any of her other histories. It is bright with talk, and character, and animation. It is a story which is not *Emma*, and which is not *Pride and Prejudice*, but something between the two, and which was written—so the Preface tells us—some years before either of them was published. In this story vague shadows of future friends seem to be passing and repassing, conversing with each other, sitting down to cards, or 'jogging along the muddy road' that led to D—in Surrey. The anteghosts, if such things exist, of a Mrs Elton, of an Elizabeth Bennet, of a Darcy, meet us, only they are not ghosts at all, but very living people, with just so much resemblance to their successors as would be found no doubt between one generation and another. A cup of gruel is prepared for the master of the house: perhaps that very cup—'thin, but not too thin'—was destined in a different metempsychosis to immortality—at least such immortality as a cup of gruel might reasonably expect...

...She has a gift of telling a story in a way that has never been surpassed. She rules her places, times, characters, and marshals them with unerring precision. Her machinery is simple but complete; events group themselves so vividly and naturally in her mind that, in describing imaginary scenes, we seem not only to read them but to live them, to see the people coming and going: the gentlemen courteous and in top-boots, the ladies demure and piquant; we can almost hear them talking to one another...Jane Austen possessed both gifts of colour and of drawing. She could see human nature as it was; with near-sighted eyes, it is true; but having seen, she could combine her picture by her art, and colour it from life.

In this special gift for organization she seems almost unequalled. Her picnics are models for all future and past picnics; her combinations of feelings, of gentlemen and ladies, are so natural and life-like that reading to criticize is impossible to some of us—the scene carries us away, and we forget to look for the art by which it is recorded...

Dear Anne Elliot!—sweet, impulsive, womanly, tender-hearted—one can almost hear her voice, pleading the cause of all true women. In those days when, perhaps, people's nerves were stronger than they are now, sentiment may have existed in a less degree, or have been more ruled by judgment, it may have been calmer and more matter-of-fact; and yet Jane Austen, at the very end of her life, wrote thus. Her words seem to ring in our ears after they have been spoken. Anne Elliot must have been Jane Austen herself, speaking for the last time. There is something so true, so womanly, about her, that it is impossible not to love her. She is the bright-eyed heroine of the earlier novels, matured, chastened, cultivated, to whom fidelity has brought only greater depth and sweetness instead of bitterness and pain.

What a difficult thing it would be to sit down and try to enumerate the different influences by which our lives have been affected—influences of other lives, of art, of nature, of place and circumstance,—of beautiful sights passing before our eyes, or painful ones: seasons following in their course—hill rising on our horizons—scenes of ruin and desolation—crowded thoroughfares—sounds in our ears, jarring or harmonious—the voices of friends, calling, warning, encouraging—of preachers preaching—of people in the street below, complaining, and asking our pity. What long processions of human beings are passing before us! What trains of thought go sweeping through our brains ! Man seems a strange and ill-kept record of many and bewildering experiences. Looking at oneself—not as oneself, but as an abstract human being—one is lost in wonder at the vast complexities which have been brought to bear upon it; lost in wonder, and in disappointment perhaps, at the discordant result of so great a harmony. Only we know that the whole diapason is beyond our grasp: one man cannot hear the note of the grasshoppers, another is deaf when the cannon sounds. Waiting among these many echoes and mysteries of every kind, and light and darkness, and life and death, we seize a note or two of the great symphony, and try to sing; and because these notes happen to jar, we think all is discordant hopelessness. Then come pressing onward in the crowd of life, voices with some of the notes that are wanting to our own part—voices tuned to the same key as our own, or to an accordant one; making harmony for us as they pass us by. Perhaps this is in life the happiest of all experience, and to few of us there exists any more complete ideal.

And so now and then in our lives, when we learn to love a sweet and noble character, we all feel happier and better for the goodness and charity which is not ours, and yet which seems to belong to us while we are near it. Just as some people and states of mind affect us uncomfortably, so we seem to be true to ourselves with a truthful person, generous-minded with a generous nature; life seems less disappointing and self-seeking when we think of the just and sweet and unselfish spirits, moving untroubled among dinning and distracting influence. These are our friends in the best and noblest sense. We are the happier for their existence,—it is so much gain to us. They may have lived at some distant time, we may never have met face to face, or we may have known them and been blessed by their love; but their light shines from afar, their life is for us and with us in its generous example; their song is for our ears, and we hear it and love it still, though the singer may be lying dead.

Some women should raise and ennoble all those who follow after,—true, gentle and strong and tender, whom 'to love is a liberal education,' whom to have known is a blessing in our past. Is not the cry of the children still ringing in our ears as when the poet first uttered her noble song?

This little book, which has come out within the last few months, tells with a touching directness and simplicity the story of a good and gifted woman, whose name has long been a household word among us, but of whose history nothing was known until this little volume appeared. It only tells the story of a country lady, of days following days tranquilly, of common events; and yet the history is deeply interesting to those who loved the writer of whom it is written; and as we turn from the story of Jane Austen's life to her books again, we feel more than ever that she, too, was one of these true friends who belong to us inalienably—simple, wise, contented, living in others, one of those whom we seem to have a right to love. Such people belong to all human-kind by the very right of their wide and generous sympathies, of their gentle wisdom and loveableness. Jane Austen's life, as it is told by her nephew, is very touching, sweet and peaceful. It is a country landscape, where the cattle are grazing, the boughs of the great elm-tree rocking in the wind: sometimes, as we read, they come falling with a crash into the sweep; birds are flying about the old house, homely in its simple rule. The rafters cross the whitewashed ceilings, the beams project into the room below. We can see it all: the parlour with the horsehair sofa, the scant, quaint furniture, the old-fashioned garden outside, with its flowers and vegetables combined, and along the south side of the garden the green terrace sloping away...

All this time, while her fame is slowly growing, life passes in the same way in the old cottage at Chawton. Aunt Jane, with her young face and her mob-cap, makes play-houses for the children, helps them to dress up, invents imaginary conversations for them, supposing that they are all grown up the day after a ball. One can imagine how delightful a game that must have seemed to the little girls. She built her nest, did this good woman, happily weaving it out of shreds, and ends, and scraps of daily duty, patiently put together; and it was from this nest that she sang the song, bright and brilliant, with quaint thrills and unexpected cadences, that reaches us even here through fifty years. The lesson her life seems to teach us is this: Don't let us despise our nests—life is as much made of minutes as of years; let us complete the daily duties; let us patiently gather the twigs and the little scraps of moss, of dried grass together; and see the result!—a whole, completed and coherent, beautiful even without the song.

We come too soon to the story of her death. And yet did it come too soon? A sweet life is not the sweeter for being long. Jane Austen lived years enough to fulfil her mission. It was an unconscious one; and unconscious teachers are the highest. They teach by their lives, even more than by their words, and their lives need not reach threescore years and ten to be complete. She lived long enough to write six books that were masterpieces in their way—to make a thousand people the happier for her industry. She lived long enough to be loved by all those of her home.

One cannot read the story of her latter days without emotion; of her patience, her sweetness, and gratitude. There is family trouble, we are not told of what nature. She falls ill. Her nieces find her in her dressing-gown, like an invalid, in an arm-chair in her bed-room; but she gets up and greets them, and, pointing to seats which had been arranged for them by the fire, says: 'There is a chair for the married lady, and a little stool for you, Caroline.' But she is too weak to talk, and Cassandra takes them away.

At last they persuade her to go to Winchester, to a well-known doctor there.

'It distressed me,' she says, in one of her last, dying letters, 'to see Uncle Henry.'

'And William Knight, who kindly attended us, riding in the rain almost the whole way. We expect a visit from them tomorrow, and hope they will stay the night; and on Thursday, which is a confirmation and a holiday, we hope to get Charles out to breakfast. We have had but one visit from *him*, poor fellow, as he is in the sick room. . . . God bless you, dear E., if ever you are ill, may you be as tenderly nursed as I have been...'

But nursing does not cure her, nor can the doctor save her to them all, and she sinks from day to day. To the end she is full of concern for others.

'As for my dearest sister, my tender, watchful, indefatigable nurse has not been made ill by her exertions,' she writes. 'As to what I owe her, and the anxious affection of all my beloved family on this occasion, I can only cry over it, and pray God to bless them more and more.'

One can hardly read this last sentence with dry eyes. It is her parting blessing and farewell to those she had blessed all her life by her presence and her love. Thank God that love is beyond death; and its benediction, still with us, not only spoken in words, but by the signs and the love of a lifetime, that does not end for us as long as we ourselves exist.

They asked her when she was near her end if there was anything she wanted.

'Nothing but death,' she said. Those were her last words. She died on the 18th of July, 1817, and was buried in Winchester Cathedral, where she lies not unremembered.

A.I.T.

(*A Book of Sibyls*, 1883, pp. 199–200)

One seems to see the picture of the unknown friend who has charmed us so long—charmed away dull hours, created neighbours and companions for us in lonely places, conferring happiness and harmless mirth upon generations to come. One can picture her as she sits erect, with her long and graceful figure, her full round face, her bright eyes cast down,—Jane Austen, 'the woman of whom England is justly proud'—whose method generous Macaulay has placed near Shakespeare. She is writing in secret, putting away her work when visitors come in, unconscious, modest, hidden at home in heart, as she was in her sweet and womanly life, with the wisdom of the serpent indeed and the harmlessness of a dove.

4. Hutton on the minor works

1871

From unsigned review of the 1871 *Memoir*, 'Miss Austen's Posthumous Pieces', *Spectator*, 22 July 1871, 891–2.

A perceptive account of the work surviving in manuscript.

...*Lady Susan*, is interesting only as the failures of men and women of genius are interesting. It exhibits, indeed, a kind of perfection in its command of English, which somehow seems to imply that the writer possesses a great fineness and delicacy of literary touch, without giving us any actual illustration of it. But there is a double fault in the literary conception. The subject was too bold, and the form was not bold enough. Lady Susan herself, who is the only person of any interest in the tale, is not simply, a flirt, she is a bad woman of a good deal of ability,—false and cruel, as well as extravagantly fond of admiration. Now Miss Austen deals best and most adequately with follies and faults rather than great vices, and it is obvious that she had not the courage to paint Lady Susan with the strength and completeness that were necessary to producing the effect she needed. Had she painted her with the freedom with which she paints Miss Crawford in *Mansfield Park*, or Wickham in *Pride and Prejudice*, Lady Susan might have been one of her most striking pictures. But it is obvious that the subject was not suited to her genius. Lady Susan is feline, velvet-pawed, cruel, false, licentious, but it does not suit Miss Austen to make us see her in that strong light. She paints her vices on the miniature scale, till they produce little more impression than very bad faults. She does not let us see her in the scenes and with the actors where her full nature would have come out. She cramps herself in dealing with a subject which required free, vigorous painting, conscious that her style succeeds best when, as she herself described herself, she is painting on ivory with a very fine brush. And consequently, *Lady Susan* is a failure. Miss Austen understood her heroine, but had not the nerve or inclination to make her fully known to us.

Then, again, the form chosen was cramping and in the wrong way. Miss Austen cramped herself in the right way,—in the way really suited to her genius,—when she made a great deal of little foibles, so much so, that the reader entered heartily into them as humorous paradoxes. That was according to her genius, which, for social traits, was microscopic. She is in the mood best suited to her when she makes the vain and vulgar Mrs Elton say in railing against the Tupmans, 'They evidently think themselves equal to my brother, Mr Suckling, who has been eleven years a resident at Maple Grove, and whose father had it before him,—*I believe, at least, I am almost sure, that old Mr Suckling had completed the purchase before his death*;' or when she makes the proud and pompous Lady Catherine De Burgh say, 'I take no leave of you, Miss Bennet, *I send no compliments to your mother*, I am most seriously displeased.' But she cramps herself the wrong way, in a way utterly unsuited to her genius, when she tries to tell a story in the indirect form of letters, according to the favourite plan of Richardson and Miss Burney,—for then she deprives herself of the freedom of manner which is her greatest charm, voluntarily surrendering the light dramatic power by which she makes human foibles so exquisitely vivid and ridiculous. *Lady Susan* is a story with a strong conception that wanted direct and rather broad handling, not only treated in far too neat and minute a fashion,—that was of the essence of its author's method,—but according to a foreign and formal pattern with which her genius had no manner of affinity. Dialogue was of the very life of her genius, which was really free in its kind, though so minute; and yet dialogue can hardly be introduced at all into an epistolary novel, and never in its easiest and raciest form. *Lady Susan* is a failure, because, with a perversity not uncommon in young genius just groping its way to the comprehension of its own powers, Miss Austen had committed the double error of choosing a subject which required a bolder style than hers, and of fettering herself in its treatment by a method which robbed her style of its greatest grace as well as power. Lady Susan is heartless as a mother, as well as treacherous and licentious in her own disposition, and we absolutely need to have her relations with her daughter and with her admirers freely described in other language than her own, in order to apprehend the full meaning of her own selfish letters, but this Miss Austen has not ventured upon in this little story. Mr Mainwaring, with whom Lady Susan's principal and worst intrigue is carried on, is always kept off the scene; and Lady Susan's daughter, whose innocent and modest disposition excites her mother to positive hatred, as well as contempt, is hardly brought into it at all,—the result being a half-realized, dim, and ineffective picture of a forbidding subject which needed strong lines and deep colours. It is interesting, however, to observe that Miss Austen taught herself by this early experiment that foibles and sins of a less deep and pronounced dye than Lady Susan's,—admitting of a slighter and at times more playful treatment,—were better suited to her genius. And it is interesting to be told that after writing *Sense and Sensibility* in the epistolary form, she reconstructed it in that freer shape in which we now have it, where there is so much more room for the play of the author's humour than there could be in a series of letters. How, for instance, could Miss Austen have imported into the letters of a sentimentalist like Marian in *Sense and Sensibility* the many humorous turns of conversation which her letters would have had to report, without either sacrificing all dramatic truth, or sacrificing the life and play of the conversation itself? No artistic mistake can be worse than for an artist to confine himself to a medium which cripples his own perceptive and imaginative powers, as Miss Austen did in her first tentative efforts to paint life through the letters of a few sharply-defined characters.

5. Leslie Stephen, 'the popularity of Miss Austen'

1876

From an unsigned article, 'Humour', *Cornhill Magazine*, 1876, xxxiii. 324–5.

Stephen (1832–1904), prominent man-of-letters, editor of the *Dictionary of National Biography*, and at this time editor of the *Cornhill*. Over the years, his views mellowed. In his *George Eliot* volume (1902) in the English Men of Letters Series, he included Jane Austen among 'the gentler and more serious observers of life' (p. 198); and Jane Austen was his chosen reading for his long, final illness.

I never, for example, knew a person thoroughly deaf to humour who did not worship Miss Austen, or, when her writings were assailed, defend themselves by saying that the assailant had no sense of humour. Miss Austen, in fact, seems to be the very type of that kind of humour which charms one large class of amiable persons; and Austenolatry is perhaps the most intolerant and dogmatic of literary creeds. To deny Miss Austen's marvellous literary skill would be simply to convict oneself of the grossest stupidity. It is probable, however, that as much skill may have been employed in painting a bit of old china as in one of Raphael's masterpieces. We do not therefore say that it possesses equal merit. And, on the same principle, allowing all possible praise to Miss Austen within her own sphere, I should dispute the conclusion that she was therefore entitled to be ranked with the great authors who have sounded the depths of human passion, or found symbols for the finest speculations of the human intellect, instead of amusing themselves with the humours of a country tea-table. Comparative failure in the highest effect is more creditable than complete success in the lower. Now the popularity of Miss Austen with non-humorous persons (I should expressly admit, to avoid any false interpretation, that she is also popular with some humorists) shows what it is which mankind really understand by humour. They are really shocked by its more powerful manifestations. They call it cynicism. They like Dickens, who was beyond all doubt a true humorist, because he was not a thoroughgoing humorist; because he could drop his humour and become purely and simply maudlin at a moment's notice; that is to say, precisely because of the qualities which offend the more refined judges and the truest humorists. They like Miss Austen, on a similar ground, because her humour (to use a vulgar, but the only phrase) is drawn so excessively mild. There is not only nothing improper in her books, nothing which could prevent them from being given by a clergyman to his daughter as a birthday present; but there is not a single flash of biting satire. She is absolutely at peace with her most comfortable world. She never even hints at a suspicion that squires and parsons of the English type are not an essential part of the order of things; if she touches upon poverty, the only reflection suggested is one of gentle scorn for people who can't keep a butler themselves or take tea with people who do so. When the amiable Fanny Price in *Mansfield Park* finds that her mother has to eat cold mutton and mend the children's clothes, her only thought is to return to her rich uncle. The harsh hideous facts with which ninety-nine out of a hundred of our fellow-creatures are constantly struggling, are never admitted into this delightful world of well-warmed country-houses.

6. 'of the second order'

1882

From unsigned obituary article for Trollope, *Times*, 7 December 1882, 9.

By the death of Mr Anthony Trollope multitudes of English-speaking people will feel that they have lost a friend. .... And if ever a novelist had a claim to this kind of widespread affectionate remembrance, it is Mr Trollope. He will scarcely rank in the future beside the great novelists of the century. Scott, Balzac, Dickens, George Sand, George Eliot, Charlotte Brontë, Thackeray, Turgue-nieff, these at least must be put in a first class to which posterity will hesitate to admit him in spite of his range and facility. Neither, we believe, will it admit Miss Austen, great as she is. She and Mr Trollope, and, perhaps, Mrs Gaskell, stand at the head of the second order. From their labour has sprung a tribe of novels in which the ways of the English middle class are described with an ease, a humour, and a tenderness of feeling which are only not the best of what the novelist's art can produce because there are certain rare and in-born gifts of genius which as it were take the heaven of our praise by force and conquer for themselves a place apart whenever they appear. Miss Austen drew the middle class of the

England of Napoleon's day; her country squires, her fashionable ladies, above all her clergymen, are as real as they can be made by the most delicate observation, expressed in a style which for its mixture of crispness, pliancy, and a kind of rippling gaiety has no rival in English. Thirty eventful years or more divided her death from the beginning of Mr Trollope's career as a novelist. But still his world is the heir of Miss Austen's. There is nobody with whom Mr Collins may be better compared than with Mr Crawley; and Anne Eliot, Catherine Morland, Emma and the delightful Elizabeth Bennet herself, are conceived in substantially the same mood, allowing for the difference of two generations, as Mary Thorne, Lucy Robarts, or Lady Lufton...

7. Pellew's 'new criticism'

From *Jane Austen's Novels* (Boston) 1883

George Pellew (1859–92), author and journalist, was born in England, came to America as a boy and went to Harvard.

Henry James saw this prize-winning Harvard dissertation as 'an attempt in scientific criticism' (see No. 8) and Howells described it as 'one of the first steps in the direction of the new criticism—the criticism which studies, classifies and registers'. The opening and closing pages are given here.

A modern critic can hardly be satisfied with taking any position other than that of an historian; for only as a contribution in some manner to the history of literature can criticism be of general service. Merely to define one's impressions of an author's writings may be entertaining, but is seldom fruitful, except as a revelation of the character of the critic. Yet it is in this way that most writers have dealt with Jane Austen. They speak of her, as men often speak of Burns, as a singular and inexplicable phenomenon, without connection with the past. But such independence is impossible, even for a poet or a novelist. In natural history, in the history of institutions or in that of fiction, the same laws hold true,—that in time every thing changes, and that this change is not from nothing into something, but by growth from what existed before, or by reaction against it. From this point of view, it is still surprising enough, that in the early part of the century, when Gothic tales and romantic poetry formed apparently the chief part of purely literary reading, a young girl living in a remote parsonage should have composed stories with such truth to nature, and such witty discrimination of character, that reputable critics have called her Shakespearian; but it would be truly miraculous, if this work had been done by the unaided force of original genius, without any connection of agreement or disagreement with previous writers, or with contemporary thought . . . .

But one rare faculty she possessed, that redeems her work from insignificance,—the faculty of describing accurately what she saw. She anticipated the scientific precision that the spirit of the age is now demanding in literature and art. People are now beginning to be dissatisfied with artificiality and exaggeration. Walt Whitman expresses the reaction against conventionality in poetry; Zola, that against conventionality in novels and the drama; and, though neither writer is able in his practice to avoid the excesses he condemns, we may believe that the art and fiction of the future will gradually be brought into ever closer relation to the facts of experience. The naturalness of Miss Austen's characters has always excited the wonder and admiration of her critics. I believe there is not a single impossible or extravagant character, however unimportant, in any of Miss Austen's greater novels. We find there an extraordinary variety of whimsical and empty-headed old ladies and old gentlemen, from Mrs Allen—who tries to console lonely Catherine Morley [sic] at the ball by vainly reiterating, 'I wish you could dance my dear; I wish you could get a partner,'—to Mr Woodhouse, with his nervous but polite anxiety lest his guests may over-eat, and need the services the next day of the 'invaluable' Perry. But no two of these good people are alike, and none of them are caricatures; and the same statement is true of the numberless vulgar men and women that throng her pages. Miss Austen, perhaps, is apt to describe persons from the outside, instead of giving us an insight into their principles of action, their thoughts and feelings. She has not, perhaps, the power of projecting herself into a character, and becoming that character for the time. But she has exquisite tact to divine how any character at any time should look and act. The natural ease and appropriateness of the conversations in these books has been often noticed, of which 'the verbose, roundabout, and parenthetic' prosing of Miss Bates has become a trite example; and one no less excellent is the conversation between Isabella Tilney and Catherine Moreland, that has been already quoted.

It is in her power of creating in artistic form another world, similar to the little world she knew, that Miss Austen's power consists. She was well aware of her own genius and its limitations, and declined Mr Clarke's well-meant but absurd suggestions to describe a literary clergyman like Beattie's minstrel, or to write an historical romance founded on the house of Saxe-Coburg. She remained uninfluenced by the romantic sense of the picturesqueness of the past, as she was uninfluenced by the romantic love of picturesque nature; and she was contented to leave it to Anne Porter to prepare the way for Scott.

The life in those country-houses may have been tedious and commonplace; but in Miss Austen's pages it is always entertaining. As we open 'Pride and Prejudice,' or 'Persuasion,' we become conscious of the charm of one of the wittiest and brightest women that ever lived; and under the spell of her humor we do not feel the absence of poetry, we forget to ask for an answer to the riddles of our existence. George Eliot or Turgenef may raise us to a higher level of thought and emotion, and in the intellectual pride of Bazaroff, or in the moral perplexities of Dorothea, may arouse a deeper and more ennobling sympathy than Jane Austen ever wished to excite, or ever can. They are, indeed, great authors in a sense in which Jane Austen is not; for they represent in typical characters the aspirations and intellectual life of a whole generation.

Jane Austen has no irresistible power to extort tears, or compel admiration; but her novels give a real though unexciting pleasure. The petty inconsistencies and social vanities of human beings are as enduring as their more impressive qualities; and it is of these that Miss Austen writes, and not, like Miss Burney, merely of the passing manners of the time. Life is often taken too seriously. Real griefs are so common, that it is grateful to turn to an author who does not make fictitious ones too pathetic. 'I love things that make me gay,' said Miss Mitford: 'therefore, amongst other reasons, I love Miss Austen.' And Miss Mitford is not the only reader who has felt this.

8. 'narrow unconscious perfection of form'

1883

Letter from Henry James to Pellew, 23 June 1883; *Henry James Letters 1875–83*, 1978, ed. Leon Edel, 422–3.

By 1883, Henry James (1843–1916) was already established as a major novelist—with *The Europeans* (1878), *Daisy Miller* (1879), *Washington Square* and *The Portrait of a Lady* (both 1881).

131 Mt. Vernon St.
June 23*d*. [1883]

My dear Pellew:

I found your thin red book on my table when I came in late last night. I read it this morning before I left my pillow—read it with much entertainment and profit. It contains many suggestive things very happily said, and I thank you much for your friendly thought in sending it to me. It is interesting as an attempt in scientific criticism of the delightful Jane—though when I read the first page or two I trembled lest you should overdo the science. But you don't overdo anything—you are indeed, I think, a little too discreet, too mild. I could have found it in me to speak more of her genius—of the extraordinary vividness with which she saw what she did see, and of her narrow unconscious perfection of form. But you point out very well all that she didn't see, and especially what I remember not to have seen indicated before, the want of moral illumination on the part of her heroines, who had undoubtedly small and second-rate minds and were perfect little she-Philistines. But I think that is partly what makes them interesting today. All that there was of them was feeling—a sort of simple undistracted concentrated feeling which we scarcely find any more. In of course an infinitely less explicit way, Emma Woodhouse and Anne Eliot give us as great an impression of 'passion'—that celebrated quality—as the ladies of G. Sand and Balzac. Their small gentility and front parlour existence doesn't suppress it, but only modifies the outward form of it. You do very well when you allude to the narrowness of Miss Austen's social horizon—of the young Martin in *Emma* being kept at a distance, etc; all that is excellent. Also in what you say of her apparent want of consciousness of nature. A friend of mine in England went to see the 'Cobb' at Lynn because in *Persuasion* it had inspired Miss A. with the unprecedented impulse of several lines of description. He said to himself that it must be wonderful, and he found it so, so that he bought a house there and remained. Do write another little red essay describing and tracing the growth of the estimate of local colour in fiction—the development of the realistic description of nature—the consciousness of places being part of the story, etc. You will do it excellently. The quotation (by 'Mr Murch') you mention on p. 26, is simply the closing sentence of Macaulay's essay on *Mme* d'Arblay!—I shall be much interested in what you do next, and remain

Very faithfully yours,
Henry James.

9. The art of Jane Austen

1885

From review-article (initialled M.A.W.) 'Style and Miss Austen', *Macmillan's Magazine*, 1885, li. 84–91; reprinted *Littell's Living Age*, 1885, clxiv. 58–64.

Mary Augustus (Mrs Humphry) Ward (1851–1920), a niece of Matthew Arnold, was a prolific novelist and reviewer and essayist. In this scathing review of Brabourne's *Letters*, we are reminded of Mrs Oliphant (*No. 42*); whilst her understanding of the novelist's art is unsurpassed.

By this publication of a newly-discovered collection of Miss Austen's letters, Miss Austen's great-nephew has done her as ill a turn as it is anybody's power to do to the author of *Pride and Prejudice*. The name of one of the nimblest, quickest, and least tiresome of mortals has been perforce associated with two volumes of half-edited matter, with letters of which she herself would never have authorised the publication, with family pedigrees of which she would have been the first person to feel the boredom and the incongruity, and literary criticisms of a kind to have set that keen wit of hers moving in its most trenchant fashion. When Lord Brabourne came into possession of those bundles of his great-aunt's letters which Mr Austen-Leigh, her first biographer, believed to have been lost, the temptation to make use of them in some way was no doubt irresistible. The virtue of literary reticence is fast becoming extinct; we have almost indeed forgotten that it is a virtue at all. To be able to persuade oneself that the world could possibly do without information which it is in one's power to give it, implies now a strength of mind so abnormal and so rare, that a modern instance of it is scarcely to be found. And the old distinction between public and private life, which still held firmly in the days when Jane Austen and Miss Ferrier refused to give their names to any production of their pens—the old personal reserve, which still forms part of the continental idea of the typical Englishman—have been so rapidly swept away during the last generation, that it would be absurd nowadays to expect of any inheritor of a great writer's correspondence that he should form the same sort of strict judgment on its claims to publication which would have been natural and possible a hundred or even fifty years ago. Taste is laxer, the public easier to please, and book-making more profitable. A modern editor of unpublished documents, by the nature of things, approaches his task in a more prodigal frame of mind. The whole mood of the present day is one of greater indulgence towards what may be called the personal side of letters than used to be the case with our grandfathers; and the seven volumes which Mr Froude has devoted to the Carlyles, and which, under all the circumstances, would have been a scandal in the days of Southey and Scott, will perhaps be accepted later on as marking the highest point of a tendency which has been long gathering strength and may not improbably soon have to fight against reaction.

Lord Brabourne, then, hardly deserves serious blame for not deciding as Mr Austen-Leigh would have probably decided twenty years ago, that the newly-discovered correspondence threw practically no fresh light on Miss Austen's personality, and, with half-a-dozen exceptions, which might have seen the light in a review, had therefore better be reserved for that family use for which it was originally intended; but he might at least have set some bounds to his confidence in the public. One small volume of these letters, carefully chosen and skilfully edited, would have been pleasant reading enough. They might have been used as illustrations of the novels, of the country society or the class relations of eighty years ago, and a few short explanations of the identity of the persons most frequently mentioned in them would have made them sufficiently intelligible to the general reader. As it is, the letters of the last fifteen years of Jane Austen's life dull the edge of whatever gentle enjoyment the reader may have derived from the sprightliness of the earlier ones, while the one literary merit which the collection possesses, its lightness and airiness of tone, is lost in the ponderous effect of the introductory chapters, with their endless string of names and wandering criticisms on the novels. Such editorial performance as this makes one sigh once more for a more peremptory critical standard than any we possess in England. What English *belles lettres* of the present day want more than anything else is a more widely diffused sense of *obligation* among the cultivators of them—obligation, if one must put it pedantically, to do the best a man can with his material, and to work in the presence of the highest ideals and achievements of his profession.

There are, however, in these volumes a few letters which were worth printing, and which do help to complete the picture already existing of Jane Austen. These are the letters written between 1796 and 1799, that is to say, during the period which witnessed the composition of *Pride and Prejudice*, *Sense and Sensibility*, and *Northanger Abbey*. Jane Austen at the time was a pretty, lively girl, very fond of dancing, deeply interested in dress, and full of the same naïf interest in the other sex with which Catherine Morland started on her Bath travels. The whole tone indeed of this early correspondence with her sister reminds one of an older and shrewder Catherine, and the ways of seeing and describing to which they bear witness are exactly those to which we owe the unflagging liveliness and gaiety of the two famous books in which the adventures of Catherine and of Elizabeth Bennett are set forth. *Northanger Abbey* especially, gay, sparkling, and rapid as it is from beginning to end, is the book in which the bright energy of Jane Austen's youth finds its gayest and freshest expression. *Pride and Prejudice* is witty and sparkling too, but it probably went through many a heightening and polishing process during the fifteen years which elapsed between the time when it was written and the time when it appeared in print; and although a great deal of it may represent the young Jane Austen, the style as a whole bears marks certainly of a fuller maturity than had been reached by the writer of *Northanger Abbey*. It is in the story of Catherine Morland that we get the inimitable literary expression of that exuberant girlish wit, which expressed itself in letters and talk and harmless flirtations before it took to itself literary shape, and it is pleasant to turn from the high spirits of that delightful book to some of the first letters in this collection, and so to realise afresh, by means of such records of the woman, the perfect spontaneity of the writer. Any one who has ever interested himself in the impulsive little heroine, who was as nearly plain as any heroine dared to be before Jane Eyre, but whose perfect good-humour and frankness won the heart of her Henry, will feel that in one or two of these newly-printed letters he comes very near to the secret of Catherine's manufacture . . . .

Lord Brabourne's book indeed only impresses upon us with fresh force what was already fairly well-known—that broadly speaking, the whole *yield* of Jane Austen's individuality is to be found in her novels. There are a certain number of facts about her which help to explain her books, and which are of use to the student of the psychological side of letters, but these were already within everybody's reach, so that the collection printed by Lord Brabourne is as a whole neither amusing nor sufficiently instructive to make it worth publication.

The triviality of the letters is easily explained. No circumstances were ever less favourable than Jane Austen's to good letter-writing. She possessed one literary instrument which she used with extraordinary skill and delicacy—the instrument of critical observation as applied to the commoner types and relations of human life. Within the limits fixed for her by temperament and circumstances she brought it to bear with unrivalled success, success which has placed her amongst English classics. But she was practically a stranger to what one may call, without pedantry, the world of ideas. The intellectual and moral framework of her books is of the simplest and most conventional kind....

In spite, however, of her narrow *Weltanschauung*, and her dearth of literary relationships, Jane Austen is a classic, and *Pride and Prejudice* will probably be read when *Corinne*, though not its author, is forgotten. Her life is a striking proof that a great novelist may live without a philosophy, and die without ever having belonged to a literary coterie. But out of the stuff of which the life was composed it was impossible to make a good letter-writer. To be a good letter-writer a man or woman must either have ideas, or sentiments strong enough to take the place of ideas, or knowledge of and contact with what is intrinsically interesting and important. Jane Austen had none of these. The graphic portraiture of men and woman seen from the outside, in which she excelled, was not possible in letters. It required more freedom, more elbow-room than letters could give. Jane Austen, in describing real people, found herself limited by the natural scruples of an amiable and gentle nature. There was a short time when the exuberance of her talent overflowed a little into her correspondence. But it soon came to an end, and for the rest of her life Jane Austen's letters were below rather than above the average in interest, point, and charm.

Miss Austen's novels are a well-worn subject. We have all read her, or ought to have read her; we all know what Macaulay and what Scott thought of her; and the qualities of her humour, the extent of her range have been pointed out again and again. Perhaps, after all, however, it may be still worth while to try and face the question which these disappointing letters bring home to one. How was it that, with all her lack of knowledge and of ideas, and with her comparative lack of passion, which so often supplies the place of both, Jane Austen accomplished work so permanent and so admirable? What is it, in a word, which makes *Pride and*

Prejudice and *Northanger Abbey* English classics, while the books of her contemporaries, Miss Ferrier and Miss Edgeworth, have practically lost their hold upon our sympathies, and are retreating year by year into a dimmer background? There are two kinds of qualities which go to the making of a classic. There are the qualities of expansion and the qualities of concentration. The great books of the world are rich in both. If you compare Chaucer's and Gower's treatment of the same theme—the subject of the *Man of Lawes Tale*, for instance—you will see not only that Chaucer's treatment is light and rapid where Gower's is heavy and prolix, but that Chaucer knew where, as the French would say, to 'lean,' where to dwell, where to expand....

The progress of literary expression during the last two hundred years has on the whole, and making due allowance for the vast stores of new material which have found their way into literature since Rousseau, been a progress towards concentration. Literature tends more and more to become a kind of shorthand. The great writers of this generation take more for granted than the great writers of the last, and the struggle to avoid commonplace and repetition becomes more and more diffused. The mind of the modern writer is on the whole most anxiously concerned with this perpetual necessity for omission, for compression. It will never describe if it can suggest, or argue if it can imply. The first condition of success in letters is nowadays to avoid vapouring, and to wage war upon those platitudes we all submit to with so much cheerful admiration in our Richardson or our Spectator.

It was her possession of the qualities of condensation that made Jane Austen what she was. Condensation in literary matters means an exquisite power of choice and discrimination—a capacity for isolating from the vast mass of detail which goes to make up human life just those details and no others which will produce a desired effect and blend into one clear and harmonious whole. It implies the determination to avoid everything cheap and easy— cheapness in sentiment, in description, in caricature. In matters of mere language it means the perpetual effort to be content with one word rather than two, the perpetual impulse to clip and prune rather than expand and lengthen. And if to this temper of self-restraint you add the imagination which seizes at once upon the most effective image or detail and realises at a glance how it will strike a reader, and a spontaneous interest in men and women as such, you have arrived at the component parts of such a gift as Jane Austen's....

[Cites a passage from *Inheritance* by Susan Ferrier]

There is no particular reason why writing of this kind should ever stop; there is nothing intimate and living in it, none of that wrestle of the artist with experience which is the source of all the labours and all the trials of art; it is all conventional, traditional, *hearsay* in fact. The qualities of concentration are altogether wanting. But now, put side by side with Gertrude's sentiment or Mrs Sinclair's remorse, some of the mental history of Jane Austen's *dramatis personae*, and the gulf which this marvellous choosing faculty digs between one writer and another will be plain at once. Anne Eliot, in *Persuasion*, has arrived at the critical moment of her fate. The man whom she had rejected seven years before has reappeared upon the scene, and as soon as she is brought in contact with him all lesser affections and inclinations, which had been filling up the time of his absence, disappear. Others might have had a chance if he had remained away, but his return, his neighbour-hood, rouses a feeling which sweep all before it. This is the situation. We may imagine, if Miss Ferrier had had to deal with it, how she would have spun it out; with what raptures, what despairs, what appeals to heaven she would have embroidered it! But Jane Austen at once seizes upon the vital points of it, and puts them before us, at first with a sober truth, and then with a little rise into poetry, which is a triumph of style.

'There was much regret,' she says, in her analysis of Anne's feelings towards the man she had resolved to sacrifice to her old lover. 'How she might have felt had there been no Captain Wentworth in the case is not worth inquiring; for there was a Captain Wentworth, and be the conclusion of the present suspense good or bad, her affection would be his for ever. Their union, she believed, could not divide her more from other men than their final separation. Prettier musings of high-wrought love and eternal constancy could never have passed along the streets of Bath than Anne was sporting with from Camden Place to Westgate Build-ings. It was almost enough to spread purification and perfume all the way.' How terse it is, how suggestive, how free from vulgarity and commonplace!

Another striking instance of this choosing instinct of hers is the description of Darcy's place, Pemberley, in *Pride and Prejudice*. There, although there is scarcely any description at all, every stroke of the pen is so managed that any reader with ordinary attention may realise, if he pleases, the whole lie of the park, the look of the house, as Elizabeth surveyed it from the opposite side of the ravine above which it stood, the relative positions of the lawns, stables, and woods. Anybody with a turn that way could sketch it with ease, and yet there is no effort, no intention to describe, nothing but a clear and vivid imagination working with that self-restraint, that concentration, which is the larger half of style. This self-restraint indeed is her important, her determining quality. In other ways she has great deficiencies. For fine instances of the qualities of expansion we must go elsewhere than to Jane Austen. Emotion, inspiration, glow, and passion are not hers; she is a small, thin classic. But classic she is; for her work is a typical English embodiment of those drier and more bracing elements of style in which French literature has always been rich, and our own perhaps comparatively poor.

M. A. W.

10. 'maiden lady realism'

1888

From signed essay, 'Turgueneff', *Fortnightly Review*, February 1888.

George Moore (1852–1933), novelist, essayist and critic, was later to abandon this 'maiden lady' Jane Austen for a writer whose eyes were open to 'the Venusberg of the drawing-room' (see No. 28).

But to whom shall we compare Turgueneff? It would be vain to speak of Miss Austen; her charm is too special, too peculiar to herself. Balzac's genius lies in his universality, Miss Austen's in her parochialism: the former was infinitely daring in attempting almost everything, the latter is infinitely daring in attempting almost nothing. She seems to have formulated her poetic system as follows: I know nothing of the natural sciences, of politics, of metaphysics, nor have I attempted to plumb the depths of the human soul; I am a maiden lady, interested in the few people with whom my lot is cast. If you care to hear how So-and-so married So-and-so I will tell you, and the simple tale I will relieve by an elderly gentleman whose faith is in gruel, and who strives to obtain converts to his favourite nourishment; but if you want to be astonished or instructed go elsewhere, I can do neither, nor will I pretend to. Now if the reader can imagine a beautifully cultivated islet lying somewhere between the philosophic realism of Balzac and the maiden lady realism of Miss Austen, he will have gone far to see Turgueneff as I see him.

11. Austenolatry

1889

Jane Austen, 'Eminent Women Series', 1889, S.F. Malden, 209–10.

This extract gives the closing paragraphs of the book and fairly represents the level of popularising appreciation on offer at this time. The quotation attributed to George Eliot is, in fact, from Lewes, 1852 (*No. 32*).

As we look back on the scanty records of Jane Austen's career, or turn from these to criticise the writings which were, in fact, her life, we cannot but feel that it was a life prematurely ended as regarded her fame, and that in the future she might have even surpassed the works we already have from her. Yet, much as we must regret that she lived to write nothing more, we cannot attach the idea of incompleteness or immaturity to anything she did write. Everything is finished to the highest point of finish; no labour has been spared, and yet nothing is laboured. George Eliot has named her 'The greatest artist that has ever written...the most perfect master over the means to her end.' Could higher praise be bestowed upon any style of writing? It is in this completeness, this absoluteness of dainty finish, joined, as it is, to a keen, delicate satire and a humour which is never coarse, that lies Jane Austen's gift; and it is one in which she has never had a rival.

It is nearly eighty years since she died, and there has been no writer since whose style, to those who know Jane Austen's well, can really challenge comparison with it for a moment. It is impossible to urge her merits on any who do not see them from her writings, 'next to Shakespeare,' as Lord Tennyson called them. Those who do appreciate her novels will think no praise too high for them, while those who do not, will marvel at the infatuation of her admirers; for no one ever cares moderately for Jane Austen's works: her readers either award them unbounded praise or find them insufferably dull. In her own day, the latter class were the larger, and reasons for this have been suggested; now, and for many years past, the tide of popular opinion has set strongly the other way, and we may believe it will continue to do so as long as novel-readers can appreciate life-like pictures of human beings who are immortal in their truth to nature, though their setting belongs to a bygone day.

12. 'no hidden meaning'

1890

Jane Austen, 'Great Writers Series', 1890, 185–91.

Goldwin Smith (1823–1910), politician and essayist. Regius Professor of Modern History, Oxford, 1858–66; then Professor of History at Cornell before settling in Toronto in 1871.

This is from the final chapter of the book. Smith voices a dry, commonsensical, middle-brow view, in contrast to Mrs Malden (No. 11), whose tones belong with Anne Thackeray and the world of the popular magazines.

Criticism is becoming an art of saying fine things, and there are really no fine things to be said about Jane Austen. There is no hidden meaning in her; no philosophy beneath the surface for profound scrutiny to bring to light; nothing calling in any way for elaborate interpretation ....

Jane Austen's characters typify nothing, for their doings and sayings are familiar and commonplace. Her genius is shown in making the familiar and commonplace intensely interesting and amusing. Perfect in her finish and full of delicate strokes of art, her works require to be read with attention, not skimmed as one skims many a novel, that they may be fully enjoyed.

But whoever reads them attentively will fully enjoy them without the help of a commentator.

Some think that they see a difference between the early and the later novels. It is natural to look for such a difference, but for ourselves we must confess that we see it not. In the first set and in the last set the style appears to us to be the same; in both equally clear, easy, and free from mannerism or peculiarity of any kind. In both there is the same freedom from anything like a straining after point and epigram, while point and epigram are not wanting when there is natural occasion for them. There are the same archness and the same quiet irony. The view of life, society, and character is essentially the same: at least, we should be surprised if any great contradiction or variation could be produced ....

In doing justice to Jane Austen and recommending her in preference to the unwholesome products of sensationalism and the careless manufactures of literary hacks, we do not mean to take a leaf from the crown of those who have dealt with nobler and more entrancing themes. The subjects which presented themselves to her were of the kind with which, and with which alone, she was singularly qualified by her peculiar temperament as as well as by her special gifts and her social circumstances to deal. But the lives of these genteel idlers after all were necessarily somewhat vapid, and void of anything heroic in action or feeling as well as of violent passion or tragic crime. Few sets of people, perhaps, ever did less for humanity or exercised less influence on its progress than the denizens of Mansfield Park and Pemberley, Longbourn and Hartfield, in Jane Austen's day. As they all come before us at the fall of the curtain, we feel that they, their lives and loves, their little intrigues, their petty quarrels, and their drawing-room adventures, are the lightest of bubbles on the great stream of existence, though it is a bubble which has been made bright for ever by the genius of Jane Austen.

13. 'the modernness of her method'

1890

From 'Jane Austen', a review of No. 12; reprinted from an unidentified source, *Criticisms* (1902), i. 21−7.

John Mackinnon Robertson (1856−1933) was a prolific polymath-writer and journalist.

Robertson takes a stringent view of Goldwin Smith's account of Jane Austen and remarks on James and Howells in considering her genius in the 'art' of the novel.

... Jane Austen's reputation is steadily on the increase.* Admired from the first by such judges as Scott and Macaulay, and later by Lewes, she has only of late years seemed to gain a really wide audience, the reason being that the wide modern development of the novel in the direction of delicacy and subtlety of character-painting has greatly multiplied the readers capable of appreciating

[*About 1887, the only editions of Jane Austen, I believe, were the unattractive one then published by Messrs. Bentley, at 6s. per volume, and the still more unattractive cheap edition issued by Messrs. Routledge. Within the past ten years, at least three new and agreeable editions have found a ready market.]

her art. To those adult readers who happen to go to her now for the first time (a conjuncture difficult to understand, but known often to occur) one of the most remarkable features of her work will be the modernness of her method. Half the time, save for the old-world intonations of her narrative style, she might be a contemporary of Mr Howells. Her art-concealing art, her lucky way of making the comic character reveal herself or himself without a word of description, is quite abreast of the latest literary craftsmanship. And, talking of Mr Howells, must we say that, while she excels him, not merely relatively to her time but absolutely, in the vitality of her comedy, she is a good deal weaker than he in her more serious work? There is no denying that, as Mr Goldwin Smith puts it, we enjoy best her fools, her sneaks, her grotesques, which will never be surpassed in this world for their combination of everyday truth with the fun of caricature. When she comes to the good people, especially the good men, she is not particularly inspired. Her moral code has all the flavor of commonplace that belonged to the serious English thought of her day: she appeals didactically—in the main, indeed, quite sensibly, but always unoriginally—to the established moral conventions, and is so much less naturally a humanist than a comédienne that she always presents to us the higher virtues and the graver vices of her personages in a narrative and non-dramatic form. And yet there is more in Macaulay's praise of the discrimination of her men characters than Mr Smith is disposed to allow. Granted that her good young men resemble each other, and her bad young men likewise, there is always something in her stiffest portraits which suggests study from the life: you feel that she had seen her character, if only she could have risen to the interest of originally handling it—if only she had not been after all an English clergyman's daughter in the period just after the French Revolution.

And yet, what can be more wonderful than her endowment and achievement as it was? Coming after Richardson, and Fielding, and Miss Burney, and Mrs Radcliffe, her work is a revelation of the possibilities of the novel in the way of the presentment of normal character independently of thrilling plot. While the possibility of the non-romantic novel was barely realised, and when the importance of observation in fiction was only vaguely acknowledged, her eye spontaneously found in the little drawing-room life of provincial England a whole world of intellectual light and shade.

She must have been a matchless observer; for surely Mr Smith obscures the point when he repudiates the notion that she as a rule put her acquaintances in her stories. She may only have pieced bits of them together, but nonetheless she transcribes life. As Mr James confesses, the novel 'lives by' the presentment of real people—if only Mr James would learn how true that is, and give us a little more of the real people! Jane Austen had the gift, not so much of 'creating' types, as Mr Smith puts it on his first page, as of delightedly transcribing character. To class her, as Mr Smith does, with 'Homer, Shakspere, Cervantes, Scott, and a few other,' is surely again a trifle indiscriminating. As well group together Titian and Raphael and Rembrandt and Hogarth and Meissonnier: there is literally all the difference in the world between such manifestations of genius. Scott's strength, for one thing, lay largely in his humorous enjoyment of Scotch character; Jane Austen's lay in her—shall we say?—smiling cynicism. For cynicism she had, though Mr Smith's affection makes him shrink from the word. When she demurely applauds the two married sisters who could retain their affection for each other though settled in the same neighbourhood, he anxiously tells us that we 'must be on our guard against taking playful irony for cynicism', because, Jane Austen being 'a member herself of a most united family, she could not really think it difficult for two sisters and their husbands to live near each other without quarrelling'. This is just a little gratuitous. Jane Austen knew, as a matter of fact, that in a very large number of cases married sisters do *not* agree when settled near each other, and she smilingly stated the fact. Indeed she has given us a set of pictures of disunited families, of families with no community of character or feeling, which at times might almost appal us when we feel how lightly she took it all. Decidedly she was cynical—in her own exquisite way.

But none of her lovers can leave her with a word which is even unreasonably associated with a repellent quality, especially when the subject is raised by such an appreciative book as Mr Goldwin Smith's. Strictly speaking, indeed, his performance does not amount to a book: with a little less exposition of the stories, it might have made a review article in the heroic days of Macaulay and Southey. It is almost impossible, indeed, to write a book on Jane Austen: you must not write treatises on miniatures. But while Mr Smith is now and then a trifle stiff, once or twice very lax in his style, and at times a little ostentatious of his own conventionality, he yet furnishes us with a masculine and intelligent account of Jane Austen, adequately warmed by appreciation and affection. The only point at which he seems to me unjust is in his criticism of 'Lady Susan'. One is half afraid to go back to that book after Mr Smith's cold words about it, but, speaking on old recollection, I am disposed to say that the world will not so willingly as he let it go out of sight; and that if it be compared with 'Ouida's' 'Moth', of which it seems to have suggested the motive, the earlier perform-ance, with its unforced power and its unadorned simplicity, will not be the one to suffer. Its plot, says Mr Smith, in his most Anglo-Saxonic manner, is 'worthy of a Parisian novelist'.* Well, is that a proof of its inferiority? Is it not the last proof of her genius that she could anticipate the modern Parisian novelist by one performance in her perfectly feminine and English way, while also anticipating the modern American novelist in her treatment of normal character? Wonderful little woman! She lived and died in the very atmosphere of unintelligence, and she has left us a body of work alive with intelligence, nay with genius, in every page, and only dulled here and there by the spirit of her time, which was too strong with her. For her there were no problems of life or society or philosophy: she took her framework as she found it, and painted what she saw within it, so far as she could venture. Would that we had such another artist to-day, with or without the same limitations!

* The British reader in general may do well to recall Coleridge's ballad 'The Three Graves' and Miss Thackeray's 'Story of Elizabeth'.

14. 'The Charm of Miss Austen'

1890

From an unsigned review by R.H. Hutton of No. 12, 'The Charm of Miss Austen', Spectator, 1890, lxiv. 403–4; reprinted Brief Literary Criticisms, 1906.

The chief interest in this fresh delineation of Miss Austen's wonderful literary power is the light it throws on the question of her secret charm for the few and her want of charm for the many,—for it cannot be denied that for a very considerable number of remarkably able men, Miss Austen wields no spell at all, though for those over whom she does wield a spell, she wields a spell of quite curious force. I believe that the secret both of her great charm for those whom she does charm, and of her complete failure to fascinate a large class of able men, is in the fineness—and, indeed, I may say, the reduced scale—of her exquisite pictures. It is not everybody who can appreciate the miniature: it is not everybody who can see life at all through a minifying instead of a magnifying medium. On the other hand, to those who can, there is a peculiar attraction in such life. You can get a glimpse of what it was in Sir Walter Scott's remark: 'The big bow-wow strain I can do myself, like any one now going; but the exquisite touch which renders ordinary commonplace things and characters interesting from the truth of the description and the sentiment, is denied to me.' That just hits the mark where it makes Scott disparage his own 'big bow-wow strain,'—in other words, the deep passions and eager ambitions which really filled his own imagination,—but it misses the mark when he supposes himself unable to touch off the truth and sentiment of commonplace situations, for no one could do it better than Scott, where the truth and sentiment of commonplace things was of a plain masculine type, like the interest of Jeanie Deans in her home, in her cows, and her dairy, or of Dinmont in his farm, or of the canny keeper, Neale Blane, in keeping well with Covenanters and Royalists alike. But what Scott really meant that he could not do, and that Jane Austen could do, was so to epitomise and yet delineate pride and meanness, and vulgarity and selfishness, and the like, as to give in one and the same sentence a glimpse of the reality and yet of the amusingness of life, to reduce its scale while really multiplying its humours. No one does this like Miss Austen. Sir Walter Scott and Fielding, and Dickens and Thackeray, and George Eliot all need considerable space for their pictures; and when you have got them, even the least literary eye can see that the scale of drawing is by no means harmonious throughout; that some passions are lifesize, and others hastily indicated by a line here and a line there; that some characters are slightly exaggerated, and others hardly made visible at all; and that while the imagination is roused and exalted by some scenes, there are others which, though necessary to the story, are not additions to its charm. But with Miss Austen this is hardly ever so. No drawing so delicate and yet so artistic has been seen in English literature. It is a selection of all that is most superficially interesting in human life, of all that is most easily appreciated without going very deep, and an exclusion of all that it takes real wear and tear of spirit to enter thoroughly into... It was hardly possible to find a finer sieve, a more effective strainer for artistic material than such a mind as this, and the result was something exquisitely interesting and attractive to those who liked the fastidious selection of social elements which such a mind instinctively made for itself, and intolerably uninteresting and unattractive to those who loved to brood over the larger enterprises, the deeper passions, the weightier responsibilities, the more massive interests at which Miss Austen hardly glanced except to convince herself that she must leave them to the care of others. The many statesmen and thinkers, and the many humorous women who love Miss Austen's books, love them because they find in them a social world like enough to the real world to be for the time eagerly lived in, and yet one relieved of the bitterest elements and infinitely more entertaining than the real world, a world which rivets the attention without wearying it, and makes life appear far less dreary and burdensome, though also far less laborious, eager, and anxious than it really is. This is the true charm of Miss Austen to those who love her, and the true source of indifference too those who do not. The former want a lively social picture in which they will be constantly amused and interested, and never required to attempt any great stretch of their powers of sympathy and imagination, one in contemplating which they can constantly laugh at the pompous self-importance of some men, and the frank selfishness of others, without grappling too closely with any of the great problems of duty or any of the great mysteries and paradoxes of faith. The anti-Austenites, on the other hand, want something very different in literature from this. The lively superficies of life is nothing to them in a mere literary mirror; they like to study it at the original sources among the smiles and frowns and flying shafts of actual society. When they take the trouble to read a book at all, they want something that excites and awakens them, that makes a kind of impression, which even the most lively society could not provide, but which they might remember in their dreams. Miss Austen's fine feminine sieve sifts away all that has most interest for such men, and leaves nothing but the aroma of society without the actual interest of personal relations. The delicate touches which the miniature preserves are interesting enough to men of this kind, if they see them in living eyes and on living lips, but when they are registered only in the fine strokes of the literary miniature they do not affect them. They expect literature to reveal something beyond even the best and most delicately sifted experiences of ordinary life; they expect it either to stir them to the very depths and electrify them, or to present them with some new mass of facts not otherwise attainable; and the delicate literary miniature painting answers neither purpose. But for those who like nothing better than to live by imagination alone among just such figures as would bore them if they were in the flesh, but only delight them in the delicately conceived field of a refined and vivid artist's canvas, Miss Austen's novels are the most perfectly amusing in the world. There is absolutely no *strain* in them, nothing but the lightest tracing of the characteristic vanities, self-deceptions, follies, and weaknesses, as well as shrewdnesses and wit of human life, so delineated as to make them all alike, seem even less important than they really are; and yet they secure all, and more than all, the charms of society to those who do not care to be themselves actors in the society they observe. If the Lady of Shalott had had Miss Austen's pictures before her, she would perhaps have been satisfied without plunging into the stream of real life; for no magic mirror ever reflected so much of it that amuses, and so little that heats and excites the soul to thirst after, and taste the reality. In Miss Austen's

world we are content to live as mere observers, while most of the
great novelists of Europe succeed in agitating the heart and
stimulating the instincts which lead to passion or action.

15. The 'provincial' Jane Austen

1891

From signed article, 'A Note on Jane Austen', *Scribner's
Magazine*, February 1891.

William Branford Shubrick Clymer, American literary journalist and editor, gave one of the most important nineteenth-
century American views on Jane Austen. Wide-ranging in its
placing of the novelist, it also offers some close-reading and
anticipates later criticism, notably Virginia Woolf (No. 31) in
seeing *Persuasion* as the opening 'of a third period'. Clymer's
comments on the scene of Louisa Musgrove's accident at
Lyme Regis can be compared with Herbert Read's (No. 35).

Scribe, mentioned on page 200, is the French playwright
Augustin Scribe (1791–1861). His plays were mediocre but
constructed with great technical efficiency.

The scrutinizing criticism to which Jane Austen has for some time
past been subjected omits explicit statement of a fundamental fact,
which it yet fully establishes by implication, namely, that she is
provincial. ... Call them what you will, Jane Austen's simple
pictures of the life she saw differ from Balzac's 'Scènes de la vie de
province,' or George Eliot's 'Scenes from Clerical Life,' or from
'Middlemarch,' which is a study of provincial life, or from 'The
House of the Seven Gables,' not so essentially in scene or incident
as in spirit. Balzac and George Eliot and Hawthorne all attempt to
let the reader into a larger world of ideas than Jane Austen ever
dreamed of. In so far as they succeed, they set astir 'that vague
hum, that indefinable echo, of the whole multitudinous life of man'

which should, it has been said, be felt to pervade a great work of fiction. In so far as Jane Austen is incapable of attempting anything of the kind, she is in one sense provincial. That is her limitation. In the recognition of that limitation lies much of her strength and of her charm—just as, conversely, Hunt's irritating weakness may be traced to his mistaking the limits of his powers.

Concentration of interest in one place and within a narrow social range, steadiness of observation, sureness of touch, firmness of handling, accurate adjustment of parts always with a view to total effect, nice discrimination of individual members of the same class, exquisite precision and high finish, permeating humor—these are among the obvious characteristics which, combining with an essentially feminine treatment—shown by her noticing, from the woman's point of view, things no man would ever think of noticing, by her women being better than her men, and by the absence of scenes between men—identify her among novelists many of whom share with her some, though perhaps none all, of these means to an artistic end. On the present inartistic generation of Americans, overrun with novels, and not keenly relishing the local flavor in provincial life, of which in this country the 'march of improvement' is rapidly effacing what vestiges remain, such qualities as those just enumerated can be expected to make no very deep impression. . . .

Jane Austen was in Mr Andrew Lang's words, 'born before Analysis came in, or Passion, or Realism, or Naturalism, or Irreverence, or Religious Open-mindedness;' she was not borne down with the sense of an all-important mission; she had no reform to preach, no faith to promulgate, no system to expound; she wrote merely because she delighted in doing what she must have felt she did well, for every page shows that she tried always to do her best. Yet, coming at about the middle of the period of a century and a half which separates us from Richardson, publishing at the precise moment when Scott was rising to his highest fame as a novelist, she is, surprised as she would have been to be told so, a significant landmark in the course of British fiction. An article attributed to Scott and an excellent article by Whately tell the story of the appearance of a new star and do full justice to its brilliance. Richardson, Fielding, and Smollett, the first novelists in England (for Defoe's stories of adventure are not precisely novels as the term is now understood), had been followed by a romantic and by a sentimental school, the former growing from Horace Walpole, through Clara Reeve and Mrs Radcliffe, to Scott; and the latter including men so dissimilar as Sterne, Mackenzie, and Goldsmith. The sentimentalists were virtually a thing of the past, and the romanticists were in full career when Jane Austen, cutting loose from both influences, set again on a firm basis the realistic study of manners taught her by Richardson and Fielding. Small and slender though it be, her work is the thread by which is traceable the continuance, through a romantic age, of the strain of realism that marks Thackeray and Trollope as descendants of Fielding and Richardson. She belongs to a small group of women who excelled in what has been well called 'fictitious biography;' of that group—comprising Miss Edgeworth, Miss Ferrier, and herself, who 'have all,' Scott says in his journal, 'given portraits of real society far superior to anything man, vain man, has produced of the like nature'—she is incontestably the finest artist. Of recent British novelists, Trollope is most obviously her inheritor, for, though he lacks her acute tact, his work is of essentially the same class as hers—high comedy of manners, and nothing else.

Unconsciously, too, she was a forerunner of another group of novelists, represented at present perhaps most completely by M. Guy de Maupassant. Could she have foreseen what was coming there is no reason to suppose she would have shrunk from the association as perturbing to maidenly susceptibilities; her minute acquaintance with Richardson, the outspoken habit of her time, a hint or two in her letters, show the likelihood that her objection to the form taken for the moment by French fiction would, like ours, be to some extent offset, would she read it, by admiration of the skill of some of the writers, all the more that she knew French. She and M. Guy de Maupassant are, indeed, in odd contrast, and yet closely alike. . . .

. . . Some of Jane Austen's scenes are as denuded of superfluity as his [Landor's], so that the meaning is to be got only on condition of mentally supplying stage-directions which are left out. The scene of Louisa Musgrove's unlucky jump is a case in point. All is hurry and agitation and movement, but for the most part merely implied in the words of the several characters. Read hastily, it is tame; read attentively, it is as rapid and close in construction, and as fully provides for every character at every moment as if it were Scribe's. The development of plot and of character by means of dialogue is as distinguishing a trait of Jane Austen as of any novelist, and is better understood by none than by her. Charles Reade and Trollope, each in his way, use dialogue very largely and very well. Reade's is dramatic in the histrionic sense that it may be put, with scarcely the change of a word, into the mouths of actors; Trollope's is the *verbatim* report of the voluminous talk of his personages; Jane Austen's differs from both in being not so literal a transcript, and in being more essentially a tissue of character manifested in speech. The whole character is shown chiefly by the dialogue in her books; the other authors need more supplementary comment to complete the character. Her way may or may not be the best; she, at any rate, is unsurpassed in that special thing; for, though perhaps nothing of hers is so concentrated and penetrating as Mr Crawley's 'Peace, woman,' to Mrs Proudie, that is an almost unique stroke in Trollope, who habitually is as diffuse as she is concise.

...the book [*Persuasion*] shows broader sympathies, deeper observation, and perhaps more perfect symmetry, balance, poise, than the others. The always flexible, unobtrusive style, in which reduction of emphasis is carried sometimes to the verge of equivocation, concealing the author, yet instinct with her presence, in none of her books approximates more nearly to Cardinal Newman's definition—'a thinking out into language.' In general, the qualities that appear in the others are in 'Persuasion' perhaps more successfully fused than before. Through it runs a strain of pathos unheard in its predecessors, which in the chapter before the last combines in harmony with the other motives in a way not suggested in the previous novels. That chapter is as well composed as Thackeray's chapters about Waterloo. As Shelley, toward the end of his life, with more complete control of his material, gave promise of more satisfying work than any he had done, so Jane Austen, always master of her material, gave evidence, in her last book, of wider scope. 'Persuasion' does not, of course, like 'Vanity Fair,' echo the distant hum of the whole of the human life; it is, however, a 'mirror of bright constancy'. Jane Austen's observation, unusually keen always—and that is no mean qualification, for has not humor its source in observation?—here unites with the wisdom of forty to make a picture softer in tone, more delicate in modelling, more mellow, than its companions of her girlhood, or than its immediate predecessors in her later period. The book marks the beginning of a third period, beyond the entrance to which she did not live to go. It is not pretended that she would, with any length of life, have produced heroic paintings of extensive and complicated scenes, for that was not her field; it may reasonably be supposed that, had she lived, her miniatures might, in succeeding years, have shown predominantly the sympathetic quality which in 'Persuasion' begins to assert itself.

Arnold says that Homer is 'rapid in movement, simple in style, plain in language, natural in thought,' and adds that he is 'also, and above all, noble.' Jane Austen, usually rapid, simple, plain, and natural, is not noble in the sense in which Arnold uses the word; nor is there quite enough of the divine madness in her method to crown her a genius. Scott, not always rapid, simple, plain, and natural, occupies the throne of nobility and genius. It is the last to which she would have aspired; her attributes are rather those of the artist. She kept her hazel eyes open in the narrow world she lived in, saw accurately and humorously its gently undulating surface, and, without exaggeration of the importance of her subject or distortion of its relations, expressed, for love of the work, and with rare skill, what she felt. The reader who, amid the conflict of our 'fierce intellectual life,' is insensible to 'the exquisite touch which renders ordinary commonplace things and characters interesting, from the truth of the description and the sentiment,' loses the unique opportunity for tranquil enjoyment afforded by the high comedy of manners of the provincial Jane Austen, the artist.

16. Realism and 'entire truthfulness'

1891

From *Criticism and Fiction*, 1891, a volume derived from Howells's monthly column in *Harper's Magazine*, 1866 onwards.

William Dean Howells (1837–1920), novelist, essayist and journalist, was Jane Austen's foremost American champion, a devotee ('the divine Jane') whose enthusiasm and affection were harnessed to considerable critical power, and the leading proponent of 'realism', both as a mode of literary treatment and as the condition of truth in art.

But what is it that gives tendency in art, then? What is it makes people like this at one time, and that at another? Above all, what makes a better fashion change for a worse; how can the ugly come to be preferred to the beautiful; in other words, how can art decay?

This question came up in my mind lately with regard to English fiction and its form, or rather its formlessness. How, for instance, could people who had once known the simple verity, the refined perfection of Miss Austen, enjoy anything less refined and less perfect?

With her example before them, why should not English novelists have gone on writing simply, honestly, artistically, ever after? One would think it must have been impossible for them to do otherwise, if one did not remember, say, the lamentable behavior of the actors who support Mr Jefferson, and their theatricality in the very presence of his beautiful naturalness. It is very difficult, that simplicity, and nothing is so hard as to be honest, as the reader, if he has ever happened to try it, must know. 'The big bow-wow I can do myself, like any one going' said Scott, but he owned that the exquisite touch of Miss Austen was denied him; and it seems certainly to have been denied in greater or less measure to all her successors...

Which brings us again, after this long way about, to the divine Jane and her novels, and that troublesome question about them. She was great and they were beautiful, because she and they were honest, and dealt with nature nearly a hundred years ago as realism deals with it to-day. Realism is nothing more and nothing less than the truthful treatment of material, and Jane Austen was the first and the last of the English novelists to treat material with entire truthfulness. Because she did this, she remains the most artistic of the English novelists, and alone worthy to be matched with the great Scandinavian and Slavic and Latin artists. It is not a question of intellect, or not wholly that. The English have mind enough; but they have not taste enough; or, rather, their taste has been perverted by their false criticism, which is based upon personal preference, and not upon principle; which instructs a man to think that what he likes is good, instead of teaching him first to distinguish what is good before he likes it. The art of fiction, as Jane Austen knew it, declined from her through Scott, and Bulwer, and Dickens, and Charlotte Brontë, and Thackeray, and even George Eliot, because the mania of romanticism had seized upon all Europe, and these great writers could not escape the taint of their time; but it has shown few signs of recovery in England, because English criticism, in the presence of the Continental masterpieces, has continued provincial and special and personal, and has expressed a love and hate which had to do with the quality of the artist rather than the character of his work.

17. Agnes Repplier on Jane Austen

1889–1931

Agnes Repplier (1855–1950) was a prolific American writer who cultivated the art of the 'familiar' essay in the tradition of Hazlitt, Leigh Hunt and Lamb (see *The Confident Years 1885–1915*, Van Wyck Brooks, 1952, 22–23).

Although her many collections of essays were published both in Britain and North America, little discussion of her work seems to have got into print. In her Presidential Address to The English Association in 1913, Anne Thackeray spoke of 'A well known critic, an American lady, Miss Fanny Repplier' ('A Discourse on Modern Sibyls', delivered 10 January 1913, *English Association Pamphlet No. 24*, p. 1). Rebecca West speaks of a school-marmish Miss Repplier in *The Strange Necessity* (1928), pp. 263–4.

(a) Jane Austen and Charlotte Brontë
From 'A Plea for Humor', *Atlantic Monthly*, February 1889;
reprinted in *Points of View*, 1891.

...Compare the harshness with which she [Charlotte Brontë]
handles her hapless curates, and the comparative crudity of her
treatment, with the surpassing lightness of Miss Austen's touch as
she rounds and completes her immortal clerical portraits. Miss
Brontë tells us, in one of her letters, that she regarded *all* curates as
'highly uninteresting, narrow, and unattractive specimens of the
coarser sex,' just as she found *all* the Belgian school-girls 'cold,
selfish, animal, and inferior.' But to Miss Austen's keen and
friendly eye the narrowest of clergymen was not wholly uninteresting, the most inferior of school-girls not without some claim to our
consideration; even the coarseness of the male sex was far from
vexing her maidenly serenity, probably because she was unac-
quainted with the Rochester type. Mr Elton is certainly narrow,
Mary Bennet extremely inferior; but their authoress only laughs at
them softly, with a quiet tolerance, and a good-natured sense of
amusement at their follies. It was little wonder that Charlotte
Brontë, who had at all times the courage of her convictions, could
not, and would not, read Jane Austen's novels. 'They have not got
story enough for me,' she boldly affirmed. 'I don't want my blood
curdled, but I like to have it stirred. Miss Austen strikes me as
milk-and-watery, and, to say truth, as dull.' Of course she did!
How was a woman, whose ideas of after-dinner conversation are
embodied in the amazing language of Baroness Ingram and her
titled friends, to appreciate the delicious, sleepy small talk, in 'Sense
and Sensibility,' about the respective heights of the respective
grandchildren?...

On the other hand, we are told that Miss Austen owned her
lively sense of humor to her habit of dissociating the follies of
mankind from any rigid standard of right and wrong; which
means, I suppose, that she never dreamed she had a mission.

(b) 'the fine, thin perfection'
From 'Literary Shibboleths', *Atlantic Monthly*, May 1890; reprinted
in *Points of View*, 1891.

... I cannot even think that Mr Howells is justified in calling the
English nation 'those poor islanders,' as if they were dancing naked
somewhere in the South Seas, merely because they love George
Eliot and Thackeray as well as Jane Austen. They love Jane Austen
too. We all love her right heartily, but we have no need to emulate
good Queen Anne, who, as Swift observed, had not a sufficient
stock of amity for more than one person at a time. We may not,
indeed, be prepared to say with Mr Howells that Miss Austen is
'the first and the last of the English novelists to treat material with
entire truthfulness,' having some reasonable doubts as to the
precise definition of truth. We may not care to emphasize our
affection for her by repudiating with one breath all her great
successors. We may not even consider 'The Newcomes' and
'Henry Esmond' as illustrating the degeneracy of modern fiction;
yet nevertheless we may enjoy some fair half-hours in the company
of Emma Woodhouse and Mr Elton, of Catherine Morland and
Elizabeth Bennet. Only, when we are searching for a shibboleth by
which to test our neighbor's intellectual worth, let not Jane
Austen's be the name, lest we be rewarded for our trouble by
hearing the faint, clear ripple of her amused laughter—that gentle,
feminine, merciless laughter—echoing softly from the dwelling-
place of the immortals.

.... And if, even to children, this joy has grown somewhat
tasteless of late years, I fear the reason lies in their lack of healthy
unconsciousness. They are taught so much they did not use to
know about the correct standing of authors, they are so elaborately
directed in their recreations as well as in their studies, that the old
simple charm of self-forgetful absorption in a book seems
well-nigh lost to them. It is not very encouraging to see a bright
little girl of ten making believe she enjoys Miss Austen's novels,
and to hear her mother's complacent comments thereon, when we
realize how exclusively the fine, thin perfection of Miss Austen's
work appeals to the mature observation of men and women, and
how utterly out of harmony it must be with the crude judgment

and expansive ideality of a child. I am willing to believe that these abnormally clever little people, who read grown-up books so conspicuously in public, love their Shakespeares, and their Grecian histories, and their 'Idylls of the King.' I have seen literature of the delicately elusive order, like 'The Marble Faun,' and 'Elsie Venner,' and 'Lamia,' devoured with a wistful eagerness that plainly revealed the awakened imagination responding with quick delight to the sweet and subtle charm of mystery. But I am impelled to doubt the attractiveness of Thackeray to the youthful mind, even when I have just been assured that 'Henry Esmond' is 'a lovely story;' and I am still more skeptical as to Miss Austen's marvelous hair-strokes conveying any meaning at all to the untrained faculties of a child.

(c) 'the secret springs'
From 'Conversation in Novels', *Essays in Miniature*, 1892.

Peacock's conversation has just been under discussion.

It is all vastly piquant and entertaining, but it is leagues away from the casual conversation, the little leisurely, veracious gossip in which Jane Austen reveals to us with merciless distinctness the secret springs that move a human heart. She has scant need to describe her characters, and she seldom takes that trouble. They betray themselves at every word, and stand convicted on their own evidence. We are not warned in advance against Isabella Thorpe. We meet her precisely as Catherine meets her in the Pump-room at Bath, where the young lady speedily opens her lips, and acquaints us in the most vivacious manner with her own callous folly and selfishness. Every syllable uttered by Mrs Norris is a new and luminous revelation; we know her just that much better than we did before she spoke. Even *Sense and Sensibility*, by no means the best of Miss Austen's novels, starts with that admirable discussion between Mr John Dashwood and his wife on the subject of his mother's and sister's maintenance. It is a short chapter, the second in the book, and at its close we are masters of the whole situation. We have sounded the feeble egotism of Mr Dashwood, and the adroit meanness of his spouse. We know precisely what degree of assistance Elinor and Marianne are likely to receive from them. We foresee the relation these characters will bear to each other during the progress of the story, and we have been shown with delicious humor how easy and pleasant is the task of self-deception. That a girl of nineteen should have been capable of such keenly artistic work is simply one of the miracles of literature; and the more we think about it, the more miraculous it grows. The best we can do is to bow our heads, and pay unqualified homage at its shrine. . . .

Lady Bertram, of *Mansfield Park*, remarking placidly from her sofa, 'Do not act anything improper, my dears; Sir Thomas would not like it,' may not exert a powerful influence for good; but who has any shadow of doubt that those are her very words? They are spoken—as they should be—to her daughters, and not to us. They are spoken—as they should be—by Lady Bertram, and not by Jane Austen. Therefore we listen with content, and take comfort in the thought that, whatever severities may be inflicted on us by the novelists of the future, it is not in the power of progress to deprive us of the past.

(d) 'bores'
From 'Ennui', *Essays in Idleness*, 1893.

Mrs Ritchie is Anne Thackeray.

Before this date, however, one English writer had given to literature some priceless illustrations of the species. 'Could we but study our bores as Miss Austen must have studied hers in her country village,' says Mrs Ritchie, 'what a delightful world this might be!' But I seriously doubt whether any real enjoyment could be extracted from Miss Bates, or Mr Rushworth, or Sir William Lucas, in the flesh. If we knew them, we should probably feel precisely as did Emma Woodhouse, and Maria Bertram, and Elizabeth Bennet,—vastly weary of their company. In fact, only their brief appearances make the two gentlemen bores so diverting, even in fiction; and Miss Bates, I must confess, taxes my patience sorely. She is so tiresome that she tires, and I am invariably tempted to do what her less fortunate townspeople would have gladly done,—run away from her to more congenial society. Surely comedy ceases, and tragedy begins, when poor Jane Fairfax escapes from the strawberry party at Donwell, and seeks, under the burning noonday sun, the blessed relief of solitude. 'We all know at times what it is to be wearied in spirits. Mine, I admit, are exhausted,' is the confession wrung from the silent lips of a girl who has borne all that human nature can bear from Miss Bates's affectionate solicitude. Perhaps the best word ever spoken upon the creation of such characters in novels comes from Cardinal Newman. 'It is very difficult,' he says, 'to delineate a bore in a narrative, for the simple reason that he is a bore. A tale must aim at condensation, but a bore acts in solution. It is only in the long run that he is ascertained.' And when he *is* ascertained, and his identity established beyond reach of doubt, what profit have we in his desolating perfections? Miss Austen was far from enjoying the dull people whom she knew in life. We have the testimony of her letters to this effect. Has not Mrs Stent, otherwise lost to fame, been crowned with direful immortality as the woman who bored Jane Austen? 'We may come to be Mrs Stents ourselves,' she writes, with facile self-reproach at her impatience, 'unequal to anything, and unwelcome to anybody;' an apprehension manifestly manufactured out of nothingness to strengthen some wavering purpose of amendment. Stupidity is acknowledged to be the one natural gift which cannot be cultivated, and Miss Austen well knew it lay beyond her grasp. With as much sincerity could Emma Woodhouse have said, 'I may come in time to be a second Miss Bates.'

(e) Re-readable
From 'In the Dozy Hours', July 1894, *In the Dozy Hours*, 1894.

Agnes Repplier has explained that in preparing for sleep, *Mansfield Park* is her reading.

Miss Austen is likewise the best of midnight friends. There stand her novels, few in number and shabby with much handling, and the god Hermes smiles upon them kindly. We have known them well for years. There is no fresh nook to be explored, no forgotten page to be revisited. But we will take one down, and re-read for the fiftieth time the history of the theatricals at Mansfield Park; and see Mr Yates ranting by himself in the dining-room, and the indefatigable lovers rehearsing amorously on the stage, and poor Mr Rushworth stumbling through his two-and-forty speeches, and Fanny Price, in the chilly little schoolroom, listening disconsolately as her cousin Edmund and Mary Crawford go through their parts with more spirit and animation than the occasion seems to demand. When Sir Thomas returns, most inopportunely, from Antigua, we lay down the book with a sigh of gentle satisfaction, knowing that we shall find all these people in the morning just where they belong, and not, after the fashion of some modern novels, spirited overnight to the antipodes, with a breakneck gap of months or years to be spanned by our drooping imaginations.

(f) Life into art
From 'Gifts', *In the Dozy Hours*, 1894.

Gifts there have been, of a humble and domestic kind, the mere recollection of which is a continual delight. I love to think of Jane Austen's young sailor brother, her 'own particular little brother,' Charles, spending his first prize money in gold chains and 'topaze crosses' for his sisters. What prettier, warmer picture can be called to mind than this handsome, gallant, light-hearted lad—handsomer, Jane jealously insists, than all the rest of the family—bringing back to his quiet country home these innocent trophies of victory? Surely it was the pleasure Miss Austen felt in that 'topaze' cross, that little golden chain, which found such eloquent expression in Fanny Price's mingled rapture and distress when *her* sailor brother brought her the amber cross from Sicily, and Edmund Bertram offered her, too late, the chain on which to hang it. It is a splendid reward that lies in wait for boyish generosity when the sister chances to be one of the immortals, and hands down to generations of readers the charming record of her gratitude and love.

(g) 'unerring taste and incomparable humor'
Signed notice, 'Jane Austen', *The Critic*, December 1900.

The elevation of *Emma*, to which she refers caustically, was certainly going on before 1890. Goldwin Smith opens ch. 5 of *Jane Austen* (1890), 'Some will think that of all Miss Austen's works *Emma* is the best' (p. 118).

In the year of grace, 1796, when Mrs Radcliffe's 'Romance of the Forest' had been already dramatized for English playgoers, and the ever-famous 'Mysteries of Udolpho' had swept its triumphant way over all the English land, Jane Austen, a girl of twenty-one, wrote in her quiet country home a story which was subsequently revised and published under the Edgeworthian title, 'Pride and Prejudice.' When we think of that year of grace, of the school of fiction then dominant, of Miss Austen's youth, upbringing, simple life, and narrow field of observation, we are forced to admit that, if the age of miracles be over now, it was by no means a thing of the past in 1796.

None of the oppressive success forced upon Mrs Radcliffe—a most modest and retiring lady—stimulated or harassed Jane Austen. Her books brought her little fame and less gold; the earnings of her lifetime falling far below the sum paid by a daring publisher for 'The Italian.' A few people read them, a very few recognized the perfection of their art. Miss Austen appears to have been well content with her modest share of fortune. She must have known the excellence of her work, and, with the tranquillity of a well-balanced nature, trusted to its finding, as all work must some day find, its one appointed place. She did not even—be it recorded with respect—exact the smallest tribute of praise or deference from her family. The restless selfishness of egotism had no place in her steadfast soul.

And now,—well now, as Mr Goldwin Smith sensibly says, 'metaphor has been exhausted' in depicting the flawlessness of Miss Austen's art and the narrowness of its boundaries. A few years ago a little school of critics, who confessed themselves pained by breadth of treatment, endeavored to exalt these half-dozen admirable novels by denying them competitors, by reducing all English fiction to one common denominator—'Emma.' The result was a temporary chilling of esteem. A sulky public observed with Marianne Dashwood, 'This is admiration of a very particular kind,' and evinced a disposition to confine itself obstinately to romance. But not even the vagaries of a bellicose enthusiasm can long stand between Jane Austen and her readers, that ever increasing body of readers, who, returning again and again to her familiar pages, find in them unfailing pleasure and recreation. If destitute of passion, they possess unerring taste and incomparable humor. If their author declines to travel far, she travels straight, and by the best of all possible paths, to her appointed goal. Her novels hold a peerless place in the world of letters, and are part of our heritage of delight.

(h) Mrs Elwood's view
From 'The Novelist', *A Happy Half Century*, 1908.

Agnes Repplier looks back to Mrs Elwood's 'genteel' account
of Jane Austen in 1843.

Ten years later 'Pride and Prejudice' made its unobtrusive
appearance, and was read by that 'saving remnant' to whom is
confided the intellectual welfare of their land. Mrs Elwood, the
biographer of England's 'Literary Ladies,' tells us, in the few
careless pages which she deems sufficient for Miss Austen's novels,
that there *are* people who think these stories 'worthy of ranking
with those of Madame d'Arblay and Miss Edgeworth'; but that in
their author's estimation (and, by inference, in her own), 'they took
up a much more humble station.' Yet, tolerant even of such
inferiority, Mrs Elwood bids us remember that although 'the
character of Emma is perhaps too manoeuvring and too plotting to
be perfectly amiable,' that of Catherine Morland 'will not suffer
greatly even from a comparison with Miss Burney's interesting
Evelina'; and that 'although one is occasionally annoyed by the
underbred personages of Miss Austen's novels, the annoyance is
only such as we should feel if we were actually in their company.'
    It was thus that our genteel great-grand-mothers, enamoured of
lofty merit and of refined sensibility, regarded Elizabeth Bennet's
relations.

(i) 'the gay cynicism'
Signed review of *Jane Austen*, R. Brimley Johnson, 1930,
Commonweal, 13 May 1931.

No man living knows more, or as much, about Jane Austen as does
Mr Johnson; and the only drawback to reading this last of his books
is that it makes us want to pause midway, and reread for the
twentieth, or the thirtieth, time one of the six immortal novels
which for a hundred years have been the solace and delight of those
who, through no merit of their own, are fitted to enjoy them. Jane

is not for all markets, and this circumstance lends a secret and unworthy zest to her faithful followers. They do not want to share their pleasure with their neighbors. It is too intimate and too individual.

Mr Johnson's careful probing shows Miss Austen to have been in the main a happy woman. This fact does not lessen our grief and resentment at the stupidity of her generation which never knew, or permitted her to know, how perfect her novels were. That she should have died before 'Persuasion' was given to the world would be starkly tragic were it not that it failed to hurt her as it would have hurt Charlotte Brontë. It hurts us now; but the gay cynicism with which Jane Austen met life was a shining armor of defense.

Did this laughing lady cherish a dim attachment for a dimly outlined gentleman whom she immortalized as Captain Wentworth? Did she reveal herself in the finely drawn portrait of Anne Elliot? The theory has taken hold of critics, and they will not let it go. Mr Johnson says that for all we know on the subject we have 'the unimpeachable authority of Cassandra'; but then it is nothing when known. A nameless Englishman whom the sisters met one summer on the Devon coast, who expressed a desire, or a determination, to meet them again the following summer, and who died in the autumn. That is all. We are grateful for the story because it inspired Kipling's vivacious poem; but there is a lack, not only of detail but of ardor, about the narrative which leaves us doubtful and dispirited. As for the more robust suitor named Bigg-Wither, we rejoice with all our hearts that Jane refused to marry him. To have had a Mrs Bigg-Wither as the author of 'Pride and Prejudice' and 'Emma' would have been more than the English-speaking world could bear.

Because Mr Johnson is so conversant with his subject, and because his book has a quietly convincing tone, we should heed what he says concerning the moderation and sanity of Miss Austen's deepest emotions. 'She regarded marriage,' he observes, 'as at once the natural and ideal consummation of life.' Yet she does not often portray married life under ideal conditions, and she does not always promise such conditions to the lovers whom she unites in her last chapters. Emma Woodhouse and Mr Knightley are, indeed, made for each other; and as much might be said for Anne Elliot and Captain Wentworth. Edmund Bertram and Fanny Price are in for a dull life, but they will never know it. Henry Tilney will, however, be acutely aware of its dulness after six months of marital experience; and it will take six years to blunt his sensibilities, and reconcile him to what Miss Austen philosophically remarks is the fate of many sensible men.

Mr Johnson's volume is an excellent piece of book-making; light to hold as are most books printed in England, and well illustrated. The fanciful maps of Longbourn, Barton, Mansfield Park, Highbury, Kellynch Hall, and Northanger Abbey are truly delightful. The reproductions of the engravings from the edition of 1833 are interesting on account of their strained and almost violent character. Henry Tilney peacefully mounting his own stairway has the aspect of a brigand, intent on murdering the justly alarmed Catherine. Zoffany's portrait of the child, Jane, is charming. One can but wish for the hundredth time that Cassandra's pudding-faced likeness (which could never have been a likeness) of her sister had been consigned to eternal oblivion.

18. Saintsbury on *Pride and Prejudice*
1894

From Preface to edition illustrated by Hugh Thomson, published by George Allen; reprinted in *Prefaces and Essays*, 1933.

George Edward Bateman Saintsbury (1845–1933) was a prolific critic and literary historian; Professor of Rhetoric and English Literature at the University of Edinburgh, 1895–1915. During this period, he attracted a large following as a genial academic ready to profess to the 'vulgar', as he facetiously called the public at large. He boasted his experience as a pedagogue at school and university.

Walt Whitman has somewhere a fine and just distinction between 'loving by allowance' and 'loving with personal love'. This distinction applies to books as well as to men and women; and in the case of the not very numerous authors who are the objects of the personal affection, it brings a curious consequence with it. There is much more difference as to their best work than in the case of those others who are loved 'by allowance', by convention, and because it is felt to be the right and proper thing to love them. And in the sect—fairly large and yet unusually choice—of Austenians or Janites, there would probably be found partisans of the claim to primacy of almost every one of the novels. To some the delightful freshness and humour of *Northanger Abbey*, its completeness, finish and *entrain*, obscure the undoubted critical facts that its scale is small, and its scheme, after all, that of burlesque or parody, a kind in which the first rank is reached with difficulty. *Persuasion*, relatively faint in tone, and not enthralling in interest, has devotees who exalt above all the others its exquisite delicacy and keeping. The catastrophe of *Mansfield Park* is admittedly theatrical, the hero and heroine are insipid, and the author has almost wickedly destroyed all romantic interest by expressly admitting that Edmund only took Fanny because Mary shocked him, and that Fanny might very likely have taken Crawford if he had been a little more assiduous; yet the matchless rehearsal-scenes and the characters of Mrs Norris and others have secured, I believe, a considerable party for it. *Sense and Sensibility* has perhaps the fewest out-and-out admirers; but it does not want them.

I suppose, however, that the majority of at least competent votes would, all things considered, be divided between *Emma* and the present book; and perhaps the vulgar verdict (if indeed a fondness for Miss Austen be not of itself a patent of exemption from any possible charge of vulgarity) would go for *Emma*. It is the larger, the more varied, the more popular; the author had by the time of its composition seen rather more of the world, and had improved her general, though not her most peculiar and characteristic dialogue; such figures as Miss Bates, as the Eltons, cannot but unite the suffrages of everybody. On the other hand, I, for my part, declare for *Pride and Prejudice* unhesitatingly. It seems to me the most perfect, the most characteristic, the most eminently quintessential of its author's works; and for this contention in such narrow space as is permitted to me. I propose here to show cause. ...

The characteristics of Miss Austen's humour are so subtle and delicate that they are, perhaps, at all times easier to apprehend than to express, and at any particular time likely to be differently apprehended by different persons. To me this humour seems to possess a greater affinity, on the whole, to that of Addison than to any other of the numerous species of this great British genus. The differences of scheme, of time, of subject, of literary convention, are, of course, obvious enough; the difference of sex does not, perhaps, count for much, for there was a distinctly feminine element in 'Mr Spectator,' and in Jane Austen's genius there was, though nothing mannish, much that was masculine. But the likeness of quality consists in a great number of common subdivisions of quality—demureness, extreme minuteness of touch, avoidance of loud tones and glaring effects. Also there is in both a certain not inhuman or unamiable cruelty. It is the custom with those who judge grossly to contrast the good nature of Addison with the savagery of Swift, the wildness of Miss Austen with the boisterousness of Fielding and Smollett, even with the ferocious practical jokes that her immediate predecessor, Miss Burney, allowed without very much protest. Yet, both in Mr Addison and in Miss Austen there is, though a restrained and well-mannered, an insatiable and ruthless delight in roasting and cutting up a fool. A man in the early eighteenth century, of course, could push this taste further than a lady in the early nineteenth; and no doubt Miss Austen's principles, as well as her heart, would have shrunk from such things as the letter from the unfortunate husband in the *Spectator,* who describes, with all the gusto and all the innocence in the world, how his wife and his friend induce him to play at blind-man's-buff. But another *Spectator* letter—that of the damsel of fourteen who wishes to marry Mr Shapely, and assures her selected Mentor that 'he admires your *Spectators* mightily'—might have been written by a rather more ladylike and intelligent Lydia Bennet in the days of Lydia's great-grandmother; while, on the other hand, some (I think unreasonably) have found 'cynicism' in touches of Miss Austen's own, such as her satire of Mrs Musgrove's self-deceiving regrets over her son. But this word 'cynical' is one of the most misused in the English language, especially when, by a glaring and gratuitous falsification of its original sense, it is applied, not to rough and snarling invective, but to gentle and oblique satire. If cynicism means the perception of 'the other side', the sense of 'the accepted hells beneath', the consciousness that motives are nearly always mixed, and that to seem is not identical with to be—if this be cynicism, then every man and woman who is not a fool, who does not care to live in a fool's paradise, who has knowledge of nature and the world and life, is a cynic. And in that sense Miss Austen certainly was one. She may even have been one in the further sense that, like her own Mr Bennet, she took an epicurean delight in dissecting, in displaying, in setting at work her fools and her mean persons. I think she did take this delight, and I do not think at all the worse of her for it as a woman, while she was immensely the better for it as an artist.

... with Miss Austen the myriad, trival, unforced strokes build up the picture like magic. Nothing is false; nothing is superfluous. When (to take the present book only) Mr Collins changed his mind from Jane to Elizabeth 'while Mrs Bennet was stirring the fire' (and we know *how* Mrs Bennet would have stirred the fire), when Mr Darcy 'brought his coffee-cup back himself,' the touch in each case is like that of Swift—'taller by the breadth of my nail'—which impressed the half-reluctant Thackeray with just and outspoken admiration. Indeed, fantastic as it may seem, I should put Miss Austen as near to Swift in some ways, as I have put her to Addison in others.

This Swiftian quality appears in the present novel as it appears, nowhere else in the character of the immortal, the ineffable Mr Collins. Mr Collins is really *great*; far greater than anything Addison ever did, almost great enough for Fielding or for Swift himself. It has been said that no one ever was like him. But in the first place, *he* was like him; he is there—alive, imperishable, more real than hundreds of prime ministers and archibishops, of 'metals, semi-metals, and distinguished philosophers.' In the second place, it is rash, I think, to conclude that an actual Mr Collins was impossible or non-existent at the end of the eighteenth century. It is very interesting that we possess, in this same gallery, what may be called a spoiled first draught, or an unsuccessful study of him, in John Dashwood. The formality, the under-breeding, the meanness, are there; but the portrait is only half alive, and is felt to be even a little unnatural. Mr Collins is perfectly natural, and perfectly alive. In fact, for all the 'miniature,' there is something gigantic in the way in which a certain side, and more than one, of humanity, and especially eighteenth-century humanity, its Philistinism, its well-meaning but hide-bound morality, its formal pettiness, its grovelling respect for rank, its materialism, its selfishness, receives exhibition. I will not admit that one speech or one action of this inestimable man is incapable of being reconciled with reality, and I should not wonder if many of these words and actions are historically true.

... Elizabeth, with nothing offensive, nothing *viraginous,* nothing for the 'New Woman' about her, has by nature what the best modern (not 'new') women have by education and experience, a perfect freedom from the idea that all men may bully her if they choose, and that most will run away with her if they can. Though not in the least 'impudent and mannish grown', she has no mere sensibility, no nasty niceness about her. The form of passion common and likely to seem natural in Miss Austen's day was so invariably connected with the display of one or the other, or both of these qualities, that she has not made Elizabeth outwardly passionate. But I, at least, have not the slightest doubt that she would have married Darcy just as willingly without Pemberley as with it, and anybody who can read between lines will not find the lovers' conversations in the final chapters so frigid as they might have looked to the Della Cruscans of their own day, and perhaps do look to the Della Cruscans of this.

And, after all, what is the good of seeking for the reason of charm?—it is there. There were better sense in the sad mechanic exercise of determining the reason of its absence where it is not. In the novels of the last hundred years there are vast numbers of young ladies with whom it might be a pleasure to fall in love; there are at least five with whom, as it seems to me, no man of taste and spirit can help doing so. Their names are, in chronological order, Elizabeth Bennet, Diana Vernon, Argemone Lavington, Beatrix Esmond, and Barbara Grant. I should have been most in love with Beatrix and Argemone; I should, I think, for mere occasional companionship, have preferred Diana and Barbara. But to live with and to marry, I do not know that any one of the four can come into competition with Elizabeth.

19. 'mistress of derision'

1894

Unsigned article, 'The Classic Novelist', *Pall Mall Gazette*, 16 February 1894; reprinted in *The Second Person Singular*, 1921; some sections used again in 'The English Women-Humorists', *North American Review*, June 1905; reprinted *The Wares of Autolycus*, 1965.

Alice Meynell (1847–1922), poet, essayist and critic, gives a significant 'depreciation'.

Jane Austen seldom begins a novel without a deliberate chapter—generally a family chapter. A masterly consciousness of her own authority gives her the right of control over her reader's impatience or slovenliness. The order of things is hers, not his, and and he must wait her time for wit. Hers are what Jeremy Taylor, even at his prayers, calls 'measures of address'. Her openings imply a firmer hold upon narrative than later novelists, with their verbless first sentences, their 'he' and 'she' for persons to be named later, thought to grasp at. The moderns would be much depressed were they required to open thus: 'The family of Dashwood had long been settled in Sussex. Their estate was large, and their residence was at Norland Park, in the centre of their property, where, for many generations, they had lived in so respectable a manner as to engage the general good opinion of their surrounding acquaintance.' We consent to read the dismal opening; we endure the pother of the unmusical words; we tolerate it all because we know that in a page or two the respectable Dashwoods will be deprived of some of the general good opinion of their surrounding acquaintance. We know that Miss Austen will make of her personages good sport for her reader, her sense of derision being equal to that of her own kin, the original Philistines. For another example, would any later author, having a Mrs Bennet to deride for our delight, consent to introduce her thus: 'Mrs Bennet was a woman of mean understanding'? But in this case Miss Austen's art loses nothing, even by the chill of that presentation.

That Jane works upon very small matters is hardly worth saying, and certainly not worth complaining of. Things are not trivial merely because they are small; but that which makes life, art, and work trivial is a triviality of relations. Mankind lives by vital relations; and if these are mean, so is the life, so is the art that expresses them because it can express no more. With Miss Austen love, vengeance, devotion, duty, maternity, sacrifice, are infinitely trivial. There is also a constant relation of watchfulness, of prudence. As the people in her stories watch one another so does Miss Austen seem to be watching them, and her curiosity is intense indeed; she realizes their colds—her female characters take a great many colds—so that one seems to hear her narrate the matter in a muffled voice, but not precisely because of her sympathy. That such close observation can work on without tenderness must be a proof of this author's exceeding cynicism.

Triviality of relations among Miss Austen's personages does not prevent a certain kind of intensity. Lying and spite among her women work at close quarters. With the men we hear of a somewhat wider range; there is, in the case of one justly rejected suitor, a suspicion, a rumour of 'Sunday travelling'; the accusation is not precisely brought home.

No one who has not read *Pride and Prejudice* and *Emma* is able to say that he knows worldliness in its own proper home. There, 'engaging the general good opinion of surrounding acquaintance' (the mouthful of thick words!) worldliness keeps its dowdy and hopeless state and ceremony. There is in almost every second page of Miss Austen, a detestable thing called, in the language of the day, 'consequence'. No slang of our own time, by the way, has ever misused a word more foolishly. To 'consequence', and to the heroine's love of it, is promptly sacrificed all that might have seemed the beginning or suggestions of spirituality. There is more that is spiritual in the heroines of to-day—in the 'female animal' herself—than in Anne, in Harriet, in Jane, in Fanny, or in any other of the young women who gossip through the pages of these famous novels. The men gossip, too; they are minutely occupied with the engagements, colds, arrowroot, tea-parties, and correspondence of the women.

All this, it may be said, relates to Miss Austen's subjects and not to her perfect art. But Miss Austen's art and her matter are made for one another. Miss Austen's art is not of the highest quality; it is of an admirable secondary quality. Her gentle spinsterly manner prevents us from perceiving at first how much of her derision—for she is mistress of derision rather than of wit or humour—is caricature of a rather gross sort. 'Lady Middleton resigned herself to the idea with all the philosophy of a well-bred woman, contenting herself with merely giving her husband a gentle reprimand on the subject five or six times every day.' Far finer is Miss Austen's success when she gains her effect by delicate persistence in reiteration. This is the way in which she enjoys Mr Woodhouse, the old gentleman in whose eyes every woman who has had the good luck to marry out of his tedious house is a 'poor dear'. His compassion makes excellent sport, of a kind, by the effect of cumulation. The author's patience and vigilance are, indeed, perfect, insomuch as they never neglect or fail to perceive an opportunity for giving the turn to his phrase, the tone to his word. And the whole thing would advance, by the slow degrees of this method, and close in a little masterpiece, but that something of the fineness, as well as something of the increase, of the result is now and then marred by Miss Austen's own explanation. She prepares her reader deliberately; she instructs him at the outset in what he would have become convinced of at the end.

Her irony is now and then exquisitely bitter. 'Who could tell'—Miss Austen is presenting the thoughts of Mrs John Dashwood in regard to her unwelcome sisters-in-law—'that they might not expect to go out with her a second time? The power of disappointing them, it was true, must always be hers. But that was not enough.' About the following little sentence there is something of the wit of surprise. It describes the joys of a young woman of the less admirable sort, lately married: 'They passed some months in great happiness at Dawlish; for she had many relations and old acquaintances to cut.' Miss Austen has a word in dismissing the inconstant Mr Willoughby: 'His wife was not always out of humour; and in his breed of horses and dogs, and in sporting of every kind, he found no inconsiderable degree of domestic felicity.'

The lack of tenderness and of spirit is manifest in Miss Austen's indifference to children. They hardly appear in her stories except to illustrate the folly of their mothers. They are not her subjects as children; they are her subjects as spoilt children, and as children through whom a mother may receive flattery from her designing acquaintance, and may inflict annoyance on her sensible friends.

The novelist even spends some of her irony upon a little girl of three. She sharpens her pen over the work. The passage is too long to quote, but the reader may refer to *Sense and Sensibility*. In this coldness or dislike Miss Austen resembles Charlotte Brontë.

Most dully expressive are Miss Austen's country houses. One description places her people in a few words in the scene that suits them with a quite subtle suitableness; and the thing is presented in words which, here again, by their very lack of music define mediocrity: 'Cleveland was a spacious, modern-built house, situated on a sloping lawn. The pleasure grounds were tolerably extensive; and, like every other place of the same degree of importance, it had its open shrubbery, and closed wood walk; a road of smooth gravel, winding round a plantation, led to the front.' There, there in the modern-built mansion was the goal of the hopes of heroines. To the shrubbery they betook themselves, in a 'hurry of spirits', or other limited forms of emotion that might make them wish to escape remark. In and out pottered the men—the men of the period, the men of so strange a sex. In the tolerably extensive grounds walked 'consequence', and its wheels marked the smooth gravel that wound round the plantation.

Before quitting the noble subject of 'consequence' let it be noted that Emma had the following hesitation about a youth she was inclined to admire (Emma was not twenty-one): 'Of pride, indeed, there was perhaps scarcely enough; his indifference to a confusion of rank bordered too much on inelegance of mind. He could be no judge, however, of the evil he was holding cheap.' It is an unheavenly world.

20. 'the greatest of them all'

1895

From 'The Demands of Art', *Courier* (Lincoln, Nebraska), 23 November 1895; reprinted *The Kingdom of Art*, ed. Bernice Slate, 1966.

Willa Cather (1876–1947), American novelist and essayist. The concluding paragraph from a reflective essay on Ouida, her novels 'one rank morass of misguided genius and wasted power'.

I have not much faith in women in fiction. They have a sort of sex consciousness that is abominable. They are so limited to one string and they lie so about that. They are so few, the ones who really did anything worth while; there were the great Georges, George Eliot and George Sand, and they were anything but women, and there was Miss Bronte who kept her sentimentality under control, and there was Jane Austen who certainly had more common sense than any of them and was in some respects the greatest of them all. Women are so horribly subjective and they have such scorn for the healthy commonplace. When a woman writes a story of adventure, a stout sea tale, a manly battle yarn, anything without wine, women and love, then I will begin to hope for something great from them, not before.

21. The heroines

1900–1

From *Heroines of Fiction*, vol. i, 1901, developed from a series of articles in *Harper's Bazar*, commencing May 1900.

Aiming at a magazine readership—with lengthy quotation and extensive story recapitulation—Howells succeeds in being introductory without any dilution to his critical argument, continued from No. 16.

JANE AUSTEN'S ELIZABETH BENNET

The fashion of Maria Edgeworth's world has long passed away, but human nature is still here, and the fiction which was so true to it in the first years of the century is true to it in the last. 'The

Absentee,' 'Vivian,' 'Ennui,' 'Helen,' 'Patronage,' show their kindred with 'Belinda,' and by their frank and fresh treatment of character, their knowledge of society, and their employment of the major rather than the minor means of moving and amending the reader, they all declare themselves of the same lineage. In their primitive ethicism they own 'Pamela,' and 'Sir Charles Grandison' for their ancestors; but they are much more dramatic than Richardson's novels; they are almost theatrical in their haste for a direct moral effect. In this they are like the Burney-D'Arblay novels, which also deal with fashionable life, with dissipated lords and ladies, with gay parties at Vauxhall and Ranelagh, with debts and duns, with balls and routs in splendid houses, whose doors are haunted by sheriff's officers, with bankruptcies and arrests, or flights and suicides. But the drama of the Edgeworth fiction tends mostly to tragedy, and that of the Burney-D'Arblay fiction to comedy; though there are cases in the first where the wrong-doer is saved alive, and cases in the last where he is lost in his sins. The author of 'Evelina' was a good but light spirit, the author of 'Belinda' was a good but very serious soul and was amusing with many misgivings. Maria Edgeworth was a humorist in spite of herself; Frances Burney was often not as funny as she meant, and was, as it were, forced into tragical effects by the pressure of circumstances. You feel that she would much rather have got on without them; just as you feel that Miss Edgeworth rejoices in them, and is not sure that her jokes will be equally blessed to you.

I

It remained for the greatest of the gifted women, who beyond any or all other novelists have fixed the character and behavior of Anglo-Saxon fiction, to assemble in her delightful talent all that was best in that of her sisters. Jane Austen was indeed so fine an artist, that we are still only beginning to realize how fine she was; to perceive, after a hundred years, that in the form of the imagined fact, in the expression of personality, in the conduct of the narrative, and the subordination of incident to character, she is still unapproached in the English branch of Anglo-Saxon fiction. In American fiction Hawthorne is to be named with her for perfection of form; the best American novels are built upon more symmetrical lines than the best English novels, and have unconsciously shaped themselves upon the ideal which she instinctively and instantly realized.

Of course it was not merely in externals that Jane Austen so promptly achieved her supremacy. The wonder of any beautiful thing is that it is beautiful in so many ways; and her fiction is as admirable for its lovely humor, its delicate satire, its good sense, its kindness, its truth to nature, as for its form. There is nothing hurried or huddled in it, nothing confused or obscure, nothing excessive or inordinate. The marvel of it is none the less because it is evident that she wrote from familiar acquaintance with the fiction that had gone before her. In her letters there are hints of her intimacy with the novels of Goldsmith, of Richardson, of Frances Burney, and of Maria Edgeworth; but in her stories there are scarcely more traces of their influence than of Mrs Radcliffe's, or any of the romantic writers whom she delighted to mock. She is obviously of her generation, but in all literature she is one of the most original and independent spirits. Her deeply domesticated life was passed in the country scenes, the county society, which her books portray, far from literary men and events; and writing as she used, amidst the cheerful chatter of her home, she produced literature of still unrivalled excellence in its way, apparently without literary ambition, and merely for the pleasure of getting the life she knew before her outward vision. With the instinct and love of doing it, and not with the sense of doing anything uncommon, she achieved that masterpiece, 'Pride and Prejudice', which is quite as remarkable for being one of several masterpieces as for its absolute excellence. There have been authors enough who have written one extraordinary book; but all Jane Austen's books are extraordinary, and 'Persuasion', 'Northanger Abbey', 'Emma', 'Mansfield Park', and 'Sense and Sensibility', are each a masterpiece, inferior only to 'Pride and Prejudice', which was written first. After the young girl of twenty had written it, she kept it half as many years longer before she printed it. In mere order of chronology it belongs to the eighteenth century, but in spirit it is distinctly of the nineteenth century, as we feel that cycle to have been when we feel proudest of it. In manners as much as in methods it is such a vast advance upon the work of her sister novelists that you wonder whether some change had not already taken place in English society which she notes, and which they fail to note.

The topics of the best fiction of any time will probably be those which decent men and women talk of together in the best company; and such topics vary greatly from time to time. There is no reason to think that Frances Burney and Maria Edgeworth were less pure-minded than Jane Austen, but they dealt with phases of human experience which she did not deal with, because their friends and acquaintances did so, without being essentially worse than hers. A tendency towards a more scrupulous tone seems to have been the effect of the general revival in religion at the close of the last century, which persisted down to that time in our own century when the rise of scientific agnosticism loosed the bonds of expression. Now again of late years men and women in the best company talk together of things which would not have been discussed during the second and third quarters of the century. One must hedge one's position on such a point with many perhapses; nothing can be affirmed with certainty; the most that can be said is that the tone if not the temper, the manners if not the morals, which have lately been called *fin de siècle*, are noticeably more akin to what was *fin de siècle* a hundred years ago, than they are to what was thought fit in polite society fifty years ago. Possibly another revival of religion will bring another change, such as the purity of Jane Austen's fiction may have forecast rather than reported. But we do not know this, and possibly again her books are what they are in matter and manner because the little world of county society which she observed was wholesomer and decenter than the great world of London society which Miss Burney and Miss Edgeworth studied.

An author is as great for what he leaves out as for what he puts in; and Jane Austen shows her mastery in nothing more than in her avoidance of moving accidents for her most moving effects. She seems to have known intuitively that character resides in habit, and that for the novelist to seek its expression in violent events would be as stupid as for the painter to expect an alarm of fire or burglary to startle his sitter into a valuable revelation of his qualities. She puts from her, therefore, all the tremendous contrivances of her predecessors, and takes her place quietly on the ground to which they were, the best of them, falteringly and uncertainly feeling their way. After De Foe and Goldsmith she was the first to write a thoroughly artistic novel in English, and she surpassed Goldsmith as far in method as she refined upon De Foe in material. Among her contemporaries she was as easily first as Shakspere among the Elizabethan dramatists; and in the high excellencies of symmetrical form, force of characterization, clearness of conception, simplicity and temperance of means, she is still supreme: that girl who began at twenty with such a masterpiece as 'Pride and Prejudice,' and ended with such a masterpiece as 'Persuasion' at forty-two!

II

The story of 'Pride and Prejudice' has of late years become known to a constantly, almost rapidly, increasing cult, as it must be called, for the readers of Jane Austen are hardly ever less than her adorers: she is a passion and a creed, if not quite a religion. A beautiful, clever, and cultivated girl is already piqued and interested if not in love with a handsome, high-principled, excessively proud man, when she becomes bitterly prejudiced against him by the slanders of a worthless beneficiary of his family. The girl is Elizabeth Bennet, the young man is Fitzwilliam Darcy, and they first meet at a ball, where he behaves with ungracious indifference to her, and afterwards at the dinners and parties of a small country neighbor-hood where persons theoretically beyond the pale of gentility are admitted at least on sufferance; the stately manners of the day are relaxed by youth and high spirits; and no doubt the academic elevation of the language lapses oftener on the lips of the pretty girls and the lively young men than an author still in her nonage, and zealous for the dignity of her style, will allow to appear in the conversation of her hero and heroine....

JANE AUSTEN'S ANNE ELIOT AND CATHARINE MORLAND

That protest already noted, that revolt against the arrogance of rank, which makes itself felt more or less in all the novels of Jane Austen, might have been something that she inhaled with the stormy air of the time and respired again with the unconsciousness of breathing. But whether she knew it or not, this quiet little woman, who wrote her novels in the bosom of her clerical family; who was herself so contentedly of the established English order; who believed in inequality and its implications as of divine ordinance; who loved the delights of fine society, and rejoiced as few girls have in balls and parties, was in her way asserting the Rights of Man as unmistakably as the French revolutionists whose volcanic activity was of about the same compass of time as her literary industry. In her books the snob, not yet named or classified, is fully ascertained for the first time. Lady Catharine de Burgh in 'Pride and Prejudice,' John Dashwood in 'Sense and Sensibility,' Mr Elton in 'Emma,' General Tilney in 'Northanger Abbey,' and above all Sir Walter Eliot in 'Persuasion,' are immortal types of insolence or meanness which foreshadow the kindred shapes of Thackeray's vaster snob-world, and fix the date when they began to be recognized and detested. But their recognition and detestation were only an incident of the larger circumstance studied in the different stories; and in 'Persuasion' the snobbishness of Sir Walter has little to do with the fortunes of his daughter Anne after the first unhappy moment of her broken engagement. . . .

JANE AUSTEN'S EMMA WOODHOUSE, MARIANNE DASHWOOD, AND FANNY PRICE

In primitive fiction plot is more important than character; as the art advances character becomes the chief interest, and the action is such as springs from it. In the old tales and romances there is no such thing as character in the modern sense; their readers were satisfied with what the heroes and heroines did and suffered.

When the desire for character arose, the novelists loaded their types with attributes; but still there was no character, which is rooted in personality. The novelist of to-day who has not conceived of this is as archaic as any romancer of the Middle Ages in his ideal of art. Most of the novels printed in the last year, in fact, are as crudely devised as those which have amused people of childish imagination at any time in the last thousand years; and it will always be so with most novels, because most people are of childish imagination. The masterpieces in fiction are those which delight the mind with the traits of personality, with human nature recognizable by the reader through its truth to himself.

The wonder of Jane Austen is that at a time when even the best fiction was overloaded with incident, and its types went staggering about under the attributes heaped upon them, she imagined getting on with only so much incident as would suffice to let her characters express their natures movingly or amusingly. She seems to have reached this really unsurpassable degree of perfection without a formulated philosophy, and merely by her clear vision of the true relation of art to life; but however she came to be what she was, she was so unquestionably great, so unmistakably the norm and prophecy of most that is excellent in Anglo-Saxon fiction since her time, that I shall make no excuse for what may seem a disproportionate study of her heroines.

I

Emma Woodhouse, in the story named after her, is one of the most boldly imagined of Jane Austen's heroines. Perhaps she is the very most so, for it took supreme courage to portray a girl, meant to win and keep the reader's fancy, with the characteristics frankly ascribed to Emma Woodhouse....

22. Henry James on Jane Austen

1905—14

(a) 'her light felicity'
'The Lesson of Balzac', 1905; reprinted, *The House of Fiction*, 62–3.

James's amusing account of the book-trade's promotion of Jane Austen is combined with his view of her as the unconscious, artless artist. Howells, for one, resented the patronising tone of this. Writing to his daughter Mildred (24 March 1906), he remarks on James giving 'a pat for the giant Jane!' (*Selected Letters*, v. 168).

...Jane Austen, with all her light felicity, leaves us hardly more curious of her process, or of the experience in her that fed it, than the brown thrush who tells his story from the garden bough; and this, I freely confess, in spite of her being one of those of the shelved and safe, for all time, of whom I should have liked to begin by talking; one of those in whose favour discrimination has long since practically operated. She is in fact a signal instance of the way it does, with all its embarrassments, at last infallibly operate. A sharp short cut, one of the sharpest and shortest achieved, in this field, by the general judgement, came out, betimes, straight at her feet. Practically overlooked for thirty or forty years after her death, she perhaps really stands there for us as the prettiest possible example of that rectification of estimate, brought about by some slow clearance of stupidity, the half-century or so is capable of working round to. This tide has risen high on the opposite shore, the shore of appreciation—risen rather higher, I think, than the high-water mark, the highest, of her intrinsic merit and interest; though I grant indeed—as a point to be made—that we are dealing here in some degree with the tides so freely driven up, beyond their mere logical reach, by the stiff breeze of the commercial, in other words of the special bookselling spirit; an eager, active, interfering force which has a great many confusions of apparent value, a great many wild and wandering estimates, to answer for. For these distinctively mechanical and overdone reactions, of course, the critical spirit, even in its most relaxed mood, is not responsible. Responsible, rather, is the body of publishers, editors, illustrators, producers of the pleasant twaddle of magazines; who have found their 'dear', our dear, everybody's dear, Jane so infinitely to their material purpose, so amenable to pretty reproduction in every variety of what is called tasteful, and in what seemingly proves to be saleable, form.

I do not, naturally, mean that she would be saleable if we had not more or less—beginning with Macaulay, her first slightly ponderous amoroso—lost our hearts to her; but I cannot help seeing her, a good deal, as in the same lucky box as the Brontës—lucky for the ultimate guerdon; a case of popularity (that in especial of the Yorkshire sisters), a beguiled infatuation, a sentimentalized vision, determined largely by the accidents and circumstances originally surrounding the manifestation of the genius—only with the reasons for the sentiment, in this latter connection, turned the other way. The key to Jane Austen's fortune with posterity has been in part the extraordinary grace of her facility, in fact of her un-consciousness: as if, at the most, for difficulty, for embarrassment, she sometimes, over her work basket, her tapestry flowers, in the spare, cool drawing-room of other days, fell a-musing, lapsed too metaphorically, as one may say, into wool-gathering, and her dropped stitches, of these pardonable, of these precious moments, were afterwards picked up as little touches of human truth, little glimpses of steady vision, little master-strokes of imagination.

(b) 'her testimony complacently ends'
'The New Novel', 1914; reprinted, *Notes on Novelists*, 1914.

So, to express it briefly, the possibility of hugging the shore of the real as it had not, among us, been hugged, and of pushing inland, as far as a keel might float, wherever the least opening seemed to smile, dawned upon a few votaries and gathered further confidence with exercise. Who could say, of course, that Jane Austen had not been close, just as who could ask if Anthony Trollope had not been copious?—just as who could *not* say that it all depended on what was meant by these terms? The demonstration of what was meant, it presently appeared, could come but little by little, quite as if each tentative adventurer had rather anxiously to learn for himself what *might* be meant—this failing at least the leap into the arena of some great demonstrative, some sudden athletic and epoch-making authority. Who could pretend that Dickens was anything but romantic, and even more romantic in his humour, if possible, than in pathos or in queer perfunctory practice of the 'plot'? Who could pretend that Jane Austen didn't leave much more untold than told about the aspects and manners even of the confined circle in which her muse revolved? Why shouldn't it be argued against her that where her testimony complacently ends the pressure of appetite within us presumes exactly to begin?

23. Mark Twain on Jane Austen

1896–c1909

Samuel Clemens (1835–1910), novelist, journalist and essayist, enjoyed himself in the character of the arch anti-Austenite, the rough-neck American democrat in collision with the genteel English spinster.

(a) From *Following the Equator* (1897), ch. 62, diary entry, on board ship, for 10 April 1896: 'Jane Austen's books, too, are absent from this library. Just that one omission alone would make a fairly good library out of a library that hadn't a book in it.'

(b) From letter 13 September 1898, first published, lacking the third sentence, in *Letters* (1917), ii. 667, ed. A. B. Paine; sentence added in 'Mark Twain and the Art of Writing', Brander Matthews, *Harper's Magazine*, October 1920: 'I haven't any right to criticise books, and I don't do it except when I hate them. I often want to criticise Jane Austen, but her books madden me so that I can't conceal my frenzy from the reader; and therefore I have to stop every time I begin. Every time I read "Pride and Prejudice" I want to dig her up and hit her over the skull with her own shin-bone.'

(c) From letter 18 January 1909 to W.D. Howells, *Mark Twain-Howells Letters* (1960), ii. 841, edd. H.N. Smith & W.M. Gibbs: (referring to Poe) 'To me his prose is unreadable—like Jane Austin's. No, there is a difference. I could read his prose on salary, but not Jane's. Jane is entirely impossible. It seems a great pity to me that they allowed her to die a natural death!' (Is Twain's spelling 'Austin' a solecism deliberately illiterate, intended to further inflame Howells?).

(d) Quoted in A.B. Paine, *Mark Twain* (1912), iii. 1500: '"When I take up one of Jane Austen's books," he said, "such as *Pride and Prejudice*, I feel like a barkeeper entering the kingdom of heaven. I know what his sensations would be and his private comments. He would not find the place to his taste, and he would probably say so."' (According to Paine, Twain said this in June 1909 on a train ride from Baltimore to Redding.)

(e) Howells recorded in *My Mark Twain* (1910), 'His prime abhorrence was my dear and honored prime favorite, Jane Austen. He once said to me... "*You* seem to think that woman could write," and he forbore withering me with his scorn, apparently because we had been friends so long, and he more pitied than hated me for my bad taste' (p. 16).

24. A.C. Bradley on Jane Austen

1911

From 'Jane Austen', a lecture first given at Newnham College, Cambridge in 1911; then to the English Association; the final text, with notes, was printed in *Essays and Studies*, 1911; and again in *A Miscellany*, 1929, where Bradley advises the reader 'to ignore the notes in reading the text'.

Andrew Cecil Bradley (1851–1935), Professor of English Literature at Liverpool, Glasgow and Oxford, is best known for his essays on Shakespeare.

This lecture is generally regarded as the starting-point for the serious academic approach to Jane Austen (notwithstanding Bradley's Janeite tone as one of the 'faithful' addressing his fellow enthusiasts). Mary Lascelles (see page 124) wrote that 'whole quotations' from it might well have headed every part of her book.

In speaking to you of Jane Austen I must assume, not only that you are familiar with her novels, but that, like myself, you belong to the faithful. That does not bind us to rank her with the very greatest novel-writers, or to prefer her works to others more ambitious and more faulty. But it does imply a perception and enjoyment of her surpassing excellence within that comparatively narrow sphere whose limits she never tries to over-pass—an excellence which, we may perhaps venture to say, gives her in that sphere the position held by Shakespeare in his. Those who lack this perception or dispute its truth may possibly be in the right; but attempts to prove that they are wrong are perfectly futile, since all the proofs rest on the perception itself. I must therefore assume that you belong to the faithful. And, if you do, you will not wish me to add another to the estimates of Jane Austen's genius; nor, on the other hand, will you ask me whether I have anything new to say. I do not know enough of Austen criticism to answer the question: nor does it matter. The faithful enjoy comparing notes; and I offer you some of mine, and wish that you could give me yours in return. . . .

There are two distinct strains in Jane Austen. She is a moralist and a humorist. These strains are often blended or even completely fused, but still they may be distinguished. It is the first that connects her with Johnson, by whom, I suspect, she was a good deal influenced. With an intellect much less massive, she still observes human nature with the same penetration and the same complete honesty. She is like him in the abstention—no doubt, in her case, much less deliberate—from speculation, and in the orthodoxy and strength of her religion. She is very like in her contempt for mere sentiment, and for that 'cant' of which Boswell was recommended to clear his mind. We remember Johnson in those passages where she refuses to express a deeper concern than she feels for misfortune or grief, and with both there is an occasional touch of brutality in the manner of the refusal. It is a question, however, of manner alone, and when she speaks her mind fully and gravely she speaks for Johnson too; as when she makes Emma say: 'I hope it may be allowed that, if compassion has produced exertion and relief to the sufferers, it has done all that is truly important. If we feel for the wretched enough to do all we can for them, the rest is empty sympathy, only distressing to ourselves' (ch. 10). Finally, like Johnson, she is, in the strict sense, a moralist. Her morality, that is to say, is not merely embodied in her plots, it is often openly expressed. She followed a fashion of the day in her abstract titles, *Sense and Sensibility*, *Pride and Prejudice*, *Persuasion*; but the fashion coincides with the movement of her mind, and she knew very well the main lesson to be drawn from the other three novels. Her explicit statements and comments are often well worth pondering, though their terminology is sometimes old-fashioned, and though her novels contain infinitely more wisdom than they formulate.

With very few exceptions the greater writers differ little in what may be called their ultimate morality; but two or three minor traits may be singled out in Jane Austen's. One is her marked distrust of any indulgence in emotion or imagination where these are not plainly subservient to the resolve to do the right thing, however disagreeable or prosaic it may be. This meets us everywhere, and it has more than one effect. It leads her to approve of such heroines as Elinor Dashwood, Fanny Price, and Anne Elliot; and we share her approval. On the other hand, for some readers, the suppression of feeling and fancy in these characters, or at least in the first two, much diminishes their charm, and even suggests the idea which Jane Austen certainly did not hold, that good sense and dutifulness are apt to be spiritless or even depressed.

Another trait is her refusal to depict those conflicts of violent passions which display, even in misdoing, the possibilities of human nature, and at once agitate and uplift us as her pictures of life never can. Like most of us she never experienced, or even witnessed, such passions, and she had the wisdom, not too common in novelists, to avoid what she did not know. Besides, 'guilt and misery' were to her 'odious subjects',* which she quitted as soon as she could. Hence, though her morality is serious and, in some points, severe, her novels make exceptionally peaceful reading. She troubles us neither with problems nor with painful emotions and if there is a wound in our minds she is not likely to probe it.

Connected with this trait is another, which has the same effect. Unlike Johnson, she was blessed with a sunny temper, and she takes a brighter view of life. If we may judge from her works, she thought that very few people are naturally ill-disposed. If you examine you find that almost always the faults of her characters are directly connected with bad training, or want of training, in youth.

---

* *Mansfield Park*, opening of ch. 48.

Her opinion of parents who spoil their children or teach them that the object of life is to have what is now called 'a good time', is obvious both in her novels and her letters. Darcy had an excellent disposition; he was *taught* to be proud. Why were the Bertram sisters what they were? Because their father was negligent and rather worldly, their mother a slug, and their aunt Mrs Norris. I do not remember one instance in Jane Austen of a child who was well brought up and turned out badly. She might have called her novels 'The Parents' Assistant in six volumes'. It is conceivable that they might still be of use; and horrible as it may appear to the modern parent that she asks him to believe on a week-day in 'the advantages of early hardship and discipline, and the consciousness of being born to struggle and endure' (*Mansfield Park, sub fin*), at least she does not ask him also to believe that his child is born bad.

The chief danger of a moralizing tendency is that it may lead the novelist to falsify human nature. I do not think it so misleads Jane Austen. She is not invariably true to human nature, but it is not her desire to edify that makes her false. There is nothing improbable in the connexion she portrays between goodness and happiness, or between error and failure. Nor do we ever think of saying that her characters are too good or too bad to be real. Somebody seems indeed to have complained that her heroines were not good enough, and she replies that pictures of perfection make her sick and wicked (*Letters*, ii, 300). The large experience of Catherine Morland led her to suspect that, though among Mrs Radcliffe's Alps and Pyreness there might be no mixed characters, 'among the English, in their hearts and habits, there was a general, though unequal, mixture of good and bad'. Jane Austen seems to have shared this suspicion. And, finally, her sympathies and antipathies never make her unjust. Indeed, in her justice she is quite Shakespearian. One example may serve for many. She must have detested Mrs Norris. We all do. Who could say a good word for her? Jane Austen could. When Sir Thomas Bertram refused to receive Maria again in his house, Mrs Norris devoted herself to the niece whose character she had done so much to spoil. She took her away to an 'establishment formed for them in another country, remote and private, where, shut up together with little society, on one side no affection, on the other no judgement, it may be reasonably supposed that their tempers became their mutual punishment.' Well, we cannot pretend to mind that much, but we realize that this intolerable woman had strong affections, and we admit that the story has implied this all along, though our hatred of her may have made us blind to it. ...

In all her novels, though in varying degrees, Jane Austen regards the characters, good and bad alike, with ironical amusement, because they never see the situation as it really is and as she sees it. This is the deeper source of our unbroken pleasure in reading her. We constantly share her point of view, and are aware of the amusing difference between the fact and its appearance to the actors. If you fail to perceive and enjoy this, you are not really reading Jane Austen. Some readers do not perceive it, and therefore fail to appreciate her. Others perceive it without enjoying it and they think her cynical. She is never cynical, and not often merely satirical. A cynic or a mere satirist may be intellectually pleased by human absurdities and illusions, but he does not feel them to be good. But to Jane Austen, so far as they are not seriously harmful, they are altogether pleasant, because they are both ridiculous and right. It is amusing, for example, that Knightley, who is almost a model of good sense, right feeling, and just action, should be unjust to Frank Churchill because, though he does not know it, he himself is in love with Emma: but to Jane Austen that is not only the way a man *is* made, but the way he *should* be made. No doubt there are plenty of things that should not be, but when we so regard them they are not comical. A main point of difference between Jane Austen and Johnson is that to her much more of the world is amusing, and much more of it is right. She is less of a moralist and more of a humorist....

Emma is a far more mature piece of work [than *NA*]. It is the most vivacious of the later novels, and with some readers the first favourite. In plot-interest it is probably the strongest of the six, and, not to speak of the more prominent persons, it contains, in Mr Woodhouse and Miss Bates, two minor characters who resemble one another in being the object equally of our laughter and our unqualified respect and affection. Jane Austen, who is said to be Shakespearian, never reminds us of Shakespeare, I think, in her full-dress portraits, but she does so in such characters as Miss Bates and Mr Allen. As for Mr Woodhouse, whose most famous sentences hang like texts in frames on the four walls of our memories, he is, next to Don Quixote, perhaps the most perfect gentleman in fiction; and under outrageous provocation he remains so. . . .

Emma is satisfactory on the more serious side of the story; but I will not dwell on that. In its main design it is a comedy, and as a comedy, unsurpassed, I think, among novels, and all the better because Jane Austen does not affront us, like Meredith in *The Egoist*, by coming forward as interpreter. Most of the characters are involved in the contrast of reality and illusion, but it is concentrated on Emma. . . .

There is every sign that in writing *Mansfield Park* Jane Austen regarded her work with unusual seriousness. This seriousness is, in part, moral, for she has deeply at heart the importance of certain truths about conduct which are embodied and occasionally enunciated in the novel. But it is at the same time artistic. She has produced a very solid and carefully considered scheme, a more organic scheme than in any other of her works. And she has bound herself to tell the truth. She renounces the pleasure of drawing semi-farcical characters; and in Lady Bertram (as later in Mr Woodhouse) she can scarcely be said even to exaggerate; she merely insists on the most salient traits, without wholly excluding the rest. Again, the conception and development of some of the main characters, of the two Crawfords, perhaps of Edmund, and notably of Fanny Price as compared with Elizabeth Bennet, is exceptionally delicate and subtle. These epithets apply also to the manner in which the influence of character on character, and of circumstances on character, is depicted. Further, we meet neither with almost incredible situations, nor with inconsistencies of character, such as may be found in *Pride and Prejudice*: for to me, at least, it is impossible to imagine those ten days during which the Wickhams stayed with the Bennets, or to believe that the Darcy of the second half of the novel could ever have behaved so totally unlike a gentleman as the Darcy of the dance where he first meets Elizabeth. And, finally, everywhere, in spite of the author's moral intentness, there is that justice to which I drew attention in the treatment of Mrs Norris. We see, for example, that, though Henry Crawford is an habitual and unfeeling lady-killer, he is capable of sincere love; and no tenderness for Fanny prevents our being told that, in spite of her love for Edmund and her repugnance to Crawford, he must have succeeded in winning her affection if for a few months he could have denied himself the pleasure of flirtation. It must be admitted, I think, that in these respects—and they are of great importance—*Mansfield Park* is considerably superior to the youthful work, and superior in some degree to *Emma* and *Persuasion*; and it is probably true that, of all the novels, it gains the most from repeated study....

25. 'complete common sense'

1913

From *The Victorian Age in Literature*, 1913, 104–5, 109–10.

Gilbert Keith Chesterton (1874–1936), Catholic apologist, critic, novelist and poet, provides a swift, sharp perception of Jane Austen's unblinkered vision.

The novel of the nineteenth century was female; as fully as the novel of the eighteenth century was male. It is quite certain that no woman could have written *Roderick Random*. It is not quite so certain that no woman could have written *Esmond*. The strength and subtlety of woman had certainly sunk deep into English letters when George Eliot began to write.

Her originals and even her contemporaries had shown the feminine power in fiction as well or better than she. Charlotte Brontë, understood along her own instincts, was as great; Jane Austen was greater. The latter comes into our present consideration only as that most exasperating thing, an ideal unachieved. It is like leaving an unconquered fortress in the rear. No woman later has captured the complete common sense of Jane Austen. She could keep her head, while all the after women went about looking for their brains. She could describe a man coolly; which neither George Eliot nor Charlotte Brontë could do. She knew what she knew, like a sound dogmatist: she did not know what she did not know—like a sound agnostic. But she belongs to a vanished world before the great progressive age of which I write....

Jane Austen was born before those bonds which (we are told) protected woman from truth, were burst by the Brontës or elaborately untied by George Eliot. Yet the fact remains that Jane Austen knew much more about men than either of them. Jane Austen may have been protected from truth: but it was precious little of truth that was protected from her. When Darcy, in finally confessing his faults, says, 'I have been a selfish being all my life, in practice *though not in theory*,' he gets nearer to a complete confession of the intelligent male than ever was even hinted by the Byronic lapses of the Brontës' heroes or the elaborate exculpations of George Eliot's. Jane Austen, of course, covered an infinitely smaller field than any of her later rivals; but I have always believed in the victory of small nationalities.

26. 'her greatness as an artist'

1913

From Unsigned review of the *Life and Letters* and *Old Friends and New Faces* by Sybil G. Brinton (continuations of the novels), *Times Literary Supplement*, 8 May 1913.

Virginia Woolf (1882–1944), novelist and critic, was probably Jane Austen's most sympathetic critic in treating questions relating to the woman novelist. The review opened on the front page of the *TLS* and carries the tone and manner of a judicial and authoritative placing.

In many ways Jane Austen must be considered singularly blessed. The manner in which from generation to generation her descendants respect her memory is, we imagine, precisely that which she would have chosen for herself—and she would have been hard to please. In 1870 the Memoir by her nephew gave us not only the facts of her life, but reproduced the atmosphere in which that life was lived so instinctively that his book can never be superseded;

and now once more the son and grandson of that nephew show themselves possessed to the full of the family taste and modesty....

But the time has come, surely, when there is no need to bring witnesses to prove Jane Austen's fame. Arrange the great English novelists as one will, it does not seem possible to bring them out in any order where she is not first, or second, or third, whoever her companions may be. Unlike other great writers in almost every way, she is unlike them, too, in the very slow and very steady rise of her reputation: it has been steady because there is probably no novelist of the nineteenth century who requires us to make so little excuse for her, and it has been slow because she has limitations of a kind particularly likely to cramp a writer's popularity. The mere sight of her six neat volumes suggests something of the reason, for when we look at them we do not remember any page or passage which so burnt itself into our minds when we read it first that from time to time we take the book down, read that sentence again, and are again exalted. We doubt whether one of her novels was ever a long toil and stumble to any reader with a splendid view at the end. She was never a revelation to the young, a stern comrade, a brilliant and extravagantly admired friend, a writer whose sentences sang in one's brain and were half absorbed into one's blood. And directly one has set down any of the above phrases one is conscious of the irony with which she would have disclaimed any such wish or intention. We can hear it in the words addressed to the nephew who had lost two chapters of his novel. 'How could I possibly join them on to the little bit (two inches wide) of ivory on which I work with so fine a brush, as produces little effect after much labour?'; and again in the famous, 'Let other pens dwell on guilt and misery. I quit such odious subjects as soon as I can.'

But however modest and conscious of her own defects she may be, the defects are there and must be recognized by readers who are as candid as Jane Austen herself would wish them to be. The chief reason why she does not appeal to us as some inferior writers do is that she has too little of the rebel in her composition, too little discontent, and of the vision which is the cause and the reward of discontent. She seems at times to have accepted life too calmly as she found it, and to any one who reads her biography or letters it is plain that life showed her a great deal that was smug, commonplace, and, in a bad sense of the word, artificial. It showed her a world made up of big houses and little houses, of gentry inhabiting them who were keenly conscious of their grades of gentility, while life itself consisted of an interchange of tea parties, picnics, and dances, which eventually, if the connexion was respectable and the income on each side satisfactory, led to a thoroughly suitable marriage. It happens very seldom, but still it does happen, that we feel that the play of her spirit has been hampered by such obstacles; that she believes in them as well as laughs at them, and that she is debarred from the most profound insight into human nature by the respect which she pays to some unnatural convention. There are characters such as the characters of Elinor Dashwood and Fanny Price which bore us frankly; there are pages which, though written in excellent English, have to be skipped: and these defects are due to the fact that she is content to take it for granted that such characters and conduct are good without trying to see them in a fresh light for herself.

But the chief damage which this conservative spirit has inflicted on her art is that it tied her hands together when she dealt with men. Her heroes were less the equals of her heroines than should have been the case, making allowance for the fact that so it must always be when a woman writes of men or a man of women. It is where the power of the man has to be conveyed that her novels are always at their weakest; and the heroines themselves lose something of their life because in moments of crisis they have for partners men who are inferior to them in vitality and character. A clergyman's daughter in those days was, no doubt, very carefully brought up, and in no other age, we imagine, were men and women less at their ease together; still, it rests with the novelists to break down the barriers; it is they who should imagine what they cannot know even at the risk of making themselves superbly ridiculous. Miss Austen, however, was so fastidious, so conscious of her own limitations, that when she found out that hedges do not grow in Northamptonshire she eliminated her hedge rather than run the risk of inventing one which could not exist. This is the more annoying because we are inclined to think that she could have run almost all the risks and triumphed. In proof of this we might quote two passages from 'Mansfield Park' (the first is quoted by Professor Bradley in his lecture to the English Association), where, forsaking her usual method, she suddenly hazards herself in a strange new atmosphere and breathes into her work a spirit of beauty and romance. Fanny Price standing at a window with

Edmund breaks into a strange rhapsody, which begins, 'Here's harmony! here's repose! here's what may leave all painting and all music behind, and what poetry only can attempt to describe!' &c. And, again, she throws a curious atmosphere of symbolism over the whole scene where Maria and Henry Crawford refuse to wait for Rushworth, who is bringing the key of the gate. 'But unluckily,' Maria exclaims, 'that iron gate, that ha-ha gives me a feeling of restraint and hardship. I cannot get out, as the starling said.'

But these limitations are noticeable only when Jane Austen is committing herself to saying seriously that such things and such people are good, which in the works of any writer is a dangerous moment, leading us to hold our breath; when she is pointing out where they are bad, weak, faulty, exquisitely absurd she is winged and inapproachable. Her heroes may be insipid, but think of her fools! Think of Mr Collins, Mr Woodhouse, Miss Bates, Mrs Norris, Mrs Bennet, and in a lesser degree of Mrs Allen, Lady Bertram, Sir William Lucas! What a light the thought of them will cast on the wettest day! How various and individual is their folly! For they are no more consistently foolish than people in real life. It is only that they have a peculiar point of view, and that when health, or economy, or ladies of title are mentioned, as must frequently happen in the world we live in, they give vent to their views to our eternal delight; but there are a great many circumstances in which they do not behave foolishly at all. Indeed, we are inclined to think that the most painful incident in any of the novels is when Miss Bates's feelings are hurt at the picnic, and, turning to Mr Knightley, she says, 'I must have made myself very disagreeable or she would not have said such a thing to an old friend.' Again, when they are discussing the study of human nature and Darcy remarks, 'But people themselves alter so much that there is something to be observed in them for ever,' Mrs Bennet's reply is surely a stroke of genius. 'Yes, indeed,' cried Mrs Bennet, offended by his manner of mentioning a country neighbourhood, 'I assure you there is quite as much of that going on in the country as in town.' Such is the light it throws upon the muddled vacuity of the poor lady's mind that she ceases to be ridiculous and becomes almost tragic in her folly.

It came so naturally to Jane Austen to describe people by means of their faults that had there been a drop of bitterness in her spirit

her novels would have given us the most consistently satirical
picture of life that exists. Open them where you will, you are
almost certain to light upon some passage exquisitely satirizing the
absurdities of life—satirizing them, but without bitterness, partly
no doubt because she was happy in her life, partly because she had
no wish that things should be other than they are. People could
never be too absurd, life never too full of humours and singularities
for her taste, and as for telling people how they ought to live,
which is the satiric motive, she would have held up her hands in
amazement at the thought. Life itself—that was the object of her
love, of her absorbed study; that was the pursuit which filled those
unrecorded years and drew out the 'quiet intensity of her nature,'
making her appear to the outer world a little critical and aloof, and
'at times very grave.' More than any other novelist she fills every
inch of her canvas with observation, fashions every sentence into
meaning, stuffs up every chink and cranny of the fabric until each
novel is a little living world, from which you cannot break off a
scene or even a sentence without bleeding it of some of its life. Her
characters are so rounded and substantial that they have the power
to move out of the scenes in which she placed them into other
moods and circumstances. Thus, if some one begins to talk about
Emma Woodhouse or Elizabeth Bennet voices from different parts
of the room begin saying which they prefer and why, and how they
differ and how they might have acted if one had been at Box Hill
and the other at Rosings, and where they live, and how their houses
are disposed, as if they were living people. It is a world, in short,
with houses, roads, carriages, hedgerows, copses, and with human
beings.

All this was done by a quiet maiden lady who had merely paper
and ink at her disposal; all this is conveyed by little sentences
between inverted commas and smooth paragraphs of print. Only
those who have realized for themselves the ridiculous inadequacy
of a straight stick dipped in ink when brought in contact with the
rich and tumultuous glow of life can appreciate to the full the
wonder of her achievement, the imagination, the penetration, the
insight, the courage, the sincerity which are required to bring
before us one of those perfectly normal and simple incidents of
average human life. Besides all these gifts and more wonderful than
any of them, for without it they are apt to run to waste, she
possessed in a greater degree perhaps than any other English

woman the sense of the significance of life apart from any personal liking or disliking; of the beauty and continuity which underlies its trivial stream. A little aloof, a little inscrutable and mysterious, she will always remain, but serene and beautiful also because of her greatness as an artist.

27. Farrer on Jane Austen

1917

'Jane Austen, *ob.* July 18, 1817', *Quarterly Review*, July 1917.

Reginald Farrer (1880–1920), employed by Foreign Office, novelist, playwright, botanist, flower-painter, traveller and writer, was famed for his expertise in Alpine plants and those of the high hills of Upper Burma, North China and Tibet. Alongside Simpson's, his essay remains one of the classic statements on Jane Austen.

JANE AUSTEN, *ob.* JULY 18, 1817

'To lounge away the time as they could, with sofas and chitchat, and Quarterly Reviews.'—'Mansfield Park,' Cap. X.

The concluding storms of a great conflict had hardly died down, when her world, almost unaware, bade farewell to Jane Austen; now, amid the closing cataclysms of a conflict yet more gigantic, we celebrate the hundredth year of her immortality. Time is the woodsman who fells the smaller trees and coppice in the forest of literature, and allows us at last to see the true proportions of its enduring giants; and the century that has passed since Jane Austen's death now sees her preeminence securely established. An early editor could only dare timidly to suggest that perhaps she might be found not wholly unworthy of a place in the same shelf with Miss Burney and Miss Edgeworth. Alas for both these, gone by now into the spare bedroom, and become the dusty curiosities of literature! Not even Jane Austen's devotion has availed to save Fanny Burney from a too-general oblivion, whereas Jane Austen herself has long since taken rank as the centre of a cult as ardent as a religion. There is no *via media*, indeed, where Jane Austen is concerned; by those who might have lent features to her fools she is vividly disliked,⋆ and by those for whom her fools were drawn, she is no less fervently adored. In water-logged trench, in cold cave of the mountains, in sickness and in health, in dulness, tribulation and fatigue, an ever-increasing crowd of worshippers flies insatiably for comfort and company perennially re-freshing, to Hartfield and Randalls, Longbourn, Northanger, Sotherton and Uppercross.

Such positions in literature are not achieved by log-rolling. Macaulay blunders, indeed, in his praise, and in the instances he selects for it; but he undoubtedly hits the bull's eye with his usual essential accuracy, when he lights on the fact that Jane Austen is comparable only with Shakespeare. For both attain their solitary and special supremacy by dint of a common capacity for intense vitalisation; both have the culminating gift of immediately projecting a living human being who is not only *a* human being, but also something much greater than any one person, a quintessentialised instance of humanity, a generalisation made incarnate and personal by genius. But the dramatist has the easier task; the novelist, unaided by actors or stage, has to impress his own imagination straight upon ours. And it is of this secret that Jane Austen is so capital a mistress; a prefatory line or two, an initial sentence, and there goes Mrs Allen or Mrs Price, a complete and complex identity, walking independently away down the ages. Even in their circumstances, too, Shakespeare and Jane Austen run curiously parallel. Our two greatest creators exist for us only in their work; and, when we search into their personal lives and tastes and tragedies, we glean nothing but a little chopped dull chaff of details in which all trace of the sacred germ is lacking. In Jane Austen's case, indeed, the disappearance of the creator into his creation is made but the completer for the abundance of superficial details with which we are provided. When the dry bones of her facts are fitted together, there results for us only a lay-figure, comfortable

---

⋆ Women often appreciate her imperfectly, because she appreciated them so perfectly, and so inexorably revealed them.

and comely, but conveying no faintest suggestion of the genuine Jane Austen.

She was obviously ill-served by her circumstances. Behind the official biographies, and the pleasant little empty letters, and the accounts of how good she was to her mother and wouldn't use the sofa, we feel always that she really lived remote in a great reserve. She praised and valued domesticity indeed, sincerely loved her own family, and made domestic instincts a cardinal virtue in all her heroes. But the praise and value are rather official than personal; her only real intimate at home was her sister Cassandra, and it is significant, that only upstairs, behind her shut door, did she read her own work aloud, for the benefit of her chosen circle in the younger generation. Yet more significant, though, is the fact that nowhere does she give any picture of united family happiness; the successful domestic unity will certainly not be successfully sought at Longbourn or Mansfield, Northanger or Kellynch. This, to any one who understands Jane Austen's preoccupation with truth, and her selection of material only from among observed facts tested by personal experience, speaks volumes, in its characteristically quiet way, for her position towards her own family. She was in it; but she was not really of it.

Even on the point of her intimacy with Cassandra there is something curiously suggestive in the fact that, after her first two novels, she never again gives us a picture of two intimately united sisters. Maria and Julia are allies only till their interests clash; Isabella is nothing to Emma; only time and trials teach Fanny to surmount her first startled disapproval of Susan; and the best that Anne can feel for Mary Musgrove is that she 'is not so repulsive and unsisterly as Elizabeth.' On the other hand, in three out of these four books, the author's delight is transferred to the relations between brother and sister—Wentworth and 'Sophy,' Henry and Eleanor, William and Fanny, and, above all, for depth of tried alliance, Crawford and Mary. Finally, she does not even die for us of anything particular, but fades out, with Victorian gentility, in a hazy unspecified decline. How much more fortunate, in her different class, is Charlotte Brontë, of whom no detail is hidden from her admirers by any such instinct for muffling things up in discretions and evasions! Even in popular language this distinction holds; no one dreams of calling the lesser writer anything but 'Charlotte Brontë,' while there still exists a whole sect of Jane

Austen's devotees, no Laodiceans either, who to this day will always talk of her as 'Miss Austen.' Which is as if one were to speak currently of Mr Milton, and Monsieur de Molière.

These fantasies of propriety, together with her own misleadingly modest allusion to the 'little piece of ivory' on which she worked, have done much to perpetuate the theory, still held among the profane, that she is a 'limited' writer. It is by no means so that her faithful see their radiant and remorseless Jane; and, though criticism depends, in the last resort, chiefly on what the critic himself brings to his subject (so that what each man comes seeking, that he will most surely find), Jane Austen's personality may be much more profitably reconstructed in her work, than from the superficial details of her life, doled out to us by her biographer. A writer's fame, in fact, relies for its permanent value on his own transpiring personality; in every line he is inevitably 'giving himself away,' and the future of his work depends on whether what he has to give possesses the salted quality of eternity. And impersonality comes as the first ingredient in the specific for immortality. The self-relevation of the writer must be as severely implicit as it is universally pervasive; it must never be conscious or obtruded.

There is, indeed, a section of writers, as of readers, who believe in frequent appearances of the author before his curtain, to make deductions from his text, and point out conclusions. This is a pandering to laziness in the reader; every meaning should be clearly discoverable in the text, without its being necessary for the author himself to dig it out for us. And to such readers as these, who want their pabulum already peptonised, Jane Austen deliberately avoids appeal. As in her own life she evaded the lionising that lesser women covet, and would assuredly have approved Cassandra's destruction of her private letters, so in her work she no less carefully avoids overt appearance on her stage. She is there all the time, indeed, but never *in propria persona*, except when she gaily smiles through the opener texture of 'Northanger Abbey,' or, with her consummate sense of art, mitigates for us the transition out of her paradises back into the grey light of ordinary life, by letting the word 'I' demurely peer forth at last, as the fantasmagoria in 'Mansfield Park,' 'Emma' or 'Northanger Abbey' begins to thin out to its final pages. Otherwise she is the most aloof of writers, and does not work 'for such dull elves' (as she says herself) as will not so far come to meet the author as to make out for themselves his conclusions and deductions.

This elimination of the author is only part of the intense concentration which the greatest writers develop in their subject. The essence of conviction, in the game of make-believe, is to convince yourself first of all, finally and absolutely. This can only be done by forgetting yourself entirely, by blotting out the whole irrelevant world from your purview, and centralising, with a single-eyed undeviating passion of conviction, upon the tale you are setting out to live. It is at this point that all living writers (with the exception of Rhoda Broughton) fail. They are telling stories in which they have either no flesh-and-blood belief of their own, or else too much; telling them with an eye to their audience and to themselves and their own pet notions, telling them, that is, objectively, not subjectively, and piling up masses of detail and explanation in order to obscure the inner lack of any completed identity between the author and his matter.

It is precisely here that Jane Austen so magnificently succeeds. Wars may be raging to their end as the background of 'Persuasion,' or social miseries strike a new facet of 'Emma'; otherwise all the vast anguish of her time is non-existent to Jane Austen, when once she has got pen in hand, to make us a new kingdom of refuge from the toils and frets of life. Her kingdoms are hermetically sealed, in fact, and here lies the strength of their impregnable immortality; it is not without hope or comfort for us nowadays, to remember that 'Mansfield Park' appeared the year before Waterloo, and 'Emma' the year after. For Jane Austen is always concerned only with the universal, and not with the particular. And it is according as they invest their souls in the former or the latter that authors eternally survive or rapidly pass away. Fashions change, fads and fancies come and go, tyrannies and empires erupt and collapse; those who make events and contemporary ideas the matter of their work have their reward in instant appreciation of their topical value. And with their topical value they die.* Art is a mysterious entity, outside and beyond daily life, whether its manifestation be by painting or sculpture or literature. If it use outside events at all, it must subdue

* After Mr Gray of Sackville Street, Jane Austen specifies no tradesman, except Broadwood, nor even dwells on any detail of fashion.

them to its medium, and become their master, not their mere vehicle. So a hundred thousand novels come and go; but Jane Austen can never be out of date, because she never was in any particular date (that is to say, never imprisoned in any), but is coextensive with human nature.

Talk of her 'limitations' is vain, and based on a misapprehension. When we speak of her as our greatest artist in English fiction we do not mean that she has the loudest mastery of any particular mood, the most clamant voice, the widest gamut of subjects; we mean that she stands supreme and alone among English writers in possession of the secret which so many French ones possess—that is, a most perfect mastery of her weapons, a most faultless and precise adjustment of means to end. She is, in English fiction, as Milton in English poetry, the one completely conscious and almost unerring artist. This is to take only the technical side of her work; her scale and scope are different matters. There is, in some quarters, a tendency to quarrel with Jane Austen because in her books there is nothing that she never intended to be there, no heroic hectorings, no Brontesque ebulliencies, no mountain or moor or 'bonny beck' (to use Charlotte Brontë's own phrase)—surely one of the monumental ineptitudes of criticism, seeing that the most elementary axiom of art is the artist's initial right to choose his own medium. We have no more right, in fact, to cavil at Jane Austen for not writing 'The Duchess of Malfi' than at Webster for not writing 'Northanger Abbey'.

At the same time, it must never be thought that limitation of scene implies limitation of human emotion. The measure of perfection has no relation to the size of its material. Perfection is one and incommensurable. Class-limitation, in fact, is no limitation of sympathy; and a breaking heart is a breaking heart, no more nor less, whether it find vent in the ululations of Tamburlaine, or in the 'almost screamed with agony' of Marianne Dashwood. Jane Austen's heroes and heroines and subject-matter are, in fact, universal human nature, and conterminous with it, though manifested only in one class, with that class's superficial limitations, in habits and manner of life.

And here another error vitiates the caviller's thought. Readers fall into two groups—the objective and the subjective. And it is only the objective class who, because emotion is not vehemently expressed by Jane Austen, will fail to realise with what profound effect it is implied. She does not expound feeling; she conveys it. With her artist's instinct, she knows that exposition by the writer destroys conviction in the reader. She has at heart, all through her life, that maxim of the French which English writers find it so impossible to assimilate—'Glissez toujours, n'appuyez pas': do your work rightly, and trust the intelligence of the reader to do the rest. When Anne again meets Wentworth there is nothing shown in the text but the little flutter given to the sentence by the repetition of the descriptive adjective in:— 'The room seemed full, full of persons and voices;' but the sensitised reader is left fairly staggering in the gale of Anne's emotion, revealed in that tiny hint more intimately than by all the paragraphs of passionate prose in which other writers would exhaustively set out the emotions of Wentworth and Anne, until no emotion at all was left in the reader. For the objective writer toils and toils outside his subject, accumulating convincing details until conviction is destroyed; the subjective gives the bare and encyclopaedic essential in a line or a word, and then goes on. And of all great writers Jane Austen is the most evocative, doing in half a dozen words (applied in exactly the proper measure, in exactly the proper place) what the sedulous subtleties of Henry James are unable to convey so clearly in as many fine-spun pages. Knightley, for instance, staying 'vigorously' on, away from Emma in Brunswick Square, gives us in one syllable more of Knightley and more of Emma than whole long paragraphs of analysis.

And among the secrets of Jane Austen's inexhaustible charm is that her work, especially in her second period, is so packed with such minute and far-reaching felicities that the thousandth reading of 'Emma' or 'Persuasion' will be certain to reveal to you a handful of such brilliant jewels unnoticed before. If she has nothing to say to those who want to sit passive while the whole story is put down plain before them like meat on a plate, she has all the more delights to unfold for those who know that the whole point of reading lies in eager cooperation with a sympathetic writer. The more rigid, in fact, the elimination of the non-essential, the more blazing the certitude with which the essential is projected. Jane Austen is even of an Elizabethan economy in her stage-settings. Modern writers pretend to reveal their characters by dint of descriptions copious as an upholsterer's catalogue; she produces her details sparingly, bit by bit, only where each is dramatically necessary to the course of character or action; often, by one of her most characteristic exquisitenesses, they are only revealed in the conversation of her persons. And, in the result, with what a life-long intimacy do we come at last to know her houses and her rooms, her gardens and shrubberies! This indirect method, too, she often chooses, to give emotions and impressions and personal pictures. Elizabeth Bennet's own delightfulness is sensibly enhanced by that of Mrs Gardiner, since she was so special a favourite there; while Elizabeth Elliot's 'something so formal and *arrangé* in her air; and she sits so upright,' though it comes quite at the end of the book, gives us an instant intimate vision of Lady Russell, besides flashing at us the whole essence of Elizabeth herself.

As for landscape, so often the stumbling-block of novelists, Jane Austen cannot be said to make any very serious use of it in her first period; but in the second, although she is far too craft-wise to fancy you can vitalise a character by dint of emotionalising its country-side and garden, she quite definitely (though still with finest economy) avails herself more and more of the outer world, not only for its value as a picture in itself—we may spend a vivid day at Sotherton—but also as playing its part in the development of her people. The squalor of Portsmouth, the autumn landscapes of Lyme and Uppercross, have a definite place in the evolution of Fanny and Anne; while the July storm which darkens the dark climax of 'Emma' is the pathetic fallacy pure and simple. It is only towards the end of her own life, that is, with the deepening of her own sympathies, that her faultless sense of fitness and relevance so far widens also as to give greater latitude to her methods of inspiring sympathy.

For it is but fair to her cruder critics to admit that Jane Austen has no taste for expressed erotics, and will thereby always seem insipid to the large crowd of readers, chiefly women, who are responsible for that perennial ill-repute of fiction against which Jane Austen herself personally launches the novelist's Magna Carta in 'Northanger Abbey,' because they read fiction principally as an erotic stimulant, and judge its merits accordingly, by the ardour of its descriptions and expressions. In this aspect of life Jane Austen has no interest. Her concern is primarily with character unfolded through love, not with that love's crudities of appetite and incident. In the supreme moments, in point of fact, humanity becomes inarticulate, and thus no longer gives material for art. Jane Austen, knowing this, is too honest to forge us false coin of phrases, and too much an artist to pad out her lines with asterisks and dashes and ejaculations. She accepts the condition, asks her reader to accept it also, and contents herself with dealing with the emotions on either side of the crucial outbreak. It is notorious how she avoids detail in her proposal-scenes; certainly not from 'ladylike' cowardice, nor from any incapacity, but merely in her artist's certainty that the epical instants of life are not to be adequately expressed in words. 'What did she say? Just what she should, of course: a lady always does.' Jane Austen, with whimsical gaiety of candour, here lays down her position once for all, and frankly tells her reader that there are matters into which neither he nor she can decently pry. That she *could* tear a passion to tatters with the best of them, indeed, is shown by Marianne Dashwood; that she never repeated the picture shows her sense of its unfitness and fatal facility, by comparison with the subtler treatments of emotion in which alone she was interested. Any red-blood writer can state passions, it takes a genius to suggest them; and Jane Austen is preeminently a clear-brained writer rather than a red-blooded one. Yet no one is left doubting Emma's feeling for Knightley, or Anne's for Wentworth, though nothing at all is said of physical attractions, and the whole effect is made by implication. But made it indubitably is, and indelibly.

On the feelings of her men, of course, Jane Austen has nothing to say at first hand, is too honest an artist to invent, and too clean a woman to attempt the modern female trick of gratifying her own passions by inventing a lover, and then identifying herself with his desires, in so far as she can concoct them. Yet it would be quite a mistake to call her men pallid or shadowy. In point of fact, they are usually carried out with all her vivid certainty, yet considered only in relation to her women, and thus, by comparison, quieter in colour, deliberately subordinate in her scheme. Even the earlier heroes will be found perfectly adapted to their place in her books, when once that place is understood; as for the later ones, they stand most definitely on legs of their own, so far as their movements in the story require. Perhaps the best of all is Knightley, not only in relation to Emma but also in himself.

Nor must it be brought against Jane Austen that she does not lard her work with sociology, religion or metaphysics. Such divagations may make a story more stirring; they certainly make it more ephemeral. And, against such writers as believe the novel is Heaven's appointed jam for the powder of their own opinions, Jane Austen decisively heads the other school, which believes that 'the book, the whole book, and nothing but the book' is the novelist's best motto. She herself pours scorn on the notion that 'Pride and Prejudice' would really be better if padded out with 'solemn nonsense about Bonaparte'; and where for once (in order to prove Fanny's brains) she ventures on irrelevant flights of rhetoric, she for once lamentably falls to earth, in those two speeches of Fanny's in the Vicarage shrubbery—deliverances false in fact, trite in thought, turgid and sententious in expression. Normally, however, she remains undistracted from the purpose of her book; and, from the first sentence, submerges herself in the single thought of the story's development, with that whole-heartedness of delight in creation for its own sake which is the prerogative of the highest genius alone, alone awakening in the reader an answering rapture of conviction and absorption. Thus it is that, to her faithful, Jane Austen has become flesh and blood of their mind's inmost fabric. Who commonly quotes Charlotte Brontë or George Eliot? But every turn and corner of life is illuminated or defined for us by some sentence of Jane Austen's; and every dim character in our 'dusty mortal days' has something of one or another in the long gallery of her creations. Thus to become the very texture of humanity's mind and talk from generation to generation, is the attainment of the supreme visualisers only; talent, at the best, can merely photograph, either from the real or from an ideal.

So far we have looked only at the literary aspect of Jane Austen. The secret of her immortality is to be found in that underlying something which is the woman herself; for, of all writers, she it is who pursues truth with most utter and undeviable devotion. The real thing is her only object always. She declines to write of scenes and circumstances that she does not know at first hand; she refuses recognition, and even condonement, to all thought or emotion that conflicts with truth, or burkes it, or fails to prove pure diamond to the solvent of her acid. She is, in fact, the most merciless, though calmest, of inconoclasts; only her calm has obscured from her critics the steely quality, the inexorable rigour of her judgment. Even Butler, her nearest descendant in this generation, never seems really to have recognised his affinity. For Jane Austen has no passion, preaches no gospel, grinds no axe; standing aloof from the world, she sees it, on the whole, as silly. She has no animosity for it; but she has no affection. She does not want to better fools, or to abuse them; she simply sets herself to glean pleasure from their folly. Nothing but the first-rate in life is good enough for her tolerance; remember Anne Elliot's definition of 'good company', and her cousin's rejoinder, 'That is not good company; that is the best.'

Everything false and feeble, in fact, withers in the demure greyness of her gaze; in 'follies and nonsense, whims and inconsistencies,' she finds nothing but diversion, dispassionate but pitiless. For, while no novelist is more sympathetic to real values and sincere emotion, none also is so keen on detecting false currency, or so relentless in exposing it. At times, even, her antagonism to conventionalities and shams betrays her almost to a touch of passion. Yet, if ever she seems cruel, her anger is but just impatience against the slack thought and ready-made pretences that pass current in the world and move her always to her quiet but destructive merriment; as in the famous outburst about Miss Musgrove's 'large fat sighings over a son whom alive no one had cared for'—a *cri de coeur* for which the author for once feels immediately bound to come before the curtain, to mitigate it with a quasi-apology quite devoid of either conviction or recantation. Nor will she hear of any reserves in honesty and candour; not only the truth, but the whole truth, must be vital to any character of whom she herself is to approve. Civilised urbane discretion, and assent to social falsehoods, make strong points in Anne's private distrust of William Elliot, and in Fanny's disapproval of Henry Crawford, artfully thrown in contrast as he is against the breezy impetuous young frankness of William Price.

She is consumed with a passion for the real, as apart from the realistic; and the result is that her creations, though obviously observed, are no less obviously generalised into a new identity of their own. She acknowledges no individual portrait, such as those in which alone such essentially unimaginative writers as Charlotte Brontë can deal. And in this intense preoccupation with character, she is frankly bored with events; the accident at Lyme shows how perfunctorily she can handle a mere occurrence, being concentrated all the time on the emotions that engender it, and the emotions it engenders. Her very style is the mirror of her temperament. Naturally enough, she both writes and makes her people speak an

English much more flowing and lucid than is fashionable in ordinary writers and ordinary life; but, allowing for this inevitable blemish, the note of her style is the very note of her nature, in its lovely limpidity, cool and clear and flashing as an alpine stream, without ebulliencies or turbidness of any kind. It is not for nothing that 'rational' is almost her highest word of praise. Good sense, in the widest meaning of the word, is her be-all and end-all; the perfect σωφροσύνη[1] which is also the perfect αὐταρκεῖα.[2]

For her whole sex she revolts against 'elegant females,' and sums up her ideal woman, not as a 'good-natured unaffected girl' (a phrase which, with her, connotes a certain quite kindly contempt), but as a 'rational creature.' The pretences of 'Vanity Fair,' for instance, to be an historical novel, fade into the thinnest of hot air when one realises, with a gasp of amazement, that Amelia Sedley is actually meant to be a contemporary of Anne Elliot. And thus one understands what a deep gulf Victorianism dug between us and the past; how infinitely nearer to Jane Austen are the sane sensible young women of our own day than the flopping vaporous fools who were the fashion among the Turkish-minded male novelists of Queen Victoria's fashions.* Take Catherine Morland, a country parson's daughter, suffered to run quite wild,† and compare her list of reading with the incredible Pinkertonian education in 'accomplishments'. Imagine Miss Pinkerton allowing Amelia Sedley to read 'Othello'; or Amelia wishing to do so, or understanding any of it if she did! At the same time, the famous outburst in 'Northanger Abbey,' shows that, in those days as well as later, 'imbecility in females is a great enhancement of their personal charms.' It is by a most curious irony of fate, indeed, that the ignorant attribute to Jane Austen and her heroines just that very primness and futility of which she, and they, are most contemptuous.

* It is but fair to add that male delight in female imbecility is as eternal as Jane Austen herself declared; and that Scott's heroines (with the exception of Diana Vernon) are generally of an insipid feebleness sinking to the lowest Victorian standards.

† Jane Austen seems to have postulated so much of intelligence in her girls, as to *prefer* for them a haphazard rather than a regular education. Elizabeth Bennet, also, was left to choose for herself whether she would learn or not; while Miss Lee's pompous curriculum at Mansfield is openly laughed at, and shown to lead to no good result, to no real education in character.

1 self-control   2 self-sufficiency

Her heroines, indeed, are out-of-door creatures, by no means fettered by conventional ignorance or innocence; and they all have minds of their own so clear and firm that, while their good-feeling remains unalienated, their judgments equally remain unconciliated. 'A knowledge, which she often wished less, of her father's character' is part of lovely gentle Anne; and even self-righteous Fanny owns to herself that *her* father was still worse than she had expected—'he swore and he drank, he was dirty and gross'—with a succinct yet comprehensive candour that would certainly not have marked any Victorian heroine's attitude towards her 'dear papa.'

And, how much nearer we are to-day Anne and Fanny than to the generation immediately behind us, is shown by the fact that Pastor Manders' ejaculation in 'Ghosts,' that it is Oswald's duty to love and honour his impossible dead father, represented such an accepted axiom to the Victorians that its obvious irony in the play was felt to be a blasphemy; whereas to us of to-day the irony has lost all point, because the axiom itself is seen as clearly to be mere nonsense, as it was seen long ago, by Fanny and Anne and Eleanor Tilney.

In fact, all the women whom Jane Austen commends are absolutely honest and well-bred in mind. Breeding is not a matter of birth or place, but of attitude towards life; Jane Austen's standard, like Anne Elliot's behaviour, is as 'consciously right as it is invariably gentle'; and, one may add, as unselfconscious about its quality as real breeding is always bound to be. Her tone of perfect quiet assurance, and taking-for-grantedness, has nowhere been equalled. Many writers, even of the great (especially nowadays, and especially among women), are too painfully at ease in their Sions of castle or country-house,* with a naive excessiveness, a solemn rapture of emphasis, that shows their inmost feeling to be really Mary Crawford's at finding herself in Mansfield Vicarage garden. Even Thackeray gloats over the silver coffee-pots at Castle Gaunt; even Henry James lingers too lovingly amid the material details of what Gertrude Atherton would call 'aristocratic' life; Jane Austen alone is as indifferent and as much at ease, wherever she goes, as those only can be who are to the manner and the matter born and bred. Note, with what decision, for instance, but with

---

* Mary Crawford 'had seen scores of great houses, and cared for none of them.'

what a lack of betraying emphasis, she reserves 'vulgar' forms, such as 'quiz' and 'beau,' and 'you was,' to the exclusive use of her vulgar characters. And how it is only her underbred women—Isabella Thorpe, Mrs Elton, Lucy Steele—who use the bare surname of a man; Jane and Elizabeth Bennet, even in their most intimate private dialogues, never talk of 'Bingley' or 'Darcy' until the familiarity has been justified by betrothal. And again, the middle-class sisters, Lady Bertram and Mrs Norris, are to each other, respectively, 'Sister' and 'Lady Bertram,' throughout their book. These are samples of the small unobtruded points that give Jane Austen's readers such unending delight.

'Lady Susan' is the first of her books to call for comment. It is not good; it is crude and hard, with the usual hardness of youth. Yet it is so important to the study of its author's career and temperament that it would be disastrous to omit it from future editions, in deference to any fancied wishes of her 'shade.' The faults of youth are really only the excesses of what are to be excellences in the matured writer; and the cold unpleasantness of 'Lady Susan' is but the youthful exaggeration of that irreconcilable judgment which is the very backbone of Jane Austen's power, and which, harshly evident in the first book, is the essential strength of all the later ones, finally protruding its bony structure nakedly again in 'Persuasion.' But 'Lady Susan' also links on to 'Mansfield Park.' For where and when did Jane Austen come into contact with the 'Smart Set' of her time? Biographies give no slightest hint; but we must not forget Miss Mitford's impression of Jane Austen as a pretty little empty-headed husband-hunting fool. However violently at variance may be this verdict from all we can divine of Jane Austen, it was evidently this unsuspectedly gay creature who foregathered at one time with the 'Souls,' in intellectual attraction and moral repulsion. For out of the same set, brilliant and heartless, which is the very scene of Lady Susan, are ultimately to be projected Henry and Mary Crawford.

With 'Sense and Sensibility' we approach the maturing Jane Austen. But it has the almost inevitable frigidity of a reconstruction, besides an equally inevitable uncertainty in the author's use of her weapons. There are longueurs and clumsinesses; its conviction lacks fire; its development lacks movement; its major figures are rather incarnate qualities than qualitied incarnations. Never again does the writer introduce a character so entirely irrelevant as

Margaret Dashwood, or marry a heroine to a man so remote in the story as Colonel Brandon. This is not, however, to say that 'Sense and Sensibility', standing sole, would not be itself enough to establish an author's reputation. The opening dialogue, for instance, between John and Fanny Dashwood—obviously belonging to the second version of the story—ranks among the finest bits of revelation that even Jane Austen has given us; and criticism stands blissfully silent before Sir John Middleton, Mrs Jennings, and the juxtaposition of Lady Middleton and Fanny Dashwood, 'who sympathised with each other in an insipid propriety of demeanour and a general want of understanding.' But its tremendous successors set up a standard beside which 'Sense and Sensibility' is bound to appear grey and cool; nobody will choose this as his favourite Jane Austen, whereas each one of the others has its fanatics who prefer it above all the rest.

But now comes the greatest miracle of English Literature. Straight on the heels of 'Lady Susan' and 'Sense and Sensibility' this country parson's daughter of barely twenty-one breaks covert with a book of such effortless mastery, such easy and sustained brilliance, as would seem quite beyond reach of any but the most mature genius. Yet, though 'Pride and Prejudice' has probably given more perfect pleasure than any other novel (Elizabeth, to Jane Austen first, and now to all time, 'is as delightful a creature as ever appeared in print,' literature's most radiant heroine, besides being the most personally redolent of her creator), its very youthful note of joyousness is also the negation of that deeper quality which makes the later work so inexhaustible. Without ingratitude to the inimitable sparkle of this glorious book, even 'Northanger Abbey,' in its different scale, must be recognised as of a more sumptuous vintage. 'Pride and Prejudice' is, in fact, alone among the Immortal Five, a story pure and simple, though unfolded in and by character, indeed, with a dexterity which the author never aimed at repeating. For, as Jane Austen's power and personality unfold, character becomes more and more the very fabric of her works, and the later books are entirely absorbed and dominated by their leading figures; whereas Darcy and Elizabeth are actors among others in their comedy, instead of being the very essence of it, like Anne or Emma. And to the reader, the difference is that, whereas he can never come to an end of the subtle delights that lurk in every sentence of the later books, there does come a point at which he has

'Pride and Prejudice' completely assimilated.

Perhaps Jane Austen never quite recovered this first fine careless rapture; still, the book has other signs of youth. It has a vice-word, 'tolerably,' and its dialogue retains traces of Fanny Burney. Compare the heavy latinised paragraphs of the crucial quarrel between Darcy and Elizabeth (the sentence which proved so indelible a whip-lash to Darcy's pride is hardly capable of delivery in dialogue at all, still less by a young girl in a tottering passion) with the crisp and crashing exchanges in the parallel scene between Elton and Emma. The later book provides another comparison. Throughout, when once its secret is grasped, the reader is left in no doubt that subconsciously Emma was in love with Knightley all the time. In 'Pride and Prejudice' the author has rather fumbled with an analogous psychological situation, and is so far from making clear the real feeling which underlies Elizabeth's deliberate-ly fostered dislike of Darcy, that she has uncharacteristically left herself open to such a monstrous misreading as Sir Walter Scott's, who believed that Elizabeth was subdued to Darcy by the sight of Pemberley. In point of fact, we are expressly told that her inevitable feeling, 'this might have been mine,' is instantly extinguished by the belief that she could not bear it to be hers, at the price of having Darcy too; while her subsequent remark to Jane is emphatically a joke, and is immediately so treated by Jane herself ('another entreaty that she would be serious', etc.), wiser than some later readers of the scene.

Sir Walter's example should be a warning of how easy it is to trip even amid the looser mesh of Jane Austen's early work. Rapid reading of her is faulty reading. As for Mr Collins and Lady Catherine, whom some are ungrateful enough to call caricatures, it must definitely be said that they are figures of fun, indeed, but by no means figures of farce. At the same time both are certainly touched with a youthful sheer delight in their absurdity which gives to them an objective ebullience not to be found in more richly comic studies such as Lady Bertram or Mr Woodhouse. Nor does Jane Austen ever again repeat the parallelism between two sisters, that makes the fabric of the two early books. Already, in her incisive treatment of Charlotte Lucas, the later Jane Austen is foreshadowed; and 'Pride and Prejudice' contains the first example of her special invention, the middle-aged married woman whose delightful presence in the middle-distance of the picture reflects an

added pleasantness on the different leading figures with which Mrs
Gardiner, Mrs Grant, Mrs Weston, and Mrs Croft are brought in
contact, as foils and confidants. Had Macaulay happed on these
examples, the proof of his contention would have been as unquestionable as its truth.

In 'Northanger Abbey' Jane Austen takes a big stride forward.
Developing her taste for technical problems, she here tackles a very
difficult one—in an artist's consciousness of the problem, indeed,
but with youth's indomitable unconsciousness of its full difficulty.
A lesser writer, or a maturer, would have either jibbed at such a
task as that of interweaving two motives, of parody and serious
drama, or would have crashed heavily through their thin ice. In
buoyancy of youth and certainty of power, Jane Austen skims
straight across the peril, and achieves a triumph so complete that
easy readers run the risk of missing both triumph and problem, in
mere joy of the book. She even allows herself to dally here with her
own delight, and personally steps forward in the tale with her three
great personal outbreaks—on Novels, on Folly in Females, and on
the Vanity of Feminine Motives in Dress. As for the reader, the
closer his study of the dovetailing of the two motives, the
profounder his pleasure. Parody rules, up to the arrival of
Catherine at Northanger, which is the pivot of the composition;
after which the drama, long-brewing out of the comic motive, runs
current with it, and soon predominates. The requisite hyphen is
provided by John and Isabella Thorpe, as differently important in
one aspect of the tale as in the other. Each moment of the drama
artfully echoes some note of the parody that had prevailed before;
and the General's final outburst is just what had been foreshadowed
long before, in burlesque, of Mrs Allen. Catherine herself suffers
by this very nicety of poise and adjustment; she is really our most
delightful of all *ingénues*, but her story is kept so constantly comic
that one has no time to concentrate on its chief figure.

Fun, too, tends to overshadow the emotional skill with which
the movement is developed. Even the processes by which
Catherine so plausibly hardens herself into her grotesque belief that
General Tilney killed his wife, even her stupefaction before the
commonplaceness of the murdered martyr's room, pale beside the
sudden comic tragedy of her awakening,★ so convincing as it is, so

★ Jane Austen loves to have her heroine taken in, either by herself or some
one else; so that author and reader can enjoy a private smile together.

completely blending the two motives of the book, and, in itself, so vibrant with an emotion as genuine as its generating causes are ridiculous. 'She raised her eyes to him more fully than she had ever done before,' is an early, but very notable, instance of Jane Austen's peculiar power of conveying intense feeling with a touch. In fact, 'Northanger Abbey' marks the point of transition between the author's first period and her second. Already character is a serious rival to the story; henceforth it becomes more and more the main motive, till finally we reach 'Persuasion,' than which no known novel of anything like equal calibre is so entirely devoid of any 'story' at all.

And now, in Jane Austen's life comes an unexpected gap. The family is moving; it goes to Bath; it goes to Portsmouth. In all those ten odd years she produces nothing, except the beginning of 'The Watsons,' which she soon dropped in an unexplained distaste, for which critics have vainly sought a reason. Was it, perhaps, because these were the crucial years of the Napoleonic war, during which its stress was most felt, and concentration on novel-writing was found to be impossible? Much more probably she was simply fretted with removals and uncongenial surroundings; and unhappy, not only in general circumstances, but also with what gleam of personal romance came abortive into her own life. Anne Elliot's distaste for Bath has a more personal note than is usual in her creator's work, and the Portsmouth scenes of 'Mansfield Park' a peculiarly *vécu* quality. Altogether one cannot but feel that in her thirties our heroine was not in health of body and spirit, nor in any environment sufficiently settled and sympathetic, to generate those floods of delight which she had hitherto poured forth. And then the family settles at Chawton. Immediately Jane Austen gets to work again; and with astounding fecundity pours forth the three supreme efforts of her maturity in the last three or four years before her death, presumably of cancer, at the age of forty-two. And not one of the three is a novel of laughter, like those of the earlier period.

'Mansfield Park' is Jane Austen's *gran rifiuto*, perhaps under the influence of the unhappiness through which she had been passing. None of her books is quite so brilliant in parts, none shows a greater technical mastery, a more audacious facing of realities, a more certain touch with character. Yet, alone of her books, 'Mansfield Park' is vitiated throughout by a radical dishonesty, that was certainly not in its author's own nature. One can almost hear the clerical relations urging 'dear Jane' to devote 'her undoubted talent to the cause of righteousness'; indeed, if dates allowed, one could even believe that Mr Clarke's unforgettable suggestion about the country clergyman had formed fruit in this biography of Edmund Bertram. In any case, her purpose of edification, being not her own, is always at cross-purposes with her unprompted joy in creation. She is always getting so interested in her subject, and so joyous in her management of it, that when her official purpose comes to mind, the resulting high sentiment or edifying speech is a wrench alike to one's attention and credulity. And this dualism of motive destroys not only the unity of the book, but its sincerity. You cannot palter with truth; one false assumption puts all the drawing and colouring out of gear.

For example, Jane Austen has vividly and sedulously shown how impossible a home is Mansfield for the young, with the father an august old Olympian bore, the mother one of literature's most finished fools, and the aunt its very Queen of Shrews; then suddenly, for edification, she turns to saying that Tom Bertram's illness converted him to a tardy appreciation of domestic bliss. Having said which, she is soon overmastered by truth once more, and lets slip that he couldn't bear his father near him, that his mother bored him and that consequently these domestic blisses resolved themselves into better service than you'ld get in lodgings, and the ministrations of the uninspiring Edmund. Worse still, because more vital in the book, is her constant deliberate weighting of the balance against Crawford and Mary, who obviously have her artist's affection as well as her moralist's disapproval (as is proved by the very violence of her outbreaks of injustice against them). The consequent strain is such that she defeats her own end by making us take their side against Edmund and Fanny. She throws away the last chance of imposing her view, when she makes Mary, *ex hypothesi* worldly, calculating and callous, not only accept a penniless dull little nobody as her brilliant brother's wife, but even welcome her with a generous cordiality of enthusiasm which sets Fanny's cold self-righteous attitude of criticism to the Crawfords in a more repellent light than ever.

The *dénouement* is an inevitable failure, accordingly. It is the harshest of those precipitate *coups de théâtre* by which Jane Austen, impatient of mere happenings, is too apt to precipitate the conclusions of her books, and jerk her reader's belief with a sudden

peripety for which no previous symptom of character had prepared
him. Indeed, 'Pride and Prejudice' and 'Northanger Abbey' are the
only two of her books which work out to an inevitable end by
means of character, and character alone. But the elopement of
Crawford and Maria is a specially flagrant fraud on the reader, a
dishonest bit of sheer bad art, meant to clear the field for Fanny,
and wrench away the story from its obvious proper end, in the
marriages of Edmund and Mary, Crawford and Fanny. However
much an author may dislike letting his 'pen dwell on guilt
and misery', this is no excuse for making Henry forfeit the woman he loves (and is winning), for the sake of another
about whom he does not care two straws. Crawford was no mere
boy, to be rushed by any married woman into a scandal so fatal to
his plans; and without some sufficient explanation one utterly
declines to believe he ever did so. Yet Jane Austen inartistically
shirks giving any reason for a perversity otherwise incredible. It
was not that she would not; her fundamental honesty told her she
could not.

Yet Henry, after all, had a very lucky miss of Fanny. How he
could ever seriously have wanted to marry her, in fact, becomes a
puzzle, for she is the most terrible incarnation we have of the
female prig-pharisee. Those who still survive of the Victorian
school, which prized a woman in proportion as she was 'little' and
soft and silly, keep a special tenderness in their hearts for Fanny
Price. Alas, poor souls, let them only have married her! Gentle and
timid and shrinking and ineffectual as she seems, fiction holds no
heroine more repulsive in her cast-iron self-righteousness and
steely rigidity of prejudice; though allowance must be made, of
course, as Jane Austen always implies it, and at least once definitely
states it, for the jealousy that taints her whole attitude to Mary. Fate
has not been kind to Mary Crawford. Her place in the book, her
creator's spasms of bias against her, combine to obscure the fact
that she is by far the most persistently brilliant of Jane Austen's
heroines. It is mere unfair Fanny-feeling to pretend she has neither
heart nor morals, but she predominates in brains; and, of all her
creator's women, she would be the most delightful as a wife—to
any man of brains himself, with income and position. For even dear
Elizabeth might sometimes seem a trifle pert beneath the polluted
shades of Pemberley, and dear Emma have her moments of trying

to direct destiny at Donwell as disastrously as she'd already done at Hartfield.

On the whole, then, 'Mansfield Park', with its unparalleled flights counteracted by its unparalleled lapses, must count lower as an achievement than 'Emma,' with its more equal movement, at a higher level of workmanship. Had it not been for its vitiating purpose, indeed, 'Mansfield Park' would have taken highest rank. Amazing, even in Jane Austen, is the dexterity of the play scenes, and the day at Sotherton; amazing even in a French realist would be the unflinching veracity with which the Portsmouth episode is treated. Only those who have tried to write, perhaps, can fully realise the technical triumphs of Jane Austen. At Sotherton she has practically her whole cast on the stage at once, yet she juggles so accurately that each character not only keeps its own due importance but continues to evolve in exactly the proper relation to all the other ones. And this *tour de force* is bettered by the play scenes, prolonged over a whole period as they are, with an even larger crowd manoeuvred simultaneously in a complicated maze of movement, that never for an instant fails to get each person into its right prominence at the required moment, without prejudice to the general figure of the dance and the particular positions of the other performers. It is a tragedy that skill so mature should here have been ruined by distracting purposes. All through 'Mansfield Park', in fact, Jane Austen is torn between the theory of what she ought to see, and the fact of what she does see. The vision is her own, the suggestion another's; and while, in talking of what she does see, she is here at her finest, in forcing herself to what she ought to see she is here at her worst; to say nothing of the harm done to her assumptions by her insight, and to her insight by her assumptions.

But now we come to the Book of Books, which is the book Emma Woodhouse.★ And justly so named, with Jane Austen's undeviating flair for the exact title. For the whole thing is Emma; there is only one short scene in which Emma herself is not on the stage; and that one scene is Knightley's conversation about her with

★ 'Heavens, let me not suppose that she dares go about Emma-Woodhouseing me!'—'Emma', Cap. XXXIII—a typical instance of a remark which, comic in itself, has a second comic intention, as showing Emma's own ridiculousness.

Mrs Weston. Take it all in all, 'Emma' is the very climax of Jane Austen's work; and a real appreciation of 'Emma' is the final test of citizenship in her kingdom. For this is not an easy book to read; it should never be the beginner's primer, nor be published without a prefatory synopsis. Only when the story has been thoroughly assimilated, can the infinite delights and subtleties of its workmanship begin to be appreciated, as you realise the manifold complexity of the book's web, and find that every sentence, almost every epithet, has its definite reference to equally unemphasised points before and after in the development of the plot. Thus it is that, while twelve readings of 'Pride and Prejudice' give you twelve periods of pleasure repeated, as many readings of 'Emma' give you that pleasure, not repeated only, but squared and squared again with each perusal, till at every fresh reading you feel anew that you never understood anything like the widening sum of its delights. But, until you know the story, you are apt to find its movement dense and slow and obscure, difficult to follow, and not very obviously worth the following.

For this is *the* novel of character, and of character alone, and of one dominating character in particular. And many a rash reader, and some who are not rash, have been shut out on the threshold of Emma's Comedy by a dislike of Emma herself. Well did Jane Austen know what she was about, when she said, 'I am going to take a heroine whom nobody but myself will much like.' And, in so far as she fails to make people like Emma, so far would her whole attempt have to be judged a failure, were it not that really the failure, like the loss, is theirs who have not taken the trouble to understand what is being attempted. Jane Austen loved tackling problems; her hardest of all, her most deliberate, and her most triumphantly solved, is Emma.

What is that problem? No one who carefully reads the first three opening paragraphs of the book can entertain a doubt, or need any prefatory synopsis; for in these the author gives us quite clear warning of what we are to see. We are to see the gradual humiliation of self-conceit, through a long self-wrought succession of disasters, serious in effect, but keyed in Comedy throughout. Emma herself, in fact, *is never to be taken seriously*. And it is only those who have not realised this who will be 'put off' by her absurdities, her snobberies, her misdirected mischievous ingenuities. Emma is simply a figure of fun. To conciliate affection for a character, not because of its charms, but in defiance of its defects, is the loftiest aim of the comic spirit; Shakespeare achieved it with his besotted old rogue of a Falstaff, and Molière with Celimène. It is with these, not with 'sympathetic' heroines, that Emma takes rank, as the culminating figure of English high-comedy. And to attain success in creating a being whom you both love and laugh at, the author must attempt a task of complicated difficulty. He must both run with the hare and hunt with the hounds, treat his creation at once objectively and subjectively, get inside it to inspire it with sympathy, and yet stay outside it to direct laughter on its comic aspects. And this is what Jane Austen does for Emma, with a consistent sublimity so demure that indeed a reader accustomed only to crude work might be pardoned for missing the point of her innumerable hints, and actually taking seriously, for example, the irony with which Emma's attitude about the Coles' dinner-party is treated, or the even more convulsing comedy of Emma's reflexions after it. But only Jane Austen is capable of such oblique glints of humour; and only in 'Emma' does she weave them so densely into her kaleidoscope that the reader must be perpetually on his guard lest some specially delicious flash escape his notice, or some touch of dialogue be taken for the author's own intention.

Yet, as Emma really does behave extremely ill by Jane Fairfax, and even worse by Robert Martin, merely to laugh would not be enough, and every disapproval would justly be deepened to dislike. But, when we realise that each machination of Emma's, each imagined piece of penetration, is to be a thread in the snare woven unconsciously by herself for her own enmeshing in disaster, then the balance is rectified again, and disapproval can lighten to laughter once more. For this is another of Jane Austen's triumphs here—the way in which she keeps our sympathies poised about Emma. Always some charm of hers is brought out, to compensate some specially silly and ambitious naughtiness; and even these are but perfectly natural, in a strong-willed, strong-minded girl of only twenty-one, who has been for some four years unquestioned mistress of Hartfield, unquestioned Queen of Highbury. Accordingly, at every turn we are kept so dancing up and down with alternate rage and delight at Emma that finally, when we see her self-esteem hammered bit by bit into collapse, the nemesis would be too severe, were she to be left in the depths. By the merciful intention of the book, however, she is saved in the very nick of time, by what seems like a happy accident, but is really the outcome of her own unsuspected good qualities, just as much as her disasters had been the outcome of her own most cherished follies.

In fact, Emma is intrinsically honest (it is not for nothing that she is given so unique a frankness of outlook on life); and her brave recognition of her faults, when confronted with their results conduces largely to the relief with which we hail the solution of the tangle, and laugh out loud over 'Such a heart, such a Harriet'! The remark is typical, both of Emma and of Emma's author. For this is the ripest and kindliest of all Jane Austen's work. Here alone she can laugh at people, and still like them; elsewhere her amusement is invariably salted with either dislike or contempt. 'Emma' contains no fewer than four silly people, more or less prominent in the story; but Jane Austen touches them all with a new mansuetude, and turns them out as candidates for love as well as laughter. Nor is this all that must be said for Miss Bates and Mr Woodhouse. They are actually inspired with sympathy. Specially remarkable is the treatment of Miss Bates, whose pathos depends on her lovableness, and her lovableness on her pathos, till she comes so near our hearts that Emma's abrupt brutality to her on Box Hill comes home to us with the actuality of a violent sudden slap in our own face. But then Miss Bates, though a twaddle, is by no means a fool; in her humble, quiet, unassuming happiness, she is shown throughout as an essentially wise woman. For Jane Austen's mood is in no way softened to the second-rate and pretentious, though it is typical of 'Emma' that Elton's full horror is only gradually revealed in a succession of tiny touches, many of them designed to swing back sympathy to Emma; even as Emma's own bad behaviour on Box Hill is there to give Jane Fairfax a lift in our sympathy at her critical moment, while Emma's repentance afterwards is just what is wanted to win us back to Emma's side again, in time for the coming catastrophe. And even Elton's 'broad handsome face,' in which 'every feature works,' pales before that of the lady who 'was, in short, so very ready to have him.' 'He called her Augusta; how delightful!'

Jane Austen herself never calls people she is fond of by these fancy names, but reserves them for such female cads or cats as Lydia Bennet, Penelope Clay, Selina Suckling, and 'the charming Augusta Hawkins.' It is characteristic, indeed, of her methods in 'Emma,' that, though the Sucklings never actually appear, we come to know them (and miss them) as intimately as if they did. Jane Austen delights in imagining whole vivid sets of people, never on the stage, yet vital in the play; but in 'Emma' she indulges herself, and us, unusually lavishly, with the Sucklings at Maple Grove, the Dixons in Ireland, and the Churchills at Enscombe. As for Frank, he is among her men what Mary Crawford is among her women, a being of incomparable brilliance, moving with a dash that only the complicated wonderfulness of the whole book prevents us from lingering to appreciate. In fact, he so dims his cold pale Jane by comparison that one wonders more than ever what he saw in her. The whole Frank-Jane intrigue, indeed, on which the story hinges, is by no means its most valuable or plausible part. But Jane Fairfax is drawn in dim tones by the author's deliberate purpose. She had to be dim. It was essential that nothing should bring the secondary heroine into any competition with Emma. Accordingly Jane Fairfax is held down in a rigid dullness so conscientious that it almost defeats another of her *raisons d'être* by making Frank's affection seem incredible.

But there is very much more in it than that. Emma is to behave so extremely ill in the Dixon matter that she would quite forfeit our sympathy, unless we were a little taught to share her unregenerate feelings for the 'amiable, upright, perfect Jane Fairfax.' Accordingly we are shown Jane Fairfax always from the angle of Emma; and, despite apparently artless words of eulogy, the author is steadily working all the time to give us just that picture of Jane, as a cool, reserved, rather sly creature, which is demanded by the balance of emotion and the perspective of the picture.* It is curious, indeed, how often Jane Austen repeats a favourite composition; two sympathetic figures, major and minor, set against an odious one. In practice, this always means that, while the odious is set boldly out in clear lines and brilliant colour, the minor sympathetic one becomes subordinate to the major, almost to the point of dulness. The respective positions of Emma, Jane, and Mrs Elton shed a flood of light back on the comparative paleness of Eleanor Tilney, standing in the same minor relation to Catherine, as against Isabella Thorpe; and the trouble about 'Sense and Sensibility' is that, while Marianne and Elinor are similarly set against Lucy, Elinor,

---

* Remember, also, that Jane Austen did herself personally hate everything that savoured of reserve and disingenuousness, 'trick and littleness.'

hypothetically the minor note to Marianne, is also, by the current and intention of the tale, raised to an equal if not more prominent position,★ thus jangling the required chord, so faultlessly struck in 'Northanger Abbey,' and in 'Emma' only marred by the fact that Jane Fairfax's real part is larger than her actual sound-value can be permitted to be.

Sentimentality has busied itself over the mellowing influences of approaching death, evident in 'Persuasion.' The only such evidences are to be found in its wearinesses and unevennesses, and in the reappearance of that bed-rock hardness which only in 'Lady Susan' stands out so naked. Jane Austen herself felt its faults more strongly than subsequent generations have done. She was depressed about the whole book. And what she meant, however much one may disagree, is plain. 'Persuasion' has its uncertainties; the touch is sometimes vague, too heavy here, too feeble there—Mrs Smith is introduced with too much elaboration, Anne Elliot with too little; balance is lost, and the even, assured sweep of 'Emma' changes to a fitful wayward beauty. This is at once the warmest and the coldest of Jane Austen's works, the softest and the hardest. It is inspired, on the one hand, by a quite new note of glacial contempt for the characters she doesn't like, and, on the other, by an intensified tenderness for those she does. The veil of her impersonality wears thin; 'Persuasion' is no Comedy, like 'Emma,' and contains no woven pattern of Austenian irony. The author allows herself to tell her tale almost openly, and, in her strait treatment of Lady Russell and the Dowager Viscountess, shows very plainly her own characteristic attitude towards the artificial claims of rank—with such decision, indeed, that one wonders why, with 'Persuasion' to his hand, Mr Goldwin Smith should have been at pains to note a mere flash of 'radical sympathy' in 'poor Miss Taylor' (where, in point of fact, there is no trace of it).

As for Mrs Clay, she is introduced with so much more emphasis than her ultimate place in the story warrants, that it looks as if she had originally been meant to play a much larger part in it. And worst of all is the violent and ill-contrived exposure of William Elliot, which is also wholly unnecessary, since we are expressly

★ The first version of the book was called 'Elinor and Marianne'; which quite clearly coming from Jane Austen, shows that Elinor was meant to be the dominant figure.

told that not even for Kellynch could Anne have brought herself to marry the man associated with it. In fact, the whole Clay-Elliot imbroglio that cuts the non-existent knot at the end of the book is perhaps the clumsiest of Jane Austen's *coups de théâtre,* though not deliberately false as that of Mansfield Park.

And yet, when everything is said and done in criticism, those who love 'Persuasion' best of all Jane Austen's books have no poor case to put forward. For 'Persuasion' is primarily Anne Elliot. And Anne Elliot is a puzzling figure in our literature. She is not a *jeune fille,* she is not gay or happy, brilliant or conspicuous; she is languidly, if not awkwardly brought on the stage, unemphasised, unemphatic. And yet Anne Elliot is one of fiction's greatest heroines. Gradually her greatness dawns. The more you know of her, the more you realise how perfectly she incarnates the absolute lady, the very counterpart, in her sex, of the καλοκἀγαθὸς [perfect gentleman] among men. And yet there is so little that is obvious to show for all this. For the book is purely a cry of feeling; and, if you miss the feeling, you miss all. It sweeps through the whole story in a vibrating flood of loveliness; yet nothing very much is ever said. Jane Austen has here reached the culminating point in her art of conveying emotion without expression. Though 'Persuasion' moves very quietly, without sobs or screams, in drawing-rooms and country lanes, it is yet among the most emotional novels in our literature.

Anne Elliot suffers tensely, hopelessly, hopefully; she never violates the decencies of silence, she is never expounded or exposed. And the result is that, for such as can feel at all, there is more intensity of emotion in Anne's calm (at the opposite pole to Marianne's 'sensibility') than in the wildest passion-tatterings of Maggie Tulliver or Lucy Snowe; and that culminating little heart-breaking scene between Harville and Anne (quite apart from the amazing technical skill of its contrivance) towers to such a poignancy of beauty that it takes rank with the last dialogue of mother and daughter in the 'Iphigeneia', as one of the very sacred things of literature that one dares not trust oneself to read aloud. And any other ending would be unbearable. So completely, in fact, do Anne and her feelings consume the book that the object of them becomes negligible. Wentworth, delightful jolly fellow that he is (with his jolly set of sailor-friends, whom Anne so wanted for hers), quite fades out of our interest, and almost out of our sight.

It is not so with the rest of the people, however. I have had curious testimony to their singular actuality. A great friend of mine, a man who never opens a book by any chance, if a newspaper be to hand, finding himself shut up for weeks in a tiny Chinese town on the borders of Tibet, was driven at last, in sheer desperation of dulness, to Jane Austen. I watched the experiment with awe and anguish. I might have spared myself. 'Emma' baffled him indeed, but 'Pride and Prejudice' took him by storm. And then, to my terror, he took up 'Persuasion'; for surely of all her works, the appeal of 'Persuasion' is the most delicate and elusive. But again I might have spared my fears. 'Persuasion' had the greatest success of all; for days, if not weeks, my friend went mouthing its phrases, and chewing the cud of its felicities. 'That Sir Walter,' he would never weary of repeating, 'he's a *nib!*' And when I tried to find out what had so specially delighted him in 'Persuasion,' he suddenly and finally summed up the whole of Jane Austen and her work:—'Why, all those people, they're—they're *real!*'

28. 'the means are as simple as the result is amazing'

1919

From *Avowals*, 1919, 33–41, 60–61.

At this point in the dialogue, George Moore has just been conjecturing on the reaction of classical Greek and Roman writers to the moderns. It leads on to an analysis of the weaknesses and strengths of *Sense and Sensibility*.

MOORE. Scott's centenary must have fallen flat, for I remember nothing of it, but I have a very distinct memory of the articles that celebrated Miss Austen's. Praise there was in plenty, and if the writers of the articles could not discover the qualities that stirred their enthusiasm, it was because they were not themselves writers of prose narrative. It may be said that nobody understands anything so intimately as the craft he practises, and though the praise of the amateur is always welcome it is the criticism of the fellow-craftsman that counts. The praise was all right and very pleasing to me, who was nevertheless puzzled and unable to explain how the gentlemen could have written so much and said so little, the subject being Miss Austen, about whom so many interesting things might be said. I should not have wished them to omit the obvious that Miss Austen was a delightful writer who described the society of which she was part and parcel; it was necessary to say as much, of course, but it was not easy to see why this very trite appreciation should be expanded into many columns when so much remained unwritten about this delightful writer who, etc. After having mentioned for the tenth time that she described the society of which she was part and parcel, I should have liked the critics to have pointed out that Miss Austen was the inventor of a new medium of literary expression; it will no doubt come as a surprise to the critics to hear from me that Miss Austen was the inventor of the formula whereby domestic life may be described; and that every one of us, without exception, Balzac and Tourguéneff as much as Mrs Henry Wood and Anthony Trollope, is indebted to her. . . .

It is many years since I have read *Pride and Prejudice*, but the two principal characters, Mr Collins and Elizabeth, are still clear to me. Mr and Mrs Bennet still keep a place in my recollection, and, unless my memory retains the good and forgets the false, this book tends towards the vase rather than the wash-tub, which is rare in English novels; but it will be safer for me to speak of *Sense and Sensibility*, which I read lately, for in that work it often seemed to me that Miss Austen is at her best and at her worst.

Her subject is what is known as County, and her narrative opens as it should open in a large commodious house situated in the middle of a park as far as possible from the high road. Miss Austen's intention in this book is to present a highly strung, romantic girl who believes the time for love is twenty or before; at two-and-twenty young women have passed the bloom of youth; and that whosoever loves once can never love again. But in setting forth the mental attitude of her young people, it seems to me that

Miss Austen falls into something like the sententiousness of Mr Waverley. She fails to see that the writing of a long exordium of common-sense is inadequate exposition, and that many pages would be needed to lead the reader into a gradual comprehension of the subject, that Elinor represents common-sense and Marianne romance. States of soul cannot be conveyed in speeches, and in speeches delivered by girls whose acquaintance we have only just made.

[Quotes passage, commencing with Elinor's speech: 'Of his sense... room this moment', ch. 4]

Elinor's resemblance to Mr Waverley in this speech is very striking, and I confess that I thought Miss Austen had succumbed to the influence of her time, and was about to put the book aside, but continued it, and fortunately, for as soon as the family reached Devon, I began to understand how the confused opening had come about: Miss Austen had found herself unable to resist the temptation to include a scene not, strictly speaking, in her subject—a grave fault with which we must, however, sympathise, the scene being one of the wittiest in literature: a dialogue between the heir, Mrs Dashwood's son, and his young wife, as to the amount Dashwood shall contribute to his mother and sisters' maintenance. The omission of this scene would have been a loss, but the book would have gained in shape, and if the pages occupied by the dialogue had been given over to an exposition of Elinor and Marianne's different mental attitudes *Sense and Sensibility* would have gained as a whole though it had lost something.

[Quotes passage 'Dear, dear Norland... to enjoy you', ch. 5]

This sententiousness—is it really sensibility?—is continued for about forty pages, and is not dropped until the sisters go with their mother to the Devonshire cottage, and our attention has relaxed considerably; but Miss Austen regains it when a young man appears whom Marianne recognises as the one she has been craving for ever since her girlhood, and within a very few weeks she is convinced that he is the only one worth living for. At last the theme becomes clear, and we perceive that the author's intention is that Marianne shall be cheated of her desire, and marry in the end a man whose years once seemed to put him among those that can no longer hope to inspire passion. Passion alone is valid, and we begin to comprehend the scheme, which is that the young man must break with her; it is essential to the story that he should, and the bringing about of the rupture, I said, will put the skill of the narrator to the finest test. The story will begin to creak in its joints if the greatest care be not taken. In about three weeks the young man expresses a desire to leave the neighbourhood, and the reason he gives for his return to London is not satisfactory; indeed, his manner alarms Marianne, and her disquiet is increased by many little incidents. So far so good, but the question has to be answered: is the author to take the reader into her confidence and tell that the young man has flirted with Marianne merely to pass the time away, his thoughts being fixed on a rich marriage, or is the author going to keep the secret from the reader, thereby appealing to that sense of curiosity which is in everyone? Strange as it may seem, Miss Austen chose to appeal to the curiosity of the reader, and we are well advanced in the novel before we hear that the young gentleman has succeeded in allying himself to money. The motive of curiosity seems to me to lie a little outside of her art, and it would have been better for her to have taken the reader into her confidence and told that young man was seeking a rich marriage, and had no intention of applying his life to the worship of a poor girl; and later on Miss Austen's inexperience in her craft leads her into a blunder that cannot be condoned. She brings back the young man after his marriage to tell Elinor that he is very sorry, and my heart failed me when I saw the scene rising up in the narrative, and prayed that it might not come to pass. But she was the first, a Giotto among women, and when she wrote there was no prose narrative for her to learn from. It is easier for us to avoid these mistakes. A writer of inferior talent—shall we say Maupassant?—would have known that the scene could not be written, for there are scenes in life that cannot be written, even if they can be proved to have happened. The writer must choose what can be written, and a worse exhibition of skill than this scene is not discoverable in literature. The young man apologised, blubbered, and went away, and with his disappearance from the book my fault-finding ends.

Remember that the theme of the book is a disappointment in love, and never was one better written, more poignant, more dramatic. We all know how terrible these disappointments are, and how they crush and break up life, for the moment reducing it to dust; the sufferer neither sees nor hears, but walks like a somnambulist through an empty world. So it is with Marianne, who cannot give up hope, and the Dashwoods go up to London in search of the young man; and every attempt is made to recapture him, and every effort wrings her heart. She hears of him, but never sees him, till at last she perceives him in a back room, and at once, her whole countenance blazing forth with a sudden delight, she would have moved towards him instantly had not her sister laid her hand on her arm, and in the page and a half that follows Miss Austen gives us all the agony of passion the human heart can feel; she was the first; and none has written the scene that we all desire to write as truthfully as she has; when Balzac and Tourguéneff rewrote it they wrote more elaborately, but their achievements are not greater. In Miss Austen the means are as simple as the result is amazing. Listen to it again. A young girl of twenty, jilted, comes up to London with her mother and sister, and she sees her lover at an assembly; he comes forward and addresses a few words more to her sister than to herself within hearing of a dozen people, and it is here that we find the burning human heart in English prose narrative for the first, and, alas, for the last time.

Miss Austen's imagination has not spent itself in this supreme scene. She can develop her motive, and the narrative is continued amid gossiping women coming and going into the house taken for the season; the drawing-room is never empty; in and out the visitors come and go, asking questions about Marianne's marriage. Each of these questions is like a burning knife thrust into the girl, and she has to keep a steady face upon it all. She has to bear with it all, listening to the chatter till she wishes herself dead, at all events in some silent world, and what is so admirable is that while the reader's heart is wrung with pity for the girl, he is amused by as good chatter as has ever been written, and a great deal of good chatter has been written by the great writers, for the power of writing chatter is the sign manual of the great writer. Perhaps the French word *boniment* will explain my meaning better; chatter, being an abstract word, does not express as much as *boniment*. The word *boniment* is associated with the showman, and the world recalls to our mind the rapid, almost incoherent, talk of the man who stands at the end of the booth, crying: walk up, walk up and see my show! Rabelais was a great master of patter, and next to him is Shakespeare. Balzac, too, could write good patter, but Mrs Jennings' patter in *Sense and Sensibility* is as good as any. She sometimes, it is true, includes an important statement in the patter, one that is necessary for the comprehension of the narrative and this to me is a mistake, for the pleasure we find in patter is merely the pleasure of words run together rapidly. You have not read *Sense and Sensibility* for a long while, Gosse, and will let me read some of Miss Austen's patter....

[Quotes Mrs Jennings, 'Well my dear...of her head', ch. 30]

GOSSE. I'm afraid I miss your point.

MOORE. We do not go into society for the pleasure of conversation, but for the pleasure of sex, direct or indirect. Everything is arranged for this end: the dresses, the dances, the food, the wine, the music! Of this truth we are all conscious now, but should we have discovered it without Miss Austen's help? It was certainly she who perceived it, and her books are permeated with it, just as Wordsworth's poems are with a sense of deity in nature; and is it not this deep instinctive knowledge that makes her drawing-rooms seem more real than anybody else's? Marianne loves beyond Juliet's or Isolde's power: and our wonder at her passion is heightened by the fact that it wears out in drawing-rooms among chaperons; the book falls on our knee, and we murmur, as we look through the silence: how simple the means and how amazing the result.

MOORE. And now another thought has come to me: that it was Miss Austen's spinsterhood that allowed her to discover the Venusberg in the modern drawing-room.

29. 'such cool perceptions'

1922

From *The Problem of Style*, 1922, 57–8.

John Middleton Murry (1889–1957), critic and essayist, edited *Rhythm, Athanaeum, Adelphi*. This brief passage comes within a discussion of the comedy of manners.

The ideal of the art as practised in England lies somewhere between Congreve and Jane Austen. Consider this passage from Jane Austen's earliest novel, *Sense and Sensibility:*

> Marianne's performance was highly applauded. Sir John was loud in his admiration at the end of every song, and as loud in his conversation with the others while every song lasted. Lady Middleton frequently called him to order, wondered how any one's attention could be diverted from the music for a moment, and asked Marianne to sing a particular song which Marianne had just finished. Colonel Brandon alone of all the party heard her without being in raptures. He paid her only the compliment of attention; and she felt a respect for him on the occasion, which the others had reasonably forfeited by their shameless want of taste. His pleasure in music, though it amounted not to that ecstatic delight which alone could sympathize with her own, was estimable when contrasted against the horrible insensibility of the others; and she was reasonable enough to allow that a man of five and thirty might well have outlived all acuteness of feeling and every exquisite power of enjoyment. She was perfectly disposed to make every allowance for the Colonel's advanced state of life which humanity required.

That is, as sportsmen would say, a perfect right and left; the two quite different birds of aberration are beautifully dropped—the social humbug of Sir John and Lady Middleton, and the romantic sensibility of Marianne. The author's point of vantage is central, and for her purpose she personifies it in Colonel Brandon. The use of anything but prose for the expression of such cool perceptions would obviously be not merely an unnecessary but a positively hampering convention. One would simply risk blurring the keen edge. These effects of contrast between the appearance and the reality, between affection and honesty, demand exactness of language; the rich reward of enhanced emotional suggestion which poetry gives in return for the judicial precision it takes away would only be an encumbrance. The style resides in the exactness with which the perceptions and the scheme to which they are referred are conveyed; these are given at the same moment—the reference to a self-consistent mode of experience is immediately perceptible. It fully satisfies our definition of a true individuality of style; the reason why it is *necessarily* prose is that the mode of experience is not predominantly emotional.

30. 'waking the Jane Austenite up'
1924

From review of the Clarendon edition of the novels edited by R.W. Chapman, *Nation and Athenaeum*, 5 January 1924, reprinted in *New Republic*, vol. xxxvii, 1924; and in *Abinger Harvest*, 1936.

E.M. Forster (1879–1970) was a novelist and essayist, whose style of social comedy—verbally and in the groupings of characters—seems to owe much to her example. Forster's confessed Janeitism here is no pose. Yet, as he shows very soon, the 'open' mouth, the 'closed' mind and the slumbering 'criticism', are part of his fool's guise; and he engages immediately in some shrewd and detailed textual commentary.

I am a Jane Austenite, and therefore slightly imbecile about Jane Austen. My fatuous expression, and airs of personal immunity—how ill they sit on the face, say, of a Stevensonian! But Jane Austen is so different. She is my favourite author! I read and re-read, the mouth open and the mind closed. Shut up in measureless content, I greet her by the name of most kind hostess, while criticism slumbers. The Jane Austenite possesses little of the brightness he ascribes so freely to his idol. Like all regular churchgoers, he scarcely notices what is being said. For instance, the grammar of the following sentence from *Mansfield Park* does not cause him the least uneasiness:

And, alas! how always known no principle to supply as a duty what the heart was deficient in.

Nor does he notice any flatness in this dialogue from *Pride and Prejudice:*

'Kitty has no discretion in her coughs,' said her father; 'she times them ill.'

'I do not cough for my own amusement,' replied Kitty fretfully. 'When is your next ball to be, Lizzy?'

Why should Kitty ask what she must have known? And why

does she say 'your' ball when she was going to it herself? Fretfulness would never carry her to such lengths. No, something is amiss in the text; but the loyal adorer will never suspect it. He reads and re-reads. And Mr R.W. Chapman's fine new edition has, among its other merits, the advantage of waking the Jane Austenite up. After reading its notes and appendixes, after a single glance at its illustrations, he will never relapse again into the primal stupor. Without violence, the spell has been broken. The six princesses remain on their sofas, but their eyelids quiver and they move their hands. Their twelve suitors do likewise, and their subordinates stir on the perches to which humour or propriety assigned them. The novels continue to live their own wonderful internal life, but it has been freshened and enriched by contact with the life of facts. To promote this contact is the chief function of an editor, and Mr Chapman fulfils it. All his erudition and taste contribute to this end—his extracts from Mrs Radcliffe and Mrs Inchbald, his disquisitions on punctuation and travel, his indexes. Even his textual criticism helps. Observe his brilliant solution of the second of the two difficulties quoted above. He has noticed that in the original edition of *Pride and Prejudice* the words 'When is your next ball to be, Lizzy?' began a line, and he suggests that the printer failed to indent them, and, in consequence, they are not Kitty's words at all, but her father's. It is a tiny point, yet how it stirs the pools of complacency! Mr Bennet, not Kitty, is speaking, and all these years one had never known! The dialogue lights up and sends a little spark of fire into the main mass of the novel. And so, to a lesser degree, with the shapeless sentence from *Mansfield Park*. Here we emend 'how always known' into 'now all was known'; and the sentence not only makes sense but illumines its surroundings. Fanny is meditating on the character of Crawford, and, now that all is known to her, she condemns it. And finally, what a light is thrown on Jane Austen' own character by an intelligent collation of the two editions of *Sense and Sensibility*! In the 1811 edition we read:

> Lady Middleton's delicacy was shocked, and in order to banish so improper a subject as the mention of a natural daughter, she actually took the trouble of saying something herself about the weather.

In the 1813 edition the sentence is omitted, in the interests of propriety: the authoress is moving away from the eighteenth century into the nineteenth, from *Love and Freindship* towards *Persuasion*.

31. 'the forerunner of Henry James and of Proust'

1923/25

From 'Jane Austen at Sixty' (Reviewing the Oxford edition of the novels), *Athenaeum*, 15 December 1923 and *New Republic* (New York), 30 January 1924; then formed the nucleus of 'Jane Austen', *The Common Reader*, 1925, incorporating passages from her reviews of *Love and Freindship* (*New Statesman*, vol. xix, 1922) and *The Watsons* (*Spectator*, vol. cxxx, 1923).

This was Virginia Woolf's longest essay on Jane Austen, of which these are the closing pages. The words dropped from the 1923 *Athenaeum* text are given as notes; the additions to it are placed in square brackets.

The balance of her gifts was singularly perfect. Among her finished novels there are no failures, and among her many chapters few that sink markedly below the level of the others. But, after all, she died at the age of forty-two. She died at the height of her powers. She was still subject to those changes which often make the final period of a writer's career the most interesting of all. Vivacious, irrepressible, gifted with an invention of great vitality, there can be no doubt that she would have written more, had she lived, and it is tempting to consider whether she would not have written differently. The boundaries were marked; moons, mountains, and castles lay on the other side. But was she not sometimes tempted to trespass for a minute? Was she not beginning, in her own gay and brilliant manner, to contemplate a little voyage of discovery?

Let us take *Persuasion*, the last completed novel, and look by its light at the books she might have written had she lived.★ There is a

★ 'to be sixty. We do not grudge it him, but her brother the Admiral lived to be ninety-one.'

peculiar beauty and a peculiar dullness in *Persuasion*. The dullness is that which so often marks the transition stage between two different periods. The writer is a little bored. She has grown too familiar with the ways of her world; [she no longer notes them freshly]. There is an asperity in her comedy which suggests that she has almost ceased to be amused by the vanities of a Sir Walter or the snobbery of a Miss Elliott. The satire is harsh, and the comedy crude. She is no longer so freshly aware of the amusements of daily life. Her mind is not altogether on her object. But, while we feel that Jane Austen has done this before, and done it better, we also feel that she is trying to do something which she has never yet attempted. There is a new element in *Persuasion*, the quality, perhaps, that made Dr Whewell fire up and insist that it was 'the most beautiful of her works.' She is beginning to discover that the world is larger, more mysterious, and more romantic than she had supposed. We feel it to be true of herself when she says of Anne: 'She had been forced into prudence in her youth, she learned romance as she grew older—the natural sequel of an unnatural beginning.' She dwells frequently upon the beauty and the melancholy of nature [upon the autumn where she had been wont to dwell upon the spring]. She talks of the 'influence so sweet and so sad of autumnal months in the country.' She marks 'the tawny leaves and withered hedges.' 'One does not love a place the less because one has suffered in it,' she observes. But it is not only in a new sensibility to nature that we detect the change. Her attitude to life itself is altered. She is seeing it, for the greater part of the book, through the eyes of a woman who, unhappy herself, has a special sympathy for the happiness and unhappiness of others, which, until the very end, she is forced to comment upon in silence. Therefore the observation is less of facts and more of feelings than is usual. There is an expressed emotion in the scene at the concert and in the famous talk about woman's constancy which proves not merely the biographical fact that Jane Austen had loved, but the aesthetic fact that she was no longer afraid to say so. Experience, when it was of a serious kind, had to sink very deep, and to be thoroughly disinfected by the passage of time, before she allowed herself to deal with it in fiction. But now, in 1817, she was ready. Outwardly, too, in her circumstances, a change was imminent. Her fame had grown very slowly. 'I doubt,' wrote Mr Austen Leigh, 'whether it would be possible to mention any other author of note whose personal obscurity was so complete.' Had she lived a few more years only, all that would have been altered. She would have stayed in London, dined out, launched out, met famous people, made new friends, read, travelled, and carried back to the quiet country cottage a hoard of observations to feast upon at leisure.

And what effect would all this have had upon the six novels that Jane Austen did not write? She would not have written of crime, of passion, or of adventure. She would not have been rushed by the importunity of publishers or the flattery of friends into slovenliness or insincerity. But she would have known more. Her sense of security would have been shaken. Her comedy would have suffered. She would have trusted less (this is already perceptible in *Persuasion*) to dialogue and more to reflection to give us a knowledge of her characters. Those marvellous little speeches which sum up, in a few minutes' chatter, all that we need in order to know an Admiral Croft or a Mrs Musgrove for ever, that shorthand, hit-or-miss method which contains chapters of analysis and psychology, would have become too crude to hold all that she now perceived of the complexity of human nature. She would have devised a method, clear and composed as ever, but deeper and more suggestive, for conveying, not only what people say, but what they leave unsaid; not only what they are, but what life is.* She would have stood farther away from her characters, and seen them more as a group, less as individuals. Her satire, while it played less incessantly, would have been more stringent and severe. She would have been the forerunner of Henry James and of Proust—but enough. Vain are these speculations; [the most perfect artist among women, the writer whose books are immortal], **died 'just as she was beginning to feel confidence in her own success.'

* 'but (if we may be pardoned the vagueness of the expression) what life is.'
** 'these speculations; she died just as'.

32. 'Novels preeminently of character'

1925

From *The Writing of Fiction*, 1925, 128–30.

Edith Wharton (1862–1937), American novelist and critic. Like James, she wrote with wide knowledge of the European novel, the French in particular; and we hear an echo of James in her observation that in *Emma* we have 'the most perfect example... of a novel in which character shapes events quietly but irresistibly'.

Novels preeminently of character, and in which situation, dramatically viewed, is reduced to the minimum, are far easier to find. Jane Austen has given the norm, the ideal, of this type. Of her tales it might almost be said that the reader sometimes forgets what happens to her characters in his haunting remembrance of their foibles and oddities, their little daily round of preoccupations and pleasures. They are 'speaking' portraits, following one with their eyes in that uncannily lifelike way that good portraits have, rather than passionate disordered people dragging one impetuously into the tangle of their tragedy, as one is dragged by the characters of Stendhal, Thackeray, and Balzac. Not that Jane Austen's characters do not follow their predestined orbit. They evolve as real people do; but so softly, noiselessly, that to follow the development of their history is as quiet a business as watching the passage of the seasons. A sense of her limitations as certain as her sense of her power must have kept her—unconsciously or not—from trying to thrust these little people into great actions, and made her choose the quiet setting which enabled her to round out her portraits as imperceptibly as the sun models a fruit. 'Emma' is perhaps the most perfect example in English fiction of a novel in which character shapes events quietly but irresistibly, as a stream nibbles away its banks.

Next to 'Emma' one might place, in this category, the masterpiece of a very different hand: 'The Egoist' of Meredith. In this book, though by means so alien to Miss Austen's delicate procedure that one balks at the comparison, the fantastic novelists, whose antics too often make one forget his insight, discarding most of his fatiguing follies, gives a rich and deliberate study of a real human being. But he does not quite achieve Jane Austen's success. His Willoughby Patterne is typical before he is individual, while every character in 'Emma' is both, and in degrees always perfectly proportioned. Still, the two books are preeminent achievements in the field of pure character-drawing, and one must turn to the greatest continental novelists—to Balzac again (as always), to Stendhal, Flaubert, Dostoievsky, Turgenev, Marcel Proust, and perhaps to the very occasional best of Trollope—to match such searching and elaborate studies.

33. 'the spirit of comedy'

1926

Extract from *Reason and Romanticism*, 1926, 182–5.

Herbert Read (1893–1968), poet, critic, academic and publisher, was a leading advocate of modernism in art and literature. In this reconsideration of the case entered against Jane Austen by Charlotte Brontë (*No. 28*), Read finds the charge 'unanswerable'.

But it is not Miss Martineau that was destined to stand as the antitype to the Brontës: a subtler and finer antagonist had been in the field for some time. It speaks a good deal for Charlotte's critical perception that she realized the implications of Miss Austen's talent as soon as she became aware of it, rather late in her life, and, though only in the privacy of her correspondence with her publisher, she then defined the limitations of that talent in terms which still remain unanswerable. In a letter written in 1850 she says: 'She does her business of delineating the surface of the lives of genteel English people curiously well. There is a Chinese fidelity, a miniature delicacy in the painting. She ruffles her reader by nothing vehement, disturbs him by nothing profound. The passions are perfectly unknown to her; she rejects even a speaking acquaintance with that stormy sisterhood. Even to the feelings she vouchsafes no more than an occasional graceful but distant recognition—too frequent converse with them would ruffle the smooth elegance of her progress. Her business is not half so much with the human heart as with the human eyes, mouth, hands, and feet. What sees keenly, speaks aptly, moves flexibly, it suits her to study; but what throbs fast and full, though hidden, what the blood rushes through, what is the unseen seat of life and the sentient target of death—this Miss Austen ignores.' The justice of that analysis remains, to confront the present sophisticated rage for Jane Austen. But it also remains the statement of an extreme position, the weakness of which would have been exceedingly patent to the precise sensibility of the author of *Pride and Prejudice*. If she had lived long enough she might have criticized *Jane Eyre* in terms almost exactly contranominal to those of Charlotte. The psychologist does not venture to take sides in such an opposition, but resorts to his theory of types, and sees here the dry bones of his structure take on perfect flesh. It would be difficult to discover a more exact illustration of the main distinction he draws between faculties directed inwards, to the observation of feeling, and faculties directed outwards, to the observation of external things. The psychologist must halt at this distinction, unless he suggests, as a scientific ideal, some harmony or balance of these tendencies. But the critic must pursue the matter to a judgement. It will not, for that purpose, suffice to identify the ordered conception of objective facts with the classical spirit, or the research of passion with the romantic spirit—though it is tempting in this case to think of Jane Austen as a typical (though rare, because feminine) embodiment of classicism, and Pater seized on *Wuthering Heights*, in preference to any work of Scott's, as the 'really characteristic fruit' of the spirit of romanticism. That only proves once more the inadequacy of these outworn shibboleths, since from another point of view *Wuthering Heights*, with its unerring unity of conception and its full catharsis of the emotions of pity and terror, is one of the very few occasions on which the novel has reached the dignity of classical tragedy. And, in the other case, it would be hard to concede the full meaning of classicism to Jane Austen's universe of undertones.

We return to Charlotte's phrase—emotion in subjection—and contend that this is the only normal sense in which the classical spirit should be endured. The rest is pedantry, academic closures, and the 'literature of our grandfathers'. To apply the distinction to Jane Austen is hardly fair: she belongs to the spirit of comedy, which has never been easily classified, always existing as a free and detached criticism of life and literature. Jane Austen, in essentials, takes her place with Congreve, if with anybody in English letters; and maybe, after all, in making her the antitype to the Brontës we are but displaying the old discordant masks side by side. Is it an equal opposition? Well, not quite. Charlotte Brontë is again the critic—'Miss Austen being, as you say, without "sentiment", without *poetry*, maybe *is* sensible, real (more *real* than *true*), but she cannot be great.' And that might be said equally well of Congreve, or of any representative of the comic spirit. It is a question of attitude. It is, finally, a question of courage—of throwing into the attempt for truth not only intelligence, spirit, faith, but also feeling, emotion, self.

34. 'a great little novelist'

1927/28

From 'Books and Persons' column, *Evening Standard*, 21 July 1927 and 22 November 1928.

Arnold Bennett (1867–1931), novelist and journalist. Apparently, Janeitism was of sufficient public interest to qualify for Bennett's popular literary column. In the second extract, it is interesting to see his agreement with Chesterton on the novelist's unblinkered view of her own society (see p. 240).

Jane Austen? I feel that I am approaching dangerous ground. The reputation of Jane Austen is surrounded by cohorts of defenders who are ready to do murder for their sacred cause. They are nearly all fanatics. They will not listen. If anybody 'went for' Jane, anything might happen to him. He would assuredly be called on to resign from his clubs. I do not want to resign from my clubs. I would sooner perjure myself. On the other hand I do not want to 'go for' Jane. I like Jane. I have read several Janes more than once. And in the reading of Jane's novels there happens to be that which can only happen in the work of a considerable author. I mean that first you prefer one novel, then you prefer another novel, and so on. Time was when I convinced myself that *Persuasion* was her masterpiece, with *Emma* a good second. Now I am inclined to join the populace and put *Pride and Prejudice* in the front, with *Mansfield Park* a good second.

But listening to the more passionate Janeites (and among them are some truly redoubtable persons), one receives the impression that in their view Jane and Shakespeare are the only two English authors who rightly count, and that Shakespeare is joined with her chiefly as a concession to the opinion of centuries. I do not subscribe to this heated notion. I do not even agree that Jane was a great novelist. She was a great little novelist. She is marvellous, intoxicating: she has unique wit, vast quantities of common sense, a most agreeable sense of proportion, much narrative skill. And she is always readable.

But her world is a tiny world, and even of that tiny world she ignores, consciously or unconsciously, the fundamental factors. She did not know enough of the world to be a great novelist. She had not the ambition to be a great novelist. She knew her place; her present 'fans' do not know her place, and their antics would without doubt have excited Jane's lethal irony. I should say that either Emily or Charlotte Brontë was a bigger novelist than Jane. The hallowed name of Brontë brings me into the Victorian era of fiction, concerning which I will, if I still survive, enrage the earnest orthodox next week.

I am not an extreme 'Janeite'; I do not feel convinced that Jane Austen was the only estimable author who ever lived. But the general level of these novels is very high. *Northanger Abbey* is the least fine; even *Sense and Sensibility* (Jane's first book) is its superior. I concede to the Janeites that their goddess at her best has never been beaten in the field of pure comedy. Continual richness! Also blunt plain speaking when the same is called for! She loved her social system—but had no (or few) illusions about it.

35. The style of the 'essayist'

1928

English Prose Style, Herbert Read, 1928, 117–20.

An analysis pointing to the inadequacy of Jane Austen's prose to render dramatic action.

Fiction did not really recover its directness for about a century, though there is an admirable concreteness about the prose of Jane Austen. There is a certain kind of economy too, but nothing so violent as speed. The characteristics, indeed, of her style are rather those of the essayist. The action is reduced to a minimum, and mind turns instead to analysis, to decoration (scene-painting), to mildly ironic comment:

[Quotes *Emma*, ch. 42, 'It was hot... without being oppressive']

Descriptive prose of this kind is not written in any mood of compulsion. A skilful writer may be able to disguise this lack of internal necessity by means of various 'tricks of the trade', and the result is merely a 'dead' perfection of phrase and rhythm. Jane Austen was not a skilled writer in this sense, and her lack of expertness betrays itself either in mere clumsiness, such as the repetition of the words 'seemed' and 'considerable' in the passage quoted here, or in a simplicity or naivety of phrasing which is perhaps the secret of the attraction which her style undoubtedly has for a large number of people.

There are many 'quiet' situations for which this style is adequate enough; but under the strain of dramatic action it becomes almost ludicrous:

[Quotes *Persuasion*, ch. 12, 'There was too much wind... the utmost rapidity']

This atmosphere of a marionnette's opera* is entirely a question

*An atmosphere that explains the charm which Jane Austen undeniably exercises on people whose particular need is to be amused in a recondite way. Such people have a sophisticated love of mere 'quaintness', and seek this quality in all the arts.

of style. In conception and development the scene is right enough; it is rendered ludicrous by polite phrases like 'sinking under the conviction', 'disengaging himself from his wife', 'every one capable of thinking felt the advantage of the idea', 'the utmost rapidity', etc., which are not congruous with the tragedy of the situation. How bathetic, too, are those apostrophes, 'The horror of that moment to all who stood around', 'O God! her father and mother!' how absurdly cooing Captain Wentworth's 'True, true'.

36. 'this comic patronage of Jane Austen'

1928

From *The Strange Necessity*, 1928, 263–64.

Rebecca West (1892–1983), novelist, essayist and journalist. The immediate point of departure is the comment by Anne Douglas Sedgwick (source unidentified). But her indignation at 'this comic patronage' might well be aimed at Garrod.

But what can one expect of a writer who astonishingly describes Jane Austen as 'tearless'? Is it really possible that anybody could read *Sense and Sensibility* or *Persuasion* without seeing behind them a face graven with weeping? 'It is dangerous to feel much unless one is great enough to feel much; and wise and charming as she is, her glance would be the pinprick to many an inflated emotion, though to many real ones she would be blind.'

Really, it is time this comic patronage of Jane Austen ceased. To believe her limited in range because she was harmonious in method is as sensible as to imagine that when the Atlantic Ocean is as smooth as a mill-pond it shrinks to the size of a mill-pond. There are those who are deluded by the decorousness of her manner, by the fact that her virgins are so virginal that they are unaware of their virginity, into thinking that she is ignorant of passion. But look through the lattice-work of her neat sentences, joined together with the bright nails of craftsmanship, painted with the gay varnish of wit, and you will see women haggard with desire or triumphant with love, whose delicate reactions to men make the heroines of all our later novelists seem merely to turn signs, 'Stop' or 'Go' oward the advancing male. And the still sillier reproach, that Jane Austen has no sense of the fundamental things in life, springs from a misapprehension of her place in time. She came at the end of the eighteenth century, when the class to which she belongs was perhaps more intelligent than it has ever been before or since, when it had dipped more deeply than comfortable folk have ever done into philosophical inquiry. Her determination not to be confused by emotion, and to examine each phenomenon of the day briskly and on its merits, was never a sign of limitation. It was a sign that she lived in the same world as Hume and Gibbon. Her cool silence on the wherefore of the why is a million times more evidential of an interest in the fundamental things of life than '"Brother, brother, how shall I know God?" sobbed Alyosha, who by this time was exceedingly drunk,' or any such sentence from those Russians.

37. The 'Divine Jane' lives on

1932

Jane Austen: Her Life and Art, 1932, 238–40.

David Rhydderch was the author of a work in Welsh; otherwise his biography is unknown.

In the book's closing pages there is an ecstatic celebration of the novelist's emergence from her 'long eclipse'. Although remote in tone from James (No. 22a) thirty years earlier, the two pieces can usefully be compared as observations on the Jane Austen world, seemingly a hive of industry, and her presence in the public mind. Rebecca West mentions this book with approval in No. 38.

Her long eclipse is now at an end. Biographies follow one another at frequent intervals. To Professor Caroline Spurgeon 'every scrap of information and every ray of light on Jane Austen are of national importance.' To the invaluable bibliography of her works by Geoffrey Keynes, her dictionary by G.L. Apperson has now been added; and Dr Chapman's edition of her letters at last proclaims the triumph of his pledge. Pilgrimages to her shrines are undertaken and illustrated, juvenilia unearthed, and collotype facsimiles in expensive editions published. Duologues and scenes from the novels are arranged and adapted for drawing-room performance. Her quotations are classified, her allusions annotated, her orthography amended, and her archaeologisms strung together. Watermarks are examined, immature fragments scrutinised and her correspondence catalogued. There are abridgments and connected extracts, scenes and selections; a questionnaire, and introductions of every hue, and wonderful shades in essays, all rich in texture and of wide research. Not forgetting her patient illustrators, the superb line drawings of Hugh Thomson, W.C. Cooke, the Brocks, Chris Hammond and A. Wallis Mills. And now, an omnibus edition of her works is in every shop window; *Pride and Prejudice, Northanger Abbey* and *Love and Freindship* have even been dramatised. The learned search for first intentions. Museums proudly exhibit her handiwork. *The Times* gives pride of place to a few unpublished letters. After her name, Mr Kipling founds a new sisterhood. There are plaques to her memory everywhere. Even the misadventure of a heroine is plaqued. In marble and oak they severally commemorate her residence in Bath and Chawton. Beside her tomb in Winchester, her name is writ on brass; and above, a Latin inscription beneath the harps of David in stained glass points her worth. The Maid of Orleans already looks down upon us; and the day is not far distant when the 'Divine Jane', like patience on a monument smiling at fame, will keep her company.

38. 'the feminism of Jane Austen'

1932

Preface, *Northanger Abbey* (Jonathan Cape), 1932; reissued 1940.

Rebecca West's reconstruction of the circumstances for the failure of the bookseller-publisher to bring out the novel leads on to a remarkable account of Jane Austen's 'indirectness' and 'feminism'.

There is a circumstance connected with the publication of *Northanger Abbey* which is among the most conspicuous oddities of literary history. Jane Austen wrote the first version of this book in 1798, when she was but twenty-three years of age, and kept it by her for five years, by which time she had brought it to the state in which we see it now. Very shortly afterwards it was bought by a bookseller, and was even announced as a forthcoming publication. But he never published it; and thirteen years later he sold it back to Jane Austen's brother Henry for exactly the ten pounds he paid for it, and no more.

Now, we must all agree with Miss Austen herself when she remarks 'that any bookseller should think it worth while to purchase what he did not think worth while to publish seems extraordinary.' It can only be explained by supposing that he was unfortunate enough to be forced by his calling into giving expression in hard cash to an attitude common enough among the readers of Jane Austen. He picked up the manuscript from his post-bag, opened it as if it were any other, and formed the opinion that it very nearly was. It was a pleasant tale about pleasant people, written in simple English; and it had the further advantage, from the point of view of the circulating libraries, that it was plainly written by a lady who wrote from her own knowledge of life as it was lived in country seats and at Bath. With all confidence, therefore, he bade the counting-house send ten pounds to the author.

But later, perhaps when he was about to send the manuscript down to the printing-press, he gave it another look, and was sharply pulled up by a suspicion that it was not what he had supposed it. He was not at all sure that the tale was as like any other as he had supposed, or so pleasant. It certainly was not the kind of tale generally accepted as pleasant at the circulating libraries, which draws tears and smiles from the reader by incidents generally accepted as having that effect. For though the people in it were pleasant enough, the author's attitude to them was not so pleasant. It was disconcerting. One did not know where one was. She seemed to be laughing at them for actions not usually considered laughable. It might even be feared that she was laughing at the reader; in which case she would certainly be laughing much harder at the business man whom she had persuaded to act as intermediary in this sarcastic assault on the public. But it might even be that the joke the manuscript was playing on him was even more impudent. It might be that there was nothing in it at all, innocuous twaddle which would strike even the circulating libraries as insipid trifling with their subscribers' intelligence; for it dealt with most ordinary people and events, and that not robustly, as Fielding and Smollett had done it, nor with sentimental excitements as Richardson and Fanny Burney had done it, but with the calm of ladies talking round a tea table. It is not to be wondered if the book-seller threw back into his drawer this manuscript that meant either far too much or far too little, told the printer's devil not to wait, and announced to himself that he might as well consider that ten pounds as good as lost.

It is worth while remembering this poor man's plight, because it draws attention to a quality in Jane Austen's work which might escape our notice: and that is its novelty. It has often been remarked that nowhere in her novels is there any mention of the Napoleonic wars that were ravaging Europe during the whole of her adult life; and though all that can legitimately be deduced from this omission is that she knew she had nothing to say about the Napoleonic wars, an attempt has been made to use it as a proof that she was an entirely intuitional and personal artist, who drew little of her power from intellectual apprehension of the world around her. But this is unjustifiable. Turn to Fanny Burney's *Evelina*, written twenty years before *Northanger Abbey*, and still so generally regarded as the standard woman's novel that Jane Austen described one of her books to a publisher as being the same length as *Evelina*: and the contrast between the two books will make one wonder if Jane Austen had not been greatly though indirectly influenced by the sceptical movement of the eighteenth century which came to a climax in the French Revolution.

The indirectness must be emphasised. Miss Austen would certainly have thought Miss Helen Maria Williams a sad goose for going to France to witness the dawn of liberty and stopping nearly long enough to get her head chopped off. But it is surely not a coincidence that a country gentlewoman should sit down and put the institutions of society regarding women through the most gruelling criticism they have ever received, just at the time when Europe was generally following Voltaire and Rousseau in their opinion that social institutions not only should but could be questioned.

For the feminism of Jane Austen, to take the expression of it in *Northanger Abbey*, was very marked. It was, I think, quite conscious; the odd attack on the Spectator at the end of Chapter Five must have been evoked by the slighting references to women common in that work. And it is very drastic; it declares that the position of woman as society dictated it was humiliating, dangerous, and founded on lying propositions. She draws us poor Catherine Morland, a good creature if ever there was one, of whom we would read with pleasure even if we did not know that when Jane describes her life as one of a country parson's brood of ten she is writing of something very near her own life as one of a country parson's brood of eight. She shows us how the good creature was flattered by the romantic conception of love and womanhood. Everywhere it was pretended that women were heroines, that men worshipped them and strove for their possession, either in the decent way that led to the altar, or by abduction and seduction, and that in any case it was disinterested desire which dictated the relationship of the sexes. To these illusions Jane Austen opposes the truth in her bitter invention of General Tilney's mercenary pursuit of Catherine and his unmannerly dismissal of her. There, it seems, were other forces operating besides the one commonly named. Men give women the incomparable protection and consequence of matrimony, but they are not above considering if there may not be a *quid pro quo* in the transaction. In fact, a wife with a dowery is better than none, and this dowery must be in gold, for, as it is pointed out in this volume on several pages, wealth of the mind counts in the female sex as a kind of poverty.

These facts shatter the conception of romantic love, and provoke among the less admirable sort of woman a counter-calculation. It is interesting to note the reality and novelty of Isabella Thorpe. Men and women writers had often drawn the coquette before, but, since they all wrote from the masculinist point of view, it was always assumed that her motive was psychological. It was to conquer men that the coquette was supposed to chop and change; but Miss Austen merrily though scornfully suggests that it was to gain as good an establishment as possible. But the tragedy is that every sensible woman had to admit that there was a lot to be said for Isabella Thorpe's aims and artifice, since there was no way of independence for women and the pleasantest way of dependence was matrimony. Husband-hunting was shameful and horrid, but there was every reason why one should join in the hunt.

There were two reasons why Jane Austen felt acutely on this subject. The first was the urgency of her own need for an establishment. Her financial position was always insecure. When her father died she and her mother and her sister were left in straitened circumstances, and so level a head must have foreseen this. Mr David Rhydderch in his interesting *Jane Austen, her Life and Art*, points out how these financial troubles are mirrored in the later novels. She must, therefore, have sometimes wished she could have been as much less than herself as would have permitted her to take a hand in the game. But there was also a force more powerful than these material considerations which made her discontented with the common attitude to love.

She was fully possessed of the idealism which is a necessary ingredient of the great satirist. If she criticised the institutions of earth it was because she had very definite ideas regarding the institutions of heaven. There is a beautiful and pathetic self-revelation in all the passages dealing with Catherine and Henry Tilney. Again and again Miss Austen makes Catherine 'give herself away' as in the scene where she bursts breathless and apologetic into the Tilneys' lodgings after John Thorpe had delivered his impertinent message to Eleanor; an enemy could be very mocking about her at such times. But Henry never goes over to the side of the enemy, he is always loyal and understanding of the stress that has compelled her to be a little foolish. It is apparent that though

Jane Austen did not want to scheme for an establishment nor to ape imbecility, she would have liked to have an eternal friend and supporter. From her drawing of Catherine Morland one knows that she would have been able to pay the price of such a benefit, and herself would have returned eternal friendship and support.

It is characteristic of Jane Austen's art that she presents this story, which was the fruit of strong feeling and audacious thought, with such perfect serenity that one accepts it as a beautiful established fact. There are those who have doubted whether *Northanger Abbey* is worthy to stand beside *Pride and Prejudice* and *Sense and Sensibility*; and it is at a disadvantage compared with these because it is the least happily proportioned of all Miss Austen's works. The satire on Mrs Radcliffe and *The Mysteries of Udolpho*, though delightful in itself, is not quite satisfactorily fused with the more important matter of the story. But this matters little in view of the many delights to be found in this book. It is sharp with Jane Austen's hate of unpleasant things, it is sweet with her love of all that is pleasant, it nourishes with her special wit that is the extremity of good sense; and her genius for character-drawing is at its happiest here. Henry Tilney and Catherine Morland are not in the least insipid because of their blamelessness; on the contrary, they are rich with the special charm that attends the conjunction of good souls and good breeding. The less admirable characters are as enjoyable, and among them Mr John Thorpe especially deserves note as a superb analysis of vulgarity and its perpetual expenditure of force to no purpose. The book contains, moreover, a wealth of those phrases which, brief and simple in themselves, evoke a whole phase of existence. On a hundredth reading Mrs Morland's gentle rebuke, 'I did not quite like, at breakfast, to hear you talk so much about the French bread at Northanger,' will bear home to one the unanalysable quality of maternal concern which is most laughed at and most missed when time has silenced it; just as Catherine's 'first view of that well-known spire which would announce her within twenty miles of home' always brings to the mind's eye and the heart's recollection whatever countryside is most familiar to them. The book has, indeed, a full measure of that character which makes the death of Jane Austen at forty-one as ominous as the death of Mozart at a slightly earlier age; since it seems to hint that too urgent a thirst for perfection can only be quenched in the grave.

39. 'sense' and 'sensibility'

1936

From 'Sense and Sensibility', *Psyche*, vol. xvi, 1936; reprinted as ch. 12 in *The Structure of Complex Words*, 1951.

William Empson (1906–1984), poet and critic, was Professor of English Literature, University of Sheffield, 1953–71.

By and large, people really do divide into those good at sense and those good at sensibility, and you must be thankful if they are good at either. So far as Caroline Thompson sets out to rebuke romanticism she is in danger of the typical romantic mistake, that of ignoring human limitations. Poor Marianne in Jane Austen is then treated as a mere social climber who made use of a fashion for sensibility. But the book is called *Sense and Sensibility*, and we are told in the first pages that Marianne after all had good sense too; therefore, after a full exposure of the errors of sensibility, the book is able to end happily, when Marianne has learned through suffering how these virtues are best combined.* The striking thing here is not that people were helpless when they used the word *sensibility* but that they balanced its fallacies by using a cognate word open to fallacies in the opposite direction; this after all is a

---

* It is perhaps fair to point out, what is rather in favour of Caroline Thompson's view, that *Sense and Sensibility* (the earliest Jane Austen novel apart from the suppressed first version of *Pride and Prejudice*) is a pretty full-blown piece of romanticism, more unlike her later books than critics generally allow. Marianne can 'scream with agony' and be convincing about it; the sensible Elinor can pass a whole morning in meditation which 'goes like a flash'. Critics are fond of saying that Jane Austen never shows men apart from women, but here (reported, to be sure, in a harangue) we have Willoughby seeing all the way in front of him, as he drives all night through storm to the supposed death-bed of Marianne, the face of deathly agony with which she had received his insults and rejection. It is a detail that you might get in Dostoevsky. But still, though she knew what she was talking about when she dealt with romantics, she was trying to hold the balance between sense and sensibility.

curious source of wisdom, and one that the linguist might well examine.

40. 'she shocks me'

1937

From 'Letter to Lord Byron', *Letters from Iceland*, 1937.

Hugh Wystan Auden (1907–73), poet and critic. Here is his much quoted snap-shot of a disconcerting Jane Austen.

> She was not an unshockable blue-stocking;
>   If shades remain the characters they were,
> No doubt she still considers you as shocking.
>
>   But tell Jane Austen, that is, if you dare,
>   How much her novels are beloved down here.
> She wrote them for posterity, she said;
> 'Twas rash, but by posterity she's read.
>
> You could not shock her more than she shocks me;
>   Beside her Joyce seems innocent as grass.
> It makes me most uncomfortable to see
>   An English spinster of the middle class
>   Describe the amorous effects of 'brass',
> Reveal so frankly and with such sobriety
> The economic basis of society.

41. Miscellanea

1871–1938

Some minor highlights of the Jane Austen literature across this period.

(a) 1871

Edward Fitzgerald to W.F. Pollock (24.12.71): 'She is capital as far as she goes: but she never goes out of the Parlour' (*Letters of Edward Fitzgerald* (1894), ii. 131).

1875

Fitzgerald to Samuel Lawrence (30.12.75), explaining why he cannot read Jane Austen: 'I cannot get on with Books about Daily Life which I find rather insufferable in practice about me' (*Letters of Edward Fitzgerald* (1980), edd. A.M. & A.D. Terhure, iii. 642).

(b) c. 1901

Joseph Conrad to H.G. Wells: 'What is all this about Jane Austen? What is there *in* her? What is it all about?' Wells supposed that Conrad found him sufficiently 'Philistine, stupid and intensely English' and thus qualified to answer these questions, which he put just after the publication of *Love and Mr Lewisham* (1900), by which he was equally baffled. (*Experiment in Autobiography* (1934), ii. 618.)

(c) 1902

Richard Garnett remarks upon the course of 'evolution by which the novel took the place of the drama in English literature. After Sheridan, its last great master, English comedy had degenerated into five-act farce. Miss Austen filled the void with a comedy that could be enjoyed apart from the theatre.' (*The Bookman* (January 1902), p. 127, review of *Jane Austen: Her Homes and Friends* (1902) by Constance Hill.)

(d) First World War

The Oxford don H.F. Brett-Smith was employed by military hospitals to advise on reading matter for the war-wounded. 'His job was to grade novels and poetry according to the "Fever-Chart". For the severely shell-shocked he selected Jane

Austen' (reported by Martin Jarrett-Kerr, letter to the *TLS*, 3 February 1984, p. 109).

(e) 1921

Edmund Wilson writing to Gilbert Troxell about Jane Austen and James Joyce: 'They share the almost unique distinction in English novels of having a sense of form.'
(*Letters on Literature and Politics 1912–1972* (1977), ed. Elena Wilson, letter dated 2.9.21, p. 74.)

(f) 1923

Virginia Woolf: 'Anybody who has had the temerity to write about Jane Austen is aware of facts: first, that of all great writers she is the most difficult to catch in the act of greatness; second, that there are twenty-five elderly gentlemen living in the neighbourhood of London who resent any slight upon her genius as if it were an insult to the chastity of their Aunts.'
('Jane Austen at Sixty', *Athenaeum*, 15 December 1923 and *New Republic*, 30 January 1924.)

(g) 1920s

Middleton Murry: 'I remember an intellectual dinner-party at which it was announced, without any manifest ill-effects upon the company, that the real test for literary taste was an admiration not for Jane Austen (as some one had suggested) but for Dickens.' (*Pencillings* (1923), p. 32.)

(h) 1938

Ezra Pound: his advice to Laurence Binyon, given 'in desperation', was that the poet should read his work to himself 'and kick out every line that isn't as Jane Austen would have written it in prose.'
(*Letters of Ezra Pound* (1951), ed. D.D. Paige, p. 403.)

(i) 1938

Yvor Winters described Jane Austen's 'frames of action' as 'so conventional as to be all but trivial' yet found her 'comment and characterisation' 'remarkably brilliant' and the novelist herself 'inescapably one of the best'.
(*Maule's Curse* (1938), reprinted in *In Defense of Reason* (1960), p. 336.)

(j) 1938

H.G. Wells: 'The English Jane Austen is quite typical. Quintessential I should call her. A certain ineluctable faded charm. Like some of the loveliest butterflies—with no guts at all'. (*The Brothers*, p. 15.)

Bibliography

A short select bibliography of works listing or describing the criticism of Jane Austen across the period 1870–1939. A more complete listing (without comment) can be found in the definitive *Bibliography of Jane Austen* (1982) by David Gilson.

Chapman, R.W., *Jane Austen: A Critical Bibliography* (1955): provides a brief compendium of extracts and quotations from a wide range of books, articles, letters, diaries, etc., touching upon Jane Austen.

Duffy, J.A.M. Jnr., 'Jane Austen and the Nineteeth-Century Critics of Fiction 1812–1913': unpublished dissertation, University of Chicago (1954): relates the course of J.A.'s reputation to criticism of the novel in general.

Link, F.M., 'The Reputation of Jane Austen in the Twentieth Century': unpublished dissertation, Boston University (1958).

Lodge, David (ed.), *Jane Austen: Emma: A Casebook* (1968): alongside Southam (1968), the earliest documentation of the critical response, this time to a single work. There is a considerable introduction and documents run from contemporary reviews to essays of the 1960s. The five other novels are treated in two further volumes in the Casebook Series: *Sense and Sensibility, Pride and Prejudice and Mansfield Park* (1976), and *Northanger Abbey and Persuasion* (1976), both edited by B.C. Southam.

Southam, B.C., *Jane Austen: The Critical Heritage* (1968): a select documentation of the critical response from J.A.'s lifetime to 1870. A considerable introduction surveys the material and looks forward briefly to criticism post-1870.

Southam, B.C., 'Jane Austen, 1775–1817', *New Cambridge Bibliography of English Literature*, ed. George Watson, vol. iii (1969). Until Gilson, this was the most complete (although selective) listing of the critical literature up to 1967.

Trilling, Lionel, 'In Mansfield Park', *Encounter* (September 1954), pp. 9–19; also *Partisan Review* (1954) xxi; reprinted in *The Opposing Self* (1955); also as 'Jane Austen and *Mansfield Park*' in

Pelican Guide to English Literature, vol. 5, *From Blake to Byron* (1957), omitting a long note on J.A. and Henry James and a long penultimate paragraph.

Trilling, Lionel, Introduction to *Emma* (1957), Riverside Edition (Boston: Houghton Mifflin); reprinted as *'Emma'*, *Encounter* (June 1957); also in *Beyond Culture*, as *'Emma* and the legend of Jane Austen'.
The opening pages of this influential essay touch upon the 'fierce partisanship' which attends the reading of J.A. and the modern reaction against 'gentle-Janeism'.

Watt, Ian (ed.), *Jane Austen: A Collection of Critical Essays* (1963): a student source-book, it carries a valuable introduction, reviewing the course of J.A. criticism.

Wright, Andrew Howell, *Jane Austen's Novels: A Study in Structure* (1953): the first substantial critical work, following *Jane Austen and Her Art* (1939) by Mary Lascelles, to carry on a dialogue with earlier critics. Includes an excellent Annotated Bibliography (revised and updated for the Peregrine Books edition, 1962), valuable for its comments and recommendations.

Select Index

In preference to a straightforward alphabetical listing of contents I have grouped the index references as follows: I. Periodicals and journals from which material has been quoted; II. Critics and reviewers; III. References to the works of Jane Austen, where there is significant comment.

II. CRITICS AND REVIEWERS, INCLUDING THOSE WHO PASSED INFORMAL COMMENT

III. THE WORKS OF JANE AUSTEN

THE CRITICAL HERITAGE SERIES

GENERAL EDITOR: B. C. SOUTHAM

Volumes published and forthcoming

ADDISON AND STEELE	Edward A. Bloom and Lillian D. Bloom
MATTHEW ARNOLD: THE POETRY	Carl Dawson
MATTHEW ARNOLD: PROSE WRITINGS	Carl Dawson and John Pfordresher
W. H. AUDEN	John Haffenden
JANE AUSTEN 1811-1870	B. C. Southam
JANE AUSTEN 1870-1940	B. C. Southam
SAMUEL BECKETT	L. Graver and R. Federman
ARNOLD BENNETT	Jame Hepburn
WILLIAM BLAKE	G. E. Bentley Jr
THE BRONTËS	Miriam Allott
BROWNING	Boyd Litzinger and Donald Smalley
ROBERT BURNS	Donald A. Low
BYRON	Andrew Rutherford
THOMAS CARLYLE	Jules Paul Seigel
CHAUCER 1385-1837	Derek Brewer
CHAUCER 1837-1933	Derek Brewer
CHEKHOV	Victor Emeljanow
CLARE	Mark Storey
CLOUGH	Michael Thorpe
COLERIDGE	J. R. de J. Jackson
WILKIE COLLINS	Norman Page
CONRAD	Norman Sherry
FENIMORE COOPER	George Dekker and John P. McWilliams
CRABBE	Arthur Pollard
STEPHEN CRANE	Richard M. Weatherford
DEFOE	Pat Rogers
DICKENS	Philip Collins
JOHN DONNE	A. J. Smith
DRYDEN	James and Helen Kinsley
GEORGE ELIOT	David Carroll
T. S. ELIOT	Michael Grant
WILLIAM FAULKNER	John Bassett
HENRY FIELDING	Ronald Paulson and Thomas Lockwood
FORD MADOX FORD	Frank MacShane
E. M. FORSTER	Philip Gardner
GEORGIAN POETRY 1911-1922	Timothy Rogers
GISSING	Pierre Coustillas and Colin Partridge
GOLDSMITH	G. S. Rousseau
THOMAS HARDY	R. G. Cox
HAWTHORNE	J. Donald Crowley
HEMINGWAY	Jeffrey Meyers
GEORGE HERBERT	C. A. Patrides
ALDOUS HUXLEY	Donald Watt
IBSEN	Michael Egan